16

D1190176

Rewired:

Research-Writing Partnerships within the Frameworks

edited by
Randall McClure

OAKTON COMMUNITY COLLEGE
DES PLAINES CAMPUS
1600 EAST GOLF ROAD
DES PLAINES, IL 60016

DATE DUE

DISCARD

Association of College and Research Libraries
A division of the American Library Association
Chicago, Illinois 2016

The paper used in this publication meets the minimum requirements of American National Standard for Information Sciences–Permanence of Paper for Printed Library Materials, ANSI Z39.48-1992. ∞

Library of Congress Cataloging-in-Publication Data

Names: McClure, Randall, editor.
Title: Rewired : research-writing partnerships in a frameworks state of mind
  / editor: Randall McClure, Pfeiffer University.
Description: Chicago : Association of College and Research Libraries, a
  division of the American Library Association, 2016.
Identifiers: LCCN 2016021641| ISBN 9780838989043 (pbk.) | ISBN
9780838989050
  (pdf)
Subjects: LCSH: Academic libraries--Relations with faculty and curriculum. |
  Academic libraries--Relations with faculty and curriculum--United
  States--Case studies. | Research--Methodology--Study and teaching (Higher)
  | Report writing--Study and teaching (Higher) | English
  language--Rhetoric--Study and teaching (Higher) | Information
  literacy--Study and teaching (Higher)
Classification: LCC Z675.U5 R467 2016 | DDC 021/.3--dc23 LC record available
at https://lccn.loc.gov/2016021641

Copyright ©2016 by the Association of College and Research Libraries.

All rights reserved except those which may be granted by Sections 107 and 108 of the Copyright Revision Act of 1976.

Printed in the United States of America.

20 19 18 17 16 5 4 3 2 1

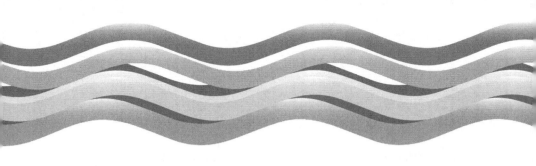

Table of Contents

DISCARD

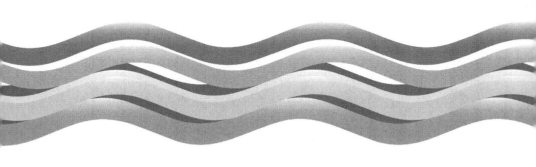

Foreword[*]

SEPARATED AT BIRTH. Why does this spring to mind when I think of information literacy and writing instruction? Wikipedia, that ever-handy resource, tells us this phrase refers to "people who are unrelated but bear a notable facial resemblance."[1] Some of us may remember the uncanny and hilarious side-by-side photos in *Spy* magazine, which first introduced this phrase in the late 1980s. For information literacy and writing instruction, I see a deeper meaning, one of family members who share DNA but who grew up in different worlds. Do they remain disconnected or can they be brought together—rewired as it were—for a happy ending?

My own aha moment for recognizing information literacy and writing instruction as separated at birth occurred at the 2015 Georgia International Information Literacy Conference. I was unfamiliar with the conference before being invited to deliver the keynote address on the ACRL Framework, and I was immediately intrigued by the conference theme: "Bringing librarians and educators into dialog with each other!"

There were a number of engaging sessions on librarian-writing instructor collaborations; two back-to-back sessions drove home, for me, the striking similarities in the knowledge practices and habits of mind in the guiding documents of the respective professional associations: the *ACRL Framework for Information Literacy for Higher Education* and the *Council of Writing Program Administrators (WPA) Framework for Success in Postsecondary Writing.*

In the first presentation, an English instructor from James Madison University told us the ACRL Framework had created a lingua franca for common conversation between librarians and writing instructors, but these partnerships wouldn't be enough to change student research and writing in the curriculum. It would take an orchestrated effort of our respective professional associations to combine forces, connect these Frameworks, and support disciplinary partnerships.

I felt he was speaking right to me as a representative of one of those parent associations, and I knew I needed to do something about this disconnect.

* This work is licensed under a Creative Commons Attribution-NonCommercial-Share-Alike 4.0 License, CC BY-NC-SA (https://creativecommons.org/licenses/by-nc-sa/4.0/).

He also cited two leading names in the field who were fostering this bilingual liaison, and I was delighted they were the presenters for the next session. Their compelling comparison of the two Frameworks provided my visual lynchpin for this separation at birth.

The conference experiences inspired me to suggest the ACRL Framework Advisory Board sponsor a two-part webcast series, in January and February 2016, on how the two Frameworks inform and support partnerships between writing instruction and information literacy practitioners. With the highest registration ever for a webcast offering, the widespread interest for this topic was clear.

Like many of us whose passion and profession is information literacy, I have often enjoyed successful partnerships with colleagues in writing studies, just as writing instructors and academic support staff have long considered librarians natural allies. But perhaps successful partnerships are more often the result of individual chemistry and less the result of a recognition of kinship by our disciplines, parent institutions, or professional associations. And it may not have been based on an attempt to have intentional conversations to better understand what we mean as we speak from our own disciplinary perspectives.

In reality, we have been living parallel lives, but raised in different cultures, speaking different languages. This image of parallel lives and its impact is captured throughout this volume, and Rosalind Bucy, Gillian Devereux, Maric Kramer, and Jenne Powers of Wheelock College do so quite eloquently in Chapter 3: "From the student perspective, librarians, writing faculty and writing center professionals may seem to exist in parallel locations, each group of 'experts' helping students with discrete parts of their academic enterprise, doing work that never intersects. When students see us working together, it helps them understand how our roles overlap and inform each other."

How do we bring these discrete pieces together? How do we develop a mutual language? Regardless of our experience with information literacy or writing instruction, we can still use help in understanding how to move across these boundaries. This inspiring book can serve as our travel guide. Randall McClure, an experienced editor and English professor with three other collections under his belt, is to be commended for his early recognition of the need for a book on the kinship between the Frameworks of information literacy and writing, and for bringing these authors together.

The fourteen chapters in this volume offer insights and experiences from more than thirty contributors who are active practitioners and partners in information and writing instruction in a variety of institutional settings. While the broad scope of the collection was intended, what may have been unforeseen is the uncanny way common language and themes repeat and reinforce each other as the authors describe the evolution of mutual understanding, the recognition of shared learning goals for students, the cultivation and inclusion of student voices, the effort to make the continuum from novice to expert more explicit, and the emergence of a teaching for transfer approach, to name a few. But the overriding theme is research and writing are iterative and interwoven processes—organic, dynamic, and continually evolving—in which we all play a role.

We knew this in our hearts, but now it is being recognized in our professional practice with the Frameworks guiding the way. I invite you to immerse yourself in this heady and invigorating collection to see how research and writing, once separated at birth, are now being rewired. Let's celebrate this reunion that was meant to be.

Sharon Mader, MLS, EdD
Dean Emeritus, University of New Orleans Library
Chair, IFLA Information Literacy Section
ACRL Visiting Program Officer for Information Literacy
New Orleans, LA

Notes

1. Wikipedia, s.v. "Separated at Birth," October 27, 2014, https://en.wikipedia.org/wiki/Separated_at_birth.

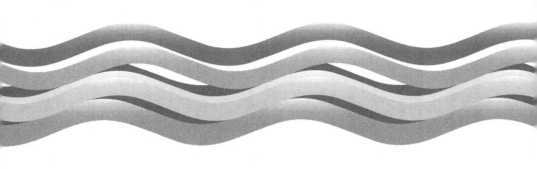

Acknowledgments

I WISH TO extend my sincere thanks to the contributors of this project for sharing their understanding of the ACRL and WPA Frameworks and for their strategies for improving library-writing partnerships. Kathryn Deiss and Erin Nevius from the Association of College and Research Libraries supported this collection, and I appreciate their belief and enthusiasm. I want to particularly thank Molly Huber for her helpful editorial assistance and proofreading along with Deanna P. Denk for her meticulous work in copy editing.

I want to also thank my colleagues at Pfeiffer University—especially David Heckel, Ashley Oliphant, and Marissa Schwalm—for their support; my Lord, our God, for His grace; and my wife, Christine, and children—Connor, Aislinn, Rowen, and Flynn—for reminding me why I write and why I live.

I dedicate this book to my mom, Marjorie Allen McDaniel, and dad, Laurence Robert McClure, for standing by me through the many seasons of my life.

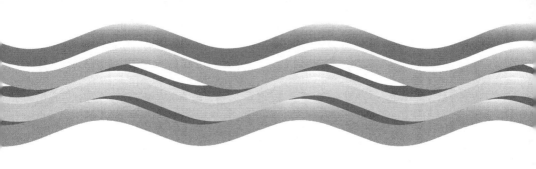

Introduction

Partnerships Rewired for the Digital Age

Randall McClure

THIS BOOK IS about partnerships, and three partnerships in particular.

First, this book is about the partnerships between college and research librarians and their colleagues in academic units across campus. From disciplines and areas one would expect—English departments, first-year writing programs, and university writing centers—to those perhaps more unexpected, such as the health sciences, courses in music, and summer bridge programs, partnerships between librarians and their colleagues across campus are as abounding as they are diverse. Now, it is true that college and research librarians have been working alongside teachers invested in writing in the disciplines for decades. What is perhaps new about these partnerships, though, is how faculty members and librarians are re-imagining their work, rewiring it if you will, for students in a world where writing is both global and largely digital. This book explores such collaborations in the digital age of researching and writing, grounding them in two recently-published frameworks documents.

The confluence, what most contributors to this book see more as confirmation than coincidence, of recent publications from both the Association of College and Research Libraries (ACRL) and the Council of Writing Program Administrators (WPA) defines the second set of partnerships in this book. While a fair number of contributors also reference the ACRL's *Information Literacy Competency Standards for Higher Education* published in 2000,[1] as well as the WPA's *Outcomes Statement for First-Year Composition*, first published in 2000[2] and revised and re-published as version 3.0 in July 2014,[3] all contributors to this book ground their partnership efforts in two documents: (1) the *Framework for Success in Postsecondary Writing* authored by the Council of Writing

Program Administrators, National Council of Teachers of English, and National Writing Project in a partnership of their own and published in 2011;[4] and (2) the ACRL's *Framework for Information Literacy for Higher Education* adopted in 2016.[5] In fact, most of our contributors see not just a partnership of key habits, skills, dispositions, and concepts in these two documents, but also a synergy and, in some cases, a sense of cross-curricular validation largely absent in the discipline-bound and subject-specific work characterizing much of higher education. Despite the continued force of the disciplinary current, the contributors to this book see, in their often side-by-side analysis of the Frameworks, incredible similarities in the organizations' views of researching and writing.

In fact, these similarities drive the third partnership in this book. While it might seem trivial to some readers, the contributors of this book opt for the term "research-writing" when discussing both the processes and the projects in which they and their students engage as the result of their partnerships or, as Kathleen Reed and Dawn Thompson of Vancouver Island University write in chapter eleven, their "dynamic duos." The contributors see, as I have argued in the past,[6] researching and writing as inseparable, interdependent and, as Stacy Kastner and Hillary Richardson from Mississippi State University write in chapter seven, "braided" processes, even in activities without a required research/source use component. Writing cannot escape research just as, in nearly all cases, researching leads to writing, whether the writing is a set of mental notes or a formal academic paper. To this end, we rewire the concept and use research-writing to highlight this partnership.

Partnerships are integral to this book. The word is not just part of the book's title, but is its organizing principle. In "Section 1: Developing a Shared Understanding," contributors provide readers with the book's foundation for the partnerships to follow.

Opening the book and framing the other chapters in the section, Brenda Refaei and M. Lauren Wahman from University of Cincinnati Blue Ash College engage one another in a discussion around both their partnership and the Frameworks. In "The Art of Conversation: Dialog between a Librarian and a Writing Program Administrator," Refaei and Wahman use a back-and-forth approach to bring to life the shared understanding of one another's work they have developed. They achieved this mutual admiration prior to the publication of the Frameworks, yet they dig deep into the documents in order to highlight the ways in which each other's professional organization discusses their respective roles working with students, often in remarkably similar ways. They write, "Having an understanding of how we each view the Frameworks [has led] into considering how to build on them to develop more dynamic curricula that fully integrates information literacy and research-writing. The Frameworks also help to actively engage in curricular conversations, using the common language found in both documents." Refaei and Wahman start this conversation in the book's opening chapter, but this dialog continues through the entire text.

In chapter two, "Interpreting the Frameworks: Faculty Constructions of Research and the Researching Student," Rick Fisher and Kaijsa Calkins from University of Wyoming extend the portrait of research-writing beyond the voices of the single librarian and writing program administrator offered in the previous chapter. Through an analysis of student learning outcomes in syllabi and course approval forms for general education advanced communication courses, those with a writing-in-the-disciplines focus, Fisher and Calkins find many faculty members still rely on dated conceptions of research-writing, continuing to align it with the traditional, print-centric research paper of yore. Their findings "reveal[] that a sizeable proportion of the courses we studied do not encourage students to see research as an ongoing, disciplinarily-embedded, socially-constructed, iterative, problem-based, and metacognitive process of growth and refinement," or the type of process that Fisher and Calkins see outlined in the Frameworks. The authors offer several suggestions to help faculty "adjust their notions and representations of research, in line with the WPA's and ACRL's perspectives of research-writing." Any reader invested in writing across the curriculum or writing in the disciplines initiatives will find this chapter of particular interest.

Whereas Fisher and Calkins provide readers with their analysis of the faculty perspective on research-writing, Rosalind Bucy, Gillian Devereux, Maric Kramer, and Jenne Powers of Wheelock College offer their collective take on the role of student voice in the Frameworks. In chapter three, "Giving Voice to Students: A Rhetorical Analysis of the Frameworks," Bucy and her Wheelock colleagues believe, much like Fisher and Calkins, the Frameworks intentionally rewire research-writing to shift focus from the traditional emphasis on the final researched product to the student's intellectual growth throughout the research-writing process. The authors of chapter three take a unique approach in making their point that "fostering and amplifying student voice is the primary objective of our work," as they examine "the usage and frequency of terms related to the idea of student voice" in the Frameworks (and the WPA Outcomes). The authors go on to offer examples of how librarians and faculty can and should collaborate at all levels of the undergraduate experience—first-year writing courses or seminars, introductory courses within the professional programs, and advanced and capstone courses—to help students develop authentic and powerful voices.

The authors of chapter three characterize research-writing at three levels of undergraduate learning; the authors of chapter four provide readers with a series of scaffolded assignments designed to bring out the habits of mind, skills, threshold concepts, and dispositions pronounced in the Frameworks.

To close out the opening section of the book, Cassie Hemstrom from University of California, Davis and Kathy Christie Anders of Texas A&M University make the foundational practical. By putting the Frameworks in direct contact with pedagogy, the authors of "In a Research-Writing Frame of Mind" draw out

> the connections that already exist between the processes of writing and researching—connections already supported and employed in composition pedagogy and assessment. The articulation of these connections should help to enable students to investigate, use, and reflect on the purposes of the process of researching as a part of scaffolded assignments, much the same way that drafting, workshopping, and revising allows students to engage knowingly and critically in the writing process.

In addition to highlighting ways these connections impact research-writing across the curriculum, the authors offer several assignment sequences as examples of researching and writing as symbiotic activities across disciplinary divides.

The highly adaptable research-writing sequences provided by Hemstrom and Anders in chapter four bridge to the specific partnerships comprising the second section of the book, aptly titled "Section 2: Partnering Research & Writing." Portraits of librarian-faculty partnerships from across the curriculum provide of avenues for readers to enter into or enhance partnerships on their own campuses.

The opening chapter of section two does what its title claims. In "Bridging the Gap: New Thresholds and Opportunities for Collaboration," Amber Lancaster, Donell Callender, and Laura Heinz, from Texas Tech University, present a case study of a library-writing studies collaboration. The authors use the Frameworks as a guide for rewiring the first-year writing course, building it around a revision of the common literature review assignment. Lancaster, Callender, and Heinz establish the goal for chapter five when they write, "Our aim in this chapter is to offer practical strategies for implementing and assessing [the Frameworks] so that others might emulate our project and advance the ideas we offer." Practicality, in fact, may be the defining characteristic of chapters in this section. Readers should be able to take the ideas and transfer them to their own locations.

Chapter six also presents a model for blending information literacy and writing designed to be easily transferred to other contexts. Authors Nancy C. DeJoy and Sara D. Miller, Michigan State University, and Brian D. Holcomb, Limestone College, detail their use of the concepts of revision, arrangement, invention, delivery, and style (RAIDS) in the creation of the disciplinary literacies assignment (DLA) in their chapter, "Integrating the Frameworks in Postsecondary Writing: Disciplinary Literacy in First-Year Composition." The authors believe the DLA "creates practical and pedagogical connections between the two Frameworks... [as it] invite[s] students to take an inquiry-based approach to building knowledge about the disciplinary literacies central to [their] major fields of study." While the assignment was developed by the authors for use in the first-year writing classroom, they suggest its use in any course where there is an opportunity to examine the "artifacts of a discipline—scholarly publications, trade articles, and primary sources such as original interviews with practitioners and educators—in order to generate knowledge about reading, writing, and researching in a [particular] field." Readers of this chapter will find a thorough discussion of RAIDS and the DLA along with their connections to both Frameworks.

Suggestions for curriculum reform are the focus of chapter seven, "Researching and Writing as Braided Processes: A Co-Curricular Model." Stacy Kastner and Hillary Richardson, from Mississippi State University, use the Frameworks as their guide to create a project-based curriculum to engage at-risk students enrolled in the summer bridge program at their school. The authors describe the development, implementation, and assessment of a pilot study that relies on a team-based, multimodal project and requires students to work together to create a hyperlinked, close historical reading of a text. This chapter not only explores a student population often overlooked in the mainstream professional literature—those conditionally-admitted—it also responds to this audience with a creative, multimodal digital mapping activity based on a traditional academic assignment yet clearly rewired for today's students.

Kastner and Richardson take the Frameworks a step further by not only using them as a guide in the curriculum development process, but also explicitly including them in the teaching and learning of the multimodal project. Doing so leads the authors to conclude "in borrowing each other's practices and by engaging so explicitly with our respective Frameworks, we not only strengthened our collaborations, but also perpetuated them." Unlike standards and other learning outcomes, the Frameworks appear to be better mapped to the classroom and, in cases like the one presented in chapter six, become part of the course content, a metaliteracy in its own right.

Whereas the authors of chapters six and seven focus on the early stages of undergraduate learning, the authors of chapter eight stretch their gaze across the totality of the undergraduate experience. In "Partnership as Process: Moving Toward an Integrated Undergraduate Writing Curriculum," Elizabeth L. Wallis, Jim Nugent, and Lori Ostergaard, Oakland University, discuss their partnered efforts to extend information literacy instruction from their first-year writing course through the undergraduate major in writing. As readers may have experienced at their own institutions, the decision to reconsider the research-writing dynamic at Oakland University resulted from an assessment project acknowledging the "faculty's recognition that [the] major curriculum was failing to prepare students for the research challenges they regularly encountered in…upper-division courses, much less the information literacy challenges they might encounter in their lives beyond the university." While the library-writing partnership had existed for some time at Oakland, the authors recognized a need to rewire it; they did so by turning to the Frameworks. In looking at their own perceptions of research-writing and the concepts, skills, habits, and dispositions outlined in the Frameworks, the authors recognized their partnership needed to be extended from curriculum design all the way through program assessment.

Chapter nine, "Metaliteracy in the Digital Landscape: Using Wikipedia for Research-Writing Across the Curriculum," takes the Frameworks even further. Authors Theresa Burress, Maribeth Clark, Sarah Hernandez, and Nova Myhill from New College of Florida, do what might have horrified librarians and faculty only a few short years ago. Believing "the principles underlying the five pillars of Wikipedia align closely with the concepts outlined in the Framework[s]…, Wikipedia [can serve] as a platform with which students can develop research and writing skills, and become metaliterate citizens," the authors describe creating library-faculty partnerships with the goal of implementing Wikipedia-based research-writing activities in introductory courses in Music, English Literature, and Sociology, along with a unique library-based independent study project. The authors contend having students practice the work of Wikipedians brings the Frameworks to life in ways ideally suited to today's digital information economy.

Chapter ten provides a second example of a library-faculty partnership in an area not often explored in the professional literature. In "Teaching the Frameworks for Writing and Information Literacy: A Case Study from the Health Sciences," Teresa Quezada, from University of Texas at El Paso (UTEP), details a partnership aimed at redesigning UTEP's technical writing course for health science majors. Quezada not only explores how the Frameworks guided changes to the research-writing elements of the course, but also discusses how hybrid instruction highlighted digital forms of researching and writing. Like others in this section, Quezada concludes "greater involvement by librarians in the course not only augments the Frameworks' prominence in the course, but also promotes student success," and she makes it clear her collaboration with library colleagues had a significant impact on student satisfaction, engagement, and retention.

Kathleen Reed and Dawn Thompson, from Vancouver Island University, in the last chapter of the section, take us to the conclusion of the undergraduate curriculum. In "Dynamic Duos: Blended Instruction and Faculty-Librarian Collaboration," Reed and Thompson consider the Frameworks from the vantage point of their partnership in a senior-level English Research Methods course. The authors discuss their use of an embedded librarian model and a co-teaching approach, one they see reflected in the shared ideas of the Frameworks. Furthermore, Reed and Thompson draw some of the strongest connections in the book between research-writing assignments, classroom activities, and the frames and habits of mind found in the Frameworks. Chapter eleven should interest readers invested in close curricular mapping, involved in the digital humanities, and intrigued by the emphasis on metacognition and metaliteracy in the Frameworks.

The chapters in section three titled "Assessing Writing & Information Literacy" do what the Frameworks do not: focus on assessment. While it is true the design of the Frameworks intentionally focuses on habits, skills, dispositions, and frames for learning, any discussion of the behaviors and skills to be nurtured in students seems incomplete without discussion of how to gauge what has been learned. The Frameworks do this largely through metacognition: through the intentional use of self-reflection in both researching and writing. The authors in section three acknowledge this while presenting readers with their methods for tying into local and national assessment programs.

Teresa Grettano and Donna Witek offer readers a clear portrait of the relationship, or dare I say partnership, between the Frameworks and assessment. In chapter twelve, "The Frameworks, Comparative Analyses, and Sharing Responsibility for Learning and Assessment," The University of Scranton authors suggest using the Frameworks in assessment allows librarians and faculty to "take more control of our pedagogical and assessment practices, to make them more intentional and meaning-driven, and to comply with outside standards while still holding true to our pedagogical beliefs." Grettano and Witek describe a mapping of student learning outcomes to the Frameworks and the results of assessment work based on this mapping. The authors situate this work within best practices for assessment and illustrate how such assessments inform their work with the curriculum and with students inside the classroom. Applying the frame/habit of metacognition to their own in the process of "closing the assessment loop," Grettano and Witek provide readers with a fresh perspective on not just the rigors, but also the possibilities of assessment.

Chapter twelve provides a robust discussion of assessment at the level of the course; chapter thirteen turns the assessment lens toward students as researchers in the digital age. In "Leveraging New Frameworks to Teach Information Appropriation," William Duffy and Rachel E. Scott, University of Memphis, and Jennifer Schnabel, The Ohio State University, examine the Frameworks as part of their work to rewire our understanding of how students can and should assess the value of the sources they locate, particularly those they find online. They write, "[C]onsidering many students now turn to the open web to conduct the initial (if not all) phases of a research project, it makes sense to reconsider the skills necessary for students to assess and in turn appropriate the various forms of information available to them with a click of the mouse." To highlight the changing nature and value of information provided to students through searches conducted online, the authors provide readers with a provocative take on the dynamic nature of information inside digital spaces. Duffy, Scott, and Schnabel dig deep inside the Frameworks to provide a fresh look on the organizations' views on information appropriation and, like other contributors to the book, offer a reworked research-writing sequence of activities, theirs clearly influenced by the field of visual rhetoric that asks students to interact with and respond to specific frames and habits of mind.

Chapter fourteen provides the appropriate close to section three and the book itself. "Can We Talk Multimodality?" by Meghan Roe and Julius Fleschner from Briar Cliff University, offers readers a glimpse of the curriculum of the future, one inspired by partnerships of all kinds. The authors explain the genesis for, the design and assessment of a new hybrid core curriculum course at their institution—CORE 131: Writing and Speaking in the Digital Age— that not only focuses on twenty-first century communication skills, but also places an emphasis on multimodality. The course pairs writing and speech with research, face-to-face with hybrid instruction, traditional assignments with multimodal ones, threshold concepts from the ACRL Framework with habits of mind from the WPA Framework, and library with writing center instruction, among others. Feedback on this fully rewired course design led the authors to conclude "[t]hese types of innovations are possible, regardless of institutional circumstances" and "[t]hrough this collaboration, we have developed stronger programs with new services that will have a long-term impact on how students approach research-writing in this increasingly digital age." This partnership, like all the others collected in this book, shows us the pie is not in the sky. It is here within reach at campuses of all shapes and sizes across the country and around the globe.

In closing, I see it only fitting to mention I owe much of my own interest in studying the information behaviors and research-writing decisions of student writers to a partnership, to a librarian colleague who approached me years ago with an interest in collecting some of my students' research papers in order to perform citation analysis in them. "You do what?" I asked. I became immediately intrigued and remain so to this day.

Before then, I did not see much more to it than the dreaded and dreary research paper, the same paper I pummeled my students with as a junior faculty member. While I probably enjoyed the research paper more than most of my colleagues (I was the department's writing specialist), I never saw it as an area of study, a venue ripe for research. Even during my doctoral work, I was only taught to teach writing. I was never trained to teach, or dare I say, enjoy, re-search-writing (an idea I have explored in other works[7]), though I was certain-ly responsible for it, often for a hundred-plus first-year students each semester.

I learned so much through what turned into a librarian-faculty collabora-tion in 2007 that it seems only fitting to pay it forward and present this set of partnerships to you. Enjoy.

Notes

1. Association of College and Research Libraries, 2000, *Information Literacy Competen-cy Standards for Higher Education*, http://www.ala.org/acrl/standards/informationlit-eracycompetency.
2. Council of Writing Program Administrators, 2000, *WPA Outcomes Statement for First-Year Composition*, http://www.in.gov/che/files/WPA_Outcomes_Statement_for_First-Year_Composition.pdf.
3. Council of Writing Program Administrators, [2000, 2008] 2014, *WPA Outcomes Statement for First-Year Composition* (3.0), http://www.wpacouncil.org/positions/out-comes.html.
4. Council of Writing Program Administrators, National Council of Teachers of English, and National Writing Project, 2011, *Framework for Success in Postsecondary Writing*, http://wpacouncil.org/framework.
5. Association of College and Research Libraries, 2016, *Framework for Information Literacy for Higher Education*, http://www.ala.org/acrl/standards/ilframework.
6. Randall McClure. "WritingResearchWriting: The Semantic Web and the Future of the Research Project," *Computers and Composition* 28, vol. 4 (December 2011): 315–326.
7. Randall McClure. "It's Not 2.0 Late: What Late Adopters Need to Know About Teach-ing Research Skills to Writers of Multimodal Texts," *The Writing Instructor* (February 2013). Accessed April 27, 2016. http://www.writinginstructor.org/mcclure-2014-03.

Bibliography

Association of College and Research Libraries. 2016. *Framework for Information Literacy for Higher Education*. Accessed April 27, 2016. http://www.ala.org/acrl/standards/ilframework.

———. 2000. *Information Literacy Competency Standards for Higher Education*. Accessed April 27, 2016. http://www.ala.org/acrl/standards/informationliteracycompetency.

Council of Writing Program Administrators. 2014. *WPA Outcomes Statement for First-Year Composition (3.0)*. Accessed April 27, 2016. http://wpacouncil.org/positions/outcomes.html.

———. 2000. *WPA Outcomes Statement for First-Year Composition*. Accessed April 27, 2016. http://www.in.gov/che/files/WPA_Outcomes_Statement_for_First-Year_Composition.pdf.

Council of Writing Program Administrators, National Council of Teachers of English, and National Writing Project. 2011. *Framework for Success in Postsecondary Writing.* Accessed April 27, 2016. http://wpacouncil.org/.

McClure, Randall. 2011. "WritingResearchWriting: The Semantic Web and the Future of the Research Project." *Computers and Composition* 28, vol. 4 (December 2011): 315–326.

———. 2013. "It's Not 2.0 Late: What Late Adopters Need to Know About Teaching Research Skills to Writers of Multimodal Texts." *The Writing Instructor* (February 2013). Accessed April 27, 2016. http://www.writinginstructor.org/mcclure-2014-03.

SECTION 1:
Developing a Shared Understanding

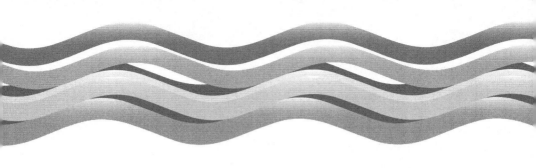

CHAPTER 1[*]

The Art of Conversation:

Dialog between a Librarian and a Writing Program Administrator

Brenda Refaei and M. Lauren Wahman
University of Cincinnati–Blue Ash

Introduction

Librarians and composition instructors have long collaborated to help students understand research processes and develop research skills, and now more than ever before are working together to engage students in research and discovery by partnering on the development of research assignments and library instruction sessions. Despite more collaboration on the ground between librarians and compositionists, it is surprising more collaboration did not occur across their respective professional organizations when working on concepts and/or learning outcomes members rely on in building curricula. In this chapter, a librarian and a writing program administrator engage in a dynamic conversation around how the new Association of College and Research Libraries

* This work is licensed under a Creative Commons Attribution 4.0 License, CC BY (https://creativecommons.org/licenses/by/4.0/).

(ACRL) *Framework for Information Literacy for Higher Education* (hereafter ACRL Framework),[1] the Council of Writing Program Administrators (WPA), National Council of Teachers of English (NCTE), and the National Writing Project's (NWP) *Framework for Success in Postsecondary Writing* (hereafter WPA Framework),[2] and the recently revised Council of Writing Program Administrators *Outcomes Statement for First-Year Composition* (hereafter WPA Outcomes)[3] inform our work with students at a two-year, open-access college.

One of our challenges is teaching students to apply and transfer their information literacy and writing skills to assignments across disciplines. Equally challenging is helping students understand the importance of lifelong learning. The Frameworks provide an opportunity to engage in conversation about knowledge transfer and student learning. They provide a powerful starting point by focusing on metacognition as a means of fostering knowledge transfer to new contexts and provide the means to help students develop ownership of this complex process.

The Frameworks define roles for librarians and writing instructors partnering in local contexts who adapt them to meet the needs of their unique student populations. Librarians and writing instructors—each with distinct roles in educating students—through increased collaboration, can build a dynamic learning environment where students are engaged as information consumers and creators. By looking through the lens of their local institutions, librarians and writing instructors can design curricula using these Frameworks to meet students where they are in the research and writing processes, encourage deeper learning, and promote the application of skills and abilities across programs and disciplines. To explain further, in this chapter we posed questions to guide our conversation with each other in our roles as librarian and college writing program administrator. Our goal is to explore how we can use the ACRL and WPA Frameworks and WPA Outcomes to shape our work with students at our two-year college. In doing so, we offer a framework for the chapters that follow and for readers looking to work with the documents on their campuses.

What do Composition Writing Instructors Understand about Librarians from Reading the ACRL Framework?

The revised ACRL Framework is a marked change from the former *ACRL Information Literacy Competency Standards for Higher Education* (hereafter ACRL Standards). Maid and D'Angelo describe how the previous ACRL Standards could be reduced as a "listing of skills that an individual can be trained (and then assessed) in with little regard for the context in which the skills are needed."[4] The new ACRL Framework is far more robust and forward thinking as it is built upon the threshold concepts in the field of information literacy. I was struck by the attention given to the social nature of knowledge construction represented as the six threshold concepts, or frames, of the discipline:

- Authority Is Constructed and Contextual
- Information Creation as a Process
- Information Has Value
- Research as Inquiry
- Scholarship as Conversation
- Searching as Strategic Exploration[5]

Each concept examines a social aspect of information literacy that goes beyond one-shot library instruction, and each calls for greater collaboration with faculty across disciplines. The threshold concepts cross disciplinary boundaries and should be embedded in the rhetorical practices of that discipline. For instance, "Authority Is Constructed and Contextual" suggests authority in one situation may not be authority in another. In composition studies, most contend that how a writer develops authority on a topic depends upon the writing context. Just as composition instructors help students examine their rhetorical situation, librarians have students analyze the credibility of the source in relation to the purpose for which it is used.

The threshold concept that most aligns the work of librarians and composition instructors at the University of Cincinnati Blue Ash College (UCBA) is "Research as Inquiry." Our composition courses are built around research assignments. As Brent has argued, "[W]riting from sources is central to the entire mission of the academy, and has resonance far beyond training students to be academics. It teaches them to engage deeply with complex texts and diverse ideas."[6] In making this comment, Brent is encouraging writing instructors to develop writing courses around research assignments. This type of assignment is central to the writing students do at all levels of our composition program. In developmental writing courses, I work with students to identify topics that are personally meaningful and develop a research question around their chosen topic so they are more willingly engaged in the labor intensive process of research-writing. Students spend a week considering topics and developing a research question. Lauren and I provide feedback to the students on the question and its scope. As the composition instructor, I discuss approaches to writing about the topic while Lauren, the instruction librarian, discusses the number and type of potential sources available. We both discuss how to evaluate source credibility, and we ask students to read the sources several times and to write summaries of the sources before they are used in their research writing projects in the basic writing course.

In the required first-year composition course, students are guided towards finding a question in their major they find intriguing. In some years, the course theme is tied to a first-year experience common reading. For instance, one year the theme was food and students were asked to research an aspect of food related to their major. Students are also asked to write about their sources as they find them: a summary of each source analyzing its credibility and discussing how it speaks to the research topic.

The knowledge practices described in the "Research as Inquiry" section of the ACRL Framework dovetail nicely with the work writing instructors do in first-year composition. We help students "formulate questions for research based on information gaps or reexamination of existing, possibly conflicting, information."[7] The questions students generate guide their work as both researchers and writers. In the first-year course, we provide guidance in research question setup so the response can be written reasonably well in five- to ten-page paper. Developing a focused research question is difficult for many first-year students because they do not yet know about the process of inquiry conducted in the academic world. They are also novices to the important conversations in their disciplines. Many students are unaware that such conversations are taking place; most courses in the disciplines present knowledge from first-year textbooks as if it were uncontested, which may be why most students choose research topics on social issues that concern them.

The ACRL Framework also suggests a continuum of learning from novice to expert. In our work with first-year students, we introduce students to ways of managing information used in their writing. Lauren and I collaborate in the development of concept maps for students' research projects. I begin by presenting a sample concept map to students, then work with them to create a class concept map. First, students are asked to brainstorm as many ideas as possible on a topics list related to a particular concept, like dogs or food. Then, students are asked to look for words that encompass some of the ideas on the list. In our example of dogs, the list might have sheepdogs, poodles, breeds, and golden retrievers, among others. I help students see that the word breeds encompasses the other words in the list. Once students understand concept mapping, they are asked to generate a concept map for their research question. A sparse concept map may indicate a student is struggling with the subject, so students with sparse maps are asked to reconsider their research topic. Students take their concept maps with them to the library instruction class.

Lauren uses the concept maps to teach students to develop keywords about their research topic during a library instruction class, providing a visual way for students to understand their research topic and identify keywords useful as part of a search. Students review their initial brainstorming in the session's first part and subsequently add or delete concepts and keywords from their maps as needed. The maps are a starting point in the search for sources. Once students have found their sources, they need to organize them.

Writing instructors and librarians mean different things, perhaps, when they say "organize information in meaningful ways."[8] In writing courses, the focus is on helping students marshal their evidence to support their theses. The evidence provided by their sources is discussed in terms of how readers will evaluate each source's credibility and quality. Therefore, students are asked to consider their readers' needs when organizing the information in their writing. Student writers analyze their audience and their purpose for writing before determining the best approach to organizing their information for their readers. In composing this chapter, it became apparent we value organizing information differently. In my writing class, where the focus is organizing information for readers in meaningful ways, it is a central course concept. Depending on the class, Lauren discusses the importance of reviewing the information gathered to identify gaps and to determine if additional information is needed. She talks with students about the type of information available in the sources and asks them to consider what value the sources will bring to their project. Lauren and her librarian colleagues will be reexamining this area as they implement the new ACRL Framework locally.

Perhaps the most difficult aspect of research-writing for first-year students is synthesizing ideas gathered from multiple sources. As the work of the Citation Project shows, students who are novice writer do not understand how to pull ideas together to create their own ideas.[9] Wells points out part of the difficulty for students is their ability to understand the sources they are reading.[10] This lack of clear understanding of their sources leads to what Howard refers to as "patch writing," which is "copying from a source text and then deleting some words, altering grammatical structures, or plugging in one-for-one synonym substitutes."[11] Howard suggests summary writing activities may help students understand more difficult analytical texts, leading to less patch writing. Students in my composition courses are asked to provide a summary of the source as well as an analysis of the source in advance of completing research-writing assignments.

By applying the ACRL "Research as Inquiry" frame, composition instructors and librarians can develop instructional activities that reinforce and support research concepts necessary for participating in the research genre and help students understand the reasons for research. In other words, the iterative research process introduces students to the exigencies that lead writers to seek information while examining the information found to determine if it fits the situation. Students learn how knowledge is socially-constructed.

In addition to identifying cognitive learning outcomes, both Frameworks suggest dispositions or habits of mind useful for students learning the threshold concepts. In the ACRL Framework section, "Research as Inquiry," among the nine dispositions listed are some matching the habits of mind in the WPA Framework. Driscoll and Wells identify four dispositions, "value, self-efficacy, attribution, and self-regulation," influencing their students' ability to transfer writing knowledge.[12] Perhaps the most important disposition is metacognition, because students must be aware of their level of understanding to take appropriate action

- rhetorical knowledge
- critical thinking
- writing processes
- knowledge of conventions
- ability to compose in multiple environments[20]

Upon reading the WPA Framework, I see some of the core concepts I embrace as a librarian are equally important to writing instructors. In the habits of mind section, familiar concepts such as performing research inquiry, gathering and evaluation of information, and citing sources are woven into the structure and clearly align with the research processes of which librarians are very familiar. Within the five experiences, elements of information literacy are certainly present. For example, the rhetorical knowledge experience includes "write and analyze a variety of types of texts to identify...the audiences and purposes for which they are intended."[21] The critical thinking and knowledge of conventions experiences also include information literacy elements such as "evaluate sources for credibility, bias, quality of evidence, and quality of reasoning"[22] and "practice various approaches to the documentation and attribution of sources."[23] Equally interesting is the WPA Framework is written using language in many ways familiar to librarians. Paired with the ACRL Framework, the WPA Framework provides common ground on which librarians can become participants with writing instructors in conversations about curriculum development and the intertwining of writing and research processes.

A critical concept—not only as part of a college education, but also once a student has graduated—is the credibility and reliability of information. For librarians, this typically refers to evaluating information sources, a core concept of the library instruction dialogue for many years. Under the previous ACRL Standards, approved in 2000, there were five standards; evaluation being the third standard. In the recently approved ACRL Framework, evaluating sources transitions into the frame, "Authority is Constructed and Contextual." Given the ever-changing information landscape, determining the credibility of information, with an emphasis on the types of authority, has become more challenging for undergraduate students.

It is an ongoing challenge, faced by both librarians and composition instructors, to get students thinking critically about sources and authority. The need is specifically recognized within the WPA Framework as one of the curiosity habits of mind; a habit is described as "...seek[ing] relevant authoritative information and recogniz[ing] the meaning and value of that information."[24] In our college writing courses, writing instructors ask students to rhetorically read their sources. They focus on the author's qualifications, the author's purpose for writing, the quality of the author's argument and evidence, and author's intended audience. Students are asked to consider their own purposes and audience as they evaluate sources and discuss the role exigence plays in determining source quality and credibility. For instance, researchers may value peer-reviewed journal sources while reporters may rely on interviews. The value of a source depends upon how effectively the student writer uses it to achieve their purpose.

When addressing evaluation of information in library instruction classes for our first-year composition course, I introduce the concept of evaluating information along with criteria (e.g. currency, relevancy, accuracy, authority, point of view) that helps students take a closer look at the source and decide on its appropriate use. Introducing evaluation of information is sometimes flipped outside the classroom where students watch a tutorial before coming to the library instruction class. Once students have an introduction to the concept, I build in time for them to apply the evaluation criteria to potential sources they have found as part of their assigned research project, sometimes pairing students and asking them to peer review each other's sources.

It is important to consider how source evaluation can be viewed as a shared responsibility between librarians and writing instructors given its presence in both Frameworks. For some librarians, partnerships with writing instructors are common and develop from a variety of experiences. From a library teaching standpoint, these collaborations may manifest as trying new activities for library instruction, flipping content, teaching multiple library instruction sessions within a semester, and being embedded in a course management system (e.g. Blackboard) to integrate library resources and provide focused research help. Alternatively, librarian-writing instructor partnerships can involve curriculum development as demonstrated in Lundstrom, Fagerheim, and Benson's case study "Librarians and Instructors Developing Student Learning Outcomes: Using Frameworks to Lead the Process,"[25] which highlights an eight-week summer workshop for curriculum development. Some librarian-writing instructor collegial relationships extend into scholarly partnerships and may take a variety of forms, including conference presentations and research projects. Dynamic conversations and significant work are taking place between librarians and writing instructors in a variety of collaborations. Such relationships take time to develop; creating a trusting and respectful environment where librarians and writing instructors can truly talk to each other about student learning is a worthwhile investment of time for both parties.

For many librarians, the question of how to start collaborating with writing instructors can be difficult. Norgaard recognized the need for more meaningful conversations between librarians and writing instructors when he stated "[w]e would do well to listen attentively to each other's voices" and continued with "this gesture ought to be more than one of courtesy, or neighborly goodwill. We need each other more than both of us may think."[26] Librarians can begin Norgaard's suggested process of "listen[ing] attentively"[27] by engaging with the WPA Framework in conjunction with the ACRL Framework. The WPA Framework provides a lens to see how the writing and research processes transect. Recognizing librarians and writing instructors have common ground can inspire meaningful conversations, supply a catalyst for curriculum development, and provide a source of strength for moving from teaching collaborations into solid partnerships focused on student success and lifelong learning.

How do the Frameworks Support and Play against Each Other?

Norgaard suggested that librarians use rhetoric and composition theory in information literacy research, as well as rhetoric and composition researchers use information literacy theories in their research.[28] He described how "any literacy is always an embedded or situated cultural practice conditioned by ideology, power, and social context."[29] The authors of the new ACRL Framework clearly adopted this view of literacy when they write that metaliteracy is foundational to the ACRL Framework in which "students are both consumers and creators of information who can participate successfully in collaborative spaces. Metaliteracy demands behavioral, affective, cognitive, and metacognitive engagement with the information ecosystem."[30] According to Norgaard, information literacy and writing are "recursive, goal-oriented, and problem-solving activit[ies] that involve a complex repertoire of strategies."[31] Both Frameworks, in fact, delineate the activities and strategies students need to learn to be responsible information users and writers.

The Frameworks provide common language, theoretical underpinnings, and pedagogical approaches that should make collaborations between writing instructors and librarians more fruitful. The ACRL Framework provides useful descriptions for students, teaching faculty, and librarians that should guide their work. It positions students as active learners in the information literacy ecology, and it imagines students creating new knowledge and responsibly using existing knowledge. The revised WPA Outcomes complement the WPA Framework and envision a writer able to adapt to new writing situations "along disciplinary, professional, and civic lines."[32] Both disciplines are preparing students for the future by giving them a skill set they can adapt to new situations. Bransford, Brown, and Cocking believe a "major goal of schooling is to prepare students for flexible adaptation to new problems and settings."[33] The threshold concepts in the ACRL Framework and the statements in the WPA Outcomes provide guidelines for students to use in writing and research tasks, as Norgaard suggests, that are "recursive, goal-setting, and problem-solving."[34] For instance, students can continually return to the rhetorical knowledge outcome in each writing task and find a new approach to addressing readers' concerns.

Teaching faculty also can return to the threshold concepts and outcomes statements to create learning environments that develop and extend their students' writing and information literacy practices. Using these two documents in concert creates a thoroughly integrated curriculum for information literacy and writing development. Both documents were created with the intent that local contexts would interpret the level of performance students should achieve. In our situation, the writing program administrator and librarian can use these documents to robustly improve the writing curriculum so it includes information literacy concepts that go beyond students' current understanding of library research. Much of the work we do in our composition classes already centers on the Burkean idea of academic writing as a conversation. In Brenda's composition classes, she discusses this conversation as a way for students to enter into their research-writing and works with Lauren to expand this metaphor to include information literacy concepts reinforced during library instruction. Lauren could ask students to diagram the conversation they are reading using a simple table in which they write how the author(s) would answer the research question and would respond to one other, thus helping students find their own place in the conversation.

McMillen and Hill use conversation as a metaphor to link composition and information literacy instruction and apply the metaphor to teaching research skills through seven principles, suggesting that research-writing is interactive, recursive, and situated in context.[35] In describing the problem with traditional research assignments, Fister advocates "recasting the research process" as "a way of tapping into a scholarly communication network. In this network scholars present new ideas, argue for new interpretations of old ideas, draw connections, point out contrasts, inquire into meaning, and interpret the signifiers of cultures in ways that construct meaning."[36] This description is remarkably similar to the research-writing as conversation metaphor developed in the ACRL Framework.

What are the Implications of the Frameworks for Composition Instructors?

The release of the revised WPA Outcomes and the new ACRL Framework come at an opportune time for writing faculty as we examine the ways we teach writing. We should consider further integrating information literacy instruction with writing instruction as they are more closely aligned in these two documents. An emerging trend in writing pedagogy is the teaching-for-transfer approach, developed by Yancey, Robertson, and Taczak,[37] in which students are taught key concepts they can apply in other writing. Students continually reflect upon these course concepts and how they use them as writers to develop their own theory of writing.[38]

This approach should consider how to incorporate some of the elements described in the new ACRL Framework so students' theories of writing would also incorporate a theory of information literacy. Concepts from the ACRL Framework could, in such a case, be added to a composition course designed for transfer. The concepts of authority, information creation, inquiry, value, conversation, and strategic searching could be integrated with the key writing concepts identified by Yancey, Robertson, Taczak "(1) audience, genre, reflection; (2) exigence, critical analysis, discourse community, knowledge; (3) context, composition, and circulation; and (4) knowledge and reflection."[39] In fact, research is a major unit in their description of their course. In piloting the teaching-for-transfer pedagogy, we could incorporate the key concepts from the ACRL Framework, including "Scholarship as Conversation," that many composition instructors already use.

What are the Implications of the Frameworks for Librarians?

The ACRL Framework presents an exciting opportunity for librarians and offers flexibility to adapt the frames, based on the needs of students, while situating concepts within the local context of their home institutions. The Task Force acknowledges this in the ACRL Framework's introduction, indicating it "is called a framework intentionally because it is based on a cluster of interconnected core concepts, with flexible options for implementation, rather than on a set of standards or learning outcomes, or any prescriptive enumeration of skills."[40] This flexibility is of particular importance given the range of skills and level of preparedness librarians see in student populations and, while liberating, it reveals larger questions for librarians in terms of unique student populations, local contexts, faculty relationships, and challenges inherent in shifting curricula and teaching practices. The expectation is more implications will surface as research in this area increases and more librarians implement the Framework in their teaching practices and instruction programs. As librarians learn what the ACRL Framework means for their students, and institutions, the true implications will become clearer with time.

As I consider the ACRL Framework's implications for my library, the WPA Framework plays an important part given the role of research processes in composition courses. The WPA Framework provides a solid structure, in conjunction with the WPA Outcomes, in which to look at first-year composition courses, and it shares common themes and language with the ACRL Framework, offering a natural starting point for research-writing conversations. Under the previous ACRL Standards, which were skill-based with a focus on standards and performance indicators, conversations with writing instructors about the role of information literacy and its part in the writing process represented a challenge given the lack of a common language. Bringing these two Frameworks together is an important opportunity to move collaboration forward and engage in a robust discussion about student learning within the context of writing and research processes.

The implications of the ACRL Framework will continue to be revealed as librarians delve further into it with questions and potential meanings for their unique student populations. Gibson and Jacobson summed it up nicely when they stated, "[t]he ongoing value of the Framework depends upon the community of information literacy librarians, their faculty colleagues, and others in the academy with a commitment to information literacy as an ongoing educational reform agenda."[41] Bringing the WPA Framework on this journey provides clarity and helps us navigate a new direction with our writing instructor partners. For many librarians, it will be an exciting journey with challenges and redirects along the way, but which ultimately delivers us to a long-awaited destination.

How Does This Conversation Influence our Work in Educating Students?

Taking part in this conversation provides starting points for how this librarian and writing program administrator plan our future work together. An initial step we recommend to any collaboration is developing a mutual understanding of the foundational documents that guide our respective programs. The ACRL Framework, WPA Framework, and the WPA Outcomes provide necessary structure and direction. Understanding how we each view the Frameworks leads into considering how to build on them a more dynamic curricula that fully integrates information literacy and research-writing. The Frameworks also help actively engage curricular conversations, using the common language found in both documents.

One way this librarian and writing program administrator can build upon these Frameworks is to more intentionally design instruction for transfer. As writing faculty think about creating a teaching-for-transfer curriculum for composition courses, composition instructors will need to engage librarians in how to integrate information literacy concepts into this new curriculum. The curriculum should include the key concepts of both disciplines. Writing instructors need to be mindful of Fister's concern that the new ACRL Framework will be reduced from its complexity into a list.[42] She has stated, "In reality these ideas about how information works and how students can participate in making meaning can't really be grasped except through sustained experience."[43] Fister seems to suggest librarians find places where they can more fully integrate information literacy instruction, and what better place than in composition classes where students are often building their writing from sources?

Exploring ways to effectively integrate information literacy into composition courses represents an important piece of our library's approach to implementing the ACRL Framework. Like many other instruction program coordinators, this librarian, along with my librarian colleagues, is in the midst of determining what the ACRL Framework means for the college, its different student populations, and for working with teaching faculty. This means situating the Framework locally to ascertain what students really need to know, determining the gaps currently in library instruction, and scaffolding those concepts appropriately for a two-year college. Situating locally also means conversations using common language with teaching faculty and other stakeholders about information literacy and the library's role in educating students. Through brainstorming sessions, faculty and student feedback, and discussions with various stakeholders about student learning outcomes, we are looking forward to reimagining curriculum using the ACRL Framework as our guide.

Conclusion

Engaging in a meaningful conversation with each other about what student success means and how librarians and writing instructors can support and inspire student learning is ultimately the goal. Librarians and writing instructors often wrestle with some of the same frustrations and challenges: getting students to apply what they learn in one course to another or from one library instruction session to the assignment itself, considering the context in which students use sources, and evaluating sources to determine authority and credibility. The question of why librarians and writing instructors are not working together more is certainly not a new one, and the reasons why working together does not always happen in the most effective way (or perhaps not at all) vary widely across institutions.

As this writing program administrator and librarian have worked together for many years, the recent launch of the ACRL Framework is prompting us to consider these important questions within our college and respective programs. While writing this chapter, we have reflected on our roles and teaching practices as well as learned from each other. In examining the respective Frameworks, it has become clear to us how they complement each other and how using them can contribute pieces to the larger puzzle of student learning. This opportunity for self-reflecting and considering new perspectives provides valuable insight into how we can work together at a more integrated level.

Notes

1.   Association of College and Research Libraries, *Framework for Information Literacy for Higher Education,* (2016). Accessed January 12, 2016. http://www.ala.org/acrl/sites/ala.org.acrl/files/content/issues/infolit/Framework_ILHE.pdf.
2.   Council of Writing Program Administrators, National Council of Teachers of English, and National Writing Project, *Framework for Success in Postsecondary Writing,* (2011). Accessed January 15, 2016. http://www.wpacouncil.org/files/framework-for-success-postsecondary-writing.pdf.
3.   Council of Writing Program Administrators, *WPA Outcomes Statement for First-Year Composition* (3.0), July 17, 2014. Accessed January 15, 2016. http://wpacouncil.org/positions/outcomes.html.
4.   Barry Maid and Barbara D'Angelo, "The WPA Outcomes, Information Literacy, and the Challenges of Outcomes-Based Curricular Design," in *Writing Assessment in the 21ˢᵗ Century: Essays in Honor of Edward M. White,* ed. Norbert Elliot and Les Perelman (New York: Hampton, 2012), 112.
5.   ACRL, Framework, 2.
6.   Douglass Brent, "The Research Paper and Why We Should Still Care," *WPA: Writing Program Administration* 37, no. 1 (2013): 50.
7.   ACRL, Framework, 7.
8.   Ibid.
9.   Rebecca Moore Howard, Tanya K. Rodrigue, and Tricia C. Serviss, "Writing from Sources, Writing from Sentences," *Writing & Pedagogy* 2, no. 2 (2010): 177–192; Sandra Jamieson, "Reading and Engaging Sources: What Students' Use of Sources Reveals about Advanced Reading Skills," *Across the Disciplines* 10, no. 4 (2013).
10. Dorothy Wells, "An Account of the Complex Causes of Unintentional Plagiarism in College Writing," *WPA: Writing Program Administration* 16, no. 3 (1993): 59–71.
11. Rebecca Moore Howard, "A Plagiarism Pentimento," *Journal of Teaching Writing* 11, (1993): 233.
12. Dana Driscoll and Jennifer Holcomb Marie Wells, "Beyond Knowledge and Skills: Writing Transfer and the Role of Student Dispositions," *Composition Forum* 26, (Fall 2012).
13. John Bransford, Ann Brown, and Rodney Cocking, *How People Learn: Brain, Mind, Experience, and School* (Washington D.C.: National Academy Press, 2000), 50.
14. Driscoll and Wells, "Beyond Knowledge."
15. WPA, Framework, 5.
16. Ibid., 1.
17. Peggy O'Neill et al., "Creating the Framework for Success in Postsecondary Writing," *College English* 74, no.6 (2012): 521.
18. WPA, Framework, 1.
19. Ibid.
20. Ibid.
21. Ibid., 6.
22. Ibid., 7.
23. Ibid., 9.
24. Ibid., 4.
25. Kacy Lundstrom, Britt Anna Fagerheim, and Elizabeth Benson, "Librarians and Instructors Developing Student Learning Outcomes: Using Frameworks to Lead the

Process," *Reference Services Review* 42, no.3 (2014): 484–498. doi:10.1108/RSR-04-2014-0007.

26. Rolf Norgaard, "Writing Information Literacy: Contributions to a Concept," *Reference & User Services Quarterly* 43, no. 2 (2003):125.

27. Ibid.

28. Ibid., 127.

29. Ibid., 126.

30. ACRL, Framework, 2.

31. Norgaard, "Writing Information Literacy," 127.

32. WPA, Outcomes.

33. Bransford, Brown, and Cocking, *How People Learn,* 77.

34. Norgaard, "Writing Information Literacy," 127.

35. Paula McMillen and Eric Hill, "Why Teach 'Research as a Conversation' in Freshman Composition Courses? A Metaphor to Help Librarians and Composition Instructors Develop a Shared Model," *Research Strategies* 20, nos.1–2 (2004): 3–22. doi:10.1016/j.resstr.2005.07.005.

36. Barbara Fister, "Teaching the Rhetorical Dimensions of Research," *Research Strategies* 11, no. 4 (1993): 211–219, http://homepages.gac.edu/~fister/rs.html.

37. Kathleen Blake Yancey, Liane Robertson, and Kara Taczak, *Writing across Contexts: Transfer, Composition, and Sites of Writing* (Boulder, Colorado: University Press of Colorado, 2014).

38. Ibid.

39. Ibid., 57.

40. ACRL, Framework, 2.

41. Craig Gibson and Trudi Jacobson, "Informing and Extending the Draft ACRL Information Literacy Framework for Higher Education: An Overview and Avenues for Research," *College & Research Libraries* 75, no. 3 (2014): 253. doi:10.5860/0750250.

42. Barbara Fister, A *College Librarian's Take on Technology* (blog). *Inside Higher Education.* https://www.insidehighered.com/blogs/library-babel-fish/naming-what-we-know-about-writing.

43. Ibid.

Bibliography

Association of College and Research Libraries. 2016. *Framework for Information Literacy for Higher Education.* Accessed January 12, 2016. http://www.ala.org/acrl/sites/ala.org.acrl/files/content/issues/infolit/Framework_ILHE.pdf.

Bransford, John D., Ann L. Brown, and Rodney R. Cocking. *How People Learn: Brain, Mind, Experience, and School.* Washington D.C.: National Academy Press, 2000.

Brent, Douglass. "The Research Paper and Why We Should Still Care." *WPA: Writing Program Administration* 37, no. 1 (2013): 33–53.

Council of Writing Program Administrators. 2014. *WPA Outcomes Statement for First-Year Composition* (3.0). Accessed January 15, 2016. http://wpacouncil.org/positions/outcomes.html.

Council of Writing Program Administrators, National Council of Teachers of English, and National Writing Project. 2011. *Framework for Success in Postsecondary Writing.*

Accessed January 15, 2016. http://www.wpacouncil.org/files/framework-for-success-postsecondary-writing.pdf.

Driscoll, Dana Lynn and Jennifer Holcomb Marie Wells. "Beyond Knowledge and Skills: Writing Transfer and the Role of Student Dispositions." *Composition Forum* 26 (Fall 2012).

Fister, Barbara. *A College Librarian's Take on Technology* (blog). *Inside Higher Education.* Accessed January 12, 2016. https://www.insidehighered.com/blogs/library-babel-fish/naming-what-we-know-about-writing.

Fister, Barbara. "Teaching the Rhetorical Dimensions of Research." *Research Strategies* 11, no. 4 (1993): 211–219. http://homepages.gac.edu/~fister/rs.html.

Gibson, Craig, and Trudi E. Jacobson. "Informing and Extending the Draft ACRL Information Literacy Framework for Higher Education: An Overview and Avenues for Research." *College & Research Libraries* 75, no. 3 (2014): 250–254. doi:10.5860/0750250.

Howard, Rebecca Moore. "A Plagiarism Pentimento." *Journal of Teaching Writing* 11 (1993): 233–245.

Howard, Rebecca Moore, Tanya K. Rodrigue, and Tricia C. Serviss. "Writing from Sources, Writing from Sentences." *Writing & Pedagogy* 2, no. 2 (2010): 177–192.

Jamieson, Sandra. "Reading and Engaging Sources: What Students' Use of Sources Reveals About Advanced Reading Skills." *Across the Disciplines* 10, no. 4 (2013).

Lundstrom, Kacy, Britt Anna Fagerheim, and Elizabeth Benson. "Librarians and Instructors Developing Student Learning Outcomes: Using Frameworks to Lead the Process." *Reference Services Review* 42, no. 3 (2014): 484–498. doi:10.1108/RSR-04-2014-0007.

Maid, Barry M., and Barbara J. D'Angelo. "The WPA Outcomes, Information Literacy, and the Challenges of Outcomes-Based Curricular Design." In *Writing Assessment in the 21st Century: Essays in Honor of Edward M. White,* edited by Norbert Elliot and Les Perelman, 101–114. New York: Hampton Press, 2012.

McMillen, Paula, and Eric Hill. "Why Teach 'Research as a Conversation' in Freshman Composition Courses? A Metaphor to Help Librarians and Composition Instructors Develop a Shared Model." *Research Strategies* 20, nos. 1–2 (2004): 3–22. doi:10.1016/j.resstr.2005.07.005.

Norgaard, Rolf. "Writing Information Literacy: Contributions to a Concept." *Reference & User Services Quarterly* 43, no. 2 (2003):124–130.

O'Neill, Peggy, Linda Adler-Kassner, Cathy Fleischer, and Anne-Marie Hall. "Creating the Framework for Success in Postsecondary Writing." *College English* 74, no. 6 (2012): 520–533.

Wells, Dorothy. "An Account of the Complex Causes of Unintentional Plagiarism in College Writing." *WPA: Writing Program Administration* 16, no. 3 (1993): 59–71.

Yancey, Kathleen Blake, Liane Robertson, and Kara Taczak. *Writing across Contexts: Transfer, Composition, and Sites of Writing.* Boulder, Colorado: University Press of Colorado, 2014.

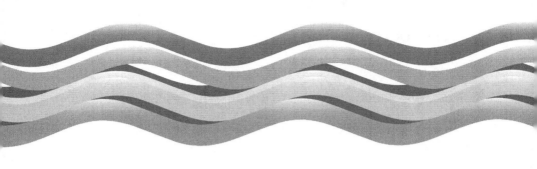

CHAPTER 2

Interpreting the Frameworks:

Faculty Constructions of Research and the Researching Student

Rick Fisher and Kaijsa Calkins
University of Wyoming

Introduction

In Fall 2015, our institution transitioned to a new set of general education requirements. During the course approval process for these new and revised general education courses, our librarians became interested in exploring ways non-library faculty planned to teach and assess research and information literacy (IL) skills. In other words, they wanted to understand how faculty construct the act of research for their students. This study contributes to composition and rhetoric scholar Karen Kaiser Lee's call for faculty and librarians to "consider what is meant by 'research' in writing assignments that students encounter across the undergraduate experience…and ascertain what sort of assignments and requirements are now in place."[1]

For the purpose of this chapter, we requested access to and were able to collect syllabi and course approval forms from all advanced communication courses offered in the general education curriculum. These courses (designated as COM3) include learning outcomes with a writing-in-the-disciplines focus. Through analysis of these course application forms, we hoped to identify common trends and gaps in faculty definitions and approaches to IL, with the larger goal of developing instructional support to deepen and extend faculty teaching in this area.

Specifically, we chose to analyze faculty descriptions of their approaches to research by coding around a set of rough binaries suggested during our examination of the documents: skills vs. discourse focus, telling vs. transforming purpose, content vs. issue orientation, and linear vs. iterative process. We believe this way of coding and analyzing the data can provide faculty—in libraries, writing and communication programs, teaching and learning centers, and the disciplines—with an understanding of research that may help them develop and support curricula in line with frameworks for twenty-first century scholars and citizens.

This chapter reviews recent scholarship about faculty approaches to research, provides a brief analysis of national frameworks meant to guide student writing and research, presents key findings from our analysis of COM3 application materials, and ends with a set of suggestions we believe useful to our campus as well as others.

Existing Research about Faculty Approaches to Research Assignments

Surveying previous scholarship by composition scholars David Russell, Stephen North, Ambrose N. Manning, and Richard L. Larson, Karen Lee's chapter in *The New Digital Scholar*[2] argues research papers, since the mid-twentieth century, have tended towards ossification that oversimplifies the research process, confines it to a "single, often laborious task," promotes an artificial and rigid process, isolates research from the writing process, and ultimately decontextualizes research activity from larger course objectives. Quoting Doug Brent, Lee notes a disconnect between research as process and research as product: "[R]esearch, the eternal ether that interpenetrates all formal inquiry, becomes 'the research paper,' a separate genre that occupies a separate little section of the course."[3]

According to Russell, this disconnect emerged as written scholarly discourse (primarily in the form of journals) associated with the German research model replaced a previously oral tradition; classrooms became sites of apprenticeship where faculty represented the larger disciplinary community. Yet, as faculty pressure to research increased, less time was available for teaching research, leading to writing which looked "toward the ideal of research, but [which was] effectively cut off from the activities of disciplinary research."[4]

As a result of this disconnect, the classroom research assignment is often characterized by a rushed, artificial process. For example, a 2010 Project Information Literacy (PIL) survey found 58 percent of students select a thesis statement early in their process. Additionally, only 55 percent of students surveyed listed "having a chance to be creative" as important during academic research (second to last among fifteen options, ahead of only "impressing parents with grade received.")[5] Another PIL report further describes a relatively rushed, linear process for most students, with three-quarters of survey respondents spending one to five hours researching before turning to writing and editing.[6] Additionally, Lee suggests students see research paper assignments as focused on informing more than analyzing,[7] further supporting the notion that classroom research, for many students, has a different focus than research in the discipline.

Dan Melzer's recent analysis of 2,101 college-level writing assignments across the curriculum updates the information presented by Lee. His study found a continuing tendency toward informative, transaction assignments, often focused on "an extremely limited view of academic discourse … asking [students] to simply display the 'right' answer or the 'correct' definition to the instructor."[8] Even at the upper level, Melzer found 61 percent of assignments were directed to "teacher-as-examiner."[9] Despite these statistics depicting an artificial process in which students prematurely settle on their stance without engaging their curiosity, Project Information Literacy's 2010 survey also determined "carrying out comprehensive research of a topic (78%) and learning something new (78%) [were] of importance to [students] too."[10]

Students appear to believe lack of clear instruction about research hinders those goals. For example, Alison Head's 2007 survey of humanities and social science majors found "nearly half of the survey sample strongly agreed with the statement that a lack of information from the assigning professor stymied them the most, sometimes keeping them from beginning an assignment at all (48%)."[11] Specifically, Head's analysis of research assignment descriptions showed "a lack of detail and guidance in many research assignment handouts. As a whole, the handouts offered little direction about (1) plotting the course for research, (2) crafting a quality paper, and (3) preparing a paper that adheres to a grading rubric of some kind."[12] She reports "[f]ew of the handouts analyzed mentioned where students were to look for research resources," and "when provided, the guidelines for crafting a quality research paper were often terse and formulaic."[13]

Additionally, the 2010 Project Information Literacy study indicates lack of clarity—both during the initial stages and during evaluation—was frustrating to students: "For over three-fourths (84%) of the students surveyed, the most difficult step of the course-related research process was getting started. Defining a topic (66%), narrowing it down (62%), and filtering through irrelevant results (61%) frequently hampered students in the sample."[14] And, nearly half of survey respondents (46 percent) said simply knowing whether they had done a good job was a struggle[15]—a percentage indicating clarity of expectations remains a significant problem for many classroom research assignments.

The lack of guidance may be explained, in part, by Michelle Simmons, who suggests faculty may struggle to make research expectations clear because they have internalized those processes and tasks: "domain-specific rhetorical processes are seen by the faculty members who work within the domain as the 'normal' or 'natural' or 'correct' way of writing, reading, or researching; and they expect their undergraduate students to be able to learn and adopt these ways of communicating without explicit instruction."[16] In other words, Simmons suggests faculty have acquired an implicit sense of good research for their discipline, but do not realize they need to unpack those assumptions about normal or correct research for their students.

Some Positive Indicators

Despite the depiction of classroom research as artificial and arhetorical, other studies provide a more positive perspective. Lee acknowledges more recent research—such as that by Melzer, Cara Hood, and James Strickland—indicates movement towards activity theory-based orientations to research, resulting in assignments engaging students in more disciplinary, discovery-based projects.[17] Additionally, Melzer characterized 17 percent of the transactional writing in his study as persuasive assignments moving students closer to working inside the discourse and often providing an audience beyond the instructor.[18] Melzer also found courses affiliated in some way with an institutional WAC program or initiative were more likely to assign a wider variety of purposes, audiences, and genres; provide interesting rhetorical situations beyond traditional exam writing; and incorporate a process approach to writing (including self-reflective writing).[19]

Specifically, in analyzing research papers as a genre, Melzer contests Russell's claim that research papers have become ubiquitous and relatively uniform;[20] in contrast, Melzer found a wide variety of genre conventions among the research-writing assignments he collected. Following Robert Davis and Mark Shadle's model, Melzer divided that variety into two general categories: the modernist paper (traditional, informative, thesis-driven, objective) and the alternative paper (which values creation of new knowledge, exploration, and originality of thought and format). Melzer reports, despite his expectations, "most of the researched writing in the study asked students to create knowledge and perform the meaning-making work of a discipline."[21] Melzer concludes with a view of the research paper genre as one of the most complex and dynamic genres in college writing, and one that instructors assign as a tool to encourage students to think critically, to introduce them to ways of thinking in the discipline, and to prepare them for the workforce.[22]

Thus, this component of Melzer's analysis highlights the ways research paper assignments, despite their flaws, may indeed promote creativity, critical thinking, and initiate students into the work of the disciplines.

In sum, the existing research on research presents a complicated, sometimes discouraging picture, but not a hopeless one. For many students, research continues to feel frustrating, artificial, and transactional; Lee ultimately claims criticisms of research assignments suggest students can find information but not "uncover new insights…as the [research] assignment was intended to do since its inception in the mid-19th century."[23] Yet, in at least some classes, faculty are developing assignments that encourage students to develop and deepen their information literacy in ways that will serve them well in their disciplinary futures.

A Brief Analysis of the Frameworks

If the previous section describes the existing situation in terms of faculty research assignments, then the two national frameworks define what it should be. Those frameworks—the *Framework for Information Literacy for Higher Education*,[24] from the Association of College and Research Libraries (ACRL), and the *Framework for Success in Postsecondary Writing*,[25] jointly developed by the Council of Writing Program Administrators (WPA), National Council of Teachers of English (NCTE), and the National Writing Project (NWP)—describe librarians' and compositionists' notions of the preferred intersections of writing and research. Thus, these Frameworks serve as aspirational documents describing how faculty should construct research for their students. Specifically, we believe the Frameworks reveal a set of shared values, including the following points of convergence:

1. Skills are subordinated to larger definitions of successful, transdisciplinary discourse practices. Both Frameworks identify concrete actions, skills, and experiences, but are situated in service to larger, more holistic goals. Thus, both documents establish claims about what academic discourse is or should be.

2. While both Frameworks are presented as transdisciplinary, each acknowledge implementation will necessarily have disciplinary differences; different disciplines will enact writing and research in different ways.

3. Researching and writing are continually developing abilities. The ACRL Framework differentiates novice and expert practices, while the WPA Framework less explicitly states "experiences are a way to foster habits of mind."[26]

4. Researching and writing are iterative, problem-based processes rather than rigid, linear pathways to re-assembling content.

5. Researching and writing are driven by rhetorical purposes and contexts. Researching and writing are conversations with others over time.

6. Researching and writing are multimodal and take place in a variety of environments.

7. Successful writing and researching involves metaliteracies/metacognition. The ACRL Framework for Information Literacy takes a metaliteracy approach which articulates IL as "an overarching set of abilities in which students are both consumers and creators of information" and who can exercise "behavioral, affective, cognitive, and metacognitive [or critical self-reflective] engagement with the information ecosystem."[27] Similarly, the WPA Framework identifies metacognition—"the ability to reflect on one's own thinking as well as on the individual and cultural processes used to structure knowledge—as an essential habit of mind for success in college writing.[28]

To sum, both the ACRL Framework and the WPA Framework value research instruction that embeds skills within larger disciplinary frames, sees information-gathering and -communicating along a continuum of expertise, acknowledges the importance of process, places research tasks in contexts of audience, purpose, and modality, and engages learners in metacognition.

Methods

Our study has the benefit of a complete but limited sample: we were able to access documentary materials for all approved COM3 courses submitted during the initial approval process (through May 2015), for a total of sixty-seven courses. Departments from all six of our university's undergraduate colleges submitted courses for review. Each course submission required a common application form and a course syllabus; in many cases, faculty included course assignment descriptions and/or assessment rubrics. These documents formed the foundation of our research.

We chose to investigate the advanced communication course in more detail because, as a course typically occurring in a student's final year, we believed it would reveal disciplinary-based assumptions about students' knowledge, skills, and habits of mind regarding information literacy. We also believe our institution's COM3 courses serve to illuminate trends likely to exist at other institutions with similar general-education courses.

While we already had access to these documents for internal assessment and planning processes, we sought and received IRB approval to use these documents for research purposes as well. We quote from application materials only in cases where we received consent to provide potentially identifiable information; in other cases, we refer to courses by general discipline or program markers.

Our Contextual Identities

Rather than claiming an objective stance for this research, we believe it important to explicitly acknowledge our invested perspectives and positions in the analytic process.[29] Though we jointly coded all data as a method to increase reliability, in this research we are not disinterested scholars; our institutional roles mean we will continue to be directly involved in curricular and faculty support activities related to COM courses in admittedly value-directed ways. Rick Fisher, at the time of writing, is the coordinator for the COM sequence and has had a substantial role guiding faculty understanding and development of the curricula reflected in the application materials being analyzed. Additionally, he teaches in the English Department, including courses in the COM sequence. Kaijsa Calkins is a subject liaison librarian for English (including the first-year writing program) whose work includes partnering with faculty to develop information literacy instruction and activities.

Theoretical Framework and Approach to Coding

At our institution, the COM application document represents what might be considered a collision of discourses: within the application materials, faculty members were asked to complete the task of synthesizing multiple discursive conceptualizations of communication and writing, research, learning/pedagogy, and performance/assessment. Thus, we saw the documents as a worthwhile site for exploring constructions of reality as well as of social roles. Our focus was less on the social roles faculty construct for themselves and instead on the ways their descriptions of research created and restricted appropriate student roles as researchers. As qualitative health-science researchers Daniel Singer and Myra Hunter define them, discourses are conversations or talk with an agenda. They are orientated towards action, aimed at establishing a particular prevailing view or social reality. Discourses govern what it is possible to think. They produce knowledge which in turn functions to maintain certain power relationships within society and influences how individuals make sense of experience.[30]

Thus, we see faculty efforts to describe research as discursive moments that can reveal subtle ways these descriptions reinforce, as well as challenge and contradict, expert ways of acting, thinking, valuing, and interacting.

Codes

Based on our interest in the construction and circulation of discourses within this set of extant texts, we inductively developed a coding scheme for this analysis. After reviewing the data, we noticed a set of emergent tensions; through further discussion, we identified three rough binaries for our coding: skills vs. discourse focus, telling vs. transforming purpose, and content vs issue orientation. Additionally, as we reviewed the ACRL and WPA Frameworks, we decided to add a process component; given the importance of process in both Frameworks, we coded the data to indicate whether a course had a primarily linear vs. iterative approach to research. We felt this binary versus coding[31] would allow us to see relationships across these perspectives.

Our binaries took vague shapes that were refined as we moved back and forth through the data. The following definitions were produced as a result of the research process, including both primary analysis and further research.

Skills vs. Discourse Focus

Many faculty who operate outside a discourse-based orientation to teaching continue to frame literacy skills as neutral, instrumental skills that can be taught in decontextualized, generalizable ways rather than skills embedded in the ideologies and epistemologies of groups operating in specific times and places. By adopting a discourse analysis perspective, we acknowledge this first binary is a false one: we see all skills as embedded in social practice of discourses.[32] But we were interested to see whether faculty representations of research provided disciplinary contextualizations for those skills and processes or whether they described research in general ways.

For example, one art course provides a number of skills tips for students as they work on their research paper/presentation; however, the instructor frames the course as an introduction to "complexities and problems of art and photography as it relates to the American West" that will lead to a "nuanced understanding of western art production." Additionally, the instructor provides guidelines for thesis statements that ground the assignment in disciplinary focuses on "historical textual evidence (historical or cultural context, historiography, biography, theory, etc.)" and/or visual analysis, and she notes the assignment thesis, structure, and research strategies will emerge through consultation with instructor and peers. Given these descriptions about what counts as evidence, and given a description of process that includes social interaction with others in the field, we categorized this class as having a discourse focus. Had the course provided only general tips for locating sources (e.g., use the library databases to locate relevant materials), we would have categorized the course as skills focused.

Telling vs. Transforming Purpose and Content vs. Issue Orientation

Both the telling vs. transforming binary and content vs. issue binary were suggested by references in Lee's chapter to previous scholarship;[33] additionally, these binaries are informed by research in problem-based learning as well as the theoretical underpinnings of Writing Across the Curriculum (WAC). Instructional technology scholar, John Savery, and cognitive psychologist, Thomas Duffy, for example, describe problem-based learning as an attempt "to relate constructivism as a theory of learning to the practice of instruction."[34] For them, this approach enacts constructivism in relationship to three propositions: (1) understanding comes through interaction with one's environment, (2) puzzlement drives learning and the cognitive representation of what is learned, and (3) knowledge evolves through social negotiations that allow individual understandings to be evaluated.[35]

Within the field of composition and rhetoric, constructivist views of writing are reflected in Writing Across the Curriculum pedagogy; as John Bean notes, WAC pedagogy "encourages the messy process whereby writers become engaged with a problem and, once engaged, formulate, develop, complicate, and clarify their ideas."[36] Bean suggests this stands in opposition to the view of writing as "information rather than as argument or analysis,"[37] and in opposition to Paulo Freire's theory of the mono-logic banking model, in which research and writing serve primarily as ways to collect and re-present objective facts.[38]

These code sets give us insight into whether research projects are problematized for students (issue orientation) and whether they encourage students to make meaning (transforming purpose) rather than reproduce accepted knowledge.

Linear vs. Iterative Process

The last code pair was motivated by the importance, in both Frameworks, of process in research-writing tasks. If these Frameworks can be taken as speaking for their professional organizations, it is evident both professions value writing and research as iterative processes. The WPA Framework identifies "developing flexible writing process" as an essential experience for post-secondary writing success: "Writing processes are not linear…. Writers learn to move back and forth through different stages of writing, adapting those stages to the situation."[39] Similarly, the ACRL's description of research as inquiry,[40] conversation,[41] and strategic exploration[42] suggests a non-linear pathway requiring iterative refinement; specifically, the ACRL Framework notes, "Research is iterative and depends upon asking increasingly complex or new questions whose answers in turn develop additional questions or lines of inquiry in any field."[43] Yet, as Lee has pointed out, a continuing problem with research assignments is they simplify the rich iterative processes of experts to a linear march through stages that poorly mimic what the ACRL Framework refers to as the "contextualized, complex experience" of non-classroom research.[44] While composition and rhetoric scholar Jennie Nelson found 95 percent of first-year composition students followed approaches she categorized as "compile information," "premature thesis," and "linear research,"[45] she argues few first-year students follow the recursive approach that aligns with the way academics describe their own approaches to research, "perhaps because few [students] have had an opportunity to experience research in this way."[46]

With this coding set, we wanted to distinguish courses/assignments that clearly encouraged students to engage in the iterative process of research and writing from those that locked students into a linear, stage-driven approach.

Limitations

Of the sixty-seven courses we reviewed, we ultimately marked twenty-two as uncategorizable. Though the application materials clearly asked faculty to describe their activities, assignments, and assessments for the COM3 research/information literacy student learning outcome, nearly a third of the courses provided so little information about research-writing that we could not assign appropriate codes. Because we were specifically analyzing faculty representations of research, some courses simply didn't include enough explanation of the research process/project for us to identify the orientation as discourse or skills. One example is a capstone course in the humanities in which the applicant described types of assignments (i.e., annotated bibliography and critical research essay) without explaining how faculty intended to facilitate/guide the research activity.

We also acknowledge some limitations to the generalizability of our analysis. First, because the primary approval document asked faculty to directly identify assignments, activities, and instruction addressing the research outcome for their advanced communication courses, we acknowledge the approval process itself may have encouraged a decontextualized approach to some descriptions of research.

Second, we cannot draw conclusions about the full framing of research activities in the courses we analyzed. Instead, we have only a snapshot of the way faculty framed research for an external approval process. However, because that process included submission of course syllabi, we believe our analysis provides important information about the ways faculty articulate the relationship of research activities to other aspects of the course. We acknowledge many of the courses that include little initial framing of disciplinary-appropriate research may ultimately provide substantial guidance in later class discussions and assignment descriptions. A syllabus can only do so much—but as an important interaction between teacher and students, the syllabus still carries a great deal of discursive power to shape students' perspectives on the purpose, nature, and value of research within the course. For the next stage of this project, we plan to conduct a number of follow-up interviews in order to gather more contextual information about perspectives revealed in the documents themselves.

Results and Discussion

Given the focus of COM3 on communication in disciplinary settings, we expected the courses we analyzed would advance students' understanding of disciplinary discourses. Our analysis reveals, however, in some cases instructors present a generalized (i.e., not discipline-specific) description of research tasks, even while other explanations of communication activity are more discourse-based.

Table 2.01 provides a graphic representation of our results. We developed this table during later stages of analysis as we struggled to meaningfully represent the results of our binary coding in a single graphic. Columns indicate purpose (i.e., telling or transforming) while rows indicate focus (i.e., discourse or skills). We found that most courses with a telling purpose viewed research with a content orientation; likewise, we found that courses with a transforming purpose would be likely to characterize research as issue-oriented. The table uses boldface to mark the few courses that didn't fit this pattern. Additionally, asterisks indicate the courses that suggested an iterative approach to research. Given the values implied in the Frameworks, we feel the asterisked courses in the top-right quadrant represent the ideal representation of research, since these courses take an iterative, discourse-based approach and ask students to do something with their research beyond merely reporting it. To maintain confidentiality of participants, we list courses by their general department/field rather than by specific course title/number.

	Purpose: Telling	Purpose: Transforming
Focus: Discourse	Chemistry,* Communication, Geography, Life Sciences, Life Sciences, Theatre, Education (7)	Economics, Art, Art*, Communication*, Econ*, Engineering, English/Writing, English/Writing, Family/Consumer Science*, History*, Political Science*, Languages, Life Sciences*, Health Sciences*, Political Science, Political Science, Religion*, Agriculture, Sociology*, Health Sciences, Education, Education, Education*, Energy Resources (24)
Focus: Skills	**Accounting, Agriculture**, Agriculture, Anthropology, Geology, Social Work, Theatre, Theatre, Zoology (9)	Economics, Agriculture, Political Science, **Sociology** (5)

Table 2.01
Course-by-Course Analysis of Focus, Purpose, Orientation, and Process

*Asterisks indicate courses that included an iterative research component.
Boldface indicates courses with a telling + issue (column 1) or transforming + content (column 2) purpose and orientation.

In addition to analysis focused on our original binaries, we also sought to identify trends related both to points of convergence between the Frameworks and to findings from previous scholarship. We provide descriptive detail about five such trends.

Overall Focus and Purpose

We were pleased more than half of the courses we analyzed (24 of 45) frame research as discourse-focused and transformative in purpose. (See the top right, shaded quadrant in Table 2.01). Many of these courses include clear rhetorical settings for the research project as well, such as this business course:

> In this senior capstone course, [business] majors interested in owning and operating their own business will develop a full-length strategic business plan for that business. This involves

writing a business plan and presenting it in-class to colleagues and faculty at the end of the semester. Students will be introduced to library databases, business resources, and course materials that will provide information and guide their strategic business plan development. The final strategic business plan will be focused on communicating each students' business idea and plan to prospective industry and financial investors.

Similarly, a capstone in life sciences provided language throughout the syllabus to frame research as central to the real work of the discipline; in the course, students produce a mock NSF-style research proposal based on service-learning projects exploring genuine field-based problems in the community. Additionally, the course included three course outcomes focused on advanced aspects of information literacy:

- Perform a thorough overview of a topic (access and assess literature) without being overwhelmed by the extent of available resources.
- Understand when and how to reference source material and recognize this process as an important part of communicating with other scholars.
- Value scientific knowledge as a tool to enact change.

In courses like these, we see instructors' descriptions of research aligning with a number of WPA and ACRL concerns. Both of these courses, for example, try to provide contexts to move students towards "genuine purposes and audiences... in order to foster flexibility and rhetorical versatility"[47] as well as encourage habits of mind like openness and persistence. The projects as described may also encourage students to consider "different types of [information] authority"[48] and engage in the process of "matching information products with their information needs."[49] Finally, in terms of establishing a discourse orientation to research, the rhetorical context of these courses affords students the opportunity to understand their research as embedded in larger conversations of and about scholarship.

In contrast, one health sciences research methods course—which we coded as skills-focused—provided extensive discourse on the overall course, but assigned activities not explicitly connected to the issues and practices of the field. Though the course requires students to collect data for statistical analysis, the prompt for this assignment does not guide students to disciplinary topics for investigation: "You could, for example, develop a Likert scale on a political topic coming out of the last election." Additionally, this course required a literature review for another, more disciplinary-focused assignment, yet provided no guidance to accomplish that review; instead, the applicant seemed to assume students have the skills for developing a lit review as well as knowledge of the disciplinary expectations for a review in this field.

In a political science course that provided clear guidance on the type of thesis/issue appropriate for the course term paper, expectations for collecting and evaluating references were less forthcoming. Despite an annotated bibliography assignment and a syllabus section labeled "research expectations," the course instructor provided primarily quantitative requirements ("8–10 scholarly sources") and general evaluative criteria ("Is the research appropriate and of high quality? Are the sources relevant and authoritative?").

Inauthentic/Incomplete Research Processes

While more than half of submissions indicate a discourse focus and a transforming purpose, far fewer faculty directly frame course research in an iterative way. This finding seems especially problematic given Lee's previous criticism of research assignments as overly static and simplified, as well as the WPA and ACRL Frameworks' emphasis on iterative composing processes.

In many courses, discussion of process addressed writing but not researching. This trend may shed light on Project Information Literacy's findings about the gap between students' writing processes and research processes in which "students had fewer techniques for conducting research and finding information than for writing papers."[50] Our analysis may explain: overall, faculty provided less explicit information for students about approaches appropriate to the research aspects of communication projects than they did about expected writing processes. In many cases, even the language around expected writing process was limited, focusing primarily on discrete activities rather than underlying goals for the process, as in this life sciences course:

> Students will be required to select and research a topic pertinent to the course and will present it in written and oral form before the end of the semester. This project should reinforce themes covered during the course (e.g., specific aspects of inflammation, degeneration, neoplasia, etc.)…Once a topic has been approved, students should prepare a written abstract of their proposed topic to be evaluated [and] present a 5 minute talk…Feedback received from the abstract and talk should be used to improve the final paper and presentation…Points will be lost for spelling or grammatical errors, and failure to cover the topic comprehensively.

Despite ACRL's assertion that "research is iterative"[51] and WPA's assertion that "writing processes are not linear,"[52] descriptions like this present the feedback stage as relatively unproblematic. In terms of WPA habits of mind, the description of research here focuses on responsibility—with heavy emphasis on requirements and expectations—and pays little attention to curiosity, openness, engagement, creativity, or flexibility that might encourage students in a more iterative exploration of their topic. In a similar way, the expectation that feedback will be "used to improve the final paper and presentation" asserts the authority of the unnamed feedback-giver(s) (the instructor? peers?) rather than drawing students into an inquiry-driven, iterative consideration of the ways "authority is constructed and contextual."[53]

Though a limited number of courses point students towards an iterative research process, the variety and creativity of non-linear processes is noteworthy. In a political science course, for example, the instructor asks students to practice, in short responses, the research writing skills they are expected to use in a final briefing paper; additionally, he requires students to revise a group research project based on feedback from disciplinary audience members during a mid-semester presentation. In another course, the instructor encourages an iterative perspective on research by asking students to update an existing article:

> All students will be provided with one journal article related to the textile industry and the environment, which may include such topics as recycling of textile materials, new technologies to cause less damage to the environment during production, etc. Each student will be expected to find a research-based article on the same/similar topic which is more current. You will write an abstract (summary) of the major points of each article, and a brief comparison summary of the two articles, indicating what changes have occurred in this topic over the last few years.

This course presents a rare case in which expectations for the writing task are not necessarily iterative (or explicitly process-based at all), but in which students are nonetheless invited to investigate the unstable nature of disciplinary knowledge.

Cases of Transforming Content and Telling Issues

In general, we found orientation (telling vs. transforming) and focus (content vs. issue) were tightly connected; in all but three cases, we coded courses as telling-content or transforming-issue. One foreign language course illustrates the type assignment we considered to be focused on transforming content:

> Prepare a biography (2–3pp.) of one of the authors on or relevant to the syllabus [as a way] to familiarize yourselves with […] biographical dictionaries, to think about what goes into a biography, and about the difficulties of writing a biography that is both reliable and interesting.

On the surface, this description is focused on content—information *about* an author or historical figure without direct concern for issues connected to that individual. Yet, that students are asked to think about matters of convention and rhetoric indicate they are nonetheless being invited to transform their research in relationship to rhetorical considerations of the genre.

In contrast, one agriculture course clearly focuses on issues in natural resource management; specifically, the syllabus indicates the course helps students "become familiar with the main concepts and concerns that shape current debates in agriculture" in order to "familiarize students with science- and practice-based information acquisition, analysis, and synthesis of possible solutions." Yet, in the minimal information provided about research in the course, the main assignments—a literature review, a group solution paper and accompanying presentation—do not indicate students are asked to transform the information they collect.

We find these few exceptions to telling-content or transforming-issue notable because we wonder whether they reveal larger disciplinary mindsets that resist assumptions about what students should *do* with content. Additionally, we suspect our coding reveals some disciplines (or instructors) may not see the content of undergraduate education as issue-based in a way requiring students to interact with previous and current debates of the field. Yet, clearly, both Frameworks emphasize the goal of transformative meaning-making. The WPA Framework, for example, suggests the habits of mind crucial to college-level learners must push the learner past merely "knowing particular facts"[54] and should promote an "active stance"[55] for learning. More forcefully, the ACRL Framework takes the position "experts see inquiry as a process that focuses on problems or questions in a discipline or between disciplines that are open or unresolved…. Many times, this process includes points of disagreement where debate and dialogue work to deepen the conversations around knowledge."[56] In both Frameworks, students are encouraged to think of information and knowledge as embedded in contextual or rhetorical settings, not as neutral content; however, our analysis suggests a number of courses we analyzed (9 of 45) take a skills-based, topic-based perspective that de-emphasizes the complexity of research activity.

Research as an (Often Implicit) Instructor-Level/ Course-Level Construct

Because the course approval process asked applicants to address seven course outcomes—only one directly focused on research—we are not entirely surprised many of the courses provided limited information about how students should approach research. Yet, the fact many of the syllabi we analyzed provided little direct framing for research processes is still important: students may have difficulty starting their research projects precisely because faculty either fail to provide clear disciplinary goals and expectations or because they assume students already know them.[57]

Further compounding this problem, expectations of the research paper genre may often be defined at the classroom discourse-community level, our findings show, which may make it hard for students to identify broader disciplinary-level expectations. Thus, our research confirms Melzer's earlier finding:

> Differences within and among disciplines—and even among instructors within the same discipline and sub-discipline—in terms of purpose, audience, research methods, what counts as evidence, how research papers are structured, and the persona that the writer is asked to take on make it difficult to generalize about the research paper.[58]

Melzer's claim, as well as Project Information Literacy data presented earlier, explains why students may struggle to adapt to new research tasks as they move between courses. Importantly, neither the WPA nor the ACRL Framework suggests schools or programs should standardize research instruction; instead, the Frameworks accept that research processes are always contextual. The ACRL encourages a flexible research approach in which learners "use various research methods, based on need, circumstance, and type of inquiry,"[59] while the WPA's goals of openness[60] and flexibility[61] similarly promote different ways of gathering information[62] as well as awareness that evidence and citation (among other conventions) depend on discipline and context.

Our analysis suggests faculty may not fully recognize the broad range of research contexts students encounter throughout their undergraduate experience, nor fully recognize or articulate their own assumptions about what is appropriate for research tasks within their courses. These are problems that libraries, writing programs, and teaching-and-learning centers will want to address.

Implications: Guidance for Faculty

Ultimately, we believe our analysis points to several implications that can promote more effective approaches to research in advanced disciplinary courses. These suggestions shed light on the ways points of convergence between the WPA and ACRL Frameworks are not being fully extended into undergraduate research experiences.

Our analysis reveals a sizeable proportion of the courses we studied do not encourage students to see research as an ongoing, disciplinarily-embedded, socially-constructed, iterative, problem-based, and metacognitive process of growth and refinement. Thus, we provide these possible pathways for encouraging faculty to adjust their notions and representations of research in line with the WPA's and ACRL's perspectives of research-writing:

1. We need to help faculty identify the specific disciplinary skills and expectations of research writing in their fields. Achieving the goal of research metaliteracy for students requires metaliteracy of faculty. While several courses in our study require a literature review, a term paper, or an annotated bibliography, for example, far fewer spell out the disciplinary goals or conventions for those documents. Especially at the advanced undergraduate level, we believe students should be developing a clear awareness of field-specific sources, evaluation methods, and functions for the research they are asked to conduct. Transdisciplinary discussion groups may help faculty explore differences among research texts across fields and recognize the peculiarities of their disciplinary research conventions.

2. We should encourage programs to articulate programmatic pathways and parameters for research activity. While there may be good reasons for individual course experiences to expose students to a variety of sub-disciplinary differences in research tasks and approaches, it should nonetheless be possible for departments and programs to describe (and justify) research skills and values central to the discipline or professional field. Students should not complete an undergraduate degree with a vague sense that research is an arbitrary, instructor-level set of preferences or requirements. Curriculum revision/redesign processes could directly invite departments and programs to articulate specific research skills, tasks, and values they expect their students to develop throughout the major curriculum.

3. We should encourage faculty members to provide a purpose and justification for research assignments in their syllabi. When students are asked to undertake research for a course, the value of that research in relationship to other course content and outcomes should be made clear. On a larger scale, faculty should also be encouraged to make

research activities of course texts more visible to students by engaging them in discussion about the types of inquiry, sources, and skills hidden in texts that may otherwise seem objective and naturalized.

4.   We must help faculty understand and extend the value of transformative and persuasive research tasks. A number of assignments we analyzed made little effort to locate students in a clear rhetorical setting. Yet, as the WPA Framework argues, writing assignments that emphasize formulaic writing for non-authentic audiences will not reinforce the habits of mind and the experiences necessary for success. [Instead,] writing activities and assignments should be designed with genuine purposes and audiences in mind ... in order to foster flexibility and rhetorical versatility.[63]

5.   We should coordinate efforts among libraries, teaching/learning centers, and writing programs. As Simmons has argued, "Librarians are simultaneously insiders and outsiders of the classroom and of the academic disciplines in which they specialize, placing them in a unique position that allows mediation between the non-academic discourse of entering undergraduates and the specialized discourse of disciplinary faculty."[64] While she argues informational literacy has much to learn from the field of Writing Across the Curriculum, some of our analysis suggests faculty do not yet see the ways both writing and research are disciplinary tasks. Coordinated efforts to provide faculty development that builds on the expertise of writing studies, information science, and learning theory can help faculty craft assignments that draw students into rich, iterative, discourse-based experiences with researching and representing the knowledge of their fields of study.

In this study, we were impressed and heartened to find many faculty at our institution teaching research in ways aligned with the values offered in the ACRL and WPA Frameworks. The ACRL describes its Framework as a holistic set of foundational ideas that provide "conceptual understandings that organize many other concepts and ideas about information, research, and scholarship into a coherent whole," and it argues "teaching faculty have a greater responsibility in designing curricula and assignments that foster enhanced engagement with the core ideas about information and scholarship within their disciplines."[65] While the WPA Framework obviously addresses research as a component of writing, this Framework also sees an essential role for research in fostering critical thinking, as well as flexible composing processes. Together, the Frameworks assert students should be encountering and conducting research in ways that move them beyond skills toward a discursive, metaliterate mindset "in which students are consumers and creators of information who can participate successfully in collaborative spaces."[66]

While we were pleased the majority of courses we studied exhibited some characteristics aligned with the ACRL and WPA Frameworks, we felt students could be further supported in internalizing the threshold concepts, habits of mind, and experiences underpinning these documents. While the majority of courses have discourse orientations, we identified a need to extend the process orientation many faculty have for writing not only to research, but also to models incorporating multiple channels of feedback that drive revision of research and writing activities. Faculty should articulate and model their own research methods and processes for their students and reveal the messy, problem-based nature of authentic scholarly research. Faculty should also discuss issues in their fields with students, as well as issues related to information, research, and communication. Those conversations should be driven by concepts from the Frameworks such as authority is constructed and contextual; there are social and financial implications of information access, particularly access to the scholarly record in a given field; and scholarship is, by its nature, made up of conversations over time (and who and how one participates in these conversations is worthy of contemplation).

Our analysis reveals the need for faculty to better frame research-writing as an opportunity to make meaning, not just assemble others' ideas into a new package, and, perhaps most importantly, to connect this purpose in all research-writing assignments with authentic and appropriate audiences.

Notes

1. Lee, "The Research Paper Project in the Undergraduate Writing Course," 59.
2. Ibid., 44–45.
3. Ibid., 45.
4. Russell, *Writing in the Academic Disciplines: A Curricular History*, 99–100.
5. Head and Eisenberg, "Truth Be Told: How College Students Seek Information in the Digital Age," 20.
6. Head, "Information Literacy from the Trenches: How do Humanities and Social Science Majors Conduct Academic Research?"
7. Lee, "The Research Paper Project," 59.
8. Melzer, "Writing Assignments Across the Curriculum: A National Study of College Writing," 22.
9. Ibid., 28.
10. Head and Eisenberg, "Truth Be Told," 4. Admittedly, these goals were less important than the pragmatic concerns with getting a good grade, finishing the assignment, passing the class, and meeting page and citation requirements.
11. Head, "Information Literacy from the Trenches," 435.
12. Ibid.
13. Ibid., 436.
14. Head and Eisenberg, "Truth Be Told," 3.
15. Ibid., 25. This struggle seemed especially problematic in the big-picture stage of task-development, see page 29.

16. Simmons, "Librarians as Disciplinary Discourse Mediators: Using Genre Theory to Move Toward Critical Information Literacy," 298.

17. Lee, "The Research Paper Project in the Undergraduate Writing Course," 56–57.

18. Melzer, "Writing Assignments Across the Curriculum," 22.

19. Ibid., see chapter 5.

20. Ibid., 43. See also Russell, *Writing in the Academic Disciplines*, 78.

21. Ibid., 49.

22. Ibid., 51.

23. Lee, "The Research Paper Project," 47.

24. ACRL, Framework.

25. WPA, Framework.

26. Ibid., 1.

27. ACRL, Framework, 2.

28. WPA, Framework, 1.

29. Starks and Trinidad. "Choose Your Method: A Comparison of Phenomenology, Discourse Analysis, and Grounded Theory."

30. Singer and Hunter, "The Experience of Premature Menopause: A Thematic Discourse Analysis," 66.

31. See, for example, Saldaña, Johnny, "Coding and Analysis Strategies" and *The Coding Manual for Qualitative Researchers*, Second Edition.

32. For further discussion of autonomous and instrumentalist views of literacy, see Street, *Literacy in Theory and Practice* and Macelo, Literacies of Power: What Americans are Not Permitted to Know.

33. I.e., Scardamalia and Bereiter's 1987 work on knowledge telling and knowledge transforming as two models of composing, and Nelson and Hayes's 1988 article about first-year students' content-driven vs. issue-driven approaches to research. For Scardamalia and Bereiter, knowledge transforming emerges from a composition process that pushes a writer beyond content space into rhetorical space where the writer must use the knowledge strategically. In their model, knowledge telling is a precursor to the ability to transform knowledge.

34. Savery and Duffy, "Problem-Based Learning: An Instructional Model and its Constructivist Framework," 135.

35. Ibid.

36. Bean, *Engaging Ideas: The Professor's Guide to Integrating Writing, Critical Thinking, and Active Learning in the Classroom*, 20.

37. Ibid., 18.

38. Freire, *Pedagogy of the Oppressed*.

39. WPA, Framework, 8.

40. ACRL, Framework, 7.

41. Ibid., 8.

42. Ibid., 9.

43. Ibid., 7.

44. Ibid., 9.

45. Nelson, "The Research Paper: 'A Rhetoric of Doing' or a 'Rhetoric of the Finished Word?'" 65–75.

46. Nelson, "The Scandalous Research Paper and Exorcising Ghosts," 10.

47. WPA, Framework, 3.

48. ACRL, Framework, 4.
49. Ibid., 5.
50. Head and Eisenberg, "Truth Be Told," 19.
51. ACRL, Framework, 7.
52. WPA, Framework, 8.
53. Ibid., 4.
54. Ibid., 4.
55. Ibid.
56. ACRL, Framework, 7.
57. Head and Eisenberg, *Assigning Inquiry: How Handouts for Research Assignments Guide Today's College Students.*
58. Melzer, "Writing Assignments Across the Curriculum," 62.
59. ACRL, Framework, 7.
60. WPA, Framework, 4.
61. Ibid., 5.
62. Ibid., 6.
63. WPA, Framework, 3. Additionally, the practice of asking students to simply re-present accepted facts (ie, telling content) can be alienating; in contrast, LeCourt argues, "Making a space for the personal… counteracts the students' perceptions that their alternative voices must be silenced within a disciplinary discourse." In "WAC as Critical Pedagogy: The Third Stage?" 401.
64. Simmons, "Librarians as Disciplinary Discourse Mediators," 298.
65. ACRL, Framework, 2.
66. Ibid.

Bibliography

Association of College and Research Libraries. 2016. *Framework for Information Literacy for Higher Education.* Accessed February 1, 2015. http://www.ala.org/acrl/sites/ala.org.acrl/files/content/issues/infolit/Framework_ILHE.pdf.

Bean, John C. *Engaging Ideas: The Professor's Guide to Integrating Writing, Critical Thinking, and Active Learning in the Classroom.* San Francisco: Jossey-Bass, 2001.

Council of Writing Program Administrators, National Council of Teachers of English, and National Writing Project. 2011. *Framework for Success in Postsecondary Writing.* Accessed February 1. 2015. http://wpacouncil.org/files/framework-for-success-postsecondary-writing.pdf.

Friere, Paolo. *Pedagogy of the Oppressed* [Pedagogía del oprimido. English]. New revised 20th-Anniversary Edition. New York: Continuum, 1993.

Head, Alison J. "Information Literacy from the Trenches: How do Humanities and Social Science Majors Conduct Academic Research?" *College & Research Libraries* 69 no. 5 (2008): 427–446. doi:10.5860/crl.69.5.427.

Head, Alison J. and Michael B. Eisenberg. *Assigning Inquiry: How Handouts for Research Assignments Guide Today's College Students.* Accessed February 1, 2015. Seattle: Project Information Literacy, 2010. http://projectinfolit.org/publications.

———. "Truth Be Told: How College Students Seek Information in the Digital Age." Seattle: Project Information Literacy, 2010. http://projectinfolit.org/publications.

LeCourt, Donna. "WAC as Critical Pedagogy: The Third Stage?" *Journal of Advanced Composition* 16 no.3 (1996): 389–405.

Lee, Karen Kaiser. "The Research Paper Project in the Undergraduate Writing Course," in *The New Digital Scholar*, eds. Randall McClure and James P. Purdy. Medford, NJ: Information Today, 2013.

Macelo, Donaldo. *Literacies of Power: What Americans are Not Permitted to Know.* Boulder, CO: Westview Press, 2006.

Melzer, Dan. "Writing Assignments Across the Curriculum: A National Study of College Writing." *College Composition and Communication* 61, no. 2 (December, 2009): 240–261.

Nelson, Jennie. "The Research Paper: 'A Rhetoric of Doing' or a 'Rhetoric of the Finished Word?'" *Composition Studies/Freshman English News* 22 no. 2 (1994): 65–75.

———. "The Scandalous Research Paper and Exorcising Ghosts," in *The Subject is Research: Processes and Practices*, eds. Wendy Bishop and Pavel Zemliansky. Portsmouth, NH: Boynton/Cook, 2001.

Nelson, Jennie and John R. Hayes. 1988. *How the Writing Context Shapes College Students' Strategies for Writing from Sources.* Technical Report 16. Berkeley: National Center for the Study of Writing and Literacy at University of California, Berkeley and Carnegie Melon University.

Russell, David R. *Writing in the Academic Disciplines: A Curricular History.* Carbondale: Southern Illinois University Press, 2002.

Saldaña, Johnny. "Coding and Analysis Strategies." In *Oxford Handbook of Qualitative Research*, ed. Patricia Leavey. New York: Oxford UP, 2014.

———. *The Coding Manual for Qualitative Researchers*, Second Edition. London; Thousand Oaks, Calif.: Sage, 2013.

Savery, John M. and Thomas M. Duffy. "Problem-Based Learning: An Instructional Model and its Constructivist Framework" in *Constructivist Learning Environments: Case Studies in Instructional Design*, ed. Brent Gayle Wilson. Englewood Cliffs, NJ: Educational Technology Publications, 1996.

Scardamalia, Marlene and Carl Bereiter. "Knowledge Telling and Knowledge Transforming in Written Composition." In *Advances in Applied Psycholinguistics*, Vol. 1, edited by Sheldon Rosenberg, 142–175. Cambridge UK: Cambridge University Press, 1987.

Simmons, Michelle Holschuh. "Librarians as Disciplinary Discourse Mediators: Using Genre Theory to Move Toward Critical Information Literacy," *portal: Libraries and the Academy* 5, no. 3 (2005): 297–311.

Singer, Daniel E. and Myra S. Hunter. "The Experience of Premature Menopause: A Thematic Discourse Analysis," *Journal of Reproductive and Infant Psychology* 17, no. 1 (1999): 63–81.

Starks, Helene and Susan Brown Trinidad. "Choose Your Method: A Comparison of Phenomenology, Discourse Analysis, and Grounded Theory," *Qualitative Health Research* 17, no. 10 (December, 2007): 1372–1380. doi:10.1177/1049732307307031.

Street, Bryan. *Literacy in Theory and Practice.* Cambridge: Cambridge University Press, 1984.

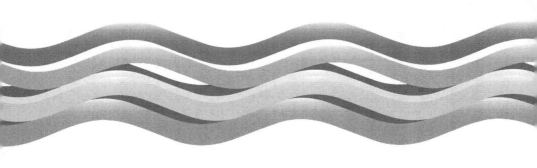

CHAPTER 3

Giving Voice to Students

A Rhetorical Analysis of the Frameworks

Rosalind Bucy, Gillian Devereux, Maric Kramer,
and Jenne Powers
Wheelock College

Introduction

Although our daily work may look different, writing center professionals, writing instructors, and reference and instruction librarians are, first and foremost, educators. We use pedagogical recommendations from our professional communities to inform, direct, and assess our work with students. Putting the professional documents guiding post-secondary writing and information literacy into conversation with each other reveals the intersections of these fields and the benefits of viewing one's work through the lens of another profession. Writing and library instruction were not intended to be conducted in isolation, but the increasing compartmentalization of higher education makes it easy to do so. Yet a writing professional and a librarian who understand each other's roles can use this conversation to improve interactions that invite emerging student voices.

* This work is licensed under a Creative Commons Attribution-NonCommercial-NoDerivatives 4.0 License, CC BY-NC-ND (https://creativecommons.org/licenses/by-nc-nd/4.0/).

While all educators contribute to the development of student voice, librarians and writing professionals have particular access to students during vital transitional moments. These transitions involve induction into new communities and modes of discourse, and the library, writing center, and writing classroom form a spatial nexus that nurtures students in the development of their authentic professional and academic voices. By designing assignments, activities, and interventions that validate student voice, educators validate a student's presence in higher education; such validation helps students develop a new identity as college students capable of engaging in academic scholarship and discourse. Many higher education researchers and professionals view first-year student success in terms of identity development. Students who identify as college students believe they will succeed as college students, and this belief has been proven to foster success in higher education.[1]

The connection between identity and success in higher education is not limited to first-year students. Students also transition from general education curricula to advanced courses required for their disciplines and once again consider their identity; the first- or second-year college student becomes an aspiring social worker, political scientist, clinical psychologist, or elementary school teacher. Again, students are asked to consider their positions in discourse communities and to view themselves as being both in professional roles and capable of contributing to the academic conversation of these communities. In the same way, students transitioning into a graduate program experience another identity shift; these students must learn to see themselves as having expertise in their field and as being capable of graduate level research and writing.

In this chapter, we focus on the usage and frequency of terms related to the idea of student voice in our rhetorical analysis of three primary documents: *The Framework for Success in Postsecondary Writing* from the Council of Writing Program Administrators, National Council of Teachers of English, and National Writing Project (WPA, NCTE, and NWP); the related *WPA Outcomes Statement for First-Year Composition*; and the *Framework for Information Literacy for Higher Education* from the Association of College and Research Libraries (ACRL).[2] This analysis informs our discussion of the emergence of student voice in the library, writing center, and other transitional spaces. It also allows us to present and reflect upon our current classroom collaborations and determine how successfully they foster student voice. Since student voice plays a crucial role in the development of postsecondary research and writing skills, fostering and amplifying student voice is the primary objective of our work. Students whose voices are heard and valued are much better positioned to develop the authoritative, authentic, and original voices they need in order to fully engage with their new communities and modes of discourse.

A Rhetorical Analysis of the WPA and ACRL Frameworks

Through education, especially higher education, students learn to adopt the conventions of discourse communities. Broadly speaking, students encounter an existing conversation and learn to add their own voices to it, making the language of the academy their own. Students pursuing higher education find themselves on the threshold of a new linguistic world, and their experiences in classes, from introductory to graduate level, usher them across this border. These experiences do not happen in isolation, as Bakhtin explains:

> As a living, socio-ideological concrete thing ... language, for the ideological consciousness, lies on the borderline between oneself and the other. The word in language is half someone else's. It becomes "one's own" only when the speaker populates it with his own intention, his own accent, when he appropriates the word, adapting it to his own semantic and expressive intention. Prior to this moment of appropriation, the word does not exist in a neutral and impersonal language (it is not, after all, out of a dictionary that the speaker gets his words!), but rather it exists in other people's mouths, in other people's contexts, serving other people's intentions: it is from there that one must take the word, and make it one's own.[3]

Students encounter academic language in these essentially social contexts; when they come to understand themselves, their ethical purposes (ethos) and their connection to these contexts, students can make this new language their own. Librarians, writing center professionals, and writing instructors can use the Frameworks to structure, guide, and assess student progress in the acquisition of academic voice, but they must recognize a superficial application of the Frameworks may create situations where skill development takes precedence over individual intellectual development.[4] Using the Frameworks in concert can avoid this problem.

When read closely in conjunction with one another, the WPA and ACRL Frameworks illustrate how writing and library professionals can cultivate spaces in which students' authentic voices are heard, nurtured, and amplified. Although each Framework constructs the idea of student voice using different words, and each situates emerging student voice differently, both Frameworks present voice as a set of contextualized choices made by authors to communicate their informed ideas and beliefs to an audience. These Frameworks speak to each other and guide their professional communities to remain student-centered as they assess their interactions, interventions, and instructional practices.

The WPA Framework does not use the word voice, but instead locates student voice within the notion of authentic audience. It has, as its explicit audience, educators who are preparing students for college success. At the same time, it shapes a vision of success in college writing having ramifications for first-year composition as well as writing in the disciplines.

The WPA Framework has three sections: an introduction; an articulation of habits of mind that support success; and a description of experiences with reading, writing, and analysis that develop those habits of mind. The authors respect the notion of writing for an authentic audience, naming audience in the introduction as "instructors who teach writing and include writing in their classes at all levels and in all subjects" along with "parents, policymakers, employers, and the general public."[5] The introduction includes the following crucial statement: "At its essence, the Framework suggests that writing activities and assignments should be designed with genuine purposes and audiences in mind."[6] The WPA Framework returns again and again to the idea of a genuine or authentic audience, and the authors argue that authentic audience is necessary for the development of habits of mind including curiosity, openness, engagement, creativity, persistence, responsibility, flexibility, and metacognition.[7]

In the descriptions of these habits of mind, audience awareness plays the largest role in developing curiosity and metacognition.[8] Curiosity involves "inquiry as a process to develop questions relevant for authentic audiences within a variety of disciplines" and communicates "to multiple audiences inside and outside school using discipline-appropriate conventions."[9] Curiosity is followed by openness and engagement, which both encourage respecting and listening to the views of others. Likewise, responsibility, as defined in this document, appears as "the ability to take ownership of one's actions and understand the consequences of those actions for oneself and others."[10] Finally, metacognition involves reflection on the choices an author makes in the interest of communicating to an authentic audience.[11] These habits, whether explicitly or implicitly performed, all involve consideration of the other, the reader, the audience.

The next section of the WPA Framework outlines the experiences supporting these explicit and implicit habits of mind. Nearly every experience described involves writing as an act necessitating consideration of audience, context, and purpose. While the WPA Framework does not directly mention student voice, it positions student writers as individuals with an important message to deliver to carefully considered readers. This section of the document begins to use the term conversation, which implies a voice in dialogue. It does not, however, address the very real challenge of finding an authentic audience in the classroom.

In 2014, the WPA issued the *WPA Outcomes Statement for First-Year Composition* which aligns with the WPA Framework.[12] In this statement, however, authentic audience does not emerge as the primary vehicle for fostering student voice. Instead, we find a particular emphasis on the act of composing and the development of students' ideas. The introductory section of this outcomes statement describes composing as "complex writing processes that are increasingly reliant on the use of digital technologies" and are "individual and social" acts that "demand continued practice and informed guidance."[13] The authors view writers' growth through an interdisciplinary lens that takes into account professional and civic goals.

The outcomes supporting the composing process include: rhetorical knowledge; critical thinking, reading, and composing; and knowledge of conventions. The outcomes represent rhetorical knowledge actively as "the ability to analyze contexts and audiences and then to act on that analysis in comprehending and creating texts."[14] The term voice is used here to represent something modulated in response to audience, which allows student writers to "develop facility in responding to a variety of situations and contexts calling for purposeful shifts in voice, tone, level of formality, design, medium, and/or structure."[15] Significantly, voice is not associated with agency; rather, as in classical rhetoric, circumstances outside the individual determine voice. In completing this discussion of rhetoric, the WPA emphasizes that students learn "the main purposes of composing in their fields."[16] While purpose may be viewed as agency, the subsequent phrase, "in their fields," reminds readers decisions may be determined by outside factors, such as the conventions of a particular discourse community.

The WPA Outcomes Statement section on critical thinking pays attention to students' ideas, asserting first-year students should "use strategies ... to compose texts that integrate the writer's ideas with those from appropriate sources."[17] The section on reading and composition processes explains the social nature of writing and revision and the value of collaboration. Like the WPA Framework, the WPA Outcomes Statement views writing as social and as active, but student voice is, again, largely absent from consideration in the text.

The ACRL Framework, on the other hand, emphasizes student voice in multiple areas related to the responsibilities of professionals and students in their ethical use of information, particularly through scholarship.[18] Through its consistent emphasis on metacognition and metaliteracy, this document encourages readers to reflect on their own voices and the ways they create, share, and use information.

Voice plays a significant role in the frame "Authority is Constructed and Contextual."[19] In this frame, the authors remind their audience that authority is determined differently by different communities and that one must understand one's position in a community in order to evaluate sources effectively, since "experts know how to seek authoritative voices but also recognize that unlikely voices can be authoritative, depending on need."[20] This frame encourages the contextualization and examination of power structures authorizing some voices over others. By associating authority with voice and considering authority as constructed and contextual, this frame empowers students to view their own voices as authoritative in certain contexts.

The frame "Information Has Value" continues the theme of empowerment by reminding us information affects the lived experiences of those who seek and employ it. Information literacy "experts understand that value may be wielded by powerful interests in ways that marginalize certain voices. However, value may [also] be leveraged for civic, economic, social, or personal gains."[21] This frame empowers the student to make decisions about information and to recognize that these decisions have real-world ramifications. This consistent view of information as power wielded by individuals acting within communities highlights the agency and ethos that must be present to create authentic student voice.

Finally, the frame "Scholarship as Conversation" legitimizes student voice in the academic context.[22] Conversations bind communities, and it is through these conversations that individuals achieve full membership. To help students understand themselves as part of the college community, their active participation in scholarly conversation must be possible. In this frame, the authors remind us established power and authority structures potentially privilege certain voices and information even though novice learners and experts at all levels can take part in the same conversation. This inequity may impact a student's ability to participate in scholarly discourse. Developing familiarity with the sources of evidence, methods, and modes of discourse in their relevant field allows novice learners to enter the ongoing conversations in that field. In addition, new forms of scholarly conversations provide more avenues in which a wide variety of individuals may have a voice in the conversation.

As writing and information literacy professionals, we have the ability to facilitate entry into this conversation through our example, our teaching, and our encouragement. As we help students navigate actual and perceived barriers to participation in scholarly and professional discourse, we validate their voices and support their transition into new forms of communication. Interestingly, the ACRL Framework, with its contextualization of authority and orientation toward community participation provides the most guidance for finding opportunities to foster the growth of student voice.

However, the WPA Framework does remind us the written word lacks power in the absence of audience and purpose. Understanding their own audiences and purposes helps students recognize the authority and power of their own voices, and the ACRL Framework connects this recognition to the dynamics of the communities in which students communicate. Using the ACRL Framework in conjunction with the WPA Framework allows library and writing professionals to encourage students to address rhetorical situations without deferring their own voices and purposes in consideration of audience and context. The idea of the scholarly conversation is central to our work with students, and an explicit focus on student voice encourages us to examine how students are positioning themselves in the academic context and how we can cultivate their full engagement with academic and professional discourse.

Putting the Frameworks into Practice

As library and writing professionals, this careful analysis of the intersections of the ACRL and WPA Frameworks provides the theoretical foundation upon which we build our practice of supporting students as they enter scholarly and professional conversations. Thus, the ACRL frame "Scholarship as Conversation" emerges as central to our efforts to foster student voice.[23] Our work with students in the writing center and at the reference desk has emphasized two additional ACRL frames: "Research as Inquiry" and "Authority is Constructed and Contextual."[24] These frames clearly connect to the habits of mind articulated in the WPA Framework, especially curiosity, openness, engagement, and responsibility.[25]

Although not directly addressed in the frame "Research as Inquiry," student voice is implied through the role of student as questioner.[26] Through their research and writing, students may be entering an ongoing and unresolved conversation where even simple questions may be viewed as disruptive. By validating students' interests and inviting exploration of authentic questions, librarians and writing professionals can help students see an opening in the conversation through which they can enter. The importance of "Research as Inquiry" for developing student voice is further emphasized by findings from a recent study conducted by Project Information Literacy (PIL).[27] In a survey of recent college graduates, PIL found only slightly more than one in four respondents felt college had helped them learn to frame and ask questions of their own.[28] These findings reveal an opportunity for collaborative teaching practices that help students develop the habits and dispositions needed to become lifelong learners. In library research consultations, we center our information searching on students' own questions. When students come to us, we spend the first few minutes of the consultation encouraging them to rephrase or to ask questions about their topics if they have not yet articulated a research question. In writing center sessions, we use open-ended questions to direct consultations and create space for students to work independently.[29] Practices such as these foster curiosity and engagement by involving students in an authentic inquiry process and giving them space to make connections and find meaning.[30]

Closely related to the idea of the student-as-questioner is the ACRL frame "Authority is Constructed and Contextual."[31] In order to make room for student voice, librarians and writing professionals benefit from examining the constructs and contexts of our own authority. When we recognize authority within students, we allow them to retain control of their research and writing processes. By encouraging students to determine the direction of a research consultation and to make decisions about what sources are relevant and authoritative for their purposes, librarians help students develop their own authentic and authoritative voices. In the writing center, we emphasize successful choices students made during the composition process, encourage students to treat their writing challenges as problems to be solved rather than mistakes to be corrected, and use body language that confirms the student's authority over the text.[32] These practices of librarians and writing professionals develop responsibility and openness in students who take ownership of their research and writing actions during consultations and examine their own perspectives in light of those of others.[33]

Integral to our shared practice is the knowledge that the library and writing center are physical spaces where students engage in academic and professional discourse. Many competing voices inhabit these spaces: the potentially authoritative voice of the professional, the seemingly more approachable voice of the peer consultant, the pervasive voice of the instructor, and the sometimes uncertain voice of the student. For decades, writing center scholarship has investigated ways to bring these voices into harmonious conversation by positioning students as the owners of authentic, original voices exercising authority over the texts they create. Foundational essays, such as Brooks' "Minimalist Tutoring," encourage both writing professionals and librarians to help students recognize their authority by establishing them as the experts of their text.[34] The focus of all our work should be communicating to students that their papers have the same value as any other piece of writing; our words and actions must tell students their writing deserves to be read and thought about with the same level of attention we would give any other written text.[35]

However, students, especially students in transitional phases of their higher education careers, can be reluctant to assume authority over their texts and the processes by which they produce them. Their desire to understand and meet instructor expectations often supersedes their desire to assume agency over ideas and express agency through their writing. In the absence of their instructor's voice and authority, students position writing teachers and librarians as authorities who will make decisions about the research and writing process for them.

To address this hesitance on the part of students, librarians and writing professionals can work together to help students with research, documentation, and citation. Faculty can be invited to participate in this process by working with professionals to negotiate the tension between their expectations and their students' individual conceptions of audience, purpose, and authority. Librarians and writing professionals who transcend traditional professional boundaries in order to instruct and empower their students encourage students to transcend the boundaries between research and writing as well as the boundaries that prevent them from fully engaging in academic discourse.

In order to completely embrace their ability to succeed in the college environment, students transitioning from high school to college, from general education courses to required courses for a particular discipline, or from introductory courses to advanced ones, need to find their authentic voices and participate in conversations, both oral and written, in which they listen to others and are heard by others. These conversations typically take place during one-on-one conferences and consultations in the library, in the writing center, and in faculty offices. The challenge we address through our collaborations is bringing these same conversations into classrooms, and other shared learning spaces, then guiding students in transition as they explore and enter the realm of scholarly and professional discourse. Our understanding of the Frameworks and our explicit goal of fostering student voice guides our close collaboration in support of transitional student learning.

Collaborations in the First-Year Classroom

The nature of assignments encountered in college can be bewildering to first-year students. Project Information Literacy's 2013 report on how college freshman conduct course research demonstrated college-level assignments "require independent choices and encourage intellectual exploration."[36] This emphasis on choice and exploration is a significant departure from the more structured assignments students encounter in high school. While many students find this new freedom exciting, most also find it challenging. One student interviewed as part of the Project Information Literacy study reported, "[T]hinking about what I'm interested in is really scary … being forced to find something that I'm passionate about is kind of daunting."[37] In addition, many students find it stressful to try to determine an instructor's expectations for an assignment; anxiety about meeting assignment requirements, combined with the challenge of exercising academic freedom, can make it difficult for students to formulate authentic research and writing questions.

It is not surprising, then, that librarians and faculty often encounter students who take a pragmatic approach when choosing a topic for a research writing assignment. Such students select topics they think will be easy to research or will please their professors. Rarely do students seriously consider their own interests when selecting a research topic. In the same way, students, especially first-year students, seldom take the time to develop their research topics into research questions, which means they often miss the opportunity to approach research as inquiry, a threshold concept identified in the ACRL Framework,[38] or to develop curiosity and openness, habits of mind encouraged in the WPA Framework.[39] Developing the habits of mind and practical skills required to understand research as inquiry is critical to the development of authentic student voice; therefore, fostering student inquiry in the first year must be a priority for both librarians and faculty who work with first-year students.

At Wheelock College, the first-year seminar course required of all students in the fall semester offers an interesting opportunity for fostering the development of student voice. This introductory general education course, taught in a variety of disciplines, focuses on building community among first-year students and recognizes that writing and learning are both individual and social; this recognition mirrors the values emphasized in the WPA Framework.[40] Many first-year seminar instructors offer non-traditional research assignments believing these offer students more opportunities to explore, question, and engage their own interests.[41] To encourage the development of student voice during instruction, librarians, writing professionals, and first-year faculty recently introduced a technique used among K–12 educators and community organizers to generate authentic research questions.

The Question Formulation Technique (QFT), developed by the Right Question Institute, is a method for generating, improving, and prioritizing questions that helps students gain confidence in their ability to ask appropriate or authentic questions.[42] Exercises like the QFT help learners "acquire strategic perspectives on inquiry and a greater repertoire of investigative methods," as indicated in the ACRL frame "Research as Inquiry."[43] The experience of developing one's own questions can be an especially powerful one in the first-year seminar where students are discovering new disciplines, exploring new discourse communities, and creating their own sense of meaning and belonging within those communities. Such activities allow students to once again engage in the habits of mind articulated in the WPA Framework, particularly curiosity and openness. Thus, collaboration between library and writing professionals in first-year seminars at Wheelock College center on bringing the QFT into the classroom.

Three different first-year seminars engaged in this question generating activity. In each case, the QFT facilitator and first-year faculty member discussed the assignment at hand and developed prompts which the students used to generate questions. In an anthropology course, students had been asked to write a short essay in which they explored and explained a symbol of a specific culture. In an American studies course, students needed to use primary sources to write an original research paper about an American leader. In a literature course, students had been asked to write a short story based on the life experiences of an individual they interviewed.

Using the QFT, students worked in groups to generate as many questions as they could about the prompts. The facilitators instructed students to write down each question, without alteration or discussion, as well as number the questions generated. Then students categorized each question as open- or closed-ended, discussed the advantages and disadvantages of each question type, and practiced changing each question type into its inverse. The facilitators then asked the groups to identify the questions they considered to be most important. Once the groups had selected three questions, they shared them with the class, along with their rationale for their choices. Rationales often included consideration of what the audience for their assignments would want or need to know. At the end of the session, students reflected on what they learned using the QFT and how they would apply what they learned when completing their assignment.

Student reflections indicated they developed an appreciation for the role of questioning as a result of their experience with the QFT, and demonstrated dispositional developments in their conception of research as inquiry,[44] in their curiosity, and in their openness to exploring questions relevant to their interests, as well as those of imagined audiences.[45] For example, many students recognized open-ended questions offer new avenues of exploration and closed-ended questions may be valuable despite their apparent simplicity.[46] Students also demonstrated "an open mind and a critical stance"[47] when they reported new understandings about how questions serve different purposes and meet the needs of different audiences depending on how they are framed rhetorically.[48]

Because the first part of the QFT focuses on generating as many questions as possible, students began to understand that the first question they develop about a topic may not be the most interesting or fruitful. This finding helps them recognize the importance of asking more than one question about a topic and of "value persistence, adaptability, and flexibility"[49] undertaking investigations in their academic, personal, and professional lives. Reflections like these were especially encouraging indicators of student progress toward the threshold concept described in the ACRL frame "Research as Inquiry," as well as the WPA Framework's habits of persistence and flexibility.[50] Valuing one's own intellectual curiosity is an important step toward developing one's own authentic voice, and the writing professionals, first-year faculty, and librarians at Wheelock College will continue incorporating the QFT into first-year seminar instruction.

Furthermore, students reported they found the QFT valuable for the immediate assignment and more general purposes. Students preparing to do interviews reported the value of distinguishing between open and closed questions and offering a variety of questions in the interview setting. Other students reported they would apply the technique to non-interview writing assignments, supporting the development of adaptable writing processes[51] and flexible habits of mind.[52] This suggests the QFT helps students understand the connections between learning, research, and writing situations and may also help them distinguish between different types of academic and professional discourse.

Collaborations in the Professional Degree Classroom

Collaborations between library and writing professionals in intermediate courses for professional degree programs, like early childhood education or social work at Wheelock College, have also included the QFT. These courses are designed to introduce students to the theories, conventions, and practices of their chosen field; they are frequently taught in a once-a-week, three-hour block, and their curriculum demands students learn a large amount of unfamiliar content in a short amount of time. Students in these courses often see themselves as novices, or even outsiders. Many of the texts they read have been written by foundational theorists or contemporary researchers, and these authors routinely use specific language containing cues and codes easily understood by those who have already been inducted into that particular discourse community.

As newcomers to these conversations in their academic and professional fields, intermediate-level students struggle to see themselves having the authority or knowledge required to engage in this new mode of discourse and often attempt to engage with it only as "it exists in other people's mouths, in other people's contexts, serving other people's intentions."[53] In these courses, students may engage with the threshold concepts articulated in the ACRL frames "Scholarship as Conversation"[54] and "Authority is Constructed and Contextual."[55] At the same time, they are developing their intellectual curiosity and openness to new ways of thinking, as well as their experiences with critical thinking that puts a "writer's ideas in conversation with those in a text in ways that are appropriate to the academic discipline or context."[56] Again, using these Frameworks in conjunction with one another supports the development of authentic student voice.

The culminating project in these intermediate courses is generally a lengthy research paper or small-scale study. Many students have never been assigned this type of research project before and rely on habits they used to write research papers in secondary school, such as beginning with a comprehensive overview of an overly broad topic. They may also try to replicate the writing style and use of language in their assigned course readings while still developing the ability to understand and contextualize the choices made by the authors of these texts.[57]

In the same way, students in the early stages of their professional degree programs, in many cases, have not yet determined their own purpose and audience. Like their first-year counterparts, they tend to select research topics based on misconceptions about instructor expectations or the perceived ease of finding enough information about a topic. Their conceptions of an appropriate research topic inform their conceptions of a successful research paper and leave little room for the development of an authentic student voice; a voice students must discover and employ before they can fully participate in their discipline's discourse community. As noted in the ACRL frame "Scholarship as Conversation," "developing familiarity with the sources of evidence, methods, and modes of discourse in the field assists novice learners to enter the conversation."[58] Likewise, second- and third-year students in these courses have only just begun to develop the critical reading, thinking, and writing skills needed to add their own voices to existing scholarly conversations.[59] Librarians and writing professionals often invite students to contribute to academic conversations associated with their chosen fields; when we do so, we teach students to equate success in their field with the ability to contribute to these conversations. Therefore, our classroom collaborations must focus on helping students develop a sense of authority, purpose, and audience as they begin the research process. Visiting the classroom early in the process to facilitate activities such as the QFT gives us the opportunity to encourage students to view their research projects as a recursive path of inquiry shaped by information searches, critical reading, and reflective writing.

To further emphasize the intersections between writing and research, the writing center director and the librarian who works most closely with the professional degree programs have begun conducting instructional sessions together. Developing authentic questions about their topics guides students not only through their research process, but also through their writing process. When we work together to help students generate, improve, and prioritize their questions by creating classroom experiences that allow students to develop habits of mind intended to foster deeper engagement with the theoretical and research literature of their chosen discipline,[60] we directly engage with concepts from the ACRL frame "Research as Inquiry" and the habits of curiosity and openness articulated in the WPA Framework.

Working with students collaboratively allows us to encourage students to identify their personal interests, the gaps in their current knowledge, and the connections between their lived experiences and their future goals from a research and writing perspective. When we plan our workshops with students, we intentionally include activities and reflective writing designed to show students "what [they] don't know is also a form of knowledge" and encourage them to "discern the shape of what [they] don't know and why [they] don't know it."[61] Encouraging students to view the gaps in their knowledge, as well as the reasons these gaps exist, as valuable encourages them to position themselves as someone possessing expertise in their field. In this way, we engage students with the concept "Authority is Constructed and Contextual," as outlined in the ACRL Framework.[62] As students learn to "acknowledge they are developing their own authoritative voices in a particular area and recognize the responsibilities this entails,"[63] they begin to see themselves as the professionals they are becoming.

Student reflections written after we used the QFT in human development courses required for professional degree programs indicate the activity reinforced not only the importance of generating research questions, but also the importance of brainstorming in a way that allows students to articulate and externalize their ideas. Students expressed feelings of being prepared or on track to write a paper that will teach them as well as their readers. Notable in these reflections, students expressed the belief they possessed the authority and skill to teach their audience. By incorporating reflective writing exercises into classroom sessions, writing professionals and librarians can aid the development of metacognitive thinking, the culminating habit of mind in the WPA Framework.[64] Reflection also encourages students to try on professional authority, conceptualize a real audience for their writing, and view themselves as contributors to scholarly and professional discourse, a key disposition in the ACRL frame "Scholarship as Conversation"[65] and a key element of rhetorical thinking espoused by both the WPA Framework and the WPA Outcomes Statement.

Students also implicitly acknowledge their ability to construct and communicate with a specific audience for a self-determined purpose in their responses to a guided reflection the writing center director uses to begin collaborative workshop sessions designed to introduce students in professional degree courses to resources particular to their field. In addition to building metacognitive skills, this exercise explicitly engages the crucial notion of authentic audience championed in the WPA Framework and reiterates the importance of connecting purpose to authentic audience in the development of student voice.[66] The exercise asks students to (anonymously) answer the following questions on an index card:

1. What is the topic of your paper?
2. Who is the audience for your paper?
3. Why are you writing this paper?

The writing center director collects the completed cards and uses categories suggested by the students' responses to sort them into groups while the librarian presents information about distinguishing between primary and secondary sources in their field and guides students through the online research guide for the course. The cards reveal 40 to 50 percent of the students identify their instructor as their audience, while another 15 to 30 percent consistently list an audience of their own design, such as "parents of adopted children" or "counselors working with foster children." A small percentage of students also identify themselves as members of the intended audience.

Responses to the question about their paper's purpose fall into a similar pattern. A small group of students indicate they are writing their paper "to get a grade" or "because it is a requirement of this course." A slightly larger group of students cite "learning" or "developing skills" as their purpose. Typically, 30 to 40 percent of students list self-determined purposes, such as "conducting research for people who share my interests," "educating parents of adopted children," or "helping teachers develop strategies for working with deaf students." This final group of responses, like the responses from students who identified a self-constructed audience, implicitly recognize the authority and authenticity of student voices. A well-facilitated class discussion addressing the range of responses and inviting students to explore the reasons for their differences helps change this implicit act of recognition into an explicit one. Following this discussion with an activity to help students locate research materials that speak to their personal interests and authentic research questions is a particularly useful way to reposition students as having authority in their discourse communities and encourages the development of student voice in the professional degree classroom. The ACRL Framework's emphasis on contextualized authority and student voice joins forces here with the WPA Framework's emphasis on using authentic audience and purpose to enhance student engagement in professional discourse communities.

Collaborations in the Advanced Classroom

Like students in professional degree courses, students in advanced arts and sciences courses are transitioning into full membership in their professional discourse communities and learning to see themselves as valid contributors to scholarly conversation.[67] Since these transitions can be stressful for students who may be unwilling to relinquish their identities as novices or who have not previously been asked to assume authority in an academic context, collaborations at this level focus on validating students' feelings of uncertainty and creating a genuine community of inquiry, again building the habit of "metacognition."[68]

Students in an advanced literature seminar were asked to write a substantial, theoretically-informed work of literary criticism. To encourage students to view themselves as literary scholars and engage in scholarly conversation during their research and writing process, the instructor and librarian monitored a research discussion board modeled after Kuhlthau's Information Search Process (ISP).[69] The instructor and librarian collaborated to create discussion prompts that would guide students through the ISP and encourage them to reflect on their experiences; these prompts paid particular attention to the stages of topic selection, pre-focus exploration, and focus formulation. Using the ISP as a model encouraged recognition of the cognitive, affective, and social dimensions of the search process—a key component of the ACRL frame "Searching as Strategic Exploration."[70] Student, instructor, and librarian participation on the board organically led to several research interventions that cultivated student voice.

Conversing and composing played integral roles in the online discussion and the development of students' scholarly voices since "conversing enables the [student] to articulate thoughts, identify gaps, and clarify inconsistencies in the process of the search" while "composing promotes thinking."[71] Students used their written responses to articulate their thoughts about their chosen topics, develop personal perspectives on those topics, share research strategies, and consider the role of the literature in developing their personal perspectives. Reflective writing such as this builds on the habits of mind articulated in the WPA Framework—especially curiosity, openness, engagement, flexibility, and metacognition[72]—students have been developing throughout their collegiate experiences with writing and research. These written reflections alerted the librarian and instructor to the need for interventions, such as recommending additional strategies for research and writing challenges or providing reassurance for students needing encouragement to continue their work. Students also expressed uncertainty about particular genres assigned in the class, such as the annotated bibliography, and in these instances, the librarian and instructor were able to clarify the disciplinary practices associated with that genre.

The collaborative nature of the discussion board helped diminish "the common experience of isolation in research projects and [enabled the students] to help one another in the process of learning."[73] The discussion board allowed the librarian and instructor to be visibly engaged in each student's project. More importantly, students demonstrated engagement[74] with and interest in each other's work, developing a practice of mutual support. Like the professionals facilitating the class, students recognized the anxiety and uncertainty their classmates experienced and intervened by sharing their own concerns, offering advice, and providing encouragement. The discussion board established a collaborative community of scholars who had become more comfortable with their own voices and expertise through repeated experiences and practice "work[ing] with others in various stages of writing."[75]

This community encouraged the students to embrace the social nature of research and engage with the knowledge practices and dispositions outlined in the ACRL frame "Scholarship as Conversation."[76] They shared their research questions and insights and responded to each other with enthusiasm and curiosity. Students also shared article citations and resources they deemed potentially helpful to their peers. Within their own community of scholars, students modeled the way expert scholars "engage in sustained discourse with new insights and discoveries occurring over time as a result of varied perspectives and interpretations."[77] Through their participation in the discussion board, students saw themselves adopting new conventions as shifts in audience and context demanded it. Students were also able to reflect on their ability to navigate different conventions and thus entered the drafting stage with more awareness of the role of their own voices in the scholarly conversation, in many ways reaching the goal writing professionals and librarians have been encouraging them to embrace throughout their foundational and intermediate experiences. At the same time, the presence in the class of students who were not humanities majors drew attention to disciplinary discourse as convention.

The discussion board invited students to approach scholarship as a conversation and also provided the librarian and instructor the opportunity to illustrate and model the method of discourse used in literary studies. The research project required students to adopt the practices and conventions of literary scholars. For some, this marked their transition from introductory to advanced scholarship in their major discipline, but for students pursuing majors in the social sciences or professional fields, this expectation demanded they learn a sophisticated scholarly practice completely separate from the discourse conventions of their primary field of study. Every student in the class found it challenging to use existing literary research to frame their projects, especially when the existing literature presented an argument or theoretical lens that differed from their own. This proved exceptionally true for students majoring in the social sciences, who were accustomed to relying on scholarly literature when providing supporting evidence for their theses. By continuing the reflective discussion even as students moved from the drafting to the revision stage, the instructor and librarian were able to highlight the students' flexible use of disciplinary conventions and the ways in which they could write differently and use research differently for different audiences and purposes.[78]

Without such sustained, supported reflection, students engaged in advanced research run the risk of losing their voices as they engage in research summary and attempt convention-bound analysis. In our roles as library and writing professionals, we have an obligation to help students understand how their unique, authentic voices can both fill and frame gaps they have identified in the existing scholarship about their topic. The research discussion board used in this advanced literature course helped students achieve that sites/ala.org.acrl/files/content/issues/infolit/Framework_ILHE.pdf; Council of Writing Program Administrators. *WPA Outcomes Statement for First-Year Composition* (3.0), July 17, 2014. Accessed March 22, 2016. http://wpacouncil.org/files/WPA%20Outcomes%20Statement%20Adopted%20Revisions[1]_0.pdf; Council of Writing Program Administrators, National Council of Teachers of English, and National Writing Project. *Framework for Success in Postsecondary Writing,* 2011. Accessed March 22, 2016. http://wpacouncil.org/files/framework-for-success-postsecondary-writing.pdf.

3.   M. M. Bakhtin, *The Dialogic Imagination: Four Essays* (University of Texas Press, 1981), 293–294.

4.   Barry M. Maid and Barbara J. D'Angelo, "The WPA Outcomes, Information Literacy, and the Challenges of Outcome-Based Curricular Design," in *Writing Assessment in the 21st Century*, ed. Norbert Elliot and Les Perelman (New York: Hampton Press, 2014), 112.

5.   WPA, Framework, 2.

6.   Ibid., 3.

7.   Ibid., 4–5.

8.   Ibid.

9.   Ibid., 4.

10. Ibid., 5.

11. Ibid.

12. WPA, Outcomes.

13. Ibid., 1.

14. Ibid.

15. Ibid.

16. Ibid., 2.

17. Ibid., 2.

18. ACRL, Framework.

19. Ibid., 4.

20. Ibid.

21. Ibid., 6.

22. Ibid., 8.

23. Ibid.

24. Ibid., 7, 4.

25. Ibid., 4.

26. Ibid., 7.

27. Alison J. Head, "Staying Smart: How Today's Graduates Continue to Learn Once They Complete College," January 5, 2016, http://projectinfolit.org/images/pdfs/2016_lifelonglearning_fullreport.pdf.

28. Ibid., 48.

29. Jeff Brooks, "Minimalist Tutoring: Making the Student Do All the Work," *The Writing Lab Newsletter* 15, no. 6 (February 1991): 1–4.

30. WPA, Framework, 4.

31. ACRL, Framework, 4.

32. Brooks, "Minimalist Tutoring: Making the Student Do All the Work."

33. WPA, Framework, 4–5.

34. Brooks, "Minimalist Tutoring: Making the Student Do All the Work."

35. Ibid., 3.

36. Alison J. Head, "Learning the Ropes: How Freshmen Conduct Course Research Once

They Enter College," Project Information Literacy, 2013, 12, http://projectinfolit.org/images/pdfs/pil_2013_freshmenstudy_fullreport.pdf.
37. Ibid., 13.
38. ACRL, Framework, 7.
39. WPA, Framework, 4.
40. Ibid., 1.
41. Robert Davis and Mark Shadle, "'Building a Mystery': Alternative Research Writing and the Academic Act of Seeking," *College Composition and Communication* 51, no. 3 (2000): 417–46, doi:10.2307/358743.
42. Dan Rothstein and Luz Santana, *Make Just One Change: Teach Students to Ask Their Own Questions* (Cambridge, MA: Harvard Education Press, 2011).
43. ACRL, Framework, 7.
44. Ibid.
45. WPA, Framework, 4.
46. ACRL, Framework, 7.
47. Ibid.
48. WPA, Framework, 6; WPA, Outcomes, 1.
49. ACRL, Framework, 7.
50. Ibid.; WPA, Framework, 5.
51. WPA, Outcomes, 2.
52. WPA, Framework, 5.
53. Bakhtin, *The Dialogic Imagination*, 293–294.
54. ACRL, Framework, 8.
55. Ibid., 4.
56. WPA, Framework, 4, 7.
57. WPA, Outcomes, 2; WPA, Framework, 7.
58. ACRL, Framework, 8.
59. WPA, Framework, 7; WPA, Outcomes, 2.
60. ACRL, Framework, 7; WPA, Framework, 4.
61. Verlyn Klinkenborg, *Several Short Sentences About Writing*, Vintage edition (New York: Vintage, 2012), 6.
62. ACRL, Framework, 4.
63. Ibid.
64. WPA, Framework, 5.
65. ACRL, Framework, 8.
66. WPA, Framework, 6.
67. ACRL, Framework, 4.
68. WPA, Framework, 5.
69. Carol C. Kuhlthau, *Seeking Meaning: A Process Approach to Library and Information Services*, 2nd ed. (Westport, CT: Libraries Unlimited, 2003).
70. ACRL, Framework, 9.
71. Kuhlthau, *Seeking Meaning*, 140.
72. WPA, Framework, 4–5.
73. Kuhlthau, *Seeking Meaning*, 135.
74. WPA, Framework, 4.
75. Ibid., 6.
76. ACRL, Framework, 8.

77. Ibid.
78. WPA, Framework, 7.

Bibliography

Association of College and Research Libraries. *Framework for Information Literacy for Higher Education,* January 11, 2016. Accessed March 22, 2016. http://www.ala.org/acrl/sites/ala.org.acrl/files/content/issues/infolit/Framework_ILHE.pdf.

Bakhtin, M. M. *The Dialogic Imagination: Four Essays.* Austin: University of Texas Press, 1981.

Bizzell, Patricia, and Bruce Herzberg. "Research as a Social Act." *The Clearing House: A Journal of Educational Strategies, Issues and Ideas* 60, no. 7 (March 1987): 303–6. doi:10.1080/00098655.1987.9959356.

Brooks, Jeff. "Minimalist Tutoring: Making the Student Do All the Work." *The Writing Lab Newsletter* 15, no. 6 (February 1991): 1–4.

Cohn, Marilyn M. "Discovering the Importance of Student Voice and Active Participation Through the Scholarship of Teaching and Learning." *Teaching and Learning Together in Higher Education,* no. 5 (2012). Accessed March 22, 2016. http://repository.brynmawr.edu/tlthe/.

Council of Writing Program Administrators. *WPA Outcomes Statement for First-Year Composition* (3.0), July 17, 2014. Accessed March 22, 2016. http://wpacouncil.org/files/WPA%20Outcomes%20Statement%20Adopted%20Revisions[1]_0.pdf.

Council of Writing Program Administrators, National Council of Teachers of English, and National Writing Project. *Framework for Success in Postsecondary Writing,* 2011. Accessed March 22, 2016. http://wpacouncil.org/files/framework-for-success-post-secondary-writing.pdf.

Davis, Robert, and Mark Shadle. "'Building a Mystery': Alternative Research Writing and the Academic Act of Seeking." *College Composition and Communication* 51, no. 3 (2000): 417–46. doi:10.2307/358743.

DeWitz, S. Joseph, M. Lynn Woolsey, and W. Bruce Walsh. "College Student Retention: An Exploration of the Relationship Between Self-Efficacy Beliefs and Purpose in Life Among College Students." *Journal of College Student Development* 50, no. 1 (2009): 19–34.

Elmborg, James K. "Critical Information Literacy: Implications for Instructional Practice." *Journal of Academic Librarianship* 32, no. 2 (2006): 192–99.

———. "Libraries in the Contact Zone: On the Creation of Educational Space." *Reference & User Services Quarterly* 46, no. 1 (2006): 56–64.

Fiumara, Gemma Corradi. *The Other Side of Language: A Philosophy of Listening.* New York: Routledge, 2013.

Head, Alison J. "Learning the Ropes: How Freshmen Conduct Course Research Once They Enter College." Project Information Literacy, 2013. Accessed March 22, 2016. http://projectinfolit.org/images/pdfs/pil_2013_freshmenstudy_fullreport.pdf.

———. "Staying Smart: How Today's Graduates Continue to Learn Once They Complete College," January 5, 2016. Accessed March 22, 2016. http://projectinfolit.org/images/pdfs/2016_lifelonglearning_fullreport.pdf.

Klinkenborg, Verlyn. *Several Short Sentences About Writing*. Vintage edition. New York: Vintage, 2012.

Kuhlthau, Carol C. *Seeking Meaning: A Process Approach to Library and Information Services*. 2nd ed. Westport, CT: Libraries Unlimited, 2003.

Maid, Barry M., and Barbara J. D'Angelo. "The WPA Outcomes, Information Literacy, and the Challenges of Outcome-Based Curricular Design." In *Writing Assessment in the 21st Century*, edited by Norbert Elliot and Les Perelman, 101–14. New York: Hampton Press, 2014.

Rothstein, Dan, and Luz Santana. *Make Just One Change: Teach Students to Ask Their Own Questions*. Cambridge, MA: Harvard Education Press, 2011.

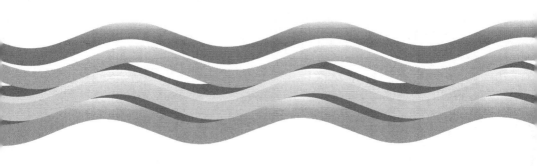

CHAPTER 4

In a Research-Writing Frame of Mind

Kathy Christie Anders
Texas A&M University

Cassie Hemstrom
University of California, Davis

Introduction

Librarians have been coordinating with composition instructors to offer information literacy instruction in composition classrooms long enough that it can no longer be considered a new trend, but rather a standard feature of many information literacy programs. Sometimes this collaboration comes in the form of a one-shot, sometimes the librarian is embedded, and sometimes the librarian is a co-instructor. Information literacy and composition are often intertwined in higher education; recently, the professional organizations associated with writing programs and with information literacy programs have developed documents to define the characteristics, habits and dispositions of successful students. The documents, the *Framework for Success in Postsecondary Writing*[1] (hereafter WPA Framework) and the *Framework for Information Literacy for Higher Education*[2] (hereafter ACRL Framework), lay out frames that describe students who write and manage information well. The publication of these two Frameworks provides an opportunity for practitioners to examine the relationship between writing and information literacy, what writing instructors often refer to as research-writing skills.

Intended for librarians and composition instructors, this chapter examines how teachers of writing and research skills can enhance their understanding of the two Frameworks as being similar and linked with one another, and by doing so become more effective teachers. We hope to make the intersections of information-using and writing that exist implicitly in practice explicit for students as we explore ways to better integrate writing and research instruction in composition and information literacy classrooms. We do so by looking at how the intersections between the Frameworks inform writing and library instruction pedagogy, and we provide examples of writing and information-using assignments based on the Frameworks.

One of our foundational claims is information literacy and writing are linked together under the view of students as information creators, partaking in the process of "information creation" as the ACRL Framework puts it.[3] To consider the research skills associated with information literacy as being separate from writing is not tenable, since writing is a form of information creation. Furthermore, much of the information that students encounter is also expressed in written language, such that the information must be considered as pieces of writing. Perhaps some will object claiming much information is visual and wordless, or is data, but it is worth noting the contemporary fields of visual and scientific rhetoric hold that visual creation and scientific communication are rhetorical in nature, and thus are not divorced from writing.

When students are evaluating information and when they are writing, they are taking rhetorical concerns into account. Rolf Norgaard has already called for a rhetoricized information literacy, but we further believe much of information literacy is inherently rhetorical in nature.[4] With this idea in mind, writing teachers and librarians can make the intersections of research and writing that implicitly exist in the minds of writing and information literacy instructors explicit for students, scholars, and administrators by addressing the WPA Framework and the ACRL Framework in their course descriptions and major assignments.

Two key frames in the WPA Framework and the ACRL Framework suggest connections between composition and research instruction, and they can be used jointly to inform practical writing classroom and library instruction pedagogy. Our chapter looks at two intersections of the two Frameworks; for each intersection we discuss how the concepts contained in those intersections interact and examine the implications of those intersections for both writing instructors and librarians. The first part of our chapter traces the theoretical and practical uses of putting the Frameworks into dialogue. In doing so, we focus on the WPA frame "Developing Flexible Writing Processes" as well as the ACRL frames "Information Creation as a Process" and "Searching as Strategic Exploration." We also consider the WPA frame "Developing Rhetorical

Knowledge" and the ACRL frames "Authority is Constructed and Contextual" and "Scholarship as Conversation."

When synthesized, these two sets of frames enable writing and library instructors to highlight the existing connections between the processes of writing and researching—connections already supported and employed in composition pedagogy and assessment. The articulation of these connections should enable students to investigate, use, and reflect on the purposes of researching as part of scaffolded assignments, much the same way drafting, workshopping, and revising allows students to engage knowingly and critically in the writing process.

Literature Review

Tying together composition and information literacy has become increasingly the norm in recent years. On a practical level, since composition classes are required of most students at nearly all U.S. colleges and universities, integrating information literacy into composition classes—through one-shots or through embedding librarians—is an efficient way to educate a large number of students early in their academic careers. Apart from those considerations, it makes sense to combine information literacy and composition because they "draw from the same intellectual well, building upon more general pedagogical developments."[5] James Elmborg notes information literacy programs have faced many of the same challenges from the academy as composition programs, but the information literacy movement could learn from Writing Across the Curriculum (WAC) programs, particularly with regard to wading into more theoretical waters.[6]

On a substantial level, composition programs and information literacy programs often aim to develop the same skills and knowledge practices of students they instruct—our analysis of the two Frameworks demonstrates this—but prior to the development of these Frameworks a good number of composition instructors and librarians had begun working together to identify and teach important skills in common, such as evaluating information for authority and bias,[7] selecting appropriate research topics, managing information, and more.[8] Despite these shared aims, there is still much work to be done putting composition instructors and librarians in conversation with one another.[9]

Several authors, in this collection and throughout the professional literature, have noted that for information literacy and composition and rhetoric to be integrated, the information literacy movement must engage in theoretical discussions about pedagogy.[10] Certainly this is true. However, the publication of the Frameworks provides a strong venue for collaboration between writing instructors and librarians. This chapter provides a rationale and sample assignment sequence that achieves the outcomes for both Frameworks, and, in doing so, also demonstrates how such collaboration can support the aims of writing programs and libraries on an institutional level.

First Intersection: Writing and Research as Processes

One of the clearest ways the Frameworks overlap is in their focus on both writing and research as processes. They are activities done over time, and students should expect both processes will have to be repeated and revised for different situations. In this section, we consider how both Frameworks present the writing and research processes, and how these processes are intertwined.

The Writing Process

The opening to *The Framework for Success in Postsecondary Writing* habit of "Developing Flexible Writing Strategies" states:

> Writing processes are not linear. Successful writers use different processes that vary over time and depend on the particular task. For example, a writer may research a topic before drafting, then after receiving feedback conduct additional research as part of revising. Writers learn to move back and forth through different stages of writing, adapting those stages to the situation. This ability to employ flexible writing processes is important as students encounter different types of writing tasks that require them to work through the various stages independently to produce final, polished texts.[11]

There are two important ideas to take away from this frame. The first, as the text clearly states, is the writing process is not linear. That is to say, there is not one set procedure through which students will move from start to finish. It is expected that students will have to cycle through the drafting, revising, and editing processes multiple times. The second idea is that the writing process is not uniform or standard. That is to say, students might not go through the same steps in the same order every time they write. For example, there may not always be time for significant revision to take place. It is important that students be flexible, as the frame states, because every writing situation will be different. Writing a ten-page report due in a month is different than writing a one-page reflection due in the next class, and both situations are different from the writing situations students might encounter in the business world. Accordingly, students must understand the importance of considering writing as a process and not view all writing situations as the same.

Likewise, these principles can be adapted when thinking about the research process,[12] as the frame implies, "a writer may research a topic before drafting, then after receiving feedback conduct additional research as part of revising."[13] It is useful for the purpose of teaching research, and particularly research as part of the writing process, to make this claim explicit in order to explore why and how research strategies, purposes, and uses can be employed and revisited. The research process is non-linear, and students may move through steps apart from a fixed order many times over. To teach students to do a fixed set of steps in a particular order is not helpful. Research situations change, and the research process for a dissertation looks very different from the research process for a two-page article summary.

Students working on large research projects will likely have to search for sources many times over, not just once at the beginning of the project. Viewing information literacy this way, a librarian would not focus on teaching students to create perfect search strings in order to acquire every necessary source at the beginning of a project; instead, a librarian might guide students through several search techniques and encourage them to engage in new searches as their research develops. Additionally, librarians can model their own research processes for students, engaging students by showing them how exciting finding and evaluating information can be.[14] Results that seem satisfactory at the beginning of a research project may not be as the project is developed and refined. By teaching students the research process is flexible, librarians prepare students for a variety of research situations without being locked into one set of steps that may or may not be appropriate for the task at hand.

Presenting the research process as flexible, another principle common to both Frameworks, also allows for more student engagement in the research process. Rather than research as fixed and external to the student, it is personal and dependent upon who is doing the research. Students must consider their research needs and context in order to decide what process will work best for them. Flexibility empowers students to make their own choices about research, rather than relying upon an external authority to dictate what steps must be followed at every turn.

The Research Process

The ACRL frame "Information Creation as a Process" begins this way:

> Information in any format is produced to convey a message and is shared via a selected delivery method. The iterative processes of researching, creating, revising, and disseminating information vary, and the resulting product reflects these differences.

The information creation process could result in a range of information formats and modes of delivery, so experts look beyond format when selecting resources to use. The unique capabilities and constraints of each creation process as well as the specific information need determine how the product is used. Experts recognize that information creations are valued differently in different contexts, such as academia or the workplace. Elements that affect or reflect on the creation, such as a pre- or post-publication editing or reviewing process, may be indicators of quality. The dynamic nature of information creation and dissemination requires ongoing attention to understand evolving creation processes. Recognizing the nature of information creation, experts look to the underlying processes of creation as well as the final product to critically evaluate the usefulness of the information. Novice learners begin to recognize the significance of the creation process, leading them to increasingly sophisticated choices when matching information products with their information needs.[15]

Teaching writing as a process is a best practices method in writing instruction, but writing instruction can further expand the definition of that process by explicitly teaching research as an iterative process built into the larger writing process. Teaching writing as a process is a component of the cognitive view of writing, an approach to writing instruction often associated with Linda Flower and John Hayes who argued for a recursive cognitive processes model for assignment sequencing.[16] Ken Hyland explains the cognitive view of writing instruction "sees writing as a problem-solving activity: how writers approach a writing task as a problem and bring intellectual range to solving it."[17] By working with librarians to develop an understanding of research as a recursive process, and by recognizing the ways in which the research process is, in fact, part of the writing process, writing instructors can employ assignments and sequences enabling students to conceptualize research as a continuing conversation, increase their audience and rhetorical awareness, and explore how the texts they produce have applicability beyond the classroom.

Writing instructors and librarians can also help students increase their ability to conduct rhetorical analysis by employing assignments requiring them to identify multiple perspectives and to understand how these might appeal to primary and secondary audiences by researching throughout the writing process to identify stakeholders and explore a discourse community.

The ACRL frame "Searching as Strategic Exploration" adds the following to this intersection of thought:

> Searching for information is often nonlinear and iterative, requiring the evaluation of a range of information sources and the mental flexibility to pursue alternate avenues as new understanding develops.[18]

By considering these two ACRL frames in conjunction as a part of the research process, writing instructors can encourage their students to go further in how they evaluate texts and select sources rhetorically. Through researching, summarizing, and synthesizing a variety of sources about a particular topic, students can gain a better understanding of sources and information as a nuanced conversation, which they can then enter into through their own writing.

Second Intersection: Rhetoric and Context

The second overlap between the two Frameworks is not as easy to piece together as process, but it is still quite powerful. Both Frameworks highlight the rhetorical nature of writing and research. As stated, the idea that information is rhetorical, whether in the form of a piece of writing or an image or graph, underlies the foundation of our analysis. This idea, as articulated in each Framework, resides at the intersection of rhetorical analysis and authority, concepts that require students to think about who is saying what and how the speaker's or writer's position affects their understanding of the information being used and created.

Rhetoric and Writing

The first habit of mind in the WPA Framework offers:

> Rhetorical knowledge is the ability to analyze and act on understandings of audiences, purposes, and contexts in creating and comprehending texts.

> Rhetorical knowledge is the basis of good writing. By developing rhetorical knowledge, writers can adapt to different purposes, audiences, and contexts. Study of and practice with basic rhetorical concepts such as purpose, audience, context, and conventions are important as writers learn to compose a variety of texts for different disciplines and purposes. For example, a writer might draft one version of a text with one audience in mind, then revise the text to meet the needs and expectations of a different audience.[19]

Contemporary writing programs teach students to analyze their rhetorical situation as they write. The audience to whom they write matters; their professors, for whom they write papers, have different expectations than their friends, for whom they write tweets. The context of their writing influences how and what they write; for example, the workplace has a different context than the academy, such that a business memo will look and be read differently than an op-ed in the school newspaper. Their purpose in writing will, of course, affect their writing. Writing intended to convince someone to buy something will look different than writing intended to explain a concept.

Perhaps this frame will sound familiar to librarians. Many of the concepts of rhetorical knowledge are interwoven into the ever popular CRAAP test, where one evaluates information for currency, relevance, authority, accuracy, and purpose.[20] For example, librarians routinely teach students to be aware of bias in the sources they choose. Like concepts, certain terms are also already shared; the term purpose is used in both fields to signal the reader, writer or researcher to consider exigency and function. Context is very much linked to currency, for which librarians also teach students to examine. In fact, as we will discuss, context plays an important role in the ACRL Framework.

What is so significant about an analysis of these similarities is it highlights librarians are teaching students to think about information rhetorically. The factors librarians teach students to consider are not arbitrary. The study of rhetoric stretches back for thousands of years. By framing information evaluation concepts as rhetorical, the artificial divide between research and writing is broken down as both are subject to rhetorical concerns. The rhetorical concept of purpose, for example, is relevant to students both as they write and as they evaluate others' writings.

The umbrella of rhetoric is also necessary as the new ACRL Framework calls upon librarians to think of students not only as information users, but also as people who partake in the information creation process, as information creators. The frame "Information Has Value" states information literate students will "see themselves as contributors to the information marketplace rather than only consumers of it."[21] This is particularly relevant to the writing classroom, where students are already treated as information creators, although they are not, generally, explicitly referred to that way. In the contemporary composition classroom, students are taught, as writers, they are always subject to rhetorical concerns, regardless of whether or not they are aware of them. A piece of writing, of course, is something librarians would consider a piece of information, and it, too, could be considered subject to rhetorical concerns.

There is a great opportunity here for librarians to bridge the gap between what students learn in the composition classroom and what they learn in the library simply by linking terms for rhetorical concepts and information literacy together. Librarians teaching information evaluation have long been teaching rhetorical analysis of information under a different name, but by speaking to the rhetorical terms students are hearing in the composition classroom, they can show how information analysis and use are closely linked to information creation.

Research and Context

The ACRL frame "Authority is Constructed and Contextual" begins:

> Information resources reflect their creators' expertise and credibility, and are evaluated based on the information need and the context in which the information will be used. Authority is constructed in that various communities may recognize different types of authority. It is contextual in that the information need may help to determine the level of authority required.[22]

The idea that a source is not a monolithic, purely objective statement of facts can be difficult for college writing students to grasp, but it is a central tenet of composition instruction. Analysis and evaluation of sources not only encourage students to consider the credibility and potential ways to use a particular source in their own writing, but also engage students in the kinds of critical thinking crucial to a successful writing process. Through analyzing the credibility of a source, students can learn to evaluate the author's ethos, identify the author's purpose in writing, and critique the rhetorical strategies and devices used in the text. This process reveals for students that authority is constructed and contextual, and it helps them see what steps they might take to construct authority in their own writing.

Writing instructors seek to foster in students the ability to read and to evaluate the credibility and appropriate use of a variety of texts, and to encourage students to identify how they are or can become an authority in writing a particular genre themselves. These interconnected outcomes of student learning, as well as the use of genre and discourse analysis pedagogies, are part of Writing Across the Curriculum (WAC) programs. Since the 1970s, writing programs have explored methods for teaching writing across the curriculum. WAC programs are not identical; William Condon and Carol Rutz state that instead, WAC "varies in its development and its manifestation from campus to campus," and "assumes certain pedagogical moves beyond the obvious difference between assigning writing and teaching writing."[23] WAC programs "[require] a complex partnership among faculty, administrators, writing centers, faculty development programs—an infrastructure that may well support general education or first-year seminar goals," and, we argue, information technology instruction.[24] They further delineate that the primary goals of foundational WAC programs are to establish "a problem-based statement of purpose," "increase writing in the curriculum," make it such that "teaching writing becomes everyone's job" (rather than just the job of writing instructors with whom students will work for one or two courses), and "understand the difference between learning to write and writing to learn."[25]

Collaborations between librarians and writing instructors to bridge the Frameworks can accomplish the goals of WAC in three ways: first, by teaching students how to "recognize different types of authorities,"[26] and understand how those authorities might be used in different ways based on different rhetorical contexts and goals; second, by extending the job of writing instruction to include librarians in their capacity of experts in teaching information literacy; and third, by valuing students (and encouraging them to value themselves) as knowledge-makers.

WAC programs value introducing students to the writing conventions, genres, and scholarly conversations across the disciplines. By working together to teach students how to recognize and analyze different authorities in different contexts, librarians and writing instructors can help students to identify, analyze, research, and write appropriate responses to a range of discipline-specific rhetorical situations using the authorities valued by the field. In composition theory and writing instruction, pedagogical approaches focused on these goals fall under the umbrella of genre analysis approaches. John Swales argues for the use of a genre analysis methodology as a means of "studying spoken and written discourse for applied ends."[27] Curricula and assignments that employ a genre approach give students "a workable way of making sense of the myriad communicative events that occur in the contemporary English-speaking academy—a sense-making directly relevant to those concerned with devising English courses," or for constructing assignments and sequences that teach writing and researching in collaboration.[28]

The goal of introducing students to the perspectives and conversations of stakeholders is shared by librarians, as is explicit in the ACRL "Authority Is Constructed and Contextual" frame and within the introduction to "Scholarship as Conversation" frame, which states: "Communities of scholars, researchers, or professionals engage in sustained discourse with new insights and discoveries occurring over time as a result of varied perspectives and interpretations."[29] One way librarians and writing instructors might achieve the shared goal of introducing students to the scholars, researchers, and professionals who engage in conversation over time and through myriad perspectives is to work together to construct and employ assignments that lead into each other and require students to regularly revisit and reexamine their research. An example of this type of assignment sequence is included at the end of this chapter.

The collaboration of writing instructors and librarians to build a genre approach assignment sequence that fosters the entwined reiterative processes of researching and writing should also have a positive impact at the institutional level. The collaboration supports a "robust, sustained WAC curriculum," aids students and the academy to recognize multiple and diverse authorities, and empowers students to see themselves as authorities by entering into scholarly conversations.[30] This collaboration is in response to and continues the call from WAC proponents to value the authority of a wide range of knowledge-makers, wherein students, faculty, and professionals "are understood to have an appropriate expertise, and tapping such expertise is understood as one important means of learning about the effects of a WAC program and then of enhancing it."[31] Drawing on the expertise of librarians enables writing instructors not only to achieve the best practices of the composition field, but also to expand writing instruction across the institution.

Furthermore, the ACRL Framework explains "developing familiarity with the sources of evidence, methods, and modes of discourse in the field assists novice learners to enter the conversation."[32] Through an assignment sequence such as the one we propose, students should recognize their own expertise as they develop familiarity with the stakeholders, conversations, and perspectives involved in a topic, come to understand the complexity and nuances of the topic, and, as a result, identify how their unique perspectives add to the conversations.

We demonstrate the intersections of the Frameworks discussed in this chapter through a sample assignment sequence, one we hope librarians and writing instructors will use to teach research as a recursive part of the writing process. We believe the assignment sequence encourages students to enter scholarly conversations as authorities. The assignments help them identify how they can present their own perspectives and the sources they have brought together in the most rhetorically-effective way for their audiences.

Sample Assignment Sequences

The following sample assignment sequence may be altered for writing courses across the curriculum. The sequence is composed of two assignments that each ask students to select a research topic and to engage in an iterative research-writing process through which they build familiarity with the subject, identify the conversations about the subject, analyze its discourse community, and insert themselves with authority into the scholarly conversation.

Assignment 1: Discourse Community Analysis

A discourse community, argues Swales, is a group of individuals having six characteristics: (1) "a broadly agreed set of common public goals," (2) "mechanisms of intercommunication among its members," (3) uses "participatory mechanisms primarily to provide information and feedback," (4) "utilizes and hence possesses one or more genres in the communicative furtherance of its aims," (5) has "acquired some specific lexis," and (6) contains "a threshold level of members with a suitable degree of relevant content and discoursal expertise."[33] An example of a discourse community can be shared with students to help them understand this concept and to model for them the analysis of a discourse community. The most helpful examples will be specific communities in conversation about a specific topic. To identify a discourse community, instructors and students can look for professional communities (such as professors, prison guards, realtors), social or societal communities (activist organizations such as Amnesty International, specific ethnic groups, etc.), civic groups (volunteers for the SPCA, a student group on campus, a political action group, etc.), or cultural communities (such as online or tabletop gaming groups, battle re-enactors, or fans of a particular show or musician).

An effective way to model discourse community analysis is to provide students with an example then ask them to walk through an examination of the key factors of a discourse community (i.e., ask students to identify the stakeholders, the gatekeepers, the jargon, shared goals, etc.) This process should enable students to become familiar with new terms and to practice using this vocabulary in a low-stakes situation. Students can then begin to identify, research, and analyze a discourse community on their own. A primary outcome of this assignment sequence is, as students continue their research process, making "new insights and discoveries…as a result of varied perspectives and interpretations."[34] This opening activity helps students realize topics are not two-dimensional, so the research they conduct will become more complex and nuanced, tuning them in to multiple and varied perspectives. An additional outcome is that this analysis and research increases their critical thinking and reading skills.

The main assignment asks students to perform a rhetorical analysis of a discourse community wherein students analyze what are the purposes of communication, how members of the community share information, and what are the genre expectations set out for the types of information produced. Students are then responsible for finding examples of writing within the discourse community, as well as outside sources about the community. This sample assignment includes the paper prompt, as well as scaffolded pre-assignments integrating ideas from the Frameworks about authority and context.

SCAFFOLDED PRE-ASSIGNMENT PROMPT

We offer the following writing activity to students in advance of the main assignment:

> Your paper assignment asks you to find three to five credible sources written by experts for your discourse community analysis. Your task for this assignment is to investigate what makes someone an expert within the discourse community, and to compare that criteria for expertise to what makes someone an expert within your current academic community. Create a list with two columns identifying and analyzing at least four characteristics of an expert in your chosen discourse community and four characteristics of an expert in your academic community. Write a brief reflection about what types of experts you will look for given your discourse community analysis assignment.

DISCOURSE COMMUNITY PAPER PROMPT

This is how we describe the main assignment to students:

> In this discourse community assignment, you will explore and analyze discourse communities within a field or discipline you are interested in entering. First, identify a specific discourse community existing within a field or discipline in which you are interested, for example, commercial real estate agents or data analysts. Next, begin primary research by contacting three to five participants in this community and conducting an email, phone, or in-person interview to learn from these participants what the goals of the community are, what sort of information is exchanged between participants, how that information is exchanged, and what types of writing of texts (genres) exist in the community to effectively convey this information and achieve these goals.

> Then, continue research by finding three to five primary examples of one of these genres. Analyze the genre for keywords or phrases that make up the lexis of the community and identify examples of how the genre achieves the goals of the community and conveys key information. Finally, continue your research by finding three to five credible sources

written by experts in or about the discourse community and use these sources to support and illustrate your discourse community analysis.

Assignment 2: Synthesis Assignment

A synthesis assignment is a unit on research many writing classes employ; this assignment allows students to begin gathering information on a particular topic on which they may work throughout a course, while also encouraging them to complicate their understanding of research. Such an assignment might ask students to research three to five credible sources on a particular topic, focusing on authors who have different points of view or relationships to the issue. Next, students typically engage with the texts by analyzing the claims, concerns, and contexts of each text. Finally, students put these texts into conversation in a paper that highlights the stakeholders, their concerns, and points of agreement or disjunction. Most students entering college writing courses tend to view issues as being black or white. By exploring the many stakeholders involved with a research topic and exploring how the conversation about the issue has progressed throughout time and through different perspectives, students learn topics are multi-faceted and that they too can add something unique to the conversation by bringing together sources in new ways to shape their own perspective on the topic.

The assignment to follow asks students to synthesize a variety of viewpoints about one particular topic. Rather than being a simple pro/con paper, the point of this assignment is for students to develop the ability to analyze multiple viewpoints, some which differ from each other only subtly, then synthesize those viewpoints. This assignment requires students work through both the writing and research processes multiple times, as well as develop the mental flexibility to accommodate a variety of perspectives and see how they intersect.

SCAFFOLDED PRE-ASSIGNMENT PROMPT

Similar to the first sample assignment, we precede the main assignment with another writing activity. We explain the preceding assignment to students this way:

> For your upcoming synthesis assignment, you will bring together several sources representing different viewpoints about a given topic. As preparation for this assignment, create a research journal about how you are finding and evaluating sources. For this pre-assignment, you will find at least six sources, four of which you will use in your synthesis assignment. For each source you find, note (1) the system you

used to perform your search (Google, the library catalog, a specific database, etc.), (2) what terms you used to find the source, and (3) why you think the source will be is useful for your paper. Please note this assignment is not expected to be a formal piece of academic writing, though it should reflect your actual research process.

SYNTHESIS PAPER PROMPT

The description we offer to students for the main assignment:

In the textbook *Navigating America,* David Moton and Gloria Dumler describe a synthesis as bringing "several sources together to make one larger point" (171).[35] A synthesis is a way to take the ideas of others and build a new text that can be your own. Synthesizing is not only a terrific critical thinking skill to develop, but also a wonderful way to academically digest the scholarship in your field to create a unique viewpoint. Synthesizing is the culmination of this whole course—when synthesizing, you use the researching and analyzing techniques you have developed over this semester to integrate the different perceptions and information available about a topic to construct and convey your own understanding of it.

For the Synthesis Essay, choose a topic and find four to five sources that represent different perspectives about that topic. Explain the perspective each source has about the issue as well as analyze why your sources might have their own particular stance on the issue, what position they have in relation to the issue, the effect the issue will have on them, their own ethos and potential effect, and their motives.

Bring your sources together to make one larger point. (If it helps, consider that your sources are having a conversation, and the larger point is the one thing they all seem to be saying.) Your essay will not be a pro/con argument, but a snapshot of one part of the conversation among your sources.

Conclusion

Both authors have experience in libraries. Both taught composition classes extensively throughout their English PhD programs, and Cassie currently teaches in a writing program and collaborates with the librarians at her university. Kathy is a librarian in a university library learning and outreach department. Both work at large public research institutions. What has been most striking about this project is finding out how often people in both libraries and composition programs are talking about the same ideas with different terms. That is to say, they are participating in different discourse communities. These different discourse communities seem to make it more difficult to collaborate on the deepest levels. However, it was striking to the authors how seamlessly they could tie together complex concepts from information literacy and rhetoric and composition when they were both speaking the same language, as it were.

At the moment, communication between the disciplines of composition studies and information studies requires a sort of code switching that adds an additional step to the collaboration process. By reviewing the Framework documents of both postsecondary writing and library science, writing instructors and librarians can together develop a method of speaking to one another that bridges disciplinary divides. This not only makes collaboration more effective, but also helps students recognize how information literacy and writing are intimately connected.

Notes

1. Council of Writing Program Administrators, National Council of Teachers of English, and National Writing Project, *Framework for Success in Postsecondary Writing* (Council of Writing Program Administrators, National Council of Teachers of English, and National Writing Project, 2011) http://wpacouncil.org/files/framework-for-success-postsecondary-writing.pdf.
2. Association of College and Research Libraries. *Framework for Information Literacy for Higher Education* (Chicago: American Library Association, 2015) http://www.ala.org/acrl/standards/ilframework.
3. Ibid.
4. Rolf Norgaard, "Writing Information Literacy in the Classroom: Pedagogical Enactments and Implications," *Reference and User Services Quarterly* 43, no. 3 (Spring 2004): 224, EBSCOHost.
5. Melissa Bowles-Terry, Erin Davis, and Wendy Holliday, "'Writing Information Literacy' Revisited: Application of Theory to Practice in the Classroom," *Reference & User Services Quarterly* 49, no. 3 (Spring 2010): 225, http://www.jstor.org//stable/20865257.
6. James Elmborg, "Information Literacy and Writing Across the Curriculum: Sharing the Vision," *Reference Services Review* 31, no.1 (2003): 68–80, doi:10.1108/00907320310460933.
7. Randall McClure and Kellian Clink, "How Do You Know That?: An Investigation of Student Research Practices in the Digital Age," *portal: Libraries and the Academy* 9, no.1 (January 2009): 115–132, doi:10.1353/pla.0.0033.
8. Wendy Holliday and Britt Fagerheim, "Integrating Information Literacy with a Se-

quenced English Composition Curriculum," *portal: Libraries and the Academy* 6, no. 2 (April 2006): 169–184, doi:10.1353/pla.2006.0023.

9. Elizabeth Birmingham et al., "First-Year Writing Teachers, Perceptions of Students' Information Literacy Competencies, and a Call for a Collaborative Approach," *Communications in Information Literacy* 2, no. 1 (2008): 2, http://www.comminfolit. org/index.php?journal=cil&page=article&op=viewArticle&path%5B%5D=Spring-2008AR1&path%5B%5D=67.

10. See Bowles-Terry, Davis, and Holliday, "'Writing Information Literacy' Revisited;" Elmborg, "Information Literacy and Writing Across the Curriculum;" and Rolf Norgaard, "Writing Information Literacy: Contributions to a Concept," *Reference and User Services Quarterly* 43, no. 2 (Winter 2003): 124–130) accessed through EBSCO-Host.

11. WPA, Framework.

12. Rolf Norgaard also articulates the need for a process-based approach to information literacy in "Writing Information Literacy." His work shows how, at a more abstract level, "rhetoricized" information literacy calls for a "process-oriented literacy" (127).

13. Ibid.

14. Elmborg, "Information Literacy and Writing Across the Curriculum," 73.

15. ACRL, Framework.

16. Linda Flower and John R. Hayes. "A Cognitive Process Theory of Writing," *College Composition and Communication* 32, no. 4 (1981): 365–387.

17. Ken Hyland, *Teaching and Researching Writing*, 2nd ed. (London: Routledge, 2013): 20.

18. ACRL, Framework.

19. WPA, Framework.

20. *Evaluating Information—Applying the CRAAP Test* (Chico: California State University, Chico, 2010) https://www.csuchico.edu/lins/handouts/eval_websites.pdf.

21. ACRL, Framework.

22. Ibid.

23. William Condon and Carol Rutz, "A Taxonomy of Writing Across the Curriculum Programs: Evolving to Serve Broader Agendas," *College Composition and Communication* 64, no. 2 (2012): 358.

24. Ibid., 358–359.

25. Ibid. 362.

26. ACRL, Framework.

27. John Swales, *Genre Analysis: English in Academic and Research Settings* (Cambridge: Cambridge University Press, 1990): 1.

28. Ibid., 1.

29. ACRL, Framework.

30. Ruth Kistler et al., "Introduction: Writing Across the Curriculum and Assessment," *Across the Disciplines* 6 (2009), http://wac.colostate.edu/ATD/assessment/kistleretal. cfm.

31. Ibid.

32. ACRL, Framework.

33. Ibid., 24–27.

34. ACRL, Framework.

35. David Moton and Gloria Dumler, *Navigating America* (New York: McGraw-Hill, 2009): 171.

Bibliography

Association of College and Research Libraries. *Framework for Information Literacy for Higher Education*. Chicago: American Library Association, 2015. Accessed March 25, 2016. http://www.ala.org/acrl/standards/ilframework.

Birmingham, Elizabeth, Luc Chinwongs, Molly R. Flaspohler, Carly Hearn, Danielle Kvanvig, and Ronda Portman. "First-Year Writing Teachers, Perceptions of Students' Information Literacy Competencies, and a Call for a Collaborative Approach." *Communications in Information Literacy* 2, no. 1 (2008) 1–17, http://www.comminfolit.org/index.php?journal=cil&page=article&op=viewArticle&path%5B%5D=Spring2008AR1&path%5B%5D=67.

Bowles-Terry, Melissa, Erin Davis, and Wendy Holliday. "'Writing Information Literacy' Revisited: Application of Theory to Practice in the Classroom." *Reference & User Services Quarterly* 49, no. 3 (Spring 2010): 225, http://www.jstor.org/stable/20865257.

Condon, William, and Carol Rutz. "A Taxonomy of Writing Across the Curriculum Programs: Evolving to Serve Broader Agendas." *College Composition and Communication* 64, no. 2 (2012): 358.

Council of Writing Program Administrators, National Council of Teachers of English, and National Writing Project. *Framework for Success in Postsecondary Writing*. Council of Writing Program Administrators, National Council of Teachers of English, and National Writing Project, 2011. Accessed March 25, 2016. http://wpacouncil.org/files/framework-for-success-postsecondary-writing.pdf.

Elmborg, James. "Information Literacy and Writing Across the Curriculum: Sharing the Vision." *Reference Services Review* 31, no.1 (2003): 68–80, doi:10.1108/00907320310460933.

Flower, Linda, and John R. Hayes. "A Cognitive Process Theory of Writing." *College Composition and Communication* 32, no. 4 (1981): 365–387.

Holliday, Wendy, and Britt Fagerheim. "Integrating Information Literacy with a Sequenced English Composition Curriculum." *portal: Libraries and the Academy* 6, no. 2 (April 2006): 169–184, doi:10.1353/pla.2006.0023.

Hyland, Ken. *Teaching and Researching Writing*. 2nd ed. London: Routledge, 2013.

Kistler, Ruth, Kathleen Blake Yancey, Kara Taczak, and Natalie Szysmanski. "Introduction: Writing Across the Curriculum and Assessment." *Across the Disciplines* 6 (2009), http://wac.colostate.edu/ATD/assessment/kistleretal.cfm.

McClure, Randall, and Kellian Clink. "How Do You Know That? An Investigation of Student Research Practices in the Digital Age." *portal: Libraries and the Academy* 9, no.1 (January 2009): 115–132, doi:10.1353/pla.0.0033.

Moton, David, and Gloria Dumler, *Navigating America*. New York: McGraw-Hill, 2009.

Norgaard, Rolf. "Writing Information Literacy: Contributions to a Concept." *Reference and User Services Quarterly* 43, no. 2 (Winter 2003): 124–130, EBSCOHost.

Norgaard, Rolf. "Writing Information Literacy in the Classroom: Pedagogical Enactments and Implications." *Reference and User Services Quarterly* 43, no. 3 (Spring 2004): 224, EBSCOHost.

Swales, John. *Genre Analysis: English in Academic and Research Settings*. Cambridge: Cambridge University Press, 1990.

SECTION 2:
Partnering Research & Writing

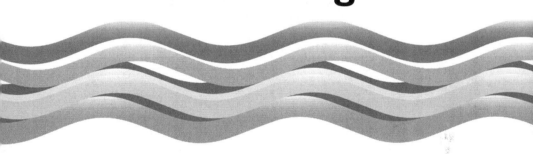

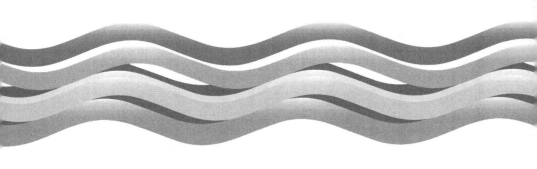

CHAPTER 5*

Bridging the Gap:

New Thresholds and Opportunities for Collaboration

Amber Lancaster, Donell Callender, and Laura Heinz
Texas Tech University

Introduction

In early November of 2014, Amber found herself submerged in grading first-year composition papers—a literature review resulting from seven weeks of research-writing activities. This seven-week endeavor included locating and assessing at least eight sources, writing an annotated bibliography, and completing several other scaffolded writing exercises. As Amber worked through grading sixty literature reviews, her level of frustration quickly grew with the products she was reading. The assignment seemed clear, but students were not *getting* it—they seemed to have selected the first eight sources they found and then tried to write a 1500-word literature review that meshed a bunch of randomly threaded ideas.

Frustrated by an obvious disconnect between her teaching and her students' learning, Amber analyzed how she might improve the way she delivers course materials to teach the literature review genre. Amber reviewed the unit materials, the textbook readings, the in-class activities, the library

* This work is licensed under a Creative Commons Attribution-NonCommercial 4.0 License, CC BY-NC (https://creativecommons.org/licenses/by-nc/4.0/).

demonstration and site visit, and the example literature reviews she offered the students. She went over her notes and instructor journal, racking her brain trying to figure out, Why don't students get this? She had several theories: students being lazy or hasty, students not reading the materials, students not having an interest in their topics, students not really being the great information consumers their generation is often labeled. She persevered and finished grading, moving on to the next unit and wrapping up the semester.

Another few weeks went by, and Amber soon let go of the less-than-perfect literature review papers, but the idea that something could be done to improve the unit and students' ability to understand the literature review genre lurked in her thoughts well into the next semester. Uncertain what the something needed to be, Amber reached out to two library colleagues. That is when she learned the Association of College and Research Libraries (ACRL) *Framework for Information Literacy for Higher Education* might be the something for which she was looking.

At about the same time Amber experienced her literature review letdown, the ACRL had published its newly revised ACRL Framework (November 12, 2014).[1] Amber listened intently about frameworks from her librarian colleagues over a cup of coffee, and the ideas started to form. She asked many questions, and she got many answers. Then she suggested a partnership—a collaborative project to revise the literature review unit—with the hope a revised unit would effectively embrace the research processes of students today and deeply emphasize the understanding of information across a network of sources.

This chapter presents a case study of this library and writing collaboration. We offer a narrative about the steps we took to integrate the ACRL Framework and to revise the first-year composition course, specifically the literature review unit. The revised course was piloted in the Fall 2015 semester. This chapter also examines the collaborative relationship between librarians and writing programs and identifies the ways the ACRL Framework complements the Council of Writing Program Administrators, National Council of Teachers of English, and National Writing Project (WPA) *Framework for Success in Postsecondary* Writing.[2] Merging the two Frameworks, we argue, more clearly defines information literacy as it is connected to the critical reading, researching, and writing skills taught in first-year composition.

Our aim in this chapter is to offer practical strategies for implementing and assessing the ACRL Framework and WPA Framework so others might emulate our project and advance the ideas we offer. We do so by presenting two aspects of the pilot project: the early consulting phase and the reformed course pilot, resulting from librarian consultation and collaboration. The early consulting section discusses how the librarian team, Donell and Laura, worked to construct information literacy objectives and matrices for assessing measurable information literacy skills connected to Amber's writing assignments. The librarian authors present the challenges they faced applying ACRL Framework threshold concepts to the course and offer guidance on putting them into practice. The section on the reformed course resulting from librarian consultations describes the outcomes of the librarian-faculty collaboration—how the course design changed to integrate both the ACRL Framework and WPA Framework. Amber explains what the reformed course looks like and discusses the challenges of putting into classroom practice the ACRL Framework's thresholds and the WPA Framework's habits of mind. In the end, our collective experiences merging the two Frameworks brought to light several practical and pedagogical considerations we hope librarians and writing instructors will explore further. Therefore, we view this chapter as a conversation starter for librarians and writing programs; we see great value, and the need for more research, in the partnerships research libraries and writing programs form.

What is in a Framework?

Much of the professional literature focusing on collaborations between faculty and academic librarians to incorporate information literacy use the *Standards for Information Literacy in Higher Education* developed by the ACRL in 1999 as their guide. The Standards' objectives define and provide outcomes for academic librarians when working with faculty to incorporate information literacy into the curriculum.

Kenedy and Monty discuss the benefits of such faculty-librarian collaboration in developing assignments that incorporate information literacy competencies.[3] Similarly, Smith and Dailey's case study concludes their collaboration enhanced the quality of research papers in an upper-division public health course with the inclusion of information literacy outcomes.[4] The ACRL reformed the Standards into the Framework in 2014 and now six concepts serve as the foundation for information literacy. Aligning these six ACRL concepts with the habits of mind found in the WPA Framework provides common ground for the composition faculty member and academic librarian when collaborating on updates to the writing curriculum. Both Frameworks focus on developing students' cognitive skills at a higher level, and concepts in both Frameworks are transformative. As we located commonalities and complementary areas of each Framework, we began to develop meaningful and dynamic assignments—one of the benefits of faculty-librarian collaboration. This notion of achieving deeper or transformative learning experiences is at the heart of our collaborative course redesign.

Librarian Consultation-Collaboration Phase: Merging Frameworks and Developing Context

In our early meetings, we discussed the existing curriculum and goals and offered an assessment of weaknesses in the course. Our aim was to identify possible causes for the disconnect between what was asked of students and what they delivered in the literature review drafts. In our own information gathering processes, Donell and Laura examined assignment descriptions, course resources, and the scaffolding approach intended to build research-writing skills, albeit in a piecemeal process. We concluded the curriculum was structured logically to introduce students to library research processes; however, the course offered little support beyond showing students where to find library resources. The curriculum included a library demonstration and a site visit tied to a scavenger hunt activity; both of these exercises are useful as they orient first-year students to the location of the library, the databases, librarians, and the reference desk. However, these were the only integrated activities involving librarians in the research process—and this was but our first change.

Our goals, as research librarians, included more than simply showing students where to find sources or how to access databases. In effective library instruction, students need contextualized activities to lead them through multiple phases of the research process: as noted in the ACRL Framework draft, "Information literacy is a spectrum of abilities, practices, and habits of mind that extend and deepen learning through engagement with the information ecosystem."[5] This exact phrasing did not make it to the final draft of the ACRL Framework; however, its meaning carries significant weight in our case. The first suggestion, then, was to develop participation activities starting with the library demonstration and site visit (still using the scavenger hunt activity), but then moving into a series of librarian-supported research activities. These activities were aimed at strengthening students' understanding of the information ecosystem; helping them engage in creative questioning, critical thinking, knowledge making; and supporting their strategic analysis of that information ecosystem.

To develop these librarian-supported research activities, we turned to the two Frameworks. With the revised ACRL Framework being relatively new to the library instruction community, we decided to begin by examining the preceding ACRL Standards paired with the typical approach to instruction. Next we matched the appropriate Framework to the existing assignments based on the desired learning traits. Following this, we decided how the ACRL and WPA Frameworks overlapped and complemented each other, and where the ACRL Framework would supplement missing or underdeveloped components in the existing curriculum.

The ACRL Standards gave us a starting point on how and where to use the ACRL Framework in the existing course; by combining them, we pieced together four library assignments. With the assignments from the course instructor, we developed the objectives as they related to the ACRL Framework. This process helped achieve a common thread between the ACRL Standards and the ACRL Framework's knowledge practices, yet we relied heavily on the knowledge practices and dispositions within each ACRL Framework. The knowledge practices and dispositions also assisted in the assessment of the ACRL Framework. In short, we matched the new Framework concepts with the old ACRL Competency Standards. Having conducted information literacy courses for first-year composition for the past ten years, we found it relatively easy to make a good match between the assignments (assessment tools) and the Framework constructs.

One advantage of the ACRL Framework is its flexibility; one can apply an entire frame or use only the knowledge practices or the dispositions to achieve the goal of the assignment. However, we felt it was important for the composition class to be introduced to the frame as a whole, then we could, by breaking it down, explain the how and why of each frame. In some cases, we developed assignments with only one connecting frame, while in other cases we developed a single assignment using two frames. This flexibility allowed us to create assignments with two parts, each part tied to one of the six ACRL frames and any overlapping WPA habits of mind.

Finally, we developed a matrix for assessing learning outcomes by using the knowledge practices from the Framework. We established a five-point rubric scale: a score of one indicated zero to one of the knowledge practices was achieved, a score of five indicated all the knowledge practices were achieved during the assignment. See Figure 5.01.

Figure 5.01
Framework Rubrics

Framework	5	4	3	2	1
Information Has Value (Assignment #2 Part 1)	Achieves 8 of the 8 Knowledge Practices (KP) Listed	Achieves 6–7 of the KP listed	Achieves 4–5 of the KP listed	Achieves 2–3 of the KP listed	Achieves 0–1 of the KP listed
Research As Inquiry (Assignment #2 Part 2)	Achieves 8 of the 8 KP Listed	Achieves 6–7 of the KP listed	Achieves 4–5 of the KP listed	Achieves 2–3 of the KP listed	Achieves 0–1 of the KP listed

Whereas the previous set of standards is considered a set of skills, the ACRL Framework is intended to be "a cluster of interconnected core concepts, with flexible options for implementation."[6] Therefore, we redesigned the literature review in the composition course so that students would finish with a solid foundation of information literacy, not merely have a step-by-step process to complete to perform research for a paper. Thus, we included the URL to the ACRL Framework in the assignments so students could obtain information about the goals of the Framework while being introduced to the research process in the course. Next, we included the pertinent frame for the appropriate activity within the assignment, including the knowledge practices and dispositions for each. We also included an explanation about the frame's intended purpose so students could successfully accomplish each task.

The goal was not to have students follow a set of instructions or list of steps to accomplish their research, but rather to have students know the why behind the instruction and, more importantly, the why behind a productive research process, which is where we believe the previous curriculum fell short. The Framework encourages a deeper look at research with the intended goal for students to better understand the why and how for doing proper research for their topics. For example, questions we wanted students to encounter included:

- Why search for information in a certain way?
- What is the benefit of doing background research about the authors?
- Why is it better to use vetted resources, such as databases, rather than the web?
- What are some strategic ways to use the web for research?
- How can a website, book, or article used for research be evaluated?
- How can an article or piece of information be determined as a good source for a particular topic?

The goal of these questions is for students to view information critically. In today's information world, students are tempted to go straight to Google to search for sources. Though students can evaluate an article via Google Scholar or other online altmetrics, they often do not question the information they are researching, resulting in articles often inappropriate for their topic. We see this more and more in composition classes and even in the one-hour credit course our librarians teach on essential scholarly research; it is the same disconnect apparent in the literature review drafts. By using the ACRL and WPA Frameworks to guide curriculum development, however, we believe we can minimize the disconnect students encounter. We believe the ACRL Framework and WPA Framework, taken together, emphasize deeper understanding of the information ecosystem—what Amber, the composition faculty, rightfully called "information across a network of sources."

Best Practices: Advancing the Pros and Avoiding the Cons

Though we see great value in the ACRL Framework in aiding the development of the four library assignments now connected to the literature review in the redesigned composition course, we experienced challenges with how the Framework is explained and how to put into context its concepts in ways students understand. In other words, a drawback to the ACRL Framework is its highly theoretical nature. We quickly realized that both Frameworks are too dense for most freshmen students and not written with that intent. The previous ACRL Standards were clear-cut, basic. The ACRL Framework draws attention to this theoretical characteristic, noting it

> is called a framework intentionally because it is based on a cluster of interconnected core concepts, with flexible options for implementation, rather than on a set of standards or learning outcomes, or any prescriptive enumeration of skills. At the heart of the framework are conceptual understandings that organize many other concepts and ideas about information, research, and conceptual scholarship into a coherent whole.[7]

The new ACRL Framework is not cut-and-dried like the old Competency Standards. Perhaps the ACRL Framework is more of a thought machine for librarians and not meant to be left to a student's interpretation, which was not the case with the competencies. Librarians and students alike could easily decipher the goals of the Standards. Consequently, we offer paraphrasing the content to make its ideas more accessible to students as a first step, and possible best practice, in adopting the new ACRL Framework.

Because the new ACRL Framework takes a theoretical approach and appears so unlike the previous Standards, many librarians may be leery of it; thus, another challenge we anticipate is nudging librarians to adopt and use it. In conversation and presentations, many librarians have criticized the ACRL Framework for not being thoroughly evaluated and researched, or for being too different from the old Standards. However, we decided to fully embrace the ACRL Framework and to compare it to the old Standards in order to seek out similarities.

Using both the old Standards as a guide (to a lesser degree) and the Framework (as they evolve into common practice) is a winning model for us. In early discussions with Amber, our writing instructor colleague, it seemed we needed to make adjustments to the library instruction and related assignments. In later discussions (after the course pilot project had begun), we learned some students were confused about the language and meaning of the ACRL Framework. As a result, we plan to include an introduction to the Framework in addition to rewording its frames to improve comprehension.

Perhaps introducing the ACRL Framework earlier in the research process would be better, such as at the library demonstration, which is the first contact students have with the librarians and the library assignments in our approach. As a second option, the writing instructor could assign readings, PowerPoint slides, or videos outside of class that reference the ACRL Framework in connection with first-year composition goals. A third option would be not to introduce the Framework at all, but rather develop outcomes specific to the assignment. This third option is also one Oakleaf has suggested: "After identifying and prioritizing the threshold concepts or additional 'big ideas' they wish to teach, librarians need to transform those concepts into learning outcomes.... After all, outcomes describe what librarians hope students will know or be able to do as a result of instruction."[8]

For those forging beyond our initial pilot project and putting into practice the ACRL Framework, we hope future iterations of course assignments will be more clear and accessible to students in the important concepts of why and how.

Reforming First-Year Composition with the ACRL and WPA Frameworks

My (Amber) initial thought, as a first-year composition instructor thinking about how the ACRL Framework would mesh with the WPA Framework, was "This makes complete sense! Easy, right?" In reality, implementing any curricular change poses a challenge for an individual instructor. Changing a standard composition course to include ACRL components poses challenges on several levels for the writing program administrator, the instructors, and its students.

The writing program administrator at our university oversees the composition program, requiring all instructors use the same textbook, a program-wide syllabus, and common assignments. Because the writing program administrator answers to senior administration and must ensure core courses meet accreditation requirements, implementing even the smallest of curriculum changes takes much work. The administrator must examine any proposed curriculum changes with numerous questions and perspectives in mind. How does the proposed change impact outcomes and assessments? How does the proposed change affect instructor workload? Students' workloads? How does the proposed change affect in-class and out-of-class activities? How does the proposed change affect institutional resources, such as the training program for teaching composition, availability of physical space for training, and budgetary aspects?

The instructor may bring concerns to the conversation including questions about the return on investment of time, effort, and resources preparing new materials, assignments and innovative activities. Will students see the value in the assignment? Will students' writing improve and their performance levels increase? What overall impact will these efforts have on my students?

The common curriculum at our university poses a unique challenge: all sections of the first-year composition course (roughly 2,500 students across seventy-two sections) are offered in hybrid format, meaning students meet for class only once a week (for one hour and twenty minutes) and are required to use a web-based model for instructional materials, assignment submissions, and writing feedback and assessment. Given this challenge, Amber had to develop the out-of-class components to avoid taxing the workload for all involved. The primary questions driving curriculum development in the ACRL and WPA Frameworks pilot project focused on complementary materials, assignments, and resources. In short, how could Amber and the library consultants delve into fundamental components of the existing curriculum so students would learn more and become independent in their academic research journey, yet prevent overhauling the course or taking up significantly more instructional class time?

In the spring of 2015, when Amber met with Donell and Laura, library faculty, to discuss the ACRL Framework and the WPA Framework, the team immediately saw several overlapping concepts. The conversations quickly moved into ways we could merge the two Frameworks and develop instructional pieces librarians could offer. In this way, librarians' instructional pieces would complement the existing curriculum without adding more to the instructor's and the students' workloads.

The consulting process took place from May 2015 to early August 2015 and produced curriculum changes employing a scaffolding approach, in which one participation activity builds on the next. We created four new library activities that tied into the existing composition curriculum. Three complemented the literature review assignment in the first half of the semester, and one complemented the transition of information from the literature review to the argument essay in the second half of the semester. Librarian consultants developed and assessed each activity for its ability to support research.

Library Activities and the ACRL and WPA Frameworks

Library Activity 1

The first library activity tasks students with attending the library database presentation, visiting the library holdings, then completing the scavenger hunt tied to the presentation. This assignment orients students to the library's resources, which they will later access for their research project. We classified this activity as a pre-literature review activity. The activity was in the existing composition course, but the revised presentation involved more collaboration with library faculty to tailor it to address the needs of the students in the context of the course and research tied to their assignments.

This activity connects with the WPA habit of mind curiosity that "is fostered when writers are encouraged to… use inquiry as a process to develop questions relevant for authentic audiences within a variety of disciplines."[9] This habit of mind aligns with the ACRL frame titled "Research as Inquiry," which is described as "an understanding that research is iterative and depends upon asking increasingly complex or new questions whose answers develop additional questions or lines of inquiry in any field."[10] To develop this first library activity in ways that move students beyond simply finding where to go to access library resources, we added a second task following the scavenger hunt.

In this second part, we task students with talking to professors in their fields or talking to experts in a specific discourse community to identify hot topics and to ask about research questions tied to those topics. This activity emphasizes that true research inquiry goes beyond the individual and connects with communities in various fields of study. Requiring students to connect with experts in the fields or disciplines in which they have an interest facilitates their selecting a research topic of interest. Thus, students stand a better chance of being invested in the research-writing process.

To further that investment, we also task students with locating two to three key articles on the topic. We ask them to explore the topic, in order to identify a research question, guided by three prompts:

- What are some hot topics or high interest topics?
- What sides of the issue/debate do you think might emerge (with further reading or research)?
- Can you locate sources to help you understand the topic?

Requiring students to use the research process as inquiry to develop a research question shifts their research experience from one of locating an answer to one of identifying the issues.

Library Activity 2

In the second library activity, we require students to locate and assess six to eight scholarly articles for their topics. This assignment guides students through getting initial sources and critically reading the sources to determine if they are suited for a literature review. This source self-assessment requires students to review their sources from the library scavenger hunt for appropriateness and is designed to encourage students to reflect upon source credentials and credibility and to encourage self-investment in selecting sources.

This activity links to the WPA habit of mind engagement that cultivates "a sense of investment and involvement in learning."[11] Fundamental to engagement are students' abilities to "make connections between their own ideas and those of others" and "find meanings new to them or build on existing meanings as a result of new connections."[12] This second library assignment, then, guides students in the assessment process to generate new ideas and make connections between sources and their own understanding of their topic.

This habit of mind aligns with two ACRL frames: "Information has Value" and "Research as Inquiry."[13] The ACRL frame "Information has Value" puts forth the notion that "value may be wielded by powerful interests in ways that marginalize certain voices. However, value may also be leveraged by individuals and organizations to effect change and for civic, economic, social, or personal gains."[14] By examining information through this ACRL frame, students learn the sources they select may advance certain voices and leave out others. The selection of the information they use and discard is itself part of an ecosystem that values some voices over others. In many ways, this idea fosters the same notion as making connections between information sources the WPA habits of mind highlight.

Similarly, engagement aligns with the ACRL frame "Research as Inquiry" by emphasizing the research process as one that examines "points of disagreement where debate and dialogue work to deepen the conversations around the knowledge."[15] This very idea is the heart of the literature review genre. We task students with critically examining the disagreements and dialogues in the scholarly conversations.

Library Activity 3

The third library activity contains two parts and calls for students to meet with a personal librarian to review the sources they selected in the second library activity, and develop a sound research plan to prepare them for the second draft of the literature review. We designed the first part to help students refine their sources and learn from the library consultant. Our goal for this activity is for students to develop a deeper understanding of selecting and using sources for academic research writing; we ask students to examine sources used in the literature review and determine their use, applicability, and appropriateness in the revised draft of the literature review.

In part two, based on the meeting with a personal librarian, we task students with removing inappropriate sources from the first draft of the literature review and then locating and adding new and more appropriate sources. Our goal in part two is for students to develop a balanced literature review that accurately presents the scholarly conversation. In this critical analysis of sources, we pose three questions to students:

- Are you hearing enough varied perspectives and interpretations?
- What perspectives might you still need to investigate and research (either more broadly or more deeply)?
- In other words, to what conversational pieces do you need to listen, follow, and present more about in the literature review to have a well-balanced conversation?

This third library assignment connects to the WPA frame of persistence,[16] which embraces the notion that writers "commit to exploring, in writing, a topic, idea, or project" and "grapple with challenging ideas, texts, processes, or projects."[17] Students are guided to see the writing and research processes as iterative and ongoing—something they explore, think about, and revisit on more than one occasion.

The WPA frame of persistence closely connects with two ACRL frames in this assignment: "Authority is Constructed and Contextual" and "Scholarship is a Conversation." The ACRL frame "Authority is Constructed and Contextual" emphasizes novices "critically examine all evidence" to "ask relevant questions about origins, context, and suitability for the current information need."[18] Furthermore, the ACRL frame "Scholarship is a Conversation" states research is "a discursive practice in which ideas are formulated, debated, and weighed against one another over extended periods of time."[19] Together, these frames highlight the need for student writers to examine and reexamine the sources, voices of authority, and ever-changing conversations emerging from these sources as they shape their own understanding within the literature.

Library Activity 4

The final library assignment serves as a transition from the literature review to the argument essay in the composition curriculum. We task students with writing a reflective summary of their consultation with the librarian in order to self-identify the next steps in their research plan. This assignment asks students to consider if they are on target with the original articles and what new information they learned from meeting with the librarian. For example, students reflect critically on the articles they have kept, added, or discarded, and the reasons why they made those decisions.

This first part of the library assignment connects to the WPA habit of mind of openness, identified as a "willingness to consider new ways of being and thinking in the world" and emphasizes the ability of students to "listen to and reflect on the ideas and responses of others."[20] Similarly, the ACRL frame "Searching as Strategic Exploration" emphasizes the notion that "information searching is a contextualized, complex experience that affects, and is affected by the cognitive, affective, and social dimensions of the searcher."[21] These perspectives illustrate an inclination to view information assessment as a negotiation between one's self and others.

Next, we task students with thinking about how changing the information context to a new writing assignment also changes the ways in which they use source materials and information. Completing the source assessment project, then, requires students to review their selected research sources from the literature review and think about how they would use the same sources in the first draft of the argument essay. By positioning their research in a new context, students should be able to identify more easily where information gaps exist—such as in their stance, the opposition to their stance, or the rebuttal to the opposition. As a primary assignment question, we ask students to explore critically the ways they would change how they use the literature.

This process of transforming information to a new context relates to the WPA habit of mind, flexibility in which students would "approach writing assignments in multiple ways, depending on the task and the writer's purpose and audience."[22] Additionally, this transformation process aligns with the ACRL frame "Information Creation as a Process," which identifies "the understanding that the purpose, message, and delivery of information are intentional acts of creation"[23] and that "the dynamic nature of information creation and dissemination requires ongoing attention to understand evolving creation processes."[24] Both the WPA and ACRL concepts complement each other by emphasizing viewing information in changing contexts. From these perspectives, this last library activity offers a useful way for students to connect one research project to another and, more importantly, see the dynamic nature of information use.

Putting into Classroom Practice a Merged Framework: How Well Did It Work?

As with any change, putting into practice the reformed course posed some challenges for Amber, the writing instructor. Determining the weight of the activities and awarding points for the work completed was a challenge. Although the librarian consultants had developed contextualized and customized activities that complemented the existing composition curriculum, the materials were outside the common course. Therefore, Amber could offer only two incentives to students for engaging in the research tasks: first was participation points (which were significantly less than the common writing assignments), and second was the value added of completing the library instructional work (emphasizing students would become better researchers and ultimately better research writers). Because the assignments' weight in points was comparably low to the common writing assignments, some students put less effort into completing these critical research exercises. As a recommended best practice, then, instructors who integrate library activities should weight such tasks appropriately. Doing so will emphasize their value and encourage students to see such activities as important to the writing projects in the composition course.

There were added instructor workload aspects tied to the delivery and assessment mechanisms of a new merged Framework. Adding the library components to the web-based courseware site (Blackboard) added to teacher prep and grading workload. However, because the librarian consultants had created a matrix for assessing students' completed work, the participation assessments required minimal time. Instructor assessments included scanning the students' submitted work and reviewing the matrix and then transferring the score from the matrix to the course gradebook. As another best practice, we recommend minimizing the challenges of administering extra assignments and grading with multiple rubrics by creating built-in rubrics in Blackboard (or other courseware) based on the matrix. Another option writing instructors might consider is adding these assessment areas to their writing rubrics. Doing so would minimize the grading workload and emphasize the library assignments as equal to the writing assignments, instead of as a supplement to the common writing assignments.

Though only anecdotal evidence at this time (our pre/post-test surveys will be analyzed for aggregated results in the Spring 2016 semester), our initial impression was the revised curriculum led by the librarian consultants has improved the teaching and learning experience tied to the literature review unit. When grading students' library assignments, pre-writing activities, annotated bibliographies, and final literature review products, the writing instructor felt students were engaged with their topics, the research process, and the writing assignments in a deeper way that illustrated critical thinking about research and the scholarly conversation that they now had joined. They finally *got* it!

Conclusion

With any curriculum reform project comes the potential for frustration—trying to figure out the best mix of old and new materials, which assignments to keep, toss out, and create new can be a challenging process. Add another layer—collaboration—and curriculum reform can quickly turn into a drawn-out process in which people endlessly debate. When this happens, the curriculum reform project can be pulled in many directions and the result can be a divided team whose compromises weaken the final product.

However, when collaboration takes the form of consultation and the curriculum reform process draws from unique areas of expertise and perspectives, the collaboration opportunities are better positioned to focus on gaps in the curriculum and how two or more teams complement (rather than compete for) ideas. This latter scenario is what we saw emerge when two librarians acted as consultants to a member of the composition faculty. In courses that couple research practices with the subject matter, who better than librarians to fill a research gap in the curriculum?

This case study pilot project has taught us that a librarian-as-consultant partnership is highly beneficial to writing programs. Our experience has shown when writing programs seek guidance from information literacy experts, the curriculum achieves a deeper connection between information literacy and the critical reading, researching, and writing skills taught in composition courses. We argue for more librarian-as-consultant partnerships, not only in writing programs, but also in higher education courses university-wide. We see these partnerships as important opportunities to bridge the gap between information literacy, college composition, and the many foundational courses that place research and writing in a network of skills within the subject matter of the course.

By synthesizing the ACRL and WPA Frameworks, we were successful in developing research and writing curricula that honed specific knowledge and skills tied to the literature review project. Students engaged more deeply with conducting research (locating, accessing, and using sources) and articulating research findings in ways more meaningful to them, and us. Synthesizing source ideas to show relationships across sources in a network, determining appropriateness of those sources in the context of that network of sources, and making new meaning from their information-seeking processes were all results clearly visible in the revised curriculum.

As with many new experiences, we find ourselves reflecting forward in a sense that we have more questions than we have answers. Therefore, we end with a few questions that surfaced through the course of our collaboration, and we offer only brief answers because of the nascent nature they present:

- How might overlapping goals of the two Frameworks shape a hybrid composition course (or any writing course) in ways that achieve deeper learning and greater ability to locate authoritative and credible resources for research-based assignments?

The Frameworks give deeper meaning to the why behind research. Instructors and librarians have more pedagogical leeway with teaching and learning as the Frameworks offer multiple lenses for examining the how and why behind information seeking. The combined Frameworks support deeper learning about how and why research-writing activities are bound.

- What challenges exist that influence application of either Framework to the first-year composition course?

We discovered students were confused by the Frameworks' structure, which is not cut-and-dried like a rubric with specific learning outcomes. However, we see this as an opportunity to interpret the Frameworks as needed for an assignment. At an institution that adopts a common syllabus for sections of the same course, however, this challenge points to where more research is needed. Applying a theoretical lens like the Frameworks to program-wide writing curricula requires careful and thorough consideration. How individual instructors interpret the use of the Frameworks in their courses and how individual students apply the Frameworks to improve their research-writing skills may achieve inconsistent results.

- What future implications might a librarians-as-consultants model offer composition programs?

Embedded librarianship is one way to take the Frameworks a step further. Online tutorials by librarians are also an option for flipped model classrooms or distance students.

- What emerging research needs surface for both disciplines as a result of librarian-instructor collaborations?

One roadblock seems to be the concept of consultation. Until there is a culture shift or change in the paradigm instructors have about librarians, librarian-as-consultant or librarian-instructor collaborations will remain unconventional. It is often thought librarians are only gatekeepers of information, or they are too busy to help instructors with classes or curriculum, or more importantly, with the instruction or pedagogy itself. Until these misconceptions are corrected, the model we present in this chapter may only exist in tiny pockets across the higher education landscape.

Notes

1. Association of College and Research Libraries. *Framework for Information Literacy for Higher Education,* February 9, 2015. http://www.ala.org/acrl/standards/ilframework.
2. Council of Writing Program Administrators, National Council of Teachers of English. *Framework for Success in Postsecondary Writing,* National Writing Project, January, 2011. http://wpacouncil.org/files/framework-for-success-postsecondary-writing.pdf.
3. Robert Kenedy and Vivienne Monty, "Faculty-Librarian Collaboration and the Development of Critical Skills through Dynamic Purposeful Learning," *Libri* 61, (2): 116–124. doi:10.1515/libr.2011.010, June 2011.
4. Meggan D. Smith and Amy B. Dailey, "Improving and Assessing Information Literacy Skills through Faculty-Librarian Collaboration," *College & Undergraduate Libraries,* 20 (2013): 314–326. doi:10.1080/10691316.2013.829370.

5. Craig Gibson and Trudi E. Jacobson, "Framework for Information Literacy for Higher Education," November 12, 2014. http://acrl.ala.org/ilstandards/wp-content/uploads/2014/11/Framework-for-IL-for-HE-draft-3.pdf.
6. ACRL, Framework, 1.
7. Ibid., 1.
8. Megan Oakleaf, "A Roadmap for Assessing Student Learning Using the New Framework for Information Literacy for Higher Education," *The Journal of Academic Librarianship* 40, (2014): 510–514. doi:10.1016/j.acalib.2014.08.001.
9. WPA, Framework, 4.
10. ACRL, Framework, 7.
11. WPA, Framework, 4.
12. Ibid., 4.
13. ACRL, Framework, 7.
14. Ibid., 6.
15. Ibid., 7.
16. WPA, Framework, 5.
17. Ibid., 7.
18. ACRL, Framework, 2.
19. Ibid., 4.
20. WPA, Framework, 1.
21. ACRL, Framework, 9.
22. WPA, Framework, 5.
23. Gibson, Framework, 6.
24. ACRL, Framework, 5.

Bibliography

Association of College and Research Libraries. *Framework for Information Literacy for Higher Education,* February 9, 2015. Accessed March 28, 2016. http://www.ala.org/acrl/standards/ilframework.

Council of Writing Program Administrators, National Council of Teachers of English. *Framework for Success in Postsecondary Writing,* National Writing Project, January, 2011. Accessed March 28, 2016. http://wpacouncil.org/files/framework-for-success-postsecondary-writing.pdf.

Gibson, Craig, and Trudi E. Jacobson. "Framework for Information Literacy for Higher Education." November 12, 2014. Accessed March 28, 2016. http://acrl.ala.org/ilstandards/wp-content/uploads/2014/11/Framework-for-IL-for-HE-draft-3.pdf.

Kenedy, Robert and Vivienne Monty. "Faculty-Librarian Collaboration and the Development of Critical Skills through Dynamic Purposeful Learning." *Libri* 61, (2): 116–124. doi:10.1515/libr.2011.010, June 2011.

Oakleaf, Megan. "A Roadmap for Assessing Student Learning Using the New Framework for Information Literacy for Higher Education." *The Journal of Academic Librarianship* 40, (2014). doi:10.1016/j.acalib.2014.08.001.

Smith, Meggan D. and Dailey, Amy B. 2013. Improving and Assessing Information Literacy Skills through Faculty-Librarian Collaboration. *College & Undergraduate Libraries,* 20.

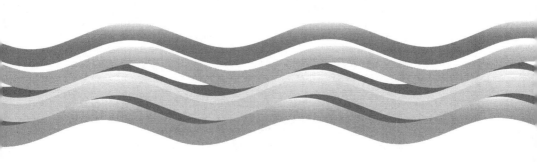

CHAPTER 6

Integrating the Frameworks in Postsecondary Writing:
Disciplinary Literacy in First-Year Composition

Nancy C. DeJoy and Sara D. Miller
Michigan State University

Brian D. Holcomb
Limestone College

Introduction

The importance of developing pedagogies that allow students to explore the concepts and practices that inform disciplinary literacy as they make the transition to higher education in the U.S. cannot be overestimated. Disciplinary literacy requires the abilities to analyze specific types of discourse and generate those types of discourse in order to effectively participate in scholarly and other conversations about subjects important within, and sometimes across, fields of study. These types of analytic, generative skills and dispositions position students to make informed decisions and to help them understand the shift away from consuming knowledge to participating in its generation. As Louise

Limberg et al. state, "Meaning in information is created through the meeting between people, practices and tools."[1]

One point along the path toward disciplinary literacy that focuses on meaning-making and is common for students today is the first-year composition course. To best help students along this path within the first-year composition course, we explore the connections between the Association of College and Research Libraries' 2015 *Framework for Literacy in Higher Education* (hereafter ACRL Framework) and the Council of Writing Program Administrators, National Council of Teachers of English, and National Writing Project's 2011 *Framework for Success in Postsecondary Writing* (hereafter WPA Framework). In doing so, we suggest how the tenets and principles of these Frameworks can be integrated in the pursuit of disciplinary literacy.

What we notice right away is integrating the two Frameworks requires a more general reconfiguration of reading and writing, one that creates a relationship between the two more focused on shifting student perspectives toward understanding knowledge creation as an engaged process.[2] Underlying both the ACRL and WPA Frameworks is a very real desire to open a space in which readers and writers are more than mere consumers who adapt to what is already known. Understanding the role of participation in the construction of knowledge (one's own knowledge and one's understanding of other's knowledge) and seeing one's own production of knowledge as an engaged process of contribution is key to expanding our ideas of literacy in ways that support success in higher education and beyond.[3]

To create a relationship in which exploring disciplinary literacy allows students to practice knowledge creation through focused engagement, we have created a disciplinary literacies assignment (DLA) built upon the concepts of revision, arrangement, invention, delivery, and style (RAIDS) offered in Appendix 6A.[4] This assignment helps students to understand texts as created artifacts, which allows them, as readers, to generate knowledge about the relevance of where those texts came from (invention), how they found their way into public spheres (delivery), and why the information they contain is organized as it is (style). The assignment also allows for a kind of rhetorical analysis focusing on how knowledge is constructed (invention), what relationships are key in the construction of that knowledge (arrangement), and what the purpose of the discourse might be (revision).

For the conceptual content of the two Frameworks to be integrated cohesively, notions of the relationship between reading and writing that assume reading is for finding pre-constructed information and writing is for communicating that information must be challenged. Using RAIDS in the context of a disciplinary literacies assignment allows us to focus on disciplinary literacy and disciplinary sources as both informational, in relation to the presentation of knowledge and its construction, and generative, in relation to the ways the presentation of information expands our understanding of the available strategies as we engage in the production of our own texts. As a result of using RAIDS as a strategy that integrates the analytic and generative aspects of literacy, we are able to integrate the Frameworks for a shared pedagogical purpose.

In this chapter, we discuss the conceptual background of a disciplinary literacies approach grounded in RAIDS and its connections to the WPA and ACRL Frameworks. We also highlight how the approach to disciplinary literacy in the assignment creates practical and pedagogical connections between the two Frameworks. The course structure, assignment design, and integrated library instruction invite students to take an inquiry-based approach[5] to building knowledge about the disciplinary literacies central to major fields of study.

Disciplinary Literacy—A Conceptual Background

Our interest with fostering disciplinary literacy is rooted in the reality that many college students change their major at least once, a move that can affect time to graduation, as well as financial and other responsibilities families and students incur when the time to graduation increases.[6] Having the opportunity to build understanding of the expectations for reading, writing, and researching, along with other factors related to careers in specific fields, helps students develop a deeper understanding of what it takes to be successful in a field beyond higher education. Research of this sort in required general education courses, especially first-year composition where research work is common, creates an opportunity for students to deepen their knowledge of a major field of study. It also helps them see similarities and differences across the major fields, supporting an orientation toward interdisciplinarity as common ground for academic conversation. Through interacting with and responding to a range of information sources—including interviews, scholarly and trade publications, and primary sources—students have the opportunity to develop an advanced understanding of the work and contributions common in the fields they choose to explore, allowing them to make more informed decisions about what major path to follow and what extracurricular experiences to pursue.

Furthermore, the approach enacts high impact practices that have been shown to increase retention and persistence rates,[7] especially practices related to undergraduate research and learning communities that invite students to study together within and across disciplines. Introducing students to the expectations for research in higher education as those relate to major fields of study allows teachers to create environments in which the work is significant beyond individual class sections and beyond the confines of first-year composition courses. From course-based technology tools common to learning management systems to social media and other more public technologies, students can share summaries of the invention, arrangement, and revision practices they find common in a discipline to reflect on their own experiences with "Information Creation as a Process"[8] and practice the habits of "Creativity," "Flexibility," and "Metacognition"[9] with students in other sections who are also interested in that discipline. The community built by these students around discussing their experiences with disciplinary practice also foregrounds the concept of "Scholarship as Conversation."[10]

Major theories of engaged learning compel us to think about how to inspire students to become oriented to research-based approaches and the development of holistic practices that connect knowledge to decision-making processes.[11] The Frameworks are well-suited to addressing and supporting these practices and approaches. Consider this tenet of the ACRL Framework: "Students have a greater role and responsibility in creating new knowledge, in understanding the contours and the changing dynamics of the world of information, and in using information, data, and scholarship ethically. Teaching faculty have a greater responsibility in designing curricula and assignments that foster enhanced engagement with the core ideas about information and scholarship within their disciplines."[12]

The WPA Framework also stresses the need for authentic contexts: "Standardized writing curricula or assessment instruments that emphasize formulaic writing for inauthentic audiences will not reinforce the habits of mind and the experiences necessary for success as students encounter the writing demands of postsecondary education."[13] These goals, when engaged within a context focusing on the transferability of skills, knowledge, and attitudes across inquiry projects, help students see the importance of understanding one's role as participatory (rather than consumptive) and contributory (rather than adaptive).[14] Participation and contribution can be practically addressed through emphasizing personal connections to purpose, information sources, and audience—in the case of the disciplinary literacies assignment, using a student's chosen major, a personal interview, and an audience of peers facing similar choices and learning goals regarding their professional futures.

Positioning the Disciplinary Literacies Assignment

It is important to set the context for a DLA in ways that support student success by helping students internalize the disciplinary practices in which the assignment invites them to engage. The first-year composition courses, which we use as examples in this chapter, begin with a memoir or literacy narrative. Students enter their first-year composition classes with histories of literacy experiences, areas of expertise, and challenges; the literacy narrative helps them build awareness of their own literacy histories, along with those of others. Students also complete an activity that builds a picture of their literacy strengths and weaknesses as a group. Specifically, students interpret their literacy histories in relation to the institutional undergraduate learning goals and the goals of the first-year composition program so they (1) begin to see the ways their current literacy supports those goals, (2) identify areas where development is needed, and (3) see how they can support one another's work. The work they do here lays a foundation for exploring disciplinary literacy as a form of developing understanding about expectations and identifying pathways to them.

The foundation of the DLA allows students to share the types of literacies they bring with them and to reflect on how relationships to their work in higher education support the "Metacognition" habit of mind in the WPA Framework: "the ability to reflect on one's own thinking as well as on the individual and cultural processes used to structure knowledge"[15] and the concept of metaliteracy from the ACRL Framework: "…students are consumers and creators of information who can participate successfully in collaborative spaces."[16] It also lays the groundwork for later discussions on the integration of advanced disciplinary literacy with students' literacy histories as we move through the full DLA.

Students next move to a project that asks them to interpret cultural meaning by looking at a specific cultural production, a project we call the cultural artifact activity. We invite students to analyze artifacts they choose themselves (UPC codes, tattoos, campus organizations, holiday traditions) as emerging from processes of production that enact values and point to community practices. Framing cultural artifacts in this way positions interviews, observations, and other primary sources of information as valid inquiry practices, preparing students to understand these methodologies as important strategies that require "Curiosity," "Openness," and the development of conventional knowledge: habits of mind and practices foregrounded in the WPA Framework.[17] These practices closely mirror the ACRL frame of "Research as Inquiry," particularly reinforcing the associated dispositions of "maintaining an open mind and a critical stance" and "valu[ing] intellectual curiosity in developing questions."[18] Additionally, recognizing artifacts as emerging from processes of production forms a direct parallel with "Information Creation as a Process," one which involves examining the "underlying processes of creation"[19] regarding information sources.

It is important to give students time during this activity to see how specific literacy practices are cultural, contextual, and best understood through inquiry, as many literacy practices are transparent in our day-to-day lives. Reflection is critical if we are to expect students to engage successfully in the disciplinary literacy assignment. Thomas Bender notes in "Do Disciplines Change?" that we must remember "disciplines provide students with unparalleled intellectual tools" and that allowing students to identify some of those early in their careers in higher education can facilitate their choices and make overt the connections across [cultural and] disciplinary forms of knowledge-making.[20] Doing so in the first-year composition course allows us to introduce students to the very different expectations for disciplinary literacy common to study in higher education in the U.S. today.

The Disciplinary Literacies Assignment

The DLA asks students to engage with sources as artifacts of a discipline—scholarly publications, trade articles, and primary sources such as original interviews with practitioners and educators—in order to generate knowledge about reading, writing, and researching in a field of their choice. The assignment is designed to help students understand the terms for becoming members of the disciplines they explore by giving them exposure to sources—print, multimedia, and people—that help them know more about what it means to be literate in that discipline. Some students may end up in internships with the people they interview for this project, others may meet a professor who helps facilitate their access to the major in which they hope to gain admittance, and still others may meet peers who become study and research partners. In this way, the assignment invites students to start doing the kind of networking that gains them entrance to the fields of study in which they are interested.

We hope this element or feature of the assignment helps even first-year composition students see themselves as participating members of a discipline and active participants in the scholarly conversations common to each one.[21] The ACRL frame of "Information Has Value"[22] comes into focus through the immediate personal value this assignment has for students. The frame indicates "information possesses several dimensions of value, including as a commodity, as a means of education, as a means to influence, and as a means of negotiating and understanding the world."[23] Viewed this way, the DLA highlights the additional, personal dimension of information's value, namely the process of researching and creating new information.

The DLA combines research skills with critical thinking, reading, and writing skills. It asks students to examine the ways communication often occurs within their chosen discipline (a major field or a projected career related to a specific discipline) and explore those forms of communication as artifacts of the discipline. To do so, students must examine a variety of communication types used and produced by practitioners of the field. At minimum, these consist of a popular or trade article, scholarly article, and professional interview. The assignment requires students to form a research question to guide their exploration. The most successful questions do not ask what kinds of communication take place, but why those forms of communication have become common within their field. A sample assignment sheet appears as Appendix 6B.

Engaging the ACRL and WPA Frameworks in Practice—The Integrated Library Session

As part of the course's careful and intentional movement toward the disciplinary literacy assignment, the semester includes one closely integrated information literacy session facilitated by a librarian during the early moments of the assignment. Although only one formal session takes place in the library, the progression of activities leading up to and within the DLA provides rich opportunity for the integration of concepts from both Frameworks. This approach grants librarians freedom to design the library session to creatively focus on Framework concepts, ask more nuanced questions, and structure the library session around notions of inquiry, discovery, and knowledge creation, concepts familiar to students from their previous activities and work with DLA. Rather than functioning as isolated instruction prior to the start of the assignment, the library session provides metacognitive support through reinforcing inquiry at a critical point in the DLA. Sample questions posed by librarians and course instructors which more fully integrate the two Frameworks are included in Appendix 6D.

The library session is designed around positioning research as a means of entering a conversation[24] through interacting with texts in order to pose questions of the texts' authors regarding their writing and information creation processes. In this case, the conversation responds to texts and centers on reading, writing, and research processes within each discipline. The session functions as one of the moments in the course where students are encouraged to identify and take up the literacy practices of the fields of study they are exploring. The session begins by having students read a popular or trade article addressing a broad disciplinary issue, such as women in STEM.

Students discuss the article to generate questions and keywords which they then use to locate disciplinary artifacts representing how that particular conversation takes place. Using an inquiry strategy to create keywords in response to the discussion of a text speaks to the disposition of "exhibiting mental flexibility and creativity"[25] through presenting an alternative to simply brainstorming synonyms for a predetermined topic. After generating keywords in a full-class discussion, students work together in small groups, drawing on one another's existing search and analysis skills to find examples of sources in their disciplines that represent various facets of conversation.

The librarian then engages students in a discussion relying on questions based on the RAIDS heuristic[26] and aiming toward uncovering the "Writing Processes," or the "multiple strategies writers use to approach and undertake writing and research" behind the sources.[27] Questions may involve rhetorical issues of "audiences, purpose, and contexts,"[28] such as who is talking to whom in the articles; what the language, style, and appearance indicate about the source's audience; and where the source was located and published. Often, questions that "situate (the writer's) ideas within different... contexts"[29] arise, such as, What do you think was the author's purpose in creating this information? or What did the author have to know in order to write this piece? Similar questions appear in Appendix 6D. Throughout the discussion, the librarian highlights and names particular facets students observe which identify and analyze the nature of the texts and the "ways that the text(s) appeal or speak to different audiences"[30] such as author, credentials, type of publication, format, and bibliography.

Through the RAIDS questions, the discussion brings the Frameworks into focus by placing specific processes of writing[31] within the broader concept of "Information Creation as a Process."[32] Asking students to think about choices the authors made regarding their writing processes, audience, eventual place of publication, and format highlights interconnections between the creation of the information and its current state. Analyzing different source formats and genres also addresses "Knowledge of Conventions[33] and "Searching as Strategic Exploration"[34] as students identify places to search (scholarly journals, professional associations, popular websites) where parts of their disciplinary conversation take place.

The students next generate questions about how the issue (for example, women in STEM) is represented in disciplinary texts: How do professional organizations address the issue, if at all? Are scholarly sources about the issue easy to access? Are there conversations about the issue prominent in popular media sources? What are the similarities and differences in how these varied sources represent the issue? By asking these questions, students discover every academic discipline addresses a variety of issues—some shared with other disciplines, some not—rather than being constituted by a finite list of absolute facts or represented in limited sources. This process is intended to foster "Openness—the willingness to consider new ways of being and thinking in the world"[35] through concentrating on helping students see disciplinary texts are not sources of objective information, but clues about the ways disciplinary practices engage invention, arrangement, and topics for revision in order to generate dialogue. Approaching sources in this manner also foregrounds the ACRL concept of "Authority is Constructed and Contextual"[36] by framing questions about a source's authority in the context of its creation process rather than using a checklist to identify whether or not a source is authoritative. Approaching a source contextually resonates with the approaches to reading and writing at the heart of the DLA and maintains students' position as readers, writers, and researchers who create new knowledge, rather than just locate someone else's knowledge.

The ACRL's "Authority is Constructed and Contextual" frame[37] is of value here, in another way, particularly when paired with the WPA concept of "Rhetorical Knowledge" that asks students to "analyz[e] a variety of types of texts."[38] Students report they have previously been told what types of sources they may and may not use, as well as that some types of information are illegitimate or forbidden, such as Wikipedia or commercial websites. The pedagogy of the library session encourages students to view every source as potentially useful, and it emphasizes the need for analysis and evaluation to determine a source's best use in the context of the researcher's needs. For example, opinion pieces may not be acceptable as factual sources in an academic work, and large, open-source encyclopedias may have inconclusive provenance, and, on some topics, may not carry the traditional authority required for academic use. However, viewed as artifacts of a discipline, they embody discussions and ideas and may have value if treated as such. This approach emphasizes the contextual nature of authority, giving permission for students to examine sources in relation to their own purposes as researchers rather than relying on a predetermined set of criteria for their acceptability.

Students typically leave the library session with practical skills and tools: a student-created list of considerations to use when identifying and analyzing texts, hands-on experience with source discovery through different search methods, and one or two texts related to their discipline. These skills and concepts are reinforced and refined in classes after the library session as students continue to locate scholarly journals in their fields and are encouraged to review the table of contents in a few issues of each journal to understand the range and scope of issues discussed within a single discipline-based publication.

After locating an article on a popular topic in their field, the task turns to understanding the ideas in the chosen article. Because most scholarly research is aimed at an audience with more disciplinary knowledge than first-year college students, the vocabulary alone can be daunting, and the baseline expectation of knowledge about the ideas within a discipline are usually not yet in place. Trying to master the information contained in a scholarly article, then, is not likely to take place within a single class session. Instead, students continue their inquiry-based method, asking questions to interact with the article rather than summarizing content as a received set of facts. They interrogate the text, make observations, and draw preliminary conclusions, activities which result in questions about disciplinary practices thus strengthening students' interaction with and connection to the disciplines they are examining. Questions about a specific text create an operational network within which students may interact with other types of sources they uncover. It also transforms the source into a rich set of observations about literacy and disciplinarity. This approach establishes a context which emphasizes "Flexibility" by enabling students to "approach writing assignments in multiple ways"[39] and encourages students to form meaning across varied situations.

Reflective Letter

Much like the impact of a single library session, the goals, achievements, and limitations of a major project are not often evident until after the work has been completed. Writing a reflective letter at the conclusion of the DLA allows students to assess their own work in relation to the goals they set for themselves and the goals of the assignment, allowing for consideration of the value of information. More importantly, this metacognitive exercise allows them to form connections between themselves, their subject, and their writing about their subject, placing their work in a context larger than the project itself and helping them understand their position as both knowledge-seeker and creator. This reflection encourages students to see themselves as participants in a scholarly conversation.

While guidelines for the reflection may be given, one of the goals of this assignment is self-awareness, so flexibility is important here to allow students to identify and explore the connections they found most meaningful. It may be helpful to ask students to reflect on each component of the assignment to be sure they do not omit discussion of some key element, but how they choose to reflect upon them is best be left to the student. A sample prompt for the reflective letter appears in Appendix 6C.

Intersections of the DLA, RAIDS, and the Frameworks

Because our use of RAIDS creates opportunities to interpret the invention, arrangement, revision, style and delivery strategies at work in texts in ways that help students build knowledge from those practices, it supports metacognitive goals across both Frameworks. To put this support in perspective, we offer relationships between the ACRL frames with the WPA habits of mind and experiences and related RAIDS elements in Appendix 6E.

When students are given reading and writing assignments with the expectation the work itself will result in raised consciousness of the ways knowledge is built and disseminated in a major field of study, metacognitive activity is suppressed. Deep knowledge of a discipline requires an understanding, not only of what is known (the content of the disciplinary literacy artifacts), but also the ways knowledge is built and communicated by members of that discipline (the methods and distribution patterns of the field). The ACRL frames of "Scholarship as Conversation"[40] and "Information Creation as a Process"[41] provide additional frames for exploring disciplinary artifacts as sources of multiple types of knowledge. For example, the goal of reading for rhetorical aspects of texts expands the invention, arrangement, and revision strategies writers have available to them. This expansion of generative strategies responds to the expectations for participation in disciplinary literacy, contributing to the conversations and research as an expansion of knowledge, rather than a report on it.

Inviting students to explore their major or academic discipline as literacy practices moves "Research as Inquiry"[42] out of the realm of the abstract, positioning research products as parts of scholarly conversation. The turn toward advanced practices in which the researcher's purpose is to participate in and contribute to an academic conversation lets students experience moving beyond simply synthesizing other people's knowledge. As students build their own knowledge of the literacy practices of the fields they explore, they often realize the information not only changes their understanding of the field, but also is important to share with peers.

Extended analysis of the literacy practices of the discipline through interaction with relevant primary and secondary sources also often inspires students to create brochures, presentations, TED-style talks, or other forms of production that make the information publicly accessible to others in a form commonly used in the discipline. They tend to be motivated to do this public knowledge sharing as an extension of their more traditional research papers. For example, one student who realized information is often disseminated through brochures in the field of criminal justice created a brochure about the major forms of literacy students could expect to define their lives as professionals. Another student, who was researching film distribution and realized stories drive that profession, wrote a paper following a day-in-the-life of two partners in the film distribution business, integrating all of the reading, writing, and researching they did to negotiate rights to distribute a film and contract with distribution sources. ACRL's description of "Research as Inquiry" indicates "[t]his process of inquiry extends beyond the academic world to the community at large, and the process of inquiry may focus upon personal, professional, or societal needs."[43] Participation in a larger community adds a personal and immediate dimension of value,[44] not just as contributors to a conversation, but also for students' own benefit. Novice learners acquire strategic perspectives on inquiry and a greater repertoire of investigative methods when they consider the value of their sources for multiple audiences and a variety of purposes.

A vital but not explicitly stated component of both "Scholarship as Conversation"[45] and "Authority Is Constructed and Contextual"[46] is conversation and authority construction occur within communities made up of actual people. It is impossible to explore either concept without making the explicit connection that humans—not faceless entities—are behind the creation and dissemination of information. The ACRL Authority frame refers to creators who hold "expertise and ability" and have voices and biases;[47] the Scholarship frame refers to "scholars, researchers, or professionals" with "varied perspectives and interpretations".[48] The DLA is, instead, explicit in its attempt to humanize information sources by connecting a disembodied text to the person or people responsible for its creation.

In addition, the attention to multiple types of information delivery in the DLA resonates strongly with students who, in the new normal of ubiquitous information-gathering instruments (smartphones, tablets, or anything with an Internet connection), use them to conduct research every day. They look up basketball scores, check the weather, find movie times, or see where their group is meeting that evening, for example. In our classes, students often recognize these information-gathering behaviors, but rarely describe them as research. The ACRL "Research as Inquiry" frame and the WPA "Curiosity" habit of mind provide a way to view these practices as interrelated through asking learners to "consider research as open-ended exploration and engagement with information"[49] and to "seek relevant authoritative information and recognize the meaning and value of that information."[50] People consult information sources to do research every day, turning that information into answers to their questions. Helping students recognize these behaviors as research is a key pedagogical move as we ask students to position themselves as researchers.

In looking up the weather, for example, the underlying question might be the following: "What should I wear today?" To find the answer, we look at the weather report, even though it does not give fashion advice. Thus, in order to answer a question, we look for information which is interpreted to form an answer, rather than looking for a pre-existing answer. This process, referred to by Head and Eisenberg as "everyday life information–seeking behavior,"[51] is completely familiar because we do it every day in a variety of contexts; this application of everyday life research is one way research in writing courses can be made more familiar. Students have been using this model all their lives; the assignment simply refocuses this information-seeking as research-based inquiry.

The disciplinary literacy research assignment allows the use of sources familiar to students, but it expands their familiarity with additional types of sources, combining the ACRL frame of "Searching as Strategic Exploration"[52] and the WPA "Creativity" habit of mind to "use methods that are new to them to investigate questions, topics, and ideas."[53] Students participate in the "evaluation of a range of information sources"[54] by exploring scholarly sources and trade publications, primary sources (such as interviews with professionals working in the field), and government sources about the quality of life issues of given professions. The assignment specifically includes scholarly research in order to help students understand knowledge production within the traditional academic context of the disciplines they choose to explore. Students are also encouraged to explore various ways knowledge is built in contexts not considered scholarly, so trade publications geared toward practitioners, popular depictions of people in the field (such as TV shows about scientists, newscasters, doctors, nurses, teachers, etc.), and interviews with people who teach and work in the field are included as appropriate sources of information. Students are not expected to come away from the DLA knowing everything they need to know without further education in their majors. What they do come away with is greater understanding of what types of reading, writing, and researching are common to in the field, how that knowledge is built and disseminated, and a bit about what the literacy lives of people who practice in those fields can be like.

Conclusion

We offer one example of the DLA in Appendix 6B. However, we recognize the DLA will, inevitably, require customization to effectively engage the Frameworks in different institutional contexts—for example, in programs where there is a two-semester first-year composition sequence and students spend the full second semester on a single research project. Despite the need for some degree of localization, connecting the DLA with the ACRL and WPA Frameworks has helped us to rethink the relationship between reading and writing in the first-year composition course, especially for students making the transition to higher education in which they will be expected to practice and internalize participatory notions of literacy. The assumptions about reading as a researcher that students bring with them to our classrooms, for example, that reading as a researcher is about finding a quote or fulfilling a requirement, may restrict or frustrate teaching and learning that invites participation and contribution, no matter how clear our individual learning goals may be. The assumptions students bring with them about writing as researchers may present similar restrictions and frustrations. Integrating outside sources as artifacts into the assignment provides a rich environment for addressing both Frameworks in ways that support the more general shift away from reading and writing as consumer activities and toward literacy as a process of engaged response and participation.

Appendix 6A: RAIDS Base

RAIDS: Revision, Arrangement, Invention, Delivery, Style

- What is invention? (In what activities did the writer have to engage to create the text?)

- What is being invented? (What ideas, practices, arguments, or worldviews are created by the text?)

- What is arrangement? (What is being put in relationship with what? What organizational pattern is being used (e.g. inductive, deductive, problem/solution, etc.?)

- What is being arranged? (How are topics, subjects, etc. being put in relation to one another?)

- What is being revised? (What ideas, practices, worldviews, etc. is the writer trying to change?)

- What is revision? (What specific strategies are engaged to help the writer achieve the revisions?)

- What styles of language have been used to meet expectations in this situation? What styles may be surprising to the reader? Might unexpected style choices be integrated successfully into the piece? Which ones? How can/does the writer help readers understand the purpose of these unexpected style choices?

- What media have been used in the communication situation? What are the benefits and obstacles of those media choices? How do delivery options affect the types of invention, arrangement, and style choices that have been/will be made?

Appendix 6B: Disciplinary Literacy Base Assignment

Writing Context: Many students come to higher education with a limited understanding of what it means to become a participating member of an academic discipline. Your purpose, in this essay, is to give students who are new to the academic discipline/field you have chosen an introduction to the expectations for writing, reading, and researching in that discipline. Ultimately, your paper should help your audience understand the ways literacies are used to create and communicate knowledge in the discipline/field you choose to explore.

Background: Earlier assignments for this course gave you opportunities to identify themes and terms for analysis so you could begin to understand and practice meeting the expectations for writing in higher education. This paper allows you to continue engaging effective invention, arrangement, revision, style, and delivery practices, especially those you can learn from reading and researching in a discipline in which you are interested. It also introduces you to the ways research and participating in important academic discussions prepare you to use literacy in successful ways in writing situations in higher educations and beyond. The guiding question for this assignment is the following: What writing, reading, and researching activities are employed in the discipline being explored? You will create your own research questions early in our class discussions of this project, and you will need to remain open to ways of gathering information beyond the goal of merely reporting what you find, ways that require interpretation and synthesis.

Requirements: Different academic disciplines have different ways of **presenting and analyzing information, different ways of building knowledge, and different ways of presenting knowledge in written forms**. This assignment gives you the opportunity to begin building your own understanding of how writing, reading, and researching operate within a discipline of interest to you. You may choose any discipline you wish to examine for this project. Whichever discipline you choose, you must engage in at least the following invention activities:

- Analyze at least one scholarly article from your discipline.

- Analyze at least one article from a trade publication related to your discipline.

- Conduct an interview with a person who teaches major courses and/or does research in your discipline.

- Conduct an interview with a person who practices in a field related to your discipline.

- Enroll on the career services website (a consultant from career services can attend class to demonstrate this system).

- Analyze an introductory piece about quality of life issues related to the literacy work done in your discipline or career field.

Your research will include additional reading and interviewing as determined by your individual projects. Papers must be at least 7–9 pages long, in 12-point font, with one-inch margins (*or the equivalent*). Your visual should communicate a specific, important piece of information; graphs and charts are commonly used for this purpose.

Appendix 6C: Prompt for Reflective Letter

Disciplinary Literacy Research Assignment

You will write your reflective letter in class. Please familiarize yourself with the prompt before class so you can write an effective response in the allotted time. Alternatively, your instructor may ask you to write the letter outside of class and submit it with your paper. In either case, be sure to respond to all the questions below and be sure to write in the form of a letter to your instructor or another audience who will prompt you to deep reflection and benefit from your response.

Note: You need not respond to the questions in the order they are asked if a different arrangement will better facilitate your process and/or lead to an engaging product.

- What were the major differences between this research project and research you have done in the past?

- What kinds of research did you do that reflects the kind of research done in the field you chose to study?

- What was the most challenging part of this project for you and how will facing that challenge affect how you do research in the future?

- What was the most enjoyable part of the project? How will that part affect how you do research in the field?

- If you could start over and do one thing differently, what would that be and why?

- What advice do you have for teachers and students starting this project in the future? (You might want to make these two separate points of reflection: advice for students and advice for teachers if that will work better for your particular reflection.)

Appendix 6D: Questions for the DLA and Integrated Information Literacy Instruction Using the RAIDS Heuristic

This chart illustrates how information literacy-specific questions can be embedded within larger questions about writing processes during the DLA.

	Sample Questions for the DLA	Sample Questions for Information Literacy-Specific Application
Revision	How does your reading of the text change your ideas about the discipline and its ways of creating and presenting knowledge? How will this affect your own writing process?	What markers of authority does the text use? What is the purpose of this text?
Arrangement	What relationships seem important? For example, are certain types of evidence used to support conclusions? Are there subjects that always come up together? What patterns of arrangement are present most often (e.g. inductive, deductive, problem/solution)? How will this affect your decisions about organizing your own text?	What does the structure of the text (i.e., sections, headings, abstract, visuals) tell you about what to expect from reading this source?
Invention	What disciplinary knowledge did the writer use to create this text? What activities did the writer need to engage in? How does this affect your ideas about the activities you will engage in to produce your text? What activities will you do that you would not have done before reading the text?	Who is the author? How are other voices represented in this text? What sources did the author use? Are they cited?

Delivery	How do members of this discipline access knowledge about the discipline and its issues? What audiences are they addressing in these different forums? How does the treatment of a topic differ according to the audience of the publication? What methods of delivery are acceptable in your current writing context?	What type of publication is this (i.e. scholarly, popular) Why? Is this text proprietary or free? How can readers locate and access it?
Style	What does the style indicate about disciplinary expectations or conventions for language and citation practices? How does that affect the citation practices and editing processes you will engage as a writer?	Who is the intended audience for this text? How is the style used to create a sense of trust or credibility for that audience

Appendix 6E: Relationship between ACRL and WPA Frames in the Context of the DLA

The WPA and ACRL goals can be engaged to support one another in a variety of ways. Here we show how they support one another in relation to the disciplinary literacy assignment and its engagement of RAIDS. The relationships between and among these concepts is fluid, and one could easily see other connections than the major connections presented here.

ACRL Frames	Authority is Constructed and Contextual	Scholarship as Conversation	Searching as Strategic Exploration	Research as Inquiry	Information Creation as a Process	Information Has Value
Related WPA Habits of Mind	Flexibility Metacognition	Metacognition	Persistence Responsibility Flexibility	Curiosity Openness Engagement Creativity	Creativity Flexibility Metacognition	Responsibility Metacognition
Related WPA Experiences	Rhetorical Knowledge Knowledge of Conventions	Rhetorical Knowledge Knowledge of Conventions Ability to Compose in Multiple Environments	Writing Processes	Critical Thinking Writing Processes	Writing Processes	Critical Thinking Knowledge of Conventions
RAIDS Concepts	Delivery Style	Invention Arrangement Delivery	Invention Revision	Revision Arrangement Invention	Revision Arrangement Invention Delivery Style	Delivery Style

Notes

1. Limberg, *Three Theoretical Perspectives on Information Literacy*, 120.
2. Miller, DeJoy, and Oberdick, "RAIDS for Research"; DeJoy, *Process This*.
3. DeJoy, *Process This*.
4. Ibid.
5. Ballenger, *The Curious Researcher*; Fink, *Creating Significant Learning Experiences*; Bain, *What the Best College Students Do*; Boyer Commission, *Reinventing Undergraduate Education*.
6. College Parents of America, *When Your College Student Changes Majors*.
7. Brownell and Swaner, *Five High Impact Practices*.
8. ACRL, Framework, 14.
9. WPA, Framework, 4–5.
10. ACRL, Framework, 20.
11. Bain, *What the Best College Students Do*; Bergen-Cico and Bylander, "Reuniting the Often Neglected Aims of a Liberal Education"; Harward, *Transforming Undergraduate Education*; Stimpson, "The Ideals of the Liberal Artisan"; Swaner, "The Theories, Contexts, and Multiple Pedagogies of Engaged Learning."
12. ACRL, Framework, 7.
13. WPA, Framework, 3.
14. DeJoy, *Process This*.
15. WPA, Framework, 5.
16. ACRL, Framework, 8.
17. WPA, Framework, 4–5, 9.
18. ACRL, Framework, 19.
19. Ibid., 14
20. Bender, "Do Disciplines Change?" 276.
21. ACRL, Framework, 20.
22. Ibid., 16.
23. Ibid.
24. ACRL, Framework, "Scholarship as Conversation," 20.
25. ACRL, Framework, "Searching as Strategic Exploration," 22.
26. Please see Appendix 6A.
27. WPA, Framework, 8.
28. Ibid., 6.
29. Ibid., 8.
30. WPA, Framework, "Rhetorical Knowledge," 6.
31. WPA, Framework, "Writing Processes," 8.
32. ACRL, Framework, 16.
33. WPA, Framework, 9.
34. ACRL, Framework, 22.
35. WPA, Framework, 4.
36. ACRL, Framework, 12.
37. Ibid.
38. WPA, Framework, 9.
39. Ibid., 5.
40. ACRL, Framework, 20.

41. Ibid., 14.
42. Ibid., 18.
43. Ibid., 18.
44. ACRL, Framework, "Information Has Value," 16.
45. ACRL, Framework, 20.
46. Ibid., 12.
47. Ibid.
48. ACRL, Framework, 20.
49. Ibid., 19.
50. WPA, Framework, 4.
51. Head and Eisenberg, "How College Students Use the Web to Conduct Everyday Life Research," Methods section.
52. ACRL, Framework, 22.
53. WPA, Framework, 5.
54. ACRL, Framework, 22.

Bibliography

Association of College and Research Libraries. 2016. *Framework for Information Literacy for Higher Education*. Accessed February 2, 2015. http://www.ala.org/acrl/standards/ilframework.

Bain, Kenneth R. *What the Best College Students Do*. Cambridge, MA: Harvard University Press, 2012.

Ballenger, Bruce P. *The Curious Researcher: A Guide to Writing Research Papers*. Eighth edition. Boston: Pearson, 2015.

Bender, Thomas. "Do Disciplines Change? Would Flipping the Curriculum Right-Side Up Lead to Change?" In *Transforming Undergraduate Education: Theory That Compels and Practices That Succeed*, edited by Harward, Donald W, 267–80. Lanham, MD: Rowman & Littlefield, 2012.

Bergen-Cico, Dessa, and Joyce Bylander. "Reuniting the Often Neglected Aims of a Liberal Education: Student Well-Being and Psycho-Social Development." In *Transforming Undergraduate Education: Theory That Compels and Practices That Succeed*, 91–108. Lanham, MD: Rowman & Littlefield, 2012.

Boyer Commission on Educating Undergraduates in the Research University. "Reinventing Undergraduate Education: A Blueprint for America's Research Universities." Stoney Brook, NY, 1998.

Brownell, Jayne E, and Lynne E Swaner. *Five High Impact Practices: Research on Learning Outcomes, Completion, and Quality*. Washington D.C.: Association of American Colleges & Universities, 2010.

Council of Writing Program Administrators, National Council of Teachers of English, and National Writing Project. 2011. *Framework for Success in Postsecondary Writing*. Accessed May 26, 2015. http://www.wpacouncil.org/files/framework-for-success-postsecondary-writing.pdf.

Dejoy, Nancy C. *Process This: Undergraduate Writing in Composition Studies*. Logan, Utah: Utah State University Press, 2004.

Fink, L. Dee. *Creating Significant Learning Experiences: An Integrated Approach to Designing College Courses* (2nd Edition). Somerset, NJ, USA: John Wiley & Sons, 2013. http://site.ebrary.com/lib/alltitles/docDetail.action?docID=10748649.

Harward, Donald W., ed. *Transforming Undergraduate Education: Theory That Compels and Practices That Succeed.* Lanham, Md: Rowman & Littlefield, 2012.

Head, Alison J., and Michael B. Eisenberg. "How College Students Use the Web to Conduct Everyday Life Research." *First Monday* 16, no. 4 (April 2, 2011). http://firstmonday.org/ojs/index.php/fm/article/view/3484.

Limberg, Louise, Olof Sundin, and Sanna Talja. "Three Theoretical Perspectives on Information Literacy." *Human IT* 11, no. 2 (2012): 93–130.

Miller, Sara D, Nancy C DeJoy, and Benjamin M Oberdick. "RAIDS for Research." In *Successful Strategies for Teaching Undergraduate Student Research*, edited by Beth Bloom and Deyrup, Marta. Rowman & Littlefield, 2013.

Stimpson, Catherine. "The Ideals of the Liberal Artisan: Notes Toward an Evolving Group Biography." In *Transforming Undergraduate Education: Theory That Compels and Practices That Succeed*, 51–72. Lanham, MD: Rowman & Littlefield, 2012.

Swaner, Lynne E. "The Theories, Contexts, and Multiple Pedagogies of Engaged Learning: What Succeeds and Why." In *Transforming Undergraduate Education: Theories that Compel and Practices that Succeed*, 73–90. Lanham, MD: Rowman & Littlefield, 2012.

"When Your College Student Changes Majors | College Parents of America." Accessed August 27, 2015. http://www.collegeparents.org/members/resources/articles/when-your-college-student-changes-majors.

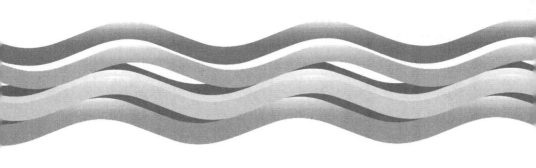

CHAPTER 7*

Researching and Writing as Braided Processes:

A Co-Curricular Model

Stacy Kastner and Hillary Richardson
Mississippi State University

Introduction to Our Partnership

In 2004, Rolf Norgaard called for a hybrid approach to information literacy education, arguing that "writing theory and pedagogy can and should have a constitutive influence on our conception of information literacy." For Norgaard, such a pedagogy requires "a partnership" characterized by "genuine intellectual engagement."[1] On college and university campuses, it is not uncommon for libraries, composition programs, and writing centers to establish partnerships in pursuit of this goal: facilitating the acquisition of research and writing as processes not meant to unbraid, but rather to be complex, demanding, and interdependent activities.[2] For example, libraries and composition programs have worked together to teach the processes of research and writing alongside one another,[3] learned the practices of each other in order to translate those into teaching moments,[4] and even co-designed entire courses.[5]

* This work is licensed under a Creative Commons Attribution-NonCommercial-NoDerivatives 4.0 License, CC BY-NC-ND (https://creativecommons.org/licenses/by-nc-nd/4.0/).

Likewise, libraries and writing centers have created sustainable partnerships in spite of institutional and organizational obstacles,[6] and they have designed co-curricular workshops targeted for specific composition courses.[7] There is a commonsense partnership between not only the practitioners who teach these processes, but also the ideas and practices of research (or information literacy) and writing, as is clearly demonstrated, we argue, by the similarities between the *Framework for Information Literacy in Higher Education*, adopted in 2015 by the Association of College and Research Libraries (ACRL),[8] and the *Framework for Success in Postsecondary Writing*, authored by the Council of Writing Program Administrators (WPA), the National Council of Teachers of English (NCTE), and the National Writing Project (NWP) in 2011 (future references of these works will be ACRL Framework and WPA Framework, respectively).[9]

As Colleen Boff and Barbara Toth explain, research and writing, and thus libraries and writing centers, demand synergetic relationships: "[I]n an academic environment, research means writing and writing means research. This understanding necessitates cooperation."[10] The difference, however, between a library collaborating with a writing center, as opposed to a writing program, is the cooperative, as Boff and Toth describe it, is therefore not driven by a grade, an official class, or even classroom space—not even a *teacher*. Instead, *librarian* and *writing tutor* collaborations happen inside libraries, writing centers, and labs, and as supplemental instruction, as extra credit, and as time spent working closely with an expert on one's own project. Whereas one typically learns alongside everyone else in the classroom and toward a due date, in the library and the writing center—ideally, of course—one learns at one's own pace and pursues one's own particular interests. It is both the counter-classroom pedagogy made possible by our support roles as librarian and writing tutor and the reality of inequality built into and maintained by educational institutions that drove us to work together on a project-based curriculum that would engage at-risk students with advanced tools, skills, and processes, through theoretical reflection concerning the nature of academic literacy as defined by the ACRL and WPA Frameworks.

Despite the fact that librarians, compositionists, and writing center specialists all seemingly agree a hybrid approach to information literacy and writing benefits students whose academic careers demand they enact this conceptualization, on many campuses, ours included, some students may take one or two writing classes before they are required or even allowed to write in conversation with researched sources, and students may receive no sustained formal instruction in how to do research or writing within their chosen disciplines. If success at the postsecondary level is characterized by the fusion of research and writing—i.e., the consumption, evaluation, synthesis, and production of information and texts as interactive processes—as library and writing center faculty, we wonder why developmental students are often discouraged, barred even, from participating in this exchange. As the editors of *Teaching Advanced Skills to At-Risk Students: Views from Research and Practice* explain:

> By reconceiving what is taught to at-risk students, and how it is taught, schools stand a better chance of engaging students from poverty and minority backgrounds in an education that will be of use to those students in their lives. It is time that we recognize the fact that the sources of disadvantage and school failure lie as much with what schools do as with what children bring to the schoolhouse door. The challenge for the future is to reappraise what disadvantaged students need and how to serve them through compensatory and other programs.[11]

Though the editors' focus in this excerpt is on pre-college students, we feel their message is equally applicable to postsecondary institutions, particularly in the context of what are framed as remedial or bridge programs for students with GPAs and test scores that suggest the students are educationally disadvantaged.

This chapter discusses our efforts at Mississippi State University to work with a group of students labeled at-risk on a project designed to engage them in the processes of reading, writing, and researching simultaneously. Often, students conceive of research and writing as related but independent processes and discrete skills, and this perception is, to some degree, maintained and confirmed by the introduction at-risk students have to these processes in separate remedial reading and writing classes, and then in separate first-year composition courses, that often do not incorporate research assignments until the last course in the sequence. Because we designed this project outside of a curriculum with established objectives and learning outcomes, we turned to our respective professional organizations' Frameworks for academic success. Throughout this chapter, references to "threshold concepts" refer to the tenets of the ACRL Framework ("Authority as constructed and contextual," "Information creation as a process," "Research as inquiry," "Scholarship as a conversation," and "Searching as strategic exploration"),[12] and references to "habits of mind" refer to the practices laid out in the WPA Framework ("Curiosity," "Openness," "Engagement," "Creativity," "Persistence," "Responsibility," "Flexibility," and "Metacognition").[13]

For readers interested in piloting a reading-research-writing hybrid experience for students on their campuses, we describe first, in this chapter, our project and its implementation, embedded as a co-curricular lab activity within a nine-week college preparation program for students identified by standardized test scores as at-risk. We next evaluate our experimental pilot, laying out the underlying questions we hoped to answer by introducing research, writing, and their shared foundations to this particular group of students, analyzing the data we collected to address such questions, and sharing what we learned based on student responses to surveys as well as our assessments of the work they produced for the collaborative project. Finally, we reflect on our attempt to design and implement a low-stakes, project-based learning experience.

Our Project

Agreeing with Norgaard that "in ways that are often deeply reciprocal, writing and information literacy can productively shape the conception of each other," we began our search for the kind of reciprocal conceptualization that might result from a library and writing center collaboration by first looking at the WPA habits of mind and the ACRL threshold concepts and then seeking opportunities to work with students on our campus over the summer term.[14]

The language of the two Frameworks strives to cultivate research and writing as habits, practices, and states of mind rather than easily standardized measures or prescriptive mandates. Furthermore, the overlap in meaning and vocabulary is plenty, with language both familiar and heady. In the threshold concepts, for instance, the explanation for the concept of "Scholarship as a conversation" reads, "Communities of scholars, researchers, or professionals engage in sustained discourse with new insights and discoveries occurring over time as a result of varied perspectives and interpretations,"[15] while "Rhetorical knowledge" within the WPA Framework is described as "the ability to analyze and act on understandings of audiences, purposes, and contexts in creating and comprehending texts."[16] The dense idea of immersing oneself in a discipline, learning the language, trends, and constructs of that conversation, and contributing to them as a way to enter that conversation appears in both Frameworks.

Additionally, the ACRL explains the "Information has value" concept by positing, "As creators and users of information, experts understand their rights and responsibilities when participating in a community of scholarship,"[17] and consequently ought to respect the rights of others, while the "Responsibility" habit of mind requires students to "act on the understanding that learning is shared among the writer and others … [and] engage and incorporate the ideas of others, giving credit to those ideas by using appropriate attribution."[18] In this instance, both collecting information and incorporating it into one's own work require similar practices and mindsets. As both Frameworks constantly refer to students as those who engage, create, and act, we wanted to give our students an opportunity to be active in the research-writing process.

We gained access to students by networking with the program leader of the Summer Development Program (SDP) at Mississippi State University (MSU). SDP is an Institution of Higher Learning (IHL) program with a consistent statewide curriculum requiring students whose ACT scores are low to attend and pass reading, writing, and math classes as well as an academic skills lab before gaining entry to postsecondary institutions in the fall. SDP students worked from 9:00 a.m. to 3:00 p.m., four days a week, for nine weeks during the summer. We met with the program leader and proposed working with students in the program during lab time—a time traditionally reserved for working on homework and hearing from guest speakers across various offices on campus, offering advice about how to navigate university life. We explained that as research librarian (Hillary) and writing center associate director and tutor (Stacy), we were interested in working with students and requiring them to engage in complicated processes and sub-processes of reading, research, and writing in a team-based, multimodal project. The project would require students to work together to create a hyperlinked, close historical reading of a text. As our university adopts a common read, the Maroon Edition, the program leader suggested this would be an ideal text for such a project and a way to provide all students in the program with the text free of charge. Similarly, because the 2015 text, *Same Kind of Different as Me*, alternated back and forth between two main narrators/authors, the text would serve us well in creating a team-based project, with each team taking responsibility for one narrator's chapters.

The SDP program director agreed to allow us three hours per week of skills lab time to work with students on this project. We split students into two teams and asked that each team build a map using Google Maps to represent different moments from each narrator's life. Each student was required to create multiple map entries in which they used an outside source to inform his or her reading of a specific person, place, or cultural artifact of interest from the common memoir. In addition to using and accurately citing the outside source, each entry required a quote and citation from the novel itself, hyperlinks within the text where appropriate, and at least one image or video clip embedded within the map entry. (See Appendix 7A for excerpts from the project description and details we discussed with students). Students worked over the course of nine weeks to build these map entries, and at the end of the program they presented their work to the university community.

We met with the students three times a week in sixty-minute blocks. Class sessions took place in either the writing center or in one of the library's computer labs, depending on the day's agenda for our meetings. We began the summer introducing students to the mapping tool (Google Maps), inviting them to navigate through personalized maps that charted our courses from childhood to our current locations on MSU's campus, then we asked students to join us by creating their own maps. Such work was an important starting point, not only because it helped students to become familiar with the technological tools we would be asking them to use, but also because it helped to establish community.

We selected Google Maps for the project for a variety of reasons. Pragmatically, it provided the immediate possibility of consumption—the possibility of an interactive readership that could extend beyond the walls of the classroom or summer semester—it facilitated the collaborative demands of the project, and it introduced students to a free digital tool with which they likely had little to no exposure.

Though we wanted to ensure students received the kinds of explicit instruction libraries and writing centers often provide within the context of course-embedded collaborations, like how to locate, use, and cite sources, our pedagogical aim was not just to keep things low-stakes and fun, but also to establish a community of scholars. As examples of the kind of low-stakes pedagogy we employed in the summer experience, learning to locate physical resources in the library took the form of a scavenger hunt, and similarly, instead of asking students to work through the novel on their own time, we gathered in the Writing Center, where students claimed couches and armchairs to read the novel aloud together. As we read, we stopped regularly to discuss what we knew about challenging vocabulary, notable people, places, events, and cultural artifacts, consulting our various mobile devices when we came across something that existed outside of our collective realm of knowledge. We used such opportunities to talk about the developing narrative of the novel and how context clues were hints to help readers gain a deeper understanding of academic texts.

For example, the first chapter of *Same Kind of Different as Me* opens with Denver's (a black man's) narrative of being dragged within an inch of his life after a group of white boys discover him helping a white woman change her tire in a Louisiana troubled by segregation and a dangerous climate of racial hatred. As Denver explains to readers, "That's just how Louisiana was in those days. Mississippi, too, I reckon, since a coupla years later, folks started tellin the story about a young colored fella names Emmitt Till who got beat till you couldn't tell who he was no more."[19] Members of the class paused in our reading to share what we knew about Till and then to investigate further, using our smart devices to identify official dates, and locations. Our conversation helped us locate Denver's narrative within a historical moment in the South and to establish specific dates and locations to guide our reading of the text—elements that eventually found their way into the students' maps.

Though students spent under thirty hours working with us and were neither required nor expected to spend any time on the project outside of our scheduled meetings, we were able to cover a lot of ground. We used individual and small group writing-to-learn strategies to talk about the threshold concepts and habits of mind and their applicability to the future college and university lives students were beginning, so as they worked through the mapping project, we were able to consistently refer to the threshold concepts and habits of mind. For example, we engaged a student frustrated by dead-end research in a conversation about the value of persistence and research as strategic exploration.

By the end of the summer, students received explicit instruction in pragmatic skills, like how to locate physical library resources, locate articles using the library's databases, cite sources using Purdue Online Writing Lab and MLA manuals, and avoid freestanding quotations. Students also received guidance in effectively working together in peer-review sessions as well as one-on-one consultations from both research librarians and writing center tutors as they built their map entries. At our last meeting, students talked about what they read, what they chose to research and why, and they presented their map entries to the chair of the English Department, SDP summer faculty, library faculty, and some of the members from the Maroon Edition Committee. Though not all of the entries were complete and many needed revision, the goal of the project was not to produce polished work, but instead, as we described to students in project materials we shared with them, to engage them in exercising and flexing their academic muscles for success. Our objective was to provide these students with a project-based experience that would expose them not only to skills and tools normally reserved for non-remedial and advanced students, but also to engage them in a hybrid conceptualization of reading, research, and writing.

Our Research Inquiries

Eight out of eleven SDP students volunteered to participate in our research. Their participation gave us permission to collect surveys at the beginning of the project and at the midpoint of the summer semester, along with the map entries they created. Demographically, SDP students did not mirror the profile of the average MSU student. In 2014, MSU had an enrollment of over twenty thousand full-time students, with close to 72 percent of MSU students being residents of the state of Mississippi.[20] The largest demographic of students enrolled at MSU is white males at 38 percent, followed closely by white females at 33 percent. In the fall of 2015, 3,471 first-time freshmen enrolled at MSU with an average ACT score of twenty-four.[21] In contrast, of the eight SDP students who volunteered to participate in this research, six were African-American females, one was an African-American male, and one was a white male. As a group, SDP students agreeing to participate in research had ACT scores ranging from twelve to seventeen, with an average composite score of thirteen, English score of twelve, and reading score of thirteen.

This was a group of students whose scores, according to the IHL's admission standards for the program, indicated they were not prepared to succeed at the postsecondary level. In addition to engaging them with college-level writing and research skills, we were interested in how these students interpreted the language used in the threshold concepts and habits of mind. In asking them directly about these concepts and habits, we were interested in better understanding:

- Their perceptions regarding their own preparedness for researching and writing at the college level.
- Their preparedness based on their reported previous experiences with and incoming understandings of research and writing.
- Their preparedness based on their understanding of language and concepts outlined in each of the respective Frameworks.
- Their preparedness based on our assessment of their final map entries.

In order to measure students' perceptions of their preparedness as well as how their prior experience prepared them for college, we administered a pre-survey using Google Forms. The pre-survey asked students: (1) on a scale of one-to-five, to rate their feelings of preparedness to participate in research and writing at the collegiate level, (2) to detail their experiences writing and researching both in school and out, focusing on genres, tools, and audiences, and (3) to describe their own research and writing processes. Additionally, we asked students to interact with language from each of the Frameworks on the pre-survey. For example, we asked students to explain, in their own words, what each of the threshold concepts meant to them, and we asked students to rate themselves as researchers and writers, both in school and out, based on the habits of mind.

In order to determine how our work with students was affecting their perceptions of their preparedness, we asked them to take a shorter survey at the mid-point of the semester. Again using Google Forms, we asked them to rate their self-perceptions of preparedness, to describe what they were learning about reading, research, and writing, and to provide a metaphor or analogy for both research and writing. Though we made space for peer-review and one-on-one research and writing consultations throughout the summer project, we did not provide students with any evaluative feedback. In fact, we conscientiously avoided it and explained to students that one of the most valuable habits for success they would need at the postsecondary level was self-motivation. Thus, in our findings section when we discuss our assessments of final mapping entries we used the same peer-review checklists students used to help one another make sure that they had all of the components needed for each of their map entries (see figure 7.01).

Our Findings and Discussion

Student Perceptions of Preparedness

In order to measure students' perceptions of preparedness for college-level research and writing, we asked students to rate themselves on both the pre-survey and mid-semester survey on a scale from one to five (with a score of 1 signifying "strongly disagree" and 5 signifying "strongly agree") in response to the following statements:

1. I feel prepared to begin doing research at the college level.
2. I feel prepared to begin writing papers at the college level.
3. I know where to get help (outside of my class) on my research paper.

At the beginning of the summer, students rated themselves fairly high with regards to all three statements. In terms of research preparation, none of students rated themselves below a 3 with an average rating of 3.6. In terms of writing preparation, though, one student rated herself at a 2, the average rating for the group was 3.5. Students seemed to feel most prepared with regards to the third statement about support services, with an average rating of 4.0. Though one student rated herself at a 2 for both writing preparation and knowing where to locate help on research papers at the beginning of the semester, by mid-summer, she raised both of these to a 3, and the average scores for all three statements rose: in terms of research from 3.6 to 3.9, in terms of writing from 3.5 to 3.9, and in terms of support services from 4.0 to 4.4.

Figure 7.01

Average Perceptions of Preparedness

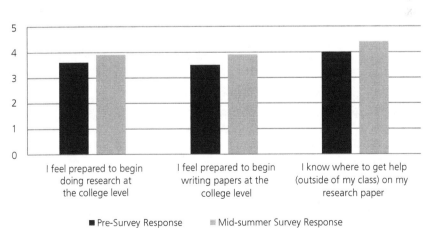

■ Pre-Survey Response   ▨ Mid-summer Survey Response

While perceptual preparedness responses suggest SDP students were aware they had room for increased knowledge regarding research-writing at the college level, both at the beginning and at the middle of the summer, they were fairly confident in their levels of preparation for academic literacy despite the fact they were participating in an admissions-contingent summer preparation program with required classes devoted to reading and writing.

Previous Experiences with Researching and Writing

The pre-survey also asked students to describe the type of research and writing they had experience with in school. In terms of writing, the majority of students mentioned note-taking for classes (six respondents) and other informal activities like "daily writing" (three), email (one), and journals (two). In terms of more sustained composing experiences, one student ambiguously referenced "papers," another mentioned "essays in English," and only two students explicitly referenced "research papers," seeming to indicate the majority of these students did not have prior experience with the kinds of sustained scholarly writing their college-level courses would require. Their responses to a question on the pre-survey, asking them to identify the tools they used most often for writing, appears to support this finding. For example, students identified pen and paper and cell phones most often (six responses identifying each), whereas a laptop was only referenced once as a writing tool most often used.

However, in response to a pre-survey question asking students to detail the kinds of research they had experience doing in school, almost every student (seven out of eight) indicated they were, indeed, required to write papers about topics using secondary sources. Responses included:

- "Looking up words seen in college books that aren't usually in high school reading and then random papers about myself or where I want to be in 10 years."
- "Creating works cited list and researching a topic."
- "The only research I really do is when I look up definitions or when I research a topic."
- "Researching a topic."
- "At school we did our research papers on a topic we picked."
- "Topics, works cited lists and citations."
- . "Researching a topic, creating a works cited pages, and world news."
- "The type of research I do for school will be, doing research on famous people, doing works cited pages, doing journal entries, doing a research paper on a topic, writing about self."

Such responses left us wondering why the responses to writing activities in school did not match research responses. Similarly, seven out of eight students identified a laptop or computer as their primary research tool (none, however, mentioned specific tools such as databases). Though such responses may reflect an issue with how students interpreted the survey question, we still wonder: if students are doing research on topics to write about with computers, then why are they most often writing in school using pen and paper? Similarly, we started to question the rigor of a research paper that is not being produced using a computer.

However, and perhaps more importantly, their pre-survey responses indicated, for us, that students already had a braided understanding of research and writing, at least when it came to describing their research experiences. For example, six out of the eight responses to our research experience question indicated these students understood research as part of a writing process, which was further confirmed by student responses to questions about writing and research processes on the pre-survey.

Few students responded to questions about their writing processes with detailed explanations regarding how they generate text, such as the following response:

> When I start my writing process, I brainstorm first. I figure out what I would like to write about and find out the most important things out of it. When I finish brainstorming, I will then make an outline of the topic and make sure I have some good supporting details to go with it. If I am writing on my smartphone, I will be free writing. I will be writing anything that comes to mind or just write how I feel about a situation or how I feel that day period.

More common were answers that discussed environments or tools. For example, one student wrote: "Well with my writing process, I don't really like using a laptop unless I got to, but I would rather use [my phone.] It's a lot easier than a laptop or a [desktop] and you can print from your phone as well, instead of worrying about a computer." Another focused on space and state of mind:

> First I procrastinate for a bit then I tell myself I need to get it done. Especially if it's for school because it HAS to get done. Then I either sit on my couch or get in my bed with my laptop and play slow indie or alternative music… I also put on my glasses because it makes me feel smarter and more productive (which probably isn't the case). Once I've started writing and get in the zone, I can't and don't stop.

It is worth noting that SDP students reported that space and environment influenced their productivity on projects. After their first visit to the writing center (a house on campus filled with comfortable furniture and natural light), students explicitly asked to meet as often as possible in this space, as opposed to the basement computer lab in the library where they regularly met for SDP classes. While the computer lab seemingly reinforced traditional, hierarchical learning structures with students sitting in rows behind large monitors facing a teacher's station, they were more likely to be distracted by cell phones and to tune out in this space, whereas in the Writing Center, students were more likely to stay on task, ask questions, and work in teams. Such anecdotal findings, when combined with student responses, suggest environment is indeed an important factor in students' composing processes.

Only the student who offered a genuine process-based writing response hinted that research ("find out the most important things") was a part of her writing process. However, when asked what their research processes entailed, half of the students responded by giving more details about their writing process, such as this response: "Well I do brainstorm before I make my outline, then I collect all my info and put it together and write out my paper on the research that I did." Another student explained, "Yes, I will be already thinking about what I am about to research and may write down the thoughts I have in my head about it. I do keep track of my research by writing it down in a notebook." While this and other responses complicate the idea that students come to college with a complex understanding of the process of research, it does, again, demonstrate students are aware of the inherent connections between researching and writing processes, even if their understandings are not nuanced.

Student Iterations of the Frameworks

Interestingly, students had no trouble explaining the relationship of the "habits of mind" and writing tasks they would be asked to do in school. For instance, in their explanation of "Responsibility," they noted the importance of producing one's own work as well as providing attribution. In our pre-survey, they were provided with a statement from the WPA Framework (i.e. "Engagement: I have a sense of investment and involvement in learning,") and a 5-point Likert scale, and they were asked to rate themselves based on each habit, according to how curious, open, responsible, etc. they thought they were. Again, they were fairly confident in themselves as researchers and writers, according to the habits of mind. On average, they rated themselves lowest in "Creativity" (3) and "Metacognition" (3.1), and highest in "Responsibility" (4.5) and "Flexibility" (4.3). We return to these ratings in our concluding reflections of the project.

Figure 7.02
Average Self-Ratings of Habits of Mind for Research-Writing

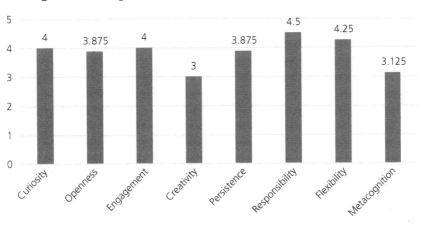

While students seemed to understand the meaning of each habit and that one needs to embody the habits of mind (e.g. "Responsibility," "Curiosity," "Persistence," etc.), there were issues, which we anticipated, with understanding the threshold concepts. Many students exhibited a surface-level understanding of certain concepts. For example, when asked to explain what "Searching as strategic exploration" meant, one student wrote, "searching takes time and patience and you have to be able to comprehend on how you bring it to your research, there is a lot to explore." On the concept of "Research as inquiry," another student wrote, "This means that the research you may find can be confusing and you may need some advice on it." While these responses demonstrate some healthy discomfort with the process of research, they acknowledge the root of the concepts: that researching and writing are not one-stop activities. Instead, both research and writing take considerable time and energy.

When asked to explain what "Scholarship as conversation" meant, however, no student demonstrated any understanding of the word "scholarship" as something other than a monetary award toward college tuition. In fact, one student simply wrote in that he had no idea what this meant. Because of this apparent lack of understanding, over the course of reading, discussing, and workshopping the mapping project, we focused on the concept of "scholarship" as both a type of academic communication and an attainable goal for these students. Regardless of this confusion, students already seemed to have an idea of research and writing as inherently related activities, as noted in their responses to questions about their own writing and research processes.

Preparedness as Suggested by Map Entries

Over the nine-week period that students worked on their map entries, we discussed not only the requirements for good scholarship (i.e. accurate citations, use of supporting evidence, etc.), but also the perceptions of oneself that would lead to producing the required elements (i.e. persistence, willingness to ask for help, creativity, etc.). We also actively participated in the maps, adding our own entries to them in the spirit of the collaborative work and as models for students. While these students' average rating of themselves regarding their level of persistence at the beginning of the semester was a 3.9 out of a possible 5 with no student rating herself below 3, we ultimately discovered the majority of these same students lacked persistence to accomplish all the required elements of the map entries. Out of the twenty-four map entries we had permission to analyze, all had accompanying visuals. Only ten, however, included the required 150-words of writing. Some entries contained only a sentence or a phrase, which could be an issue of timing, persistence, or even confusion. Though six entries almost met the requirements and thus were assessed as needing improvement, eight were simply incomplete. Similarly, only five map entries included a works cited entry for the novel even though seventeen entries included information from the novel. See table 7.01, the peer-review document that we also used to evaluate students' final products, for the overall assessments of their map entries.

Table 7.01
Tallies from Peer Review Document When Used in Final Assessment of Student Maps

	NO	YES	YES (but needs improvement)
Does the map entry have a descriptive title?	3	15	6
Does the map entry have an image or video that makes sense/helps readers to better understand the topic that is being mapped?	0	22	2
Does the map entry have 150-words of writing, explaining what that point is?	8	10	6
Does the map entry include information from the novel?	7	16	1
Is there an in-text citation for the novel?	12	6	6
Is the in-text citation for the novel correct?	19	4	1

Is there a Works Cited entry for the novel?	19	5	
Is the Works Cited entry for the novel correct?	19	4	1
Does the map entry include information from a source that is not the novel?	4	13	7
Is there an in-text citation for this other source?	16	4	4
Is the in-text citation for this other source correct?	21	2	1
Is there a Works Cited entry for this other source?	16	6	2
Is the Works Cited entry for this other source correct?	22		2
Is it clear to you where the writer is using information from her/his own head and where the writer is using information s/he located using research?	5	13	6
Is there a link that readers can click on somewhere in the map entry that will lead readers to additional (and relevant) information?	10	10	4

While we cannot point to one reason in particular, we speculate the large number of entries with missing or incomplete components is because the mapping project was neither tied to students' for-credit work, nor was it required to pass the Summer Development Program. Because their completion of the program did not hinge on this project and they exclusively worked on the project during their three hours per week with us, several students neglected essential parts of the project, either by doing them hastily or omitting them altogether, as was often the case with citations. This absence was most evident in components that involved an output of scholarship. For instance, while most students were able to collect research on a cultural element from our common read, select a place to plot it on the map, and associate it with an image, video, or hyperlink, several students struggled to effectively incorporate that research with their own words through quotations, paraphrasing, and accurate citations. Some of their mapped entries consisted of only an image, a reference to the novel, and a reference to a webpage like Wikipedia. A few of the entries even unintentionally plagiarized content. Having addressed these issues many times within our meetings, we speculate our co-curricular status played a large part in some students' incomplete entries, along with the short amount of time we had with the students (nine weeks; less if you subtract the time it took to introduce the My Map application, threshold concepts and habits of mind, and read the novel together).

In the future, even though we value the low-stakes learning environment and believe there is a serious need for co-curricular support outside the classroom, our pilot suggests it might benefit students more if we tied the research project to an assignment in one of their for-credit classes within the SDP program. Yet at the end of the semester, we were impressed to find that even without any kind of formal credit—besides our insistence that this experience would be beneficial to students and introduce them to skills, tools, processes, and habits necessary for their success in the university—students still contributed more than thirty map entries.

Our Reflections and Ideas for Further Research

As a pilot project with an experimental curriculum, guided by at least one Framework that has itself received criticism,[22] there is no doubt we made positive strides closing the fabricated gap between research and writing, and we engaged students in an experience requiring them to exercise research and writing skills they otherwise would have had no exposure to in their summer program. Particularly for SDP instructors and co-curricular instructors (librarians and tutors), the project served as a reminder that we are all working through similar processes and toward similar ends. Furthermore, the project introduced the habits and concepts of researching—a practice that defines our academic environment—to students who entered a program with little to no research experience.

In participating in this project ourselves, we discovered the language of the WPA Framework was easily understood and interpreted by most students. However, we did not have this same experience introducing students to the language of the ACRL Framework. As previously noted, students more readily absorbed the language of the WPA Frameworks likely because the language constructing them is familiar to students. Students exhibited more confidence and understanding in the questionnaire and discussions regarding the WPA Frameworks, so much so that they may have brushed them off as common-sense precepts. Even though both the ACRL and WPA Frameworks iterate writing and research require a continual, deliberate cultivation of practices and mindsets, students were less engaged in references to the ACRL Frameworks, and even though we described them for just under nine weeks, they seemed not to have a firm grasp on the language or the concepts.

Though they are not identical, the WPA habits of mind can greatly inform the work of librarians in how they relate threshold concepts to students and to teaching faculty. They provide accessible language for librarians, teachers, *and students*, encouraging not just the absorption of scholarship, but also its production. They create opportunities for library instruction to be less tool-based and more process-oriented, whereas traditionally, libraries have been more concerned with the tools of information (i.e. citation formats and catalog records) or, to use Elmborg's terminology, the "grammar of information."[23] However, as Emily Drabinski notes, our collaboration moves instruction of research and writing "away from the master of standard grammar … and toward the development of student writers capable of using language to intervene productively in their world."[24] Privileging the power of creating knowledge over the tools that enable its creation not only improves our teaching, but also affords agency to all students but especially those enrolled in remedial or bridge programs like SDP.

Should librarians reading the WPA Framework document cross out "write" and replace it with "research," they might find more accessible material for campus discussions about research and information literacy. Instead, we advocate librarians, writing teachers, and writing tutors on college campuses ignite a dialogue between the WPA Framework and the ACRL Framework; our experience confirmed that doing so greatly enriched our understanding of information literacy and writing, concepts and practices with which our students struggle.

Since the debut of the ACRL Frameworks in February 2015, debates about whether or not undergraduate students (some even include graduate students and non-library faculty) should be exposed to them in the raw have offered widely varying opinions. Several participants in the *ACRL Framework for Information Literacy for Higher Education* listserv, "acrlframe," debated whether or not the language of the frames in an IL classroom was too full of jargon (i.e. "reflective discovery" and "sustained discourse") for first-year students. One participant called the language "forbidding," while another participant, who introduced frames as they were written, argued the "language of the frames resonated with students and they had very insightful responses."[25] Similarly, we found discussing the ACRL Framework in tandem with the WPA Framework was insightful. The language in the ACRL Framework helped unpack the complexities of the WPA habits of mind our students seemed to oversimplify because the language was too accessible or familiar. For example, students rated themselves high in "Responsibility" while routinely neglecting to add necessary citations in their map entries. Based on this discovery, we believe their confused responses regarding the idea of "Scholarship as conversation" a more accurate measure of their current relationship with and understanding of research-writing at the postsecondary level.

While the implementation of the project itself brought about positive change in the minds of the instructors and students involved, the products that students created demonstrate our experimental curriculum could use improvement in certain areas—some within our control and some outside of it. For example, students began the summer with strong perceptions of themselves as researchers and writers and those perceptions remained mid-semester, even as they struggled with complicated research-writing processes and products. At the end of this project, we continue to contemplate how student misperceptions of their preparedness for college-level researching and writing might be addressed in ways that both sustain and challenge that self-confidence. Similarly, because we were working within a state-regulated program with explicit requirements, none of which included the capabilities to consume or produce writing with a research component, our co-curricular situation only allowed for a low-stakes project that would not be graded or required for the completion of the program. Our experience indicated such external motivation—a grade—may, indeed, encourage student persistence. Despite the incomplete and sometimes pilfered constructions within some students' entries, other students used this project as an opportunity to be curious, to practice "Research as inquiry," and so forth. In their mid-semester survey responses about research, they gave responses like "[R]esearch to me is like solving a mystery," "Research is like being Nancy Drew," and about writing, "Writing can be fun sometimes," and "Writing is like a maze, you have to go through so much." They also showed comfort in asking for help, did not hesitate to use the workshop time as a space to explore and experiment, and showed leadership in passing on their newfound learning to other students in the class.

As anyone designing a course will know, student performance (including the final project) was not the only take-away from this collaborative experience. During the nine-week semester, we had the enriching experience of designing not only the final assignment's goals and requirements together, but also the in-class exercises that provided scaffolding for the assignment. While this work led to more intentional discussions about the habits of mind and the threshold concepts, it also—and perhaps more importantly—provided a window into each other's methods of implementing those concepts into classroom deliverables. In short, this was an important and valuable learning experience for us as well. For librarians who are only recently wrestling with translating new, complex threshold concepts, teaching students to integrate someone else's scholarship into their own writing can be a transferable process through their research. Additionally, at the end of our experiment, we were happy to find that the writing instructor for the SDP course was contemplating implementing this multimodal, collaborative, and hybrid approach into her middle school English Language Arts classroom in the fall, and a graduate student who worked one-on-one with SDP students through the Writing Center would go on to propose this mapping method as a useful pedagogical tool for literature teachers in one of her graduate seminar papers.

In working so closely together, we also invited several of our writing center and library colleagues to join several sessions of our class as resident experts and guides. In other words, although we were the primary point-persons for the students, we demonstrated there were several experts available to help them throughout their research-writing. This it-takes-a-village approach created our own community of scholars that included instructors, librarians, and tutors, as well as students. Because librarians and writing center tutors at MSU and elsewhere work closely together already, and even share some of the same physical spaces, it was valuable to add another layer of collaboration to our project. Additionally, starting in the fall semester, writing center tutors and librarians began co-teaching campus workshops that used similar strategies. So in borrowing each other's practices and by engaging explicitly with our respective Frameworks, we not only strengthened our collaborations, but also perpetuated them. Through this project, we have opened a door into each other's practices and professional conversations. In the coming semesters, it is our hope to continue this dialogue and refine our approaches to imparting them to students, faculty, and staff of all abilities on our campus.

Appendix 7A: Assignment Directions Given to Summer Development Program Students

General Description and Purpose/Intended Outcomes of Project

Using the My Maps Google application, you will be responsible for mapping the Maroon Edition, Same Kind of Different As Me. Think of the map as a context map—you will locate people, places, events, and artifacts that we read about in the text on a map of the U.S., and, based on research, you'll provide information about each of them (using writing to introduce that information and to cite where it came from). This project is designed to engage you in exercising/flexing your academic muscles for success—the processes you will go through in order to generate this map, in other words, will help you to understand

- Authority as Constructed/Contextual
- Information Creation as a Process
- Research as Inquiry
- Scholarship as a Conversation
- Searching as Strategic Exploration will give you experience with
  → Analyzing and acting on an understanding of audiences, purposes, and contexts in creating and comprehending texts (Rhetorical Knowledge)
  → Analyzing a situation or text and making thoughtful decisions based on that analysis (Critical Thinking)
  → Multiple strategies to approach and undertake writing and research (Writing Processes)
  → Formal and Informal Conventions
  → Composing in Multiple Environments and will also require you to be
    ◆ Curious
    ◆ Open
    ◆ Engaged
    ◆ Creative
    ◆ Persistent
    ◆ Responsible
    ◆ Flexible
    ◆ Reflective

Project Specifics

Working in two teams, one team will map Denver's story and one team will map Ron's story. As we read the book in the Writing Center, take note of notable people, places, events, and cultural artifacts that come up in each narrator's respective chapters (literally, circle these things, earmark pages, use sticky notes, take notes in the margins, etc.). Each team member will need to contribute/build at least three different kinds of entries. As a class, we'll "present" the map to the Maroon Edition committee and staff and faculty of the Summer Development Program at the end of the summer.

Map Entry Requirements

1. A short paragraph (no less than 150 words) that explains the significance of this point (the information module you're building) to the character's narrative and the whole novel—how does this extra information you are providing relate to the novel? Each paragraph will need to include:
   a. a quote, summary, or paraphrase from the novel, and
   b. a quote, summary, or paraphrase from a secondary source.
   Note: each of these items (from the book or from a source) will need to include an in-text citation and works cited (MLA) or referenced (APA) entry.
2. An appropriate photo or video representing this point.
3. A link (or links) to external content, either separate from the paragraph or embedded in your paragraph.

Notes

1. Rolf Norgaard, "Writing Information Literacy: Contributions to a Concept," *Reference & User Services Quarterly,* 43, no. 2 (2003): 124.
2. Barbara Fister, "Common Ground: The Composition/Bibliographic Instruction Connection," in *Proceedings from ACRL's Academic Libraries: Achieving Excellence in Higher Education,* ed. Thomas Kirk (Chicago: Association of College and Research Libraries, 1992), 154.
3. Jean Sheridan, "Making the Library Connection with Process Writing," in *Writing-Across-the-Curriculum and the Academic Library: A Guide for Librarians, Instructors, and Writing Program Directors,* ed. Jean Sheridan (Westport, CT: Greenwood Press, 1995): 71–94.
4. Ross LaBaugh, "Talking the Discourse: Composition Theory," in *Writing-Across-the-Curriculum,* 71–94.
5. Jeanne Armstrong, "Designing a Writing Intensive Course with Information Literacy and Critical Thinking Outcomes," *Reference Services Review,* 38, no. 3 (2010): 445–457.

6.   Lea Currie and Michele Eodice, "Roots Entwined: Growing a Sustainable Collabo-
      ration," in *Centers for Learning: Writing Centers and Libraries in Collaboration*, eds.
      James Elmborg and Sheril Hook. (Chicago: Association of College and Research
      Libraries, 2005): 42–60.

7.   Sheril Hook, "Teaching Librarians and Writing Center Professionals in Collabora-
      tion: Complementary Practices," in *Centers for Learning*, 21–41.

8.   Association of College and Research Libraries. *Framework for Information Literacy
      for Higher Education*. (February 2015): http://www.ala.org/acrl/standards/ilframe-
      work. Hereafter cited as ACRL.

9.   Council of Writing Program Administrators, National Council of Teachers of En-
      glish, and National Writing Project. *Framework for Success in Postsecondary Writing*.
      (January 2011): http://wpacouncil.org/files/framework-for-success-postsecond-
      ary-writing.pdf. Hereafter cited as WPA.

10.   Colleen Boff and Barbara Toth, "Better-Connected Student Learning: Research and
      Writing Clinics at Bowling Green State University," In *Centers for Learning*, 149.

11.   Barbara Means, Carol Chelemer, and Michael S. Knapp, "Preface," In *Teaching
      Advanced Skills to At-Risk Students: Views from Research and Practice*, ed. Barbara
      Means, Carol Chelemer, and Michael S. Knapp (San Francisco: Jossey-Bass Publish-
      ers, 1991), xiii.

12.   ACRL, Framework, n.p.

13.   WPA, Framework.

14.   Rolf Norgaard, "Writing Information Literacy in the Classroom: Pedagogical Enact-
      ments and Implications," *Reference & User Services Quarterly* 43, no. 3 (2004): 221.

15.   ACRL, Framework, 8.

16.   WPA, Framework, 1.

17.   ACRL, Framework, 6.

18.   WPA, Framework, 5.

19.   Ron Hall, Denver Moore, and Lynn Vincent. *Same Kind of Different as Me*. (Nash-
      ville, Tennessee: Thomas Nelson, 2006): 3.

20.   Office of Institutional Research and Effectiveness, Mississippi State University, "Pock-
      et Factbook" (Fall 2014). http://www.ir.msstate.edu/factbook_pocket14.pdf.

21   ———, "First-time Freshman ACT Average by Gender & Race" (October 2015).
      http://www.ir.msstate.edu/enroll_ftf_act_avg_gender_race_fa10_fa15.pdf.

22.   Ian Beilin, "Beyond the Threshold: Conformity, Resistance, and the ACRL Infor-
      mation Literacy Framework for Higher Education," *In the Library with the Lead
      Pipe* (February 25, 2015): 1–9.; Kim Leeder Reed, "Square Peg in a Round Hole?
      The Framework for Information Literacy in the Community College Environment,"
      Journal of Library Administration 55, no. 3 (2015): 235–248. doi:10.1080/01930826.20
      15.1034052.

23.   James Elmborg, "Critical Information Literacy: Implications for Instructional Prac-
      tice," *Journal of Academic Librarianship* 32, no. 2 (2006): 197.

24.   Emily Drabinski, "Toward a Kairos of Library Instruction," *Journal of Academic
      Librarianship* 40 (2014): 483.

25.   Jody Caldwell, "Info Lit Definitions for Students," acrlframe listserv—*ACRL Frame-
      work for Information Literacy for Higher Education* (August 2015): http://lists.ala.org/
      sympa/arc/acrlframe/2015-08/msg00003.html.

Bibliography

Armstrong, Jeanne. "Designing a Writing Intensive Course with Information Literacy and Critical Thinking Outcomes." *Reference Services Review* 38, no. 3 (2010): 445–457.

Association of College and Research Libraries. 2016. *Framework for Information Literacy for Higher Education.* Accessed February 25, 2015. http://www.ala.org/acrl/standards/ilframework.

Beilin, Ian. "Beyond the Threshold: Conformity, Resistance, and the ACRL Information Literacy Framework for Higher Education." *In the Library with the Lead Pipe* (February 25, 2015): 1–9.

Boff, Colleen and Barbara Toth, "Better-Connected Student Learning: Research and Writing Clinics at Bowling Green State University." In *Centers for Learning: Writing Centers and Libraries in Collaboration*, 148–57. Edited by James Elmborg and Sheril Hook. Chicago: Association of College and Research Libraries, 2005.

Caldwell, Jody. "Info Lit Definitions for Students." *acrlframe listserv – ACRL Framework for Information Literacy for Higher Education.* Accessed February 25, 2015. http://lists.ala.org/sympa/arc/acrlframe/2015-08/msg00003.html.

Council of Writing Program Administrators, National Council of Teachers of English, and National Writing Project. *Framework for Success in Postsecondary Writing.* Accessed February 25, 2015. wpacouncil.org/files/framework-for-success-postsecondary-writing.pdf.

Currie, Lea and Michele Eodice. "Roots Entwined: Growing a Sustainable Collaboration." In *Centers for Learning: Writing Centers and Libraries in Collaboration*, 42–60. Edited by James Elmborg and Sheril Hook. Chicago: Association of College and Research Libraries, 2005.

Drabinski, Emily. "Toward a Kairos of Library Instruction." *Journal of Academic* Librarianship 40 (2014): 480–5.

Elmborg, James. "Critical Information Literacy: Implications for Instructional Practice." *Journal of Academic Librarianship* 32, no. 2 (2006): 192–9.

Fister, Barbara. "Common Ground: The Composition/Bibliographic Instruction Connection." In *Proceedings from ACRL's Academic Libraries: Achieving Excellence in Higher Education*, 154–58. Edited by Thomas Kirk. Chicago: Association of College and Research Libraries, 1992.

Hall, Ron, Denver Moore, and Lynn Vincent. *Same Kind of Different as Me.* Nashville, Tennessee: Thomas Nelson, 2006.

Hook, Sheril. "Teaching Librarians and Writing Center Professionals in Collaboration: Complementary Practices." In *Centers for Learning: Writing Centers and Libraries in Collaboration*, 21–41. Edited by James Elmborg and Sheril Hook. Chicago: Association of College and Research Libraries, 2005.

LaBaugh, "Talking the Discourse." In *Writing-Across-the-Curriculum and the Academic Library: A Guide for Librarians, Instructors, and Writing Program Directors*, 23–32. Edited by Jean Sheridan. Westport, CT: Greenwood Press, 1995.

Means, Barbara, Carol Chelemer, and Michael S. Knapp. *Teaching Advanced Skills to At-Risk Students: Views from Research and Practice.* San Francisco: Jossey-Bass Publishers, 1991.

Norgaard, Rolf. "Writing Information Literacy: Contributions to a Concept." *Reference & User Services Quarterly,* 43, no. 2 (2003): 124–30.

———. "Writing Information Literacy in the Classroom: Pedagogical Enactments and Implications." *Reference & User Services Quarterly* 43, no. 3 (2004): 220–6.

Office of Institutional Research and Effectiveness, Mississippi State University. "Pocket Factbook." Accessed February 25, 2015. http://www.ir.msstate.edu/factbook_pocket14.pdf.

———. "First-time Freshman ACT Average by Gender & Race." (October 2015). http://www.ir.msstate.edu/enroll_ftf_act_avg_gender_race_fa10_fa15.pdf.

Reed, Kim Leeder. "Square Peg in a Round Hole? The Framework for Information Literacy in the Community College Environment." *Journal of Library Administration* 55, no. 3 (2015): 235–248. doi:10.1080/01930826.2015.1034052.

Sheridan, Jean. "Making the Library Connection with Process Writing." In *Writing-Across-the-Curriculum and the Academic Library: A Guide for Librarians, Instructors, and Writing Program Directors*, 71–94. Edited by Jean Sheridan. Westport, CT: Greenwood Press, 1995.

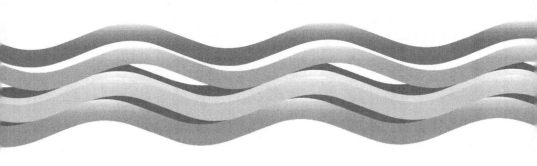

CHAPTER 8[*]

Partnership as Process:

Moving Toward an Integrated Undergraduate Writing Curriculum

Elizabeth L. Wallis, Jim Nugent, and Lori Ostergaard
Oakland University

If libraries continue to evoke, for writing teachers and their students, images of the quick field trip, the scavenger hunt, the generic, stand-alone tutorial, or the dreary research paper, the fault remains, in large part, rhetoric and composition's failure to adequately theorize the role of libraries and information literacy in its own rhetorical self-understanding and pedagogical practice.
—*Rolf Norgaard*[1]

If writing instructors have undertheorized IL [Information Literacy] in relation to writing, this is, in part, because of librarians' failure to articulate the contributions that our theoretical tradition can make to rhetoric and composition and, by extension, learning in general.
—*Melissa Bowles-Terry*[2]

* This work is licensed under a Creative Commons Attribution-NonCommercial-ShareAlike 4.0 License, CC BY-NC-SA (https://creativecommons.org/licenses/by-nc-sa/4.0/).

Introduction

The epigraphs illustrate how libraries and first-year writing programs can seem to be working at cross-purposes when they are not engaged in active communication and collaboration. Disconnects such as these are particularly troubling as our intellectual and pedagogical approaches are seemingly unanimous: reading between the ACRL's *Framework for Information Literacy for Higher Education* (hereafter ACRL Framework) and the Council of Writing Program Administrators' *Outcomes Statement for First-Year Writing* (hereafter WPA Outcomes), it is clear that very little separates librarians and first-writing instructors and administrators in their approaches to information literacy and student success. And yet, this ideological match is not always manifested in our institutional relationships. In this chapter, we describe how we resisted working at cross-purposes at Oakland University by forming a fruitful partnership between the department of writing and rhetoric and the university library. In the course of our collaboration, we have come to recognize the commonality of our intellectual and pedagogical approaches, most particularly as evidenced by the ACRL Framework and WPA Outcomes Statement. Recognizing the need to work with one another, we have come to see opportunities to improve the teaching of information literacy not just within the first-year writing curriculum, but also within Oakland University's burgeoning undergraduate major in writing and rhetoric.

Oakland University (OU) is a Carnegie-ranked Doctoral Research University (DRU) located approximately twenty-five miles north of Detroit. It is home to twenty thousand students—a population that is largely working class, is fairly diverse, mostly commutes to school, predominantly works part-time while attending, and includes a sizeable portion of transfer students.[3] The department of writing and rhetoric is relatively new, having been established as an independent department in 2008. The department administers a first-year writing program consisting of four courses: WRT 104: Supervised Study, WRT 102: Basic Writing, WRT 150: Composition I, and WRT 160: Composition II. Central to this program are Composition I and Composition II, which are the two largest courses in the institution and deliver approximately twenty-four thousand course hours to twenty-three hundred students annually. As part of Composition II, the university library and the department of writing and rhetoric have a longstanding partnership aimed at introducing information literacy skills to OU students early in their academic careers.

The department also offers an undergraduate major in writing and rhetoric. This major was created simultaneously with the establishment of the independent department in 2008[4] and includes three tracks offering specialized study in professional writing, writing studies, and writing for digital media. The professional writing track prepares students "to be critical, ethical, and capable practitioners of writing within a broad range of professional contexts."[5] The writing studies track prepares students for graduate study in composition-rhetoric and eventual careers as writing instructors, and the writing for digital media track prepares students to write for online contexts, including writing for social media.

In this chapter, we describe how our first-year writing program and the library instruction associated with that program have been shaped by the WPA's *Framework for Success in Postsecondary Writing* (hereafter WPA Framework) and the ACRL Framework. We also describe the first assessment of our writing and rhetoric major, outlining the assumptions about research and information literacy that were revealed by that assessment and discussing our approach to addressing those assumptions. We conclude the chapter by outlining our plans for incorporating information literacy instruction throughout the curriculum in the major.

Using the *Framework for Success in Postsecondary Writing* to Shape First-Year Writing

Although instructors' approaches vary, all of Oakland's first-year writing courses share common, program-wide goals that were shaped by the WPA Outcomes. Thus, our first-year classes emphasize rhetorical knowledge, critical analysis, and knowledge of conventions.[6] Each course in the first-year writing program also has its own set of course-specific learning outcomes[7] that scaffold the study of what we call the four Rs: rhetoric, research, revision, and reflection. The only required course in the program, Composition II, is further shaped by two university general education goals and three so-called cross-cutting capacities:

The writing knowledge foundation area prepares students to demonstrate:
- knowledge of the elements, writing processes, and organizing strategies for creating analytical and expository prose
- effective rhetorical strategies appropriate to the topic, audience, context and purpose

Cross-cutting capacities:
- effective communication
- critical thinking
- information literacy

To date, only the basic writing class (WRT 102) has been explicitly redesigned to address the recommendations within the WPA Framework, although the department will engage in a discussion of the WPA Framework during a professional development meeting later this year. The WRT 102 course was revised three years ago in an effort to shift the course away from a historically remedial approach that was consistent with what William B. Lalicker refers to as a "prerequisite model,"[8] and what Shawna Shapiro identifies as a "traditional remedial model."[9] This was the same year the WPA Framework was published, and we used this document to shape our revisions to this course. Prior to the department's revision, the basic writing course provided students with skills-based, grammar-focused, current-traditional instruction emphasizing error correction, workbook exercises, and grammar drills; it offered at-risk students little preparation for the challenges of writing in advanced courses in their majors or even our own major in writing and rhetoric. Shifting the focus of our basic writing course to encompass habits of mind, reflective practices, and a study of research, rhetoric, and writing practices has helped us transform this developmental class from one existing in a programmatic or "institutional quarantine"[10] to one conforming to the pedagogical values and learning outcomes of the other courses in our first-year curriculum.

Using the *Framework for Information Literacy for Higher Education* to Shape FYW Library Instruction in our First-Year Writing Curriculum

In a similar effort to align curriculum with broader philosophy, the library faculty undertook an evaluation of the library instruction goals for Composition II to ensure the module aligns with the ACRL Framework. The student learning outcomes (SLOs) for the library instruction portion of WRT 160 were developed by the library's Committee on Instruction (COI) with input from the wider library faculty. These SLOs were developed in conjunction with the ACRL *Information Literacy (IL) Competency Standards for Higher Education* (hereafter ACRL IL Standards), which define the information literate student in detail as one who "determines the nature and extent of the information needed," "accesses needed information effectively and efficiently," "evaluates information and its sources critically and incorporates selected information into his or her knowledge base and value system," "uses information effectively to accomplish a specific purpose," and "understands many of the ethical, legal and socio-economic issues surrounding information and information technology."[11]

Teaching all of these IL skills in approximately one hour of face-to-face instruction and brief supplementary online tutorials is unfeasible, so the library faculty found it necessary to focus on which skills were most vital to first-year writing students learning to write a research paper. The student learning outcomes that came out of these discussions are divided into two broad goals and seven outcomes:

Goal 1: Students will learn the importance of using an effective search strategy. At the end of the IL modules, students will be able to

- apply effective keyword search skills to find results in an online database,
- identify at least two methods for finding resources related to a specific database record, and
- demonstrate at least two strategies for broadening or narrowing a research topic based on search results.

Goal 2: Students will gain an understanding of the value of resource evaluation. At the end of the IL modules, students will be able to

- identify the main uses of, and reasons to use, at least two types of information sources available via the library;
- evaluate any source—print or digital—for authority, currency, relevancy, accuracy, objectivity, and appropriateness to their level of research;
- read and interpret a database record to determine an item's publication date, publication type, and general topic; and
- evaluate database search results for relevancy to their research topics.

These outcomes have served WRT 160 students well since their adoption. Assessment data is reviewed by the COI annually to affirm student attainment of the outcomes reaches 80 percent or higher, and past research has shown the library's instruction efforts are equally effective face-to-face and online.[12] However, since these WRT 160 library instruction outcomes were put into place, the ACRL developed and published its own Framework, the essential concepts of which are: "Authority Is Constructed and Contextual," "Information Creation as a Process," "Information Has Value," "Research as Inquiry," "Scholarship as Conversation," and "Searching as Strategic Exploration."[13]

Because the WRT 160 Library Instruction SLOs were initially designed to align with the ACRL IL Standards, it was necessary to evaluate the outcomes as they relate to the new Framework in order to determine if any changes were necessary. As shown in Table 8.01, the COI determined five of six of the concepts in the ACRL Framework are covered by the existing WRT 160 student learning outcomes. The remaining frame, "Information has Value," can be considered a higher order concept more appropriately covered in library instruction sessions with upper-level courses and graduate courses; therefore, the members of the Committee on Instruction concluded the Library's existing WRT 160 SLOs are quite effective in relation to both the ACRL IL Standards and the new Framework.

Table 8.01
Comparison of Frames and Student Learning Outcomes

Frames	Student Learning Outcomes						
	1.a.	1.b.	1.c.	2.a.	2.b.	2.c.	2.d.
Authority Is Constructed and Contextual				x	x		
Information Creation as a Process				x	x		
Information Has Value							
Research as Inquiry	x	x	x	x	x	x	x
Scholarship as Conversation				x	x		
Searching as Strategic Exploration	x	x	x	x	x		

Partnering to Improve Information Literacy in the First-Year Writing Program

Historically, the library and the department of writing and rhetoric have engaged in a number of successful partnerships related to the first-year writing program. The publication of the ACRL Framework has provided us with the exigency to extend those partnerships in the following ways:

1. Two of this chapter's authors presented on the WPA and ACRL Frameworks at a meeting of the department's First-Year Writing Committee last fall, asking the full- and part-time faculty on that committee to begin developing professional development materials and workshops centered on the Frameworks as well as to review the first-year program goals in order to determine where IL, in particular, fits within our program.

2. The writing and rhetoric librarian presented the morning workshop at the writing and rhetoric department's annual spring conference. This workshop included an introduction to the ACRL Framework, a breakout session on ways to incorporate the Framework into first-year writing courses, and a discussion of how to scaffold IL instruction throughout the first-year writing program.

3. The authors are collaborating on an information literacy chapter for our required, first-year writing textbook, *Grizz Writes*.[14] This textbook is required in all three of our first-year writing courses. Our chapter introduces information literacy, providing students with a summary of the ACRL Framework and a rationale for the various research dispositions it outlines.

Using the ACRL Framework to Shape the Bachelor's Program in Writing and Rhetoric

The partnership between the library and the first-year writing program has been longstanding; in fact, senior faculty members in both units are unable to identify when this partnership began. Despite this, there has been little collaboration between the library and the department in our still relatively new writing and rhetoric major. Like many battlefield alliances, the partnership we describe formed in response to a crisis. The crisis was fueled by the writing and rhetoric department faculty's recognition that our major curriculum was failing to prepare students for the research challenges they regularly encountered in our upper-division courses, much less the information literacy challenges they might encounter in their lives beyond the university. As we demonstrate, the completion of our first major assessment report occurred around the same time as the publication of the ACRL Framework, thus creating an opportune moment to expand the instructional partnership between the library and the department to include the writing and rhetoric major.

In 2014, the department of writing and rhetoric performed a detailed assessment of its major program, evaluating the capstone portfolios from eight of the program's graduates that year (although seemingly small, this sample represents 100 percent of the capstone students that year). The portfolios were analyzed for nine objectives, including rhetorical knowledge, research processes, writing processes, and ethical collaboration. Research processes scored low in this assessment, although about average for all areas evaluated (3.1 on a five-point scale). This low score troubled many of our faculty and was considered one of the most significant findings of the assessment. An unexpected secondary finding was deemed even more troubling for faculty working in our professional writing and digital media tracks. This secondary finding related to the fact that our assessment committee elected to assess only academic research papers in the senior portfolios and did so using a rubric originally designed to assess papers from our first-year writing program.

In other words, while students in professional writing and digital media employed research to develop their course projects, none of those projects were evaluated in the program assessment; only traditional research essays composed primarily in our the academic-focused core courses were evaluated. Thus, our assessment revealed not only were writing and rhetoric majors struggling to locate, analyze, and synthesize research, but our very definitions of research and writing may have been tied narrowly to academic contexts, suggesting that our BA program was patterned on our first-year, general education program.

This assumption about the academic focus of our major and the assessment committee's corresponding inattention to work performed in the pre-professional tracks of the major (and that serve the majority of our majors) is evidenced throughout the assessment report, but especially in the close analysis of the students' portfolios treated to extended critiques for the following:

- lack of intellectual depth (topic)
- lack of effective organization and synthesis (audience)
- lack of understanding of academic contexts for research-based writing (context)
- lack of critical analysis and use of source material to support a claim (purpose)
- lack of appropriate language use and evidence of editing/proofreading (ethos)

In fact, five of the eight portfolios were analyzed for deficiencies because they scored below a three in an overall rating of the quality of writing. In the assessment report shared with the department, samples of these students' work were closely evaluated to demonstrate our majors' specific struggles with writing. The report critiqued one paper in one sample portfolio for its "lack of understanding of academic conventions for research-based writing," including the criticism that the paper's "reference citations are not written in conventional American Psychological Association (APA) style."[15] While APA is the style specified in our curricula for the Composition II course, faculty teaching in the professional writing and writing for digital media tracks teach research and citation practices that vary widely based on the rhetorical situations which authors composing professional, technical, and digital texts address.

As the assessment committee reported:

> An analysis of a student's work notes that the portfolio includes a link to a collaborative video produced for WRT 233: Digital Storytelling and a printout of the PowerPoint slides for a final presentation in WRT 342: History of Rhetoric.... In addition, so much of the work submitted was personal writing, including two literacy narratives and reflective blog posts related to the capstone project, that it was nearly impossible to evaluate how [this student] engaged in critical analysis of sources and used cited source material as evidence to support analytical claims.[16]

In other words, the variety of genres this digital media student produced was viewed by the assessment committee as an assessment problem rather than a demonstration of the student's rhetorical ability, as there was a "limited sample of...academic writing" documented in the portfolio.[17] An assessment that valued the range of research and compositions our majors engaged in during their programs of study might have provided insights into how research and an understanding of rhetorical principles were employed in each of the genres included in this student's portfolio, and perhaps, celebrated the ways this student addressed multiple audiences, purposes, and mediums with his work.

The assessment committee also identified a number of issues in the preparation of student portfolios for assessment. For example, the committee noted it "had no information about the assignment requirements at the time the portfolios were assessed, which might have accounted for students' selection of sources, specific organizational strategies, assumed audience, etc."[18] In other words, the committee acknowledged the original assignment description and intended audiences for each work they assessed might account for the some of the issues they identified with the writing. However, this acknowledgment neither informed the critique of these papers, nor impacted the choice of rubrics used to assess these works.

The possible bias in favor of academic research practices revealed by this report surprised many of us, but the overall results of the assessment should have surprised no one: research and information literacy are only briefly touched upon and are otherwise absent from our undergraduate program goals. Our faculty may have read between the lines in developing their courses or may have assumed information literacy instruction was happening in the first-year courses or in "somebody else's" course in the major, but research practices are not immediately foregrounded in our writing major program goals.

Program Goals

This program strives to develop students':
- abilities as critical readers, writers, and thinkers in academic and non-academic contexts
- abilities as literate agents working independently and collaboratively
- abilities as engaged participants in their local and national communities
- abilities as effective users of technologies of literacy
- understanding of the histories, theories, research methods, ethics, and conventions of literate acts and practices
- use of that understanding to produce their own works for audiences, purposes, and contexts

So while our curriculum does prepare students to be users of the technologies of literacy, information literacy itself is not overtly mentioned anywhere in our program goals.

As illustrated in the Table 8.02, our assessment committee's (generous) interpretation of these goals incorporated research, but only as a part of students' demonstrated ability to compose collaboratively and as a part of the overall writing process. Information literacy was not mentioned in a department whose commitment to (1) critical thinking, (2) collaboration, (3) community engagement, (4) technological literacy, (5) disciplinary practices, and (6) rhetoric was reflected clearly in both its goals and learning outcomes. In sum, information literacy and research practices remain surprisingly marginal to our major in writing and rhetoric, and our assessment practices were informed by a very limited conception of research practices constrained within academic contexts.

Table 8.02
Comparison of Program Goals with Student Learning Outcomes

	Program Goals	Student Learning Outcomes (SLOs) that Correspond with Each Goal *(Majors will...)*
1	to develop students' abilities as critical readers, writers, and thinkers in academic and non-academic contexts	• apply rhetorical analysis to communicative practices, written or otherwise • articulate the professional and academic possibilities for a degree in writing and rhetoric
2	to develop students' abilities as literate agents working independently and collaboratively	• engage in ethical collaborations in academic and non-academic contexts • engage in research processes in independent and collaborative research
3	to develop students' abilities as engaged participants in their local and national communities	• discuss the role of writing and rhetoric in the public sphere • apply classroom learning to activities beyond the classroom, which may include 1) service to specific communities as civic-minded rhetors, 2) workplace applications, or 3) pre-professional experiences
4	to develop students' abilities as effective users of technologies of literacy	• apply various technologies and media to produce effective digital texts
5	to develop students' understanding of the histories, theories, research methods, ethics, and conventions of literate acts and practices	• incorporate discussion of the histories and theories of rhetoric

Table 8.02

Comparison of Program Goals with Student Learning Outcomes

	Program Goals	Student Learning Outcomes (SLOs) that Correspond with Each Goal *(Majors will…)*
6	to have students use that understanding to produce their own works for audiences, purposes, and contexts	• apply writing processes (including researching, prewriting, drafting, peer reviewing, revising, and reflecting) to compose a variety of texts for multiple audiences, media, and contexts

Although troubling, the attitudes and assumptions about research and information literacy revealed within our own program assessment may not be unusual for new writing major programs around the country. Indeed, only a small number of the writing majors detailed in the 2009 Conference on College Composition and Communication "Writing Majors at a Glance" database tout the importance of information literacy in the descriptions of the majors included. A few programs note "we live in an Information Age" (York College) and an "information-rich economy" (University of Central Florida), while others opine that "in today's competitive world, information is power" (Barry University). There is also at least some mention of a need for a writing major that will "prepare students for the information rich workplace" (University of Central Arkansas).[19] Only a handful of BA programs included in this database (6 of 71) mention the importance of information literacy, though often without using the phrase information literacy (within their major descriptions), and only some of these further note that information retrieval, evaluation, and synthesis are essential skills for majors. Nonetheless, the major requirements, course titles, and course descriptions within those majors emphasize the importance of conveying, shaping, or communicating information through a study of information management, information design, information architecture, and information technologies.

Given very few of the programs included in this database explicitly mention information literacy, we can assume these skills are not being prioritized within the curricula. Even as many first-year writing programs have partnered extensively with libraries to provide students with foundational information literacy skills, it is not clear how or how much the writing majors documented in the database build upon those foundational skills. It is true program descriptions and outcomes do not always capture the invisible curricula of individual courses and programs of study, but in the curricula of many undergraduate degree programs—our major included—information literacy appears to remain a one-way street. These programs uniformly make room in their curricula for teaching students to communicate information outward through a variety of genres and media, but they rarely make room expressly for instruction in information evaluation, analysis, and synthesis. While this is not true of all writing majors, we can certainly contend our own program has not done enough to prepare students with the skills to "perform efficient, high-level, accurate research in the digital world."[20]

While the 2009 database of writing majors does not reflect recent developments in writing majors and it cannot account for the revisions many of those original programs have made over the past seven years (our own program included), it does suggest many programs fail to provide students with meaningful and challenging experiences locating, interpreting, evaluating, and working with information. As the epigraphs opening this chapter attest, and as James K. Elmborg notes in his 2006 *Writing Lab Newsletter* article, "[W]e seem to have erected an invisible intellectual wall between those who teach students to write and those who teach students to research."[21] In OU's writing and rhetoric program, we may have marginalized information literacy instruction, relegating it to first-year writing. The ACRL Framework reminds us that information literacy is vital to the success of our majors and provides us with a rationale for integrating this instruction into our undergraduate degree program.

As we demonstrate, thinking about how we teach information literacy in our major at OU—or, indeed, wondering if we have been teaching it at all—has led to some generative rethinking about everything from course requirements and scaffolding to professional development and assessment.

Partnering to Improve Information Literacy in the BA Program in Writing and Rhetoric

The methods the assessment committee employed and the conclusions it reached in its report demonstrated some surprising assumptions our writing and rhetoric faculty members held about what defines research writing in our degree program. Nevertheless, the distribution of the assessment report during a department retreat in December 2014 provided the kairotic moment to begin discussing substantive revisions to the major that will begin to correct this oversight.

Some of the suggested revisions require additional partnerships between faculty in the library and faculty in the department so we may incorporate information literacy instruction more directly into the major. The most significant of these revisions will bookend information literacy through modules or assignments designed to be delivered in both the gateway courses for the three tracks of the major and in the capstone course taken by students from all three tracks. The modules for the gateway courses will be tailored for each of the three tracks: Writing Studies, Professional Writing, and Writing for Digital Media. Each module will be developed collaboratively by the writing and rhetoric librarian in partnership with the writing faculty who teach within each track. The modules will then be offered by the gateway course instructor.

All three courses will prepare students to locate secondary sources, assess the credibility of those sources, place those sources into a larger conversation within the field, and synthesize those sources with their own research. However, because the library module for each gateway course will be tailored to the respective track of the major, each gateway will place additional emphasis on the ACRL Framework concepts that are vital to students' success within that track. This instruction will culminate in an increased focus on information literacy practices in the capstone course:

- Information Literacy Module: Introduction to Writing Studies (WRT 329). The Writing Studies track of the major prepares students for graduate study in composition-rhetoric. For this track, students need to be prepared to engage in "Research as Inquiry"[22] by conducting primary research that is predominantly qualitative—ethnography, participant-observation, interview, survey, etc.—and conforms to standards for the ethical use of human subjects. Of particular importance in this course is the construction of "Scholarship as Conversation"; thus, the curriculum is designed to introduce students to significant and ongoing conversations within the field—including the conversations resulting from frameworks documents—demonstrate how they should situate their own research questions within that conversation, and teach them how to "evaluate contributions made by others" in the field.[23] Students in this gateway course also need to know how to conduct effective secondary research that employs peer-reviewed research studies. The major research projects in this class are, typically, a survey of the job market within the field of composition-rhetoric and a study that employs archival sources.[24] While the first project introduces students to the realities of present-day working conditions for writing faculty, the second provides them with first-hand experience analyzing "changes in scholarly perspective over time on a particular topic within" the discipline of composition-rhetoric.[25]

- Introduction to Writing for Digital Media (WRT 232). Students preparing to study in the Writing for Digital Media track of the major need to understand ethical practices for working with human subjects, and they need to recognize the value of the information they work with and be familiar with issues of copyright and fair use. Of particular importance to students studying digital media is the recognition of "Authority as Constructed and Contextual":[26] Research assignments in the Digital Media track make use of secondary sources, although students in this class may also need to conduct primary research online and make use of a broad array of peer-reviewed, authoritative sources in combination with non-peer-reviewed, popular sources. The information literacy module for this course will prepare students to be flexible researchers who recognize "Searching as Strategic Exploration"[27] and "Information Creation as a Process,"[28] and who can adapt to new and varied standards for information quality.

- Introduction to Professional Writing (WRT 331). Often, technical and professional writers are called upon to take difficult concepts from primary research sources and communicate them to lay audiences. As such, it is vital for these students to understand "Information Has Value"[29] and to recognize the information they construct may be employed differently by various users, stakeholders, and audiences. Students in this pre-professional track should recognize "Information Creation as a Process"[30] in which rhetors may be called upon to address gaps in their users' understanding, design information to simultaneously meet the needs of expert and lay audiences, and document their own creative processes. Technical and professional writers must have well-developed primary and secondary research skills. In terms of primary research, professional writers must be capable interviewers and be proficient in researching their end users and audiences. In addition, these students must be able to "articulate the purpose and distinguishing characteristics of copyright, fair use, open access, and the public domain."[31]

- Capstone Course (WRT 491). Information literacy instruction and individualized research consultations have been incorporated into the capstone course for our majors who are working on thesis projects or professional internships. Ideally, these consultations will serve to reemphasize the ACRL Framework and demonstrate the value of the concepts associated with that document to students' individual internship experiences or theses.

In addition to these larger curricular measures, our partnership includes a number of other new approaches and initiatives to be pursued in the near future. First, we plan to implement annual "shared workshops"[32] where librarians and writing and rhetoric faculty discuss research assignments, plagiarism prevention, and students' abilities to evaluate source credibility, among others. Our first shared workshop opened up a discussion between faculty in the library and in writing about current needs and future workshop topics. Second, the department of writing and rhetoric has decided to include librarians on future assessment committees, both for first-year writing and the major. This change should enable librarians to see how students employ information in their texts so they can better serve student researchers and help writing faculty to develop more effective research assignments and IL lesson plans. Finally, we plan to seek further opportunities for collaboration in research and publication.

Conclusion

A key goal for the library and the department of writing and rhetoric is to remain attuned to opportunities strengthening our existing partnership efforts and to collaborate on new endeavors. It is all too easy to stay confined within our respective institutional silos, even as important policy documents such as the *Framework for Information Literacy for Higher Education* and the *Framework for Success in Postsecondary Writing* remind us we are working toward the same intellectual and pedagogical ends. But this inclination toward insularity can prevent us from seeing opportunities to work together, such as the surprising and productive collaboration we have begun with Oakland University's writing and rhetoric major.

Appendix 8A: First-Year Writing Program Goals

The goal of the first-year writing program is to introduce students to the reading and writing of academic discourse in the context of critical thinking. In all of our first-year writing courses, we present strategies including analytic and critical reading that are useful in academic and civic writing situations. We expect students to understand they are emerging scholars involved in academic dialogue rather than reporters summarizing the experts; we encourage real research writing for a particular purpose/audience, where students engage with their topics as contributors to a discussion of key issues and ideas. This kind of academic research is a process, and the course structure and instruction should emphasize process at least equally with product. By the end of the first-year sequence of writing courses, we expect students to demonstrate the following abilities:

Rhetorical Knowledge

- understand how rhetorical contexts shape reading and writing
- analyze a writing situation in terms of audience, topic and purpose
- recognize and use a variety of technologies to address a range of audiences
- develop rhetorical strategies appropriate to context such as print, oral, visual, or digital communication
- apply these rhetorical skills to personal, academic, professional, and public writing

Critical Analysis

- use writing and reading for global and local inquiry, learning, thinking, and communicating
- understand the relationships among language, knowledge, and power in the public and political sphere
- demonstrate an ability to negotiate and integrate diverse perspectives
- read print, visual, and electronic sources analytically and critically
- understand principles of locating and evaluating information with the aid of computer technology
- complete extended research projects incorporating multiple sources to support sustained discourse for an argumentative, persuasive or critical purpose

- understand a writing assignment as a series of tasks, including finding, evaluating, analyzing, and synthesizing appropriate primary and secondary sources
- be aware it usually takes multiple drafts to create and complete a successful text, understanding writing as an open process that permits writers to use later invention and re-thinking to revise their work
- develop flexible strategies for generating, revising, editing, and proofreading
- understand the collaborative and social aspects of writing processes, including the use of online communication
- solicit and balance/integrate peer feedback but accept responsibility for one's own submitted work

Knowledge of Conventions

- frame clear and focused discourses using relevant detail and analysis
- write conventional, academically appropriate English, showing control of sentence structure, voice, tone, and diction
- meet exacting standards of form including proper citation and documentation of sources in some recognized system (MLA or APA format, e.g.)
- control such surface features as syntax, grammar, punctuation, and spelling, as appropriate for the rhetorical context
- understand how conventions are affected by shifting from print to visual to digital modes of communication
- use both words and images to construct and critique arguments and convey knowledge

Appendix 8B: Course-Specific Learning Objectives for First-Year Writing

WRT 102: Basic Writing

- approach writing as a multi-step, recursive process requiring feedback
- compose their texts to address the rhetorical situation
- demonstrate an ability to synthesize information/ideas in and between various texts—written, spoken, and visual
- reflect on their own writing processes and evaluate their own learning
- adapt their prior knowledge and learning strategies to a variety of new writing and reading situations in college and beyond
- develop the habits of mind of effective college writers and readers

WRT 104: Supervised Study

- interpret the rhetorical situation (audience, context, purpose) a writing assignment asks students to address
- identify the requirements of a specific writing assignment
- use a variety of techniques to generate ideas and to draft, organize, revise, edit, and reflect on their writing
- recognize and correct patterns of error in standard edited English that interfere with or distort meaning
- produce academic prose that demonstrates an understanding of college-level argumentation (or other course-specific writing tasks)

WRT 150: Composition I

- analyze rhetorical situations (writer, text, context, purpose, audience) in a variety of genres and media
- define and enact appropriate rhetorical strategies, including kairos, ethos, logos, pathos, to communicate ideas in a variety of genres
- apply rhetorical knowledge to gain a better understanding of a professional discourse community
- develop strategies for reading rhetorically, evaluating, and respond-

ing to a variety of texts, including visual, electronic, written and verbal texts
- reflect on their own writing processes, evaluate their own learning, transfer and adapt their learning to new settings, and develop the habits of mind of effective college writers
- employ writing as a process of making meaning, requiring multiple drafts and revisions
- demonstrate syntactic fluency and control of language conventions, including awareness of sentence and paragraph structure
- exhibit accurate use of and rhetorical purpose for documentation systems, generally MLA

WRT 160: Composition II

- make connections with the broader community through activities related to civic and community engagement on and/or off campus
- demonstrate familiarity with basic rhetorical, ethical, and methodological conventions of academic disciplines (such as humanities, sciences, social sciences) to prepare them for further study in their chosen discipline
- demonstrate the ability to locate and analyze scholarly sources critically and synthesize them to produce various academic genres which include print, visual, digital, or oral elements

In addition to reinforcing the outcomes from WRT 150, WRT 160 will instill in students a basic understanding of:
- primary research methods (quantitative and qualitative) appropriate for academic scholarship
- secondary research strategies for locating and evaluating sources both through library databases and through external online databases appropriate for academic scholarship
- ethical considerations in academic scholarship, including responsibility to human subjects, non-biased use of language, fair and accurate use of sources, appropriate documentation, and larger rhetorical purposes of civic engagement
- stylistic conventions for integrating secondary and primary research to arrive at new knowledge in academic disciplines, including familiarity with APA format

Notes

1. Rolf Norgaard, "Writing Information Literacy: Contributions to a Concept," *Reference and User Services Quarterly* 43, no. 2 (2003): 124.
2. Melissa Bowles-Terry, Erin Davis, and Wendy Holliday, "'Writing Information Literacy' Revisited: Application of Theory to Practice in the Classroom," *Reference and User Services Quarterly* 49, no. 3 (2010): 225.
3. Felicia Chong and Jim Nugent, "A New Major in the Shadow of the Past: The Professional Writing Track at Oakland University," *Programmatic Perspectives* 7, no. 2 (2015): 173.
4. Lori Ostergaard and Greg A. Giberson, "Unifying Program Goals: Developing and Implementing a Writing and Rhetoric Major at Oakland University," *Composition Forum* 22 (2010), http://compositionforum.com/issue/22/oakland.php, paragraph 3.
5. Chong and Nugent, "A New Major," 177.
6. See Appendix 8A.
7. See Appendix 8B.
8. William B. Lalicker, "A Basic Introduction to Basic Writing Program Structures: A Baseline and Five Alternatives," *Basic Writing eJournal* 1, no. 2 (1999), http://bwe.ccny.cuny.edu/Issue%201.2.html#bill, paragraph 3.
9. Shawna Shapiro, "Stuck in the Remediation Rut: Confronting Resistance to ESL Curriculum Reform," *Journal of Basic Writing* 30, no. 2 (2011): 42.
10. Mike Rose, "The Positive Purpose of Remediation: Getting to the Core of Higher Education," *About Campus* 14, no. 5 (2009): 4.
11. Association of College and Research Libraries, *Information Literacy Competency Standards for Higher Education*, 2000, http://ww.ala.org/acrl/sites/ala.org.acrl/files/content/issues/infolit/Framework_ILHE.pdf.
12. Katie Greer, Amanda Nichols Hess, and Elizabeth W. Kraemer, "The Librarian Leading the Machine: A Reassessment of Library Instruction Methods," *College & Research Libraries* (2016): forthcoming.
13. Association of College and Research Libraries, *Framework for Information Literacy for Higher Education*, 2015, http://www.ala.org/acrl/standards/ilframework.
14. Lori Ostergaard and D.R. Hammontree, ed. *Grizz Writes: A Guide to First-Year Writing at Oakland University*. (Southlake, TX: Fountainhead Press, 2015).
15. Department of Writing and Rhetoric, "WRT Major Assessment Report," (Report, Oakland University, 2014), 10.
16. Ibid., 11.
17. Ibid., 11.
18. Ibid., 4.
19. Committee on the Major in Rhetoric and Composition, "Writing Majors at a Glance," *Conference on College Composition and Communication,* 2009, http://www.ncte.org/library/NCTEFiles/Groups/CCCC/Committees/Writing_Majors_Final.pdf.
20. Alison J. Head and John Wihbey, "At Sea in a Deluge of Data," *The Chronicle of Higher Education* 60, no. 41 (July 18, 2014), http://www.chronicle.com/article/At-Sea-in-a-Deluge-of-Data/147477, paragraph 10.
21. James K. Elmborg, "Locating the Center: Libraries, Writing Centers, and Information Literacy," *Writing Lab Newsletter* 30, no. 6 (2006), 7.
22. ACRL, Framework, 7.

23. Ibid., 8.
24. Lori Ostergaard, "Working with Disciplinary Artifacts: An Introductory Writing Studies Class for Writing Majors," *Composition Studies* 43, no. 2 (2015).
25. ACRL, Framework, 8.
26. Ibid., 4.
27. Ibid., 9.
28. Ibid., 5.
29. Ibid., 6.
30. Ibid., 5.
31. Ibid., 6.
32. Elmborg, "Locating the Center," 11.

Bibliography

Association of College and Research Libraries. 2016. *Framework for Information Literacy for Higher Education*. Accessed October 19, 2015. http://www.ala.org/acrl/standards/ilframework.

Association of College and Research Libraries. 2000. *Information Literacy Competency Standards for Higher Education*. Accessed October 19, 2015. http://www.ala.org/acrl/standards/informationliteracycompetency.

Bowles-Terry, Melissa, Erin Davis, and Wendy Holliday. "'Writing Information Literacy' Revisited: Application of Theory to Practice in the Classroom." *Reference and User Services Quarterly* 49, no. 3 (2010): 225–230.

Chong, Felicia, and Jim Nugent. "A New Major in the Shadow of the Past: The Professional Writing Track at Oakland University." *Programmatic Perspectives* 7, no. 2 (2015): 173–188.

Committee on the Major in Rhetoric and Composition. "Writing Majors at a Glance." *Conference on College Composition and Communication*. 2009. Accessed July 27, 2010. http://www.ncte.org/library/NCTEFiles/Groups/CCCC/Committees/Writing_Majors_Final.pdf.

Council of Writing Program Administrators, National Council of Teachers of English, and National Writing Project. 2011. *Framework for Success in Postsecondary Writing*. http://www.wpacouncil.org/files/framework-for-success-postsecondary-writing.pdf.

Council of Writing Program Administrators. *WPA Outcomes Statement for First-Year Composition (v3.0)*. 2014. http://wpacouncil.org/files/WPA%20Outcomes%20Statement%20Adopted%20Revisions%5B1%5D_0.pdf.

Department of Writing and Rhetoric. "WRT Major Assessment Report." Report, Oakland University, December 1, 2014.

Elmborg, James K. "Locating the Center: Libraries, Writing Centers, and Information Literacy." *Writing Lab Newsletter* 30, no. 6 (2006): 7–11.

Greer, Katie, Amanda Nichols Hess, and Elizabeth W. Kraemer. "The Librarian Leading the Machine: A Reassessment of Library Instruction Methods." *College & Research Libraries* (2016): forthcoming.

Head, Alison J., and John Wihbey. "At Sea in a Deluge of Data." *The Chronicle of Higher Education* 60, no. 41 (July 18, 2014). Accessed October 31, 2015. http://www.chronicle.com/article/At-Sea-in-a-Deluge-of-Data/147477.

Lalicker, William B. "A Basic Introduction to Basic Writing Program Structures: A Baseline and Five Alternatives." *Basic Writing eJournal* 1, no. 2 (1999). Accessed January 24, 2014. http://bwe.ccny.cuny.edu/Issue%201.2.html.

Norgaard, Rolf. "Writing Information Literacy: Contributions to a Concept." *Reference and User Services Quarterly* 43, no. 2 (2003): 124–130.

Ostergaard, Lori, and D.R. Hammontree, ed. *Grizz Writes: A Guide to First-Year Writing at Oakland University*. Southlake, TX: Fountainhead Press, 2015.

Ostergaard, Lori, and Greg A. Giberson. "Unifying Program Goals: Developing and Implementing a Writing and Rhetoric Major at Oakland University." *Composition Forum* 22 (2010). http://www.compositionforum.com/issue/22/oakland.php.

Ostergaard, Lori. "Working with Disciplinary Artifacts: An Introductory Writing Studies Class for Writing Majors." *Composition Studies* 43, no. 2 (2015): 150–171.

Rose, Mike. "The Positive Purpose of Remediation: Getting to the Core of Higher Education." *About Campus* 14, no. 5 (2009): 2–4.

Shapiro, Shawna. "Stuck in the Remediation Rut: Confronting Resistance to ESL Curriculum Reform." *Journal of Basic Writing* 30, no. 2 (2011): 24–52. http://files.eric.ed.gov/fulltext/EJ988209.pdf.

CHAPTER 9

Metaliteracy in the Digital Landscape:

Using Wikipedia for Research-Writing Across the Curriculum

Theresa Burress, Maribeth Clark, Sarah
Hernandez, and Nova Myhill
New College of Florida

Introduction

Twenty-first century college students have been exposed to electronic media from a young age, and K–12 schools now regularly teach children how to create multimedia presentations. Although most students are taught about the reliability of information available electronically, their information literacy skills are not fully matured by the time they enroll in college, in part because the scope of information literacy continues to evolve and expand. In 2013, the United Nations Educational, Scientific and Cultural Organization (UNESCO) clarified their definition of information literacy to include media literacy in an attempt to acknowledge new opportunities and challenges presented by the vast digital ecosystem. UNESCO now defines media and information literacy as "a set of competencies that empowers citizens to access, retrieve, understand, evaluate and use, create, as well as share information and media content in all formats, using various tools, in a critical, ethical and effective way, in order to participate and engage in personal, professional and societal activities."[1] Such a definition suggests our highest societal ideals may be out of reach for those who lack information literacy skills, equating the acquisition of such skills with the power to participate effectively in democratic processes. If UNESCO's definition and goals are taken seriously, then it seems to us that undergraduate students need support not only to write well and understand the use of evidence, but also to collaborate with others to produce and share content across the digital landscape.

We believe Wikipedia is a resource that teachers should use toward the end goal of information literacy today. As most people with access to the Internet know, Wikipedia is a free, web-based encyclopedia written by a community of volunteers using collaborative wiki technology.[2] With more than five million articles in the English-language Wikipedia, as well as several million more articles written in 290 different languages,[3] Wikipedia has become the largest encyclopedia in the world,[4,5] a ubiquitous resource consulted by millions of people.[6] Wikipedia operates under a set of principles called the five pillars, which guide volunteer author and editor contributions as follows: (1) it is an encyclopedia, (2) its content is written from a neutral point of view, (3) content is free to use, edit, or distribute, (4) editors treat each other with civility and respect, and (5) there are no firm rules.[7]

The advent and growth of Wikipedia presents professors and researchers with new challenges, some of which we also see as opportunities. Since Wikipedia is free to anyone with Internet access, it is globally accessible. Because its contributors are not limited to formally-recognized experts, articles can be authored and edited by anyone. Although these inclusive conditions pose a challenge to academic authority, academe has begun to adapt to and engage with Wikipedia, in part because as participation in the wiki grows, the value of its shared knowledge increases, as do the stakes for those who do not know how to evaluate its content.

Because the principles underlying the five pillars of Wikipedia align closely with the concepts outlined in the *Framework for Information Literacy for Higher Education*[8] and *The Framework for Success in Postsecondary Writing*[9] (see table 9.01), Wikipedia serves as a platform with which students can develop research and writing skills, and become metaliterate[10,11] citizens. While in many colleges and universities, librarians advance information literacy primarily through one-shot workshops taught in first-year composition courses, faculty and librarians at New College of Florida have been experimenting with Wikipedia-based coursework suitable to the learning environment of a small liberal arts college. In this chapter, we share our experience with a collaborative approach to information literacy where librarians and faculty offer Wikipedia-based course assignments and projects tailored to the needs of individual courses within various subject disciplines.

Table 9.01
Key Principles Underlying the Five Pillars of Wikipedia as Mapped to Similar Principles in the Frameworks

Wikipedia Tenets*	ACRL Framework**	WPA Framework***
"Wiki" technology; talk pages	Scholarship as Conversation	Engagement: Make connections between their own ideas and those of others
Free: Respect copyright; no plagiarism	Information Has Value	Responsibility: Give credit to others' ideas
Identify information gaps	Research as Inquiry	Curiosity: Use inquiry as a process to develop questions
No original research; verifiability	Searching as Strategic Exploration	Openness: Practice different ways of gathering, investigating information
Neutral point of view; use credible sources	Authority is Constructed and Contextual	Flexibility: Conventions are dependent upon discipline and context
Synthesize and summarize; Be bold! Revert! Discuss!	Information Creation as a Process	Creativity: Take risk by exploring new questions, topics, ideas

* Wikimedia Foundation, "Wikipedia: Five Pillars."

** Association of College and Research Libraries, *Framework for Information Literacy for Higher Education*.

*** Council of Writing Program Administrators, National Council of Teachers of English, *Framework for Success in Postsecondary Writing*.

Case Studies

New College of Florida is a small, public, liberal arts honors college offering its students the option of taking introductory courses in a variety of disciplines designed to develop skills in critical inquiry, including intensive research-writing projects. While one-shot library instruction sessions are developed for introductory courses in some disciplines, a small group of faculty coordinated with a librarian, one trained as the campus Wikipedia ambassador, to experiment with using Wikipedia as a means to introduce information literacy skills.

While New College faculty recognize media and information literacy are important components of twenty-first century university training, it is a challenge to integrate skills-based instruction such as a library workshop into limited classroom time without sacrificing content. However, as faculty adopt teaching practices emphasizing active learning, Wikipedia provides a platform offering students the opportunity to engage in the process of information creation, including meaningful dialog with each other and the world outside of the college. In addition, the range of subjects covered is broad enough to address a wide variety of disciplines and interests of faculty, allowing for the development of transferable skills while being flexible enough to accommodate the diverse scope and pedagogical approach of each course.

During the 2014–2015 academic year, professors teaching introductory courses in music, literature, and sociology each offered assignments requiring students to contribute to Wikipedia. In addition, the humanities librarian was the instructor of record for three students who chose to contribute to Wikipedia as the focus of their Independent Study Projects (ISPs) during the January inter-term. For each Wikipedia assignment and ISP, the librarian conducted one or more workshops where the intended learning outcomes were for students to:

- become familiar with the five pillars of Wikipedia
- communicate with fellow Wikipedians via talk pages
- begin adding content to Wikipedia using WikiCode

One benefit of using Wikipedia to teach metaliteracy[12,13] skills is many students are familiar with Wikipedia and thus positive about the idea of contributing content, even if they are unfamiliar with the technical aspects of WikiCode. In an informal poll of the fifteen–twenty students in each course, every student reported they knew of Wikipedia and had used it as a resource prior to the assignment. A series of national studies titled Project Information Literacy,[14] which investigates the information-seeking behavior of college students, shows Wikipedia to be the fifth most heavily used resource for students doing course-related work. For everyday life research, Wikipedia moves up into the number two spot (84 percent), second only to search engines (95 percent), including Google. Despite their familiarity with and dependence on the resource, few students in the courses reported having edited Wikipedia and fewer had active accounts prior to the assignment.

In the following sections, we describe the course projects using Wikipedia and reflect on the faculty experience and that of their students.

Contemplating Bias, Documenting Sources

In Music and the Environment, a first- and second-year writing course focused on sound and place, the professor used the Wikipedia pillar and core content policy of neutral point of view as the entry point for students to make a contribution to Wikipedia. As information on this pillar explains, "[A]rticles must not take sides, but should explain the sides, fairly and without editorial bias."[15] In other words, the neutral point of view invites synthesis and summary. These concepts, found in the column Wikipedia Tenets in table 9.01, relate to the Association of College & Research Librarians' "Information Creation as a Process" frame,[16] as well as the risk-taking involved in creativity by exploring new questions, topics, and ideas, a habit of mind articulated by the Council of Writing Program Administrators' (WPA) Framework.[17] Unbiased synthesis and summary are two difficult types of writing college students should master as part of the larger project of academic writing, which often involves, in contrast to writing for Wikipedia, taking a position. Before students make a claim, however, they need to explore their options and have some mastery of content. Writing for Wikipedia, then, can represent a type of writing appropriate to the early stages of research, where students gain an understanding of a subject through describing it in prose and documenting the source.

The following describes two different structures for student contributions to Wikipedia, both of which benefited from the support of New College's humanities librarian, who serves as the campus Wikipedia ambassador. In the first example, students chose the article of their focus and worked independently on the writing. In the second, the class worked together on one article to which all students contributed while working in pairs and small groups. In both situations, the librarian provided an introduction to the structure and coding language of Wikipedia, use of the sandbox as a place to experiment, and use of the citation generator for footnotes. She was also available for individual consultation as students experienced difficulties.

The first time Wikipedia was integrated into this course, with the guiding premise of neutrality in mind, it was described as an exercise in descriptive writing. Students were asked to find a Wikipedia article related to a reading assigned for the course. It could be about an author of one of the articles, a piece of music or a genre, a performer or composer, or a concept. Once students chose a topic, they drafted an informal, low-stakes analysis of the existing article articulating its positive qualities as well as what aspects needed improvement and what gaps could be filled. After completing this analysis, they re-drafted the article with changes and citation of the material on which they drew.

The class had some success with the assignment. One student focused on "listening," an article on the physiology of the ear and how we hear. She added a new Wikipedia page on the topic to address what Roland Barthes has called "listening as a psychological act."[18] Two other students, staying with the spirit of the class but finding information outside of the assigned readings to enhance their article, added information to Wikipedia about the sounds of animals—one focusing on the cry of the common loon and the other on the bellowing of the American alligator—information that had not been addressed in the Wikipedia articles as they originally found them. A number of students were drawn to articles on genres of popular music, such as glitch, or artists who create noise music, like Masami Akita.

Not all members of the class were successful in their contributions. One student contributed to the Wikipedia article on "silence" and saw all her work eliminated as the original author, an experienced and committed Wikipedian, scrubbed her additions from the page. Students also found ways to avoid the assignment by editing the prose without contributing to the content, or by adding a works list to an article about a sound artist rather than revising the body of the article. In all cases, students observed the workings of the online community, had an opportunity to engage in information creation as a process, and gained, as a result, a more nuanced appreciation of the encyclopedia's strengths and weaknesses.

The assignment was subsequently revised to better capture the essence of collaborative authorship the Wikipedian community embodies and to model the community of Wikipedians on a local scale. During fall 2015, all students contributed to the same article: "sound studies." Jonathan Sterne's *The Sound Studies Reader* (SSR),[19] an eclectic collection of readings on this interdisciplinary subject, served as the basis of the assignment. The publication consists of forty-four readings organized into six sections. Sterne provided an overarching introduction to the volume and a brief introduction to each of the six sections. Students formed teams of two or three and collaborated on the construction of six new sections for the article, each corresponding to a section of the reader, and a revision of the introduction to the article. The final outcome lacked polish, but the class enriched the list of citations for further reading, and added three new subsections to the discussion.

Three groups did not feel brave enough to post their work; this reflected fear and anxiety over the process that surprised us. We had hoped envisioning Wikipedia as an audience for their writing would make the task of summarizing more meaningful and purposeful. Perhaps for some students it did. For another group, however, prone to anxiety over their writing, they were frozen by the prospect of public display of their work.

These Wikipedia assignments continue to evolve as we learn to model the outcomes we want for our students and trust in students' capacity to engage successfully with each other and with Wikipedia as a platform. Considering what is meant by neutral point of view and relating it to verifiability and the prohibition against original research (i.e., content that does not advance a position) becomes the measure of good summary, effective description, appropriate documentation, and a good encyclopedia article.

An assignment that asks students to contribute to Wikipedia can put them in a position of power. It stands as an invitation to find something wrong, or if not wrong, to identify information gaps and weaknesses. This activity models the information literacy frame "Research as Inquiry,"[20] where the real work of scholars takes place: evaluating the state of the scholarship, albeit on a small scale, and working to improve its representation on the web. Working with Wikipedia moves the student from writing for a professor to writing for the sake of providing people access to information. Summarizing can seem like busywork as a small, stand-alone assignment; when the summary contributes a missing point of view to a Wikipedia article, though, the parameters of the activity become more meaningful, more representative of a community of scholars learning as they share knowledge, an element of the "Scholarship as Conversation" frame.[21,22] The hard part of this process is supporting students as they accept this power and encouraging them to take a risk and engage fearlessly in creation. This process involves taking risks, and not all students are prepared to take these risks. For those who can be persuaded to join the community of Wikipedians, who accept the challenges of contributing to a community of volunteer information-constructors, the rewards can be great.

Student Engagement in a Survey Course

At first glance, an introductory twentieth-century British and American drama course is a peculiar fit for a Wikipedia-based assignment. Where Wikipedia requires a neutral point of view, the main goal of this course is to teach students how to write essays that make and support debatable claims. Where Wikipedia expects its contributors to rely primarily on secondary sources, this course emphasizes close work with primary sources, substantially to the exclusion of secondary criticism. And a survey course, with its mandate to cover a century or more of work in one semester, is the type of course in which the necessity of presenting an enormous amount of content creates a significant barrier to a skills-based assignment that would take away, at minimum, two class periods from that content. Despite these challenges, developing a Wikipedia assignment for this course offered a way to strengthen student engagement in "Scholarship as Conversation"[23] by requiring participation in various scholarly communities. The assignment also required beginning students to develop the research skills, specifically by "determining the credibility of sources"[24] and making effective use of secondary sources to synthesize ideas[25] that are crucial to their academic success.

The starting point was the vast amount of relevant material the class does not cover. In previous iterations, each student was required to research a major playwright whose work was not covered in the class and present a short oral report on the significance of that playwright in the context of one or two of the assigned plays. The goal was not only to increase the range of authors with which the class gained some familiarity, but, more importantly, to have students teach each other and allow them to occupy a position of expertise. In practice it's very hard to become an expert, even for five minutes, on something you haven't been taught, particularly when you don't know how to find the right kind of sources. Therefore, restructuring this assignment to center around editing a Wikipedia entry was appealing on several levels. First, the students used Wikipedia regularly as a point of entry when researching a new topic, but most of them had been instructed previously that Wikipedia is not a reliable source and should not be treated as an authority the way scholarly essays or traditional print encyclopedia entries are. Second, because of its collaborative authorship, individual Wikipedia entries vary widely in quality and, more importantly, some fields have better coverage than others. Wikipedia coverage on contemporary drama, particularly coverage specific to the content of this course, is generally very weak, which offers a number of important pedagogical opportunities. To these ends, the Wikipedia assignment for this course was an attempt to improve the students' research skills in a context that tied library instruction to a specific assignment. Students actively practiced "Information Creation as a Process"[26] by contributing to the authoring information on drama available to Wikipedia users.

The first part of the assignment was for students to select an appropriate Wikipedia entry on drama to revise. Students chose a playwright from the list the professor had used to assign oral report subjects in the earlier iteration of the assignment, and then went to Wikipedia and found an entry on a play by that author that could easily be improved. The students examined and compared multiple entries to determine what a successful article, by Wikipedia's editorial standards, looked like, and mostly avoided the small number of extremely famous works that had comprehensive entries. Instead, most students chose articles specifically flagged as needing additional sources or verification; some chose articles that were not flagged but lacked a section, such as "production history" or "reception" that other articles had. Two students attempted to create new entries for plays mentioned in the Wikipedia entry for a specific playwright, but which lacked their own articles. Looking at a range of articles with the goal of determining deficiencies, identifying information gaps, and finding suitable models helped the students to approach Wikipedia (and hopefully other sources as well) with the evaluative mindset described in the "Research as Inquiry" frame.[27] Starting with entries that failed to meet Wikipedia's own standards helped the students to see scholarship as a conversation in which they could participate.

While the idea of scholarship as conversation can be abstract to undergraduates, Wikipedia's talk pages literalize this concept. After the students chose their articles for revision and created their accounts, the librarian spent a class session training them to use the talk pages and their sandboxes, where most of the work of the assignment was completed. Because the assignment goals centered on research and content rather than style, students were not required to publish their revisions. Instead, the professor and students engaged in peer review and evaluation, using the Wikipedia sandboxes available within each editor account. The professor's criteria for evaluation were timeliness, accuracy, readability, and utility, which match up with Wikipedia's own principles (see table 9.01). Ultimately, the sandbox served as a safe space for students to experiment and to collaborate by peer reviewing one another's work using the associated talk pages. This form of collaboration was important in giving students a specific context for their research as well as a better understanding of scholarship as conversation.

The guidelines provided to students for revising their selected Wikipedia entries were very loose, but the one hard and fast requirement was to add two references. As a tertiary source, Wikipedia serves to point readers to diverse sources of information, and locating additional sources is a basic skill in information literacy. This task was a relatively easy way for students to add value to the entries, and it was a simple illustration of how their contributions improved the entry. We encouraged students to publish their revisions if they were so inclined, and some did, with mixed results. The assignment's focus on scholarship as a conversation and information creation as a process made use of Wikipedia's tools to allow students to easily share their research in process within the classroom community, but did not emphasize Wikipedia's larger community and readership as the arbiters of the value of the research; to do so would have placed undue emphasis on what was a relatively small assignment in the larger scheme of the course.

It is worth thinking about how working with Wikipedia is both compatible and incompatible with the goals of a course that is already pulling in two directions—the content-based period survey of literature and the skills-based introductory writing course. One concern with adding assignments with significant technical components not directly related to course content is that working out these aspects of assignments takes time that would otherwise be spent working with primary sources. Many faculty members find the idea of incorporating work with Wikipedia into their courses attractive, but they have not tried to do so due to concerns about the time involved. Almost all training on our campus is provided by the librarian, supplemented by Wikipedia's own very usable online tutorials; all the professor needs to do is guide the process and evaluate the results, but we should not underestimate the amount of time required to so. This relatively small assignment has a timeline that stretches from the second to the final week of the semester and includes the dedication of two full class periods, which has the effect of giving it prominence far out of proportion with its significance in the course as a whole.

Developing Writing Skills for Global Citizens

Our next example is drawn from a work organization course where students learn about various expressions of economic democracy. The Professor determined a Wikipedia project would encourage students to strengthen their research-writing skills, as well as the synthesizing skills that were the focus of the course. The assignment has now been attempted twice, first in 2013 and second in 2015. In addition to the content, students learn to weave various scholars' work into a cohesive piece with a central thesis; the skill is developed through four short essays written throughout the semester. In each essay, students are expected to select a topic from the previous month's readings and weave the various authors' research to address one topic. By the time the students write their final research project, they had developed the synthesizing skills necessary for the Wikipedia entry.

Students were instructed to conduct research on a specific topic of their choosing and contribute such knowledge to Wikipedia. Students were guided throughout various steps in the research process: identifying their topic and narrowing it down by the second week; submitting an initial bibliography by the fourth week; presenting an initial report of their findings mid-semester; presenting their findings to the class three weeks before the end of the semester; and submitting the final work at the end of the semester. In 2015, a step was added between choosing the topic and gathering the bibliography, where students had to identify whether or not there were information gaps in Wikipedia regarding their topic. This exercise taught students how to identify gaps in existing information and ascertained that all students could contribute various strands of new information. Students' topics ranged from the experiences in workers' councils in Germany, unionization of sex workers in the U.S., cooperatives in various parts of the world and in different time periods, to the Kibbutz and other forms of communal economic organizations.

The Wikipedia exercise as designed addresses all elements of the WPA Framework. Curiosity and creativity are a part of the process of identifying their research topic. Seeking various information sources (openness), recognizing authorship (responsibility), and seeing the way the various sources are in conversation (engagement) are a part of their research-writing process. In addition, students see the benefits of an interdisciplinary approach to understand the content (flexibility).[28] As noted later, the skills described in the ACRL Framework[29] are also developed through this exercise.

In the early part of the semester, students received instructions on the Wikipedia project and were taught how to sign up for a Wikipedia account. In the second week of the course, the librarian offered a workshop on Wikipedia, explaining to students the process of writing their drafts in the sandbox, the process of posting the editions into Wikipedia, the various parts of each Wikipedia page, and the general approach to writing a Wikipedia entry. Students were informed the librarian was their resource person for all technical questions regarding the Wikipedia project in addition to offering guidance in the research for content.

We developed a Wikipedia course page and students signed up for it. Students could choose to have a login name that preserved their anonymity in the Wikipedia community. Because they had to sign up for the course, we were able to keep track of their contributions to Wikipedia. Students' contributions were evaluated on the basis of the modifications and additions offered to the Wikipedia pages. The first time around, we dedicated fifteen minutes of class time to the initial introduction to Wikipedia, where our librarian explained how to create a Wikipedia account. A week later, we dedicated a entire class period so the librarian could explain the principles of Wikipedia[30] and its technical aspects. After that, students continued to consult with the librarian to have their technical and research challenges addressed.

In both iterations, students appeared to gain a fairly nuanced understanding of the possibilities and limitations of Wikipedia as a source of information. During the course of their projects, students discovered broken links to cited sources, the need for more supportive evidence and for greater scope in the information being offered, the challenges in determining the title of each article, and the difficulties in handling the various terms used to refer to their topics and subtopics. In addition, in order to learn about their topics, they had to engage in the more traditional approach to gathering academic information. With guidance from librarians, they identified the most useful search engines and search terms and found reliable sources. In order to upload their information into Wikipedia, students also had to become acquainted with basic coding and the technical framework of Wikipedia.

In various ways, students were able to use their synthesizing skills. Students used their sources to strengthen the reliability of the information contained in the existing entries, modified sections to better match the academic literature's findings, and offered paragraphs with new information arising from their research. They wrote more extensive syntheses of their findings in the encyclopedic style of Wikipedia, filling the gaps they had identified earlier. It was evident the four earlier essays served as good exercise for the final Wikipedia entry, as their contributions brought together nicely their various sources into a unified and cohesive story. In order to do this, students strengthened their critical thinking skills, assessing what was important and relevant to share. In the process, students came to understand the rules guiding the encyclopedic writing expected in Wikipedia.

This exercise also gave students the opportunity to strengthen their skills in the frames of information literacy. As they selected a topic and explored the gaps in Wikipedia, they came to see "Research as Inquiry."[31] To gain the knowledge necessary to fill these gaps, students learned to identify reliable academic sources. With the support of our librarians, they learned to search strategically,[32] identifying the more relevant search engines and sources. Since they needed to synthesize their findings and share them in Wikipedia's global world, they became aware of the fact that scholarship is a conversation[33] among these researchers and that "Authority is Constructed and Contextual."[34] Because their syntheses needed to have the supportive evidence and hence cite their sources, students' awareness that "Information has Value"[35] was reinforced. Their contributions to Wikipedia made them aware the creation of information involves a careful scientific process. Furthermore, through their contributions in Wikipedia, students learned how to produce and share knowledge in a collaborative fashion.

Through this assignment, students in this course have come to understand being part of their society, both locally and globally, they can be sources of knowledge through information resources such as Wikipedia.

Supporting Research-Writing through Independent Study Projects

As these fall Wikipedia assignments progressed, the librarian successfully put forward a proposal to act as the instructor of record for an Independent Study Project (ISP) course called "Become a Wikipedian" during the January 2015 inter-term. Three students signed up, and she used the previous assignments from the other courses discussed in this chapter as models to develop a standalone course[36] on Wikipedia. They met as a group three times: the first week for a Wikipedia workshop, the second week for a library research workshop, and then for a final meeting where the students presented their contributions and reflected on the process. As the librarian prepared for these workshops, she engaged with the draft ACRL Framework and modified the workshop discussion to connect the "Scholarship as Conversation" frame[37] with the collaborative editing process generally, and with regard to the talk pages specifically. The process of information creation and the "Research as Inquiry" frame[38] fit nicely into the subsequent discussion of how the students would identify information gaps and thus improve their articles. The library workshop was an opportunity to delve more deeply into the "Searching as Strategic Exploration" frame,[39] as the group discussed the importance of using different strategies depending upon the scope and search capabilities of each research database.

Because the intent of the ISP is for students to work independently, and because the students were each working in completely separate disciplines, the peer review aspect of this project was not very successful. However, because of the small size of the group, the Wikipedia Education Program staff offered to assist in reviewing the student contributions before they were published, and this review gave the students excellent editorial feedback regarding their contributions.

Conclusion: Outcomes and Assessment Possibilities

These examples show teachers, librarians, and students using Wikipedia in significantly different ways, emphasizing varying aspects of information literacy. The range of learning objectives these assignments support suggests the flexibility of this type of assignment, which can be applied in a broad range of disciplines across the curriculum. At the same time, each of these assignments and projects contain common interests and goals achieved with diverse approaches. Strengthening research skills is a key learning outcome pursued in all assignments and projects, with students charged with evaluating article quality, identifying information gaps and appropriate resources to fill those gaps, and developing a sense of "Research as Inquiry."[40] Strengthening writing skills is another key learning outcome of the Wikipedia course assignments, and concepts from the WPA Framework will be incorporated into the next Independent Study Project. The assignments and projects also provided opportunities to experience collaboration and peer review in different ways: via interaction amongst the students, feedback from the broader Wikipedian community, or review by the Wikipedia Education Program staff.

The shift college students make from being primarily consumers of information to becoming producers and disseminators of knowledge is central to their education. Dedicated classroom time, such as in the sequenced workshops described in this chapter, is necessary to address the metaliteracy skills relevant to the discipline-specific goals of each course. Wikipedia, as a collaboratively produced work, offers an experimental model for creating public knowledge, the benefits of which appear to outweigh the sacrifice of the small amount of content each course has traded for it.

Other benefits related to this experience have to do with communication. As faculty involved with this process, we have shared assignments with one another and benefited from the experience of feedback from each other. As faculty connecting with our librarian colleague, we have supported her in the development of her instruction, providing her information about our goals that may make it possible for future information literacy instruction to be more focused and effective over time. Furthermore, it becomes possible to see commonalities and to contribute to the development of student learning outcomes for general education that cut across disciplines.

As a platform for collaboration and experimentation, Wikipedia's mission and operating principles align nicely to advance the global definition of information literacy, as well as the ACRL and WPA Frameworks in their expanded goals of developing savvy information consumers and information creators engaged in the context of the global community.

Notes

1.   UNESCO, *Global Media and Information Literacy Assessment Framework: Country Readiness and Competencies*, 29.
2.   Leuf and Cunningham, *The Wiki Way: Quick Collaboration on the Web*.
3.   Wikimedia Foundation, "Wikipedia: About."
4.   Dalby, *The World and Wikipedia: How We Are Editing Reality*, 42.
5.   Wikimedia Foundation, "Wikipedia Statistics: Words."
6.   Wikimedia Foundation, "Wikimedia Report Card."
7.   Wikimedia Foundation, "Wikipedia: Five Pillars."
8.   ACRL, Framework.
9.   WPA, Framework.
10. Mackey and Jacobson, "Reframing Information Literacy as a Meta Literacy."
11. Mackey and Jacobson, *Metaliteracy: Reinventing Information Literacy to Empower Learners*.
12. Mackey and Jacobson, "Reframing Information Literacy as a Meta Literacy."
13. Mackey and Jacobson, *Metaliteracy: Reinventing Information Literacy to Empower Learners*.
14. Head, "Project Information Literacy: What Can Be Learned about the Information-Seeking Behavior of Today's College Students?" 477–478.
15. Wikimedia Foundation, "Wikipedia: Neutral Point of View."
16. ACRL, Framework, 5.
17. WPA, Framework, 4–5.
18. Barthes, "Listening," 245.
19. Sterne, *The Sound Studies Reader*.
20. ACRL, Framework, 7.
21. Heidi Jacobs has written that the challenge to using Wikipedia for teaching information literacy lies in casting it as a problem, with which students then engage. See Jacobs "Posing the Wikipedia 'Problem': Information Literacy and the Praxis of Problem-Posing in Library Instruction."
22. ACRL, Framework, 8.
23. Ibid.
24. Ibid., 4.
25. Ibid., 7.
26. Ibid., 5.
27. Ibid., 7.
28. WPA, Framework, 4–5.

29. ACRL, Framework.
30. Wikimedia Foundation, "Wikipedia: Five Pillars."
31. ACRL, Framework, 7.
32. Ibid., 9.
33. Ibid., 8.
34. Ibid., 4.
35. Ibid., 6.
36. See the archived Wikipedia course page: https://en.wikipedia.org/wiki/Education_Program:New_College_of_Florida/Become_a_Wikipedian_(January_2015).
37. Ibid., 8.
38. Ibid., 7.
39. Ibid., 9.
40. Ibid., 7.

Bibliography

Association of College and Research Libraries. *Framework for Information Literacy for Higher Education*, 2016. Accessed March 1, 2016. http://www.ala.org/acrl/sites/ala.org.acrl/files/content/issues/infolit/Framework_ILHE.pdf.

Barthes, Roland. "Listening." In *The Responsibility of Forms*, 245–60. New York: Hill and Wang, 1985.

Council of Writing Program Administrators, National Council of Teachers of English, and National Writing Project. *Framework for Success in Postsecondary Writing*, 2011. Accessed March 1, 2016. http://www.wpacouncil.org/files/framework-for-success-postsecondary-writing.pdf.

Dalby, Andrew. *The World and Wikipedia: How We Are Editing Reality*. Draycott: Siduri Books, 2009.

Head, Alison J. "Project Information Literacy: What Can Be Learned about the Information-Seeking Behavior of Today's College Students?" *ACRL 2013 Proceedings: Advancing Learning. Transforming Scholarship*, 2013, 472–82. http://www.ala.org/acrl/sites/ala.org.acrl/files/content/conferences/confsandpreconfs/2013/papers/Head_Project.pdf.

Jacobs, Heidi. "Posing the Wikipedia 'Problem': Information Literacy and the Praxis of Problem-Posing in Library Instruction." In *Critical Library Instruction: Theories and Methods*, edited by Maria T. Accardi, Emily Drabinski, and Alana Kumbier, 179–97. Duluth: Library Juice Press, 2010.

Leuf, Bo, and Ward Cunningham. *The Wiki Way: Quick Collaboration on the Web*. Boston: Addison-Wesley, 2001.

Mackey, Thomas P., and Trudi E. Jacobson. *Metaliteracy: Reinventing Information Literacy to Empower Learners*. Chicago: American Library Association, 2014.

———. "Reframing Information Literacy as a Meta Literacy." *College & Research Libraries* 72, no. 1 (2011): 62–78.

Sterne, Johnathan, ed. *The Sound Studies Reader*. New York and London: Routledge, 2012.

UNESCO. *Global Media and Information Literacy Assessment Framework: Country Readiness and Competencies*. Paris, 2013.

Wikimedia Foundation. "Wikimedia Report Card," 2015. Accessed March 1, 2016. http://
    reportcard.wmflabs.org/.
———. "Wikipedia Statistics: Words," 2014. Accessed March 1, 2016. https://stats.wikime-
    dia.org/EN/TablesDatabaseWords.htm.
———. "Wikipedia: About." *Wikipedia*, 2015. Accessed March 1, 2016. http://en.wikipe-
    dia.org/wiki/Wikipedia:About.
———. "Wikipedia: Five Pillars," 2015. Accessed March 1, 2016. https://en.wikipedia.org/
    wiki/Wikipedia:Five_pillars.
———. "Wikipedia: Neutral Point of View," 2016. Accessed March 1, 2016. https://
    en.wikipedia.org/wiki/Wikipedia:Neutral_point_of_view.

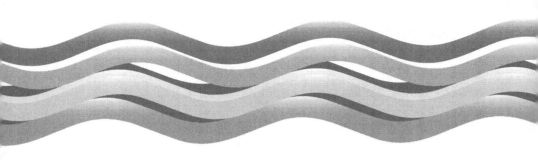

CHAPTER 10

Teaching the Frameworks for Writing and Information Literacy:

A Case Study from the Health Sciences

Teresa Quezada
University of Texas at El Paso

Introduction

The resurgence of rhetorical concepts in the college composition classroom means university students are introduced to traditional rhetorical concepts regarding ethos or authority as well as concepts of appropriate writing conventions. At the University of Texas at El Paso (UTEP), first-year composition students are also introduced to concepts such as discourse communities and genres that then lead to discussions of writing conventions. Students are asked to analyze textual as well as different media to foster analytical skills, and research projects usually become the basis for additional projects where students are asked to present information in different media and for persuasive purposes. Thus for me, the knowledge practices, dispositions, and habits of mind articulated in the *Framework for Information Literacy for Higher Education* (hereafter ACRL Framework) and *The Framework for Success in Postsecondary Writing* (hereafter WPA Framework), developed by the Association of College and Research Libraries (ACRL) and the Council of Writing Program Administrators (WPA), the National Council of Teachers of English (NCTE), and the National Writing Project (NWP) respectively, have been inherent in writing courses.

Although the Framework documents articulate previously implicit learning objectives and goals for the writing classroom, the knowledge practices, dispositions, and habits of mind seem to have been identified by other disciplines seeking to foster those dispositions in writing intensive disciplinary courses and in their students. For example, Krest and Carle assert that "writing courses within content areas are the very places instructors can most effectively integrate writing, research and critical thinking, and emphasize the specific developmental skills that neither content nor generic writing courses can cover."[1] Malcolm also described writing in a sociology course as "the most powerful tool for learning that is available to teachers…Through writing, students must engage the material, struggle with it and make sense of it."[2] Students in Malcolm's courses also began analyzing alternative and visual media to include editorial cartoons, comic strips, and advertisements in an effort to "energize[] students, making them more likely to care about completing a strong analysis."[3] ESL scholarship also grappled with preparing students to enter academic conversations in different genres as exemplified by Shih's comments that "[s]tudents write in a variety of forms"[4] and that students write to demonstrate knowledge while instructors use writing to prompt "independent thinking, researching and learning."[5] Furthermore, Shih recognized writing instruction must prepare students "to learn to gather and interpret data according to methods and standards accepted in their fields, to bring an increasing body of knowledge to bear on their interpretations, and to write in specialized formats."[6] Although the terms vary slightly from those used in the WPA Framework document, they certainly foreshadow expectations such as the ability to analyze and understand audiences to create appropriate texts, the ability to make thoughtful decisions based on analysis, and the ability to identify and compose given the field's conventions.[7]

Although the conversation regarding these dispositions and habits of mind may have emerged as higher education grappled with developing analytical university graduates, those concepts were also discussed by compositionists and the dispositions and habits were introduced into the writing classroom as outcomes statements were developed. *The Instructor Guide to Undergraduate Rhetoric and Writing Studies* 17th edition, developed by the Rhetoric and Writing Studies program at UTEP articulates that the learning outcomes for first year students "are designed to meet the outcomes statement created by the Council of Writing Program Administrators" adopted in April 2000 and amended in July 2008.[8] The WPA Outcomes preceded the Framework documents and were the first step in making the dispositions and habits of mind explicit within the writing classroom. One further piece of evidence that the habits of mind and information literacy have been curricular elements in UTEP's undergraduate writing course is the inclusion of workshops with instructional librarians in many first-year writing courses. However, the faculty-librarian partnerships at UTEP were often informal, and developed through word-of-mouth information among the faculty and doctoral students working as assistant instructors in the Rhetoric and Writing Studies (RWS) program. I had participated in such informal arrangements with two instructional librarians for my first-year courses and had discovered their usefulness to incoming university students. Those experiences led me to seek more opportunities to expose students to information literacy in upper-division courses as well and a formalized opportunity arose when the UTEP Library established a Library Information Literacy Course Enhancement Grant.

The course enhancement initiative encouraged instructors to enhance their courses—usually those with significant research projects—by collaborating with interested librarians to provide greater continuity and emphasis on information literacy as a learning objective in the course. As Lindstrom and Shonrock indicate, faculty-librarian partnerships must share common goals, include competent instructors and librarians for the specific tasks, and the collaborators must communicate throughout the planning process and as the course progresses to ensure a successful teaching collaboration and to provide a fertile learning environment for the students.[9] The Library Information Literacy Grant at my school provided a formalized process where instructors and librarians could communicate and collaborate through course design, during course delivery, and after course completion. Perhaps, most importantly, the grant heralded the library and university's commitment to provide resources for instructor-librarian collaborations. Integration into specific courses is not new; as Lindstrom and Shonrock report, recent librarian integration into specific courses at Butler University's College of Business Administration, the University of Auckland Business School, and Penn State University have resulted in long-lasting and effective librarian–instructor relationships.[10] The UTEP library's goal was to foster similar on-going, long-lasting instructor-librarian partnerships by introducing faculty to the resources available to students and faculty and illustrating how those resources could enhance courses.

This chapter focuses on the formalized and explicit instructor-librarian collaboration in a specialized section of technical writing, and how that partnership initiated curricular and pedagogical changes that brought the Frameworks to the forefront of course design. I discuss how the work in the classroom, the library, and the learning management system cultivated the abilities, habits, and practices of mind advanced by the Framework documents.

Technical Writing Course for Health Science Majors

The Technical Writing course at UTEP is a junior/senior level course taught by the Rhetoric and Writing Studies (RWS) program faculty; it is generally available to any interested student, but it specifically satisfies the writing requirement for students in health science programs such as nursing, kinesiology, social work, and health promotions. RWS undergraduate faculty redesigned the course during the 2013–2014 academic year to emphasize rhetorical principles, align course objectives with technical communication goals, differentiate the course from Workplace Writing (another course taught by RWS faculty at the time and required by the College of Business Administration for its students) and provide uniform guidance to advanced RWS doctoral students who also teach the course. Redesign efforts for Technical Writing relied on the Society of Technical Communication's (STC) core competencies, and the resulting course objectives and outcomes merged both an STC and RWS Studies perspective.[11] Not only were course objectives and outcomes revised, but also a variety of available technical writing textbooks were reviewed by undergraduate RWS faculty. As a result, two major textbooks were recommended that reflected the revised course objectives and outcomes. Instructors could then choose one of the two recommended textbooks and adhere to the course objectives and outcomes.

I taught a section of Technical Writing during the fall 2014 semester, and the section was specifically reserved for students accepted into health science majors. The goal for the course was to address this population's disciplinary writing needs more directly rather than teach an overview of technical writing that lacked disciplinary specificity. Such a specialized section had only been offered once before as an online course, and the offering for the fall 2014 semester was a hybrid section where the class met with the instructor once a week for eighty minutes and the remaining coursework was completed online. The RWS program was piloting the hybrid format to allow greater scheduling flexibility to the target student population whose degree plans frequently called for courses with labs and thus limited scheduling options.

Armed with the revised course objectives and learning outcomes, a colleague's syllabus, and a general understanding of the course's target student population, I aligned the newly revised learning objectives with the health science specialization. Given the specialization, I selected texts that specifically addressed writing in the health professions: Barbara Heifferon's *Writing in the Health Professions* and Charles Abraham and Marieke Kools's *Writing Health Communication: An Evidence-Based Guide.* These two books offered what the recommended textbooks could not: the document types health professionals are most likely to encounter in their professions as well as an overview of responsible writing in the health disciplines.

The revised course description and learning objectives for the course presented to students in the syllabus were the following:

Course Description
The primary goal of English 3359 is to develop students' effective communication in technical writing within professional health care contexts. This effective communication is based on an awareness of and appreciation for discourse communities as well as knowledge specific to subject matter, genre, rhetorical strategy, and writing process.

The class presents an approach to communication that helps students determine the most effective strategies, arrangements, and media. You will produce a variety of documents and presentations to gain more confidence and fluency in visual, oral, and written communication.

Another goal of English 3359 is to strengthen your self-learning skills. This means you will be required to work independently to be fully prepared for class and for the writing projects you must complete.[12]

Learning Objectives
In this course, [students] will
- analyze the rhetorical situation and define the users and/or audience as well as the tasks that the information must support
- apply rhetorical principles to plan and design effective technical documents for diverse media
- research appropriate sources that inform your writing
- compose content appropriate for the users and genre
- revise and edit written work for accuracy, clarity, coherence and appropriateness, and document resources in the health care environment

- apply technological and visual rhetorical skills (e.g., document design, graphics, computer documentation, electronic editing, and content management applications) in the composing process
- publish, deliver, and archive the composed documents as required
- consider the ethical dimension of composing and working within health care organizations
- recognize and respect various cultural attitudes toward and conventions for health care communications
- understand what health literacy is and how it will influence writing
- develop accurate reporting and recording skills of health issues
- work critically and collaboratively to complete projects[13]

Thus, the course retained the RWS perspective that, similarly to the ACRL, recognizes students' increased responsibility to create new knowledge by utilizing pertinent information in a world flooded with data.[14] As a service course, however, the objectives were designed to prepare students to write documents they were likely to encounter in their professions and to incorporate subject-specific content for specific audiences and purposes.

As envisioned, students would write about medical and health issues rather than address general research topics. This focus meant that students' research would similarly have to be focused and they would have to critically evaluate sources applicable to their specific disciplines, often those collected in specialized databases. Further, the medical field's protean nature demanded that students learn to locate current and relevant sources and learn to discern the value these sources had for them as both consumers of technical information and future mediators and interpreters of that information to their patients and clients. Information literacy, therefore, became a critical component of the course. Fortunately, I had collaborated with two instructional librarians from the UTEP Library for my first-year composition courses in prior years, so I knew I could rely on their assistance in this upper-division course. My reliance on librarian instruction was further cemented when the UTEP Library announced a campus-wide Library Information Literacy Course Enhancement Grant late in the spring of 2014 to further faculty-librarian collaboration in specific courses during the summer and fall 2014 terms.

Library Information Literacy Course Enhancement Grant: Designing the Course

Since the Technical Writing section for health science majors had only been offered once before and the fall 2014 semester was the first time I taught the course, I came to realize, as Artman, Frisicaro-Pawlowski and Monge argue, that enabling students to take advantage of information resources available to them had to be a "prominent goal in [the course's] pedagogy and curriculum design."[15] I applied for the Library Information Literacy Course Enhancement Grant proposing to integrate the instructional librarians into the course and modify both pedagogy and curriculum to emphasize information literacy within the health sciences. The first step was to include both instructional librarians as instructors on Blackboard, the course's learning management system (LMS). The course included librarian-led workshops during class time to introduce students to medical and legal databases that address ethical and legal issues in the health care industry. As students were introduced to content-specific databases, they also learned about information timelines and the impact those timelines have on the nature of the information available. Students also learned that as the information matures, it is presented in different genres with different levels of review, perspective, and credibility.

I was awarded the grant early in the summer of 2014 and immediately began collaborating with the instructional librarians to restructure the course calendar and revise assignments that would emphasize literacy concepts and allow for librarian-student interactions. The course design also worked to counter the perception that seems to persist, according to Artman, Frisicaro-Pawlowski and Monge, that the research process is separate from the writing process.[16] The first step I took to link research and writing was to schedule librarian-led workshops inside the library when the major research project was introduced and again mid-point through the students' research efforts. Several scaffolding exercises designed to help students formulate research questions and organize their research were originally scheduled, and those remained as part of the course since they also strengthened the bond between researching and writing.

As the course design proceeded, the librarians and I agreed fostering students' direct access to the librarians was critical. To allow for student-librarian interactions, both librarians were added to the course LMS and several discussion posts where students were required to interact with the librarians were developed. Given the hybrid nature of the course, discussions were primarily written exchanges that further emphasized the link between researching and writing.

To gauge the students' understanding of information production and researching, I devised an end-of-term assignment requiring students to locate an innovation in the health field that had been introduced in the previous 12–18 months and propose a research plan based on the investigative practices they had learned earlier in the semester. Although students were not required to consult librarians for this assignment, they were encouraged to review the materials previously presented and ask the instructor and/or the librarians questions about researching, source relevancy and credibility, and audience as they developed their research plan.

Developing assignments and scheduling librarian intervention was only the beginning of the grant's impact on course design, curriculum, and pedagogy, however. As I developed the course to support the grant's intent and goals, I found my curriculum and pedagogy addressed the Frameworks explicitly. I discuss how the Frameworks, the revised curriculum, and the resulting pedagogy aligned in the next section.

Aligning Curriculum and Pedagogy with the Frameworks

As initially designed, course readings and assignments cultivated students' curiosity, one of the WPA habits of mind, by allowing them to research topics within their disciplines. Since the students had already been exposed to their disciplinary content, and in some instances were close to completing their degree program, they understood notions of authority and its construction[17] within the health sciences field. However, I had the opportunity to complicate that understanding through explorations into concepts* such as audience, purpose, contexts, and culture. For example, students were introduced to the impact cultural differences have on information creation and consumption and audience expectations. I intended that exposure to cultural differences would lead students to consider alternative ways to think about their future patients/clients and realize that their interactions would be informed not only by their own culture, but also by their audience's culture. Further, the course and workshops highlighted information creation and value, concepts found in the ACRL Framework. The workshops introduced students to information relevance and timeliness, and these factors impacted students' research and ultimate credibility as they consumed, assimilated, synthesized, and dissem-

---

* These notions further several experiences recommended by the WPA Framework including "Developing Rhetorical Knowledge," "Developing Critical Thinking Through Writing, Reading, and Research," "Developing Flexible Writing Processes," and "Developing Knowledge of Conventions."

inated information to various audiences. To this end, the course assignments were designed to help students recognize that their research would result in conversations—another key element in the ACRL Framework—with scholars, colleagues, other professionals involved in the medical treatment of their clients/ patients, the community at large, and individual clients/patients.

Readings and Other Resources

As previously indicated, the course texts were selected because they addressed the specific writing genres and environments the target students would encounter in their professions. However, the text authors also demonstrated an affinity for the Frameworks. Heifferon, in particular, addresses ACRL frames of authority, information creation and value, and research as inquiry in chapters that address audience and context analysis, ethics, and multicultural environments.[18] Additional readings and videos also complicated the WPA and ACRL notions of authority and knowledge construction for students.[19] Students were provided resources to guide their citation efforts and to help students properly attribute information in their assignments. Students viewed videos to introduce them to concepts of literacy, both in its traditional understanding and as it pertains to health information. The following detailed discussion of the workshops, course assignments based on readings, other resources, and the overall course objectives and their relationship to the Framework documents responds to the fundamental question for this chapter: In what ways does your teaching, in the classroom and in the library, work to cultivate the desired abilities, habits, and practices of mind advanced by the Framework documents?

Librarian-Led Workshops

Two library workshops were scheduled during the semester. Although this is not much more than the oft-criticized one-shot instruction, the hybrid nature of the course did not allow for much flexibility since the class met only once a week for eighty minutes and the remainder of the coursework was completed online. Both sessions however, incorporated several methods discussed in the Hsieh, Dawson, Hoffmann, Titus and Carlin study, including the limited preview method, and active learning during the session.[20] Although the Hsieh et al. study investigated the methods independently of one another, in class, students were encouraged to preview existing library guides, which ideally provided a refresher to students into general library resources and access. During the first workshop, students learned the Boolean connectors, attempted phrase searching, and completed a worksheet to practice search techniques similar to the active learning method Hsieh et al. employed.[21]

The first workshop was scheduled as students were exploring and narrowing their research topic and was intended to help them refine the topic based on available information. Since the course did not focus on primary investigation and research methods, students were encouraged to identify topics that would yield robust, credible, and relevant resources. The second workshop focused specifically on medical and legal databases and helped students further refine their inquiries.

Both workshops were developed and led by the instructional librarians, with additional commentary provided by the instructor to emphasize course requirements or to answer course-specific questions. The ACRL Framework heavily informed the sessions, as the librarians led students from general research to specific research strategies as well as helped students understand the information's value, authority, and relevance. As the librarians explained how information is created and refined over time, students were introduced to the different modes of reporting they could expect to find depending on the issue's timeline. For example, students learned as a topic initially becomes newsworthy, initial reports can be located in news outlets such as newspapers or weekly magazines. Information in these modes is limited to reporting basic facts and is usually reported by journalists rather than subject matter experts. As the topic matures, greater effort is spent on analyzing other instances where similar issues have occurred and information then appears in other genres, such as trade magazines, where the authors may be practitioners rather than generalists, as is the case of news reports. As more time elapses, published materials begin exploring causes and effects; the analysis portion becomes more robust and information can appear as scholarly articles. Scholars and researchers write the latter sources; research methodologies for these sources are also typically more rigorous and final texts are usually subjected to greater scrutiny through peer review.

Understanding the life cycle of issues allows students to develop knowledge practices articulated in the Frameworks. For example, students learn researching a new topic may mean they will not find much analysis and will have to rely on journalistic reporting. Recognizing the value of this research, given the topic's life cycle, enables students to recognize how "Authority Is Constructed and Contextual," that it has value, and that "Information Creation is a Process."[22]

Similarly, to Artman, Frisicaro-Pawlowski and Monge's observations, the librarians and I found students were unfamiliar with multiple resources at their disposal despite the fact they had conducted research within their disciplinary fields prior to taking the writing course.[23] Since the course is a junior/senior level course, students should have completed first-year composition courses where research projects are critical components. Even assuming some students might have tested out of first-year composition courses, my expectation, borne out by students' responses to an initial assessment asking them to describe their previous writing experiences, was that students had completed research projects in courses both within and outside their disciplines. However, few students indicated familiarity with databases dedicated specifically to medical literature. The activity-based workshop which called for students to identify key phrases and different terms to research their topic seemed to provide students with a new strategy to begin their research. As such, the workshops served to teach the ACRL framework "Searching as Strategic Exploration" since students learned how to narrow or expand their key phrases, and consequently their research results, based on the scope of their proposed research.[24]

Assignments

As expected for a writing course, both major and minor assignments were designed so students would respond in writing. While the response genres varied, and some were specifically designed to foster an understanding of workplace conventions, students were expected to connect readings with their experiences and other courses along with the response environment, thus fostering metacognition and reflection as encouraged by the WPA Framework.[25] This section discusses the relevant assignments and how they cultivated habits and practices articulated in both Frameworks.

Discussion Board Postings

The first assignment was a short, 250- to 300-word discussion post visible by all students in the class asking them to describe their positive and negative writing experiences, articulate their expectations for the course, and identify issues they wanted to learn about writing in general. My goal was to instill a sense of reflection and engagement in the course as well as to establish a sense of responsibility for learning. Students responded with comments regarding improving grammar and mechanics; however, they added comments about missing something in previous writing courses and wanting to learn about writing professionally and efficiently. Reflecting on their experiences and voicing their expectations seemed to set a comprehensive Framework-based environment in the course by encouraging engagement, persistence, responsibility, flexibility and metacognition—the habits of mind the WPA Framework hopes to foster.[26]

A second discussion post asked students to consult with one of the course librarians after the first of two librarian-led workshops. The initial workshop re-introduced the students to library resources, timeliness of information, and basic searching parameters such as Boolean searches. As a result of the initial workshop and the online library guide resources available through the LMS, students were expected to narrow their topic selection for the research assignments to two or three issues. To help students refine their topics, they consulted librarians and were asked to discuss databases, quality of sources, and appropriateness of sources as well as receive help identifying other sources if needed. Despite the prompts for consultation with the librarians, students' comments were disappointingly superficial. Most students requested confirmation that medical databases were appropriate for their research. From their comments, it became evident the consultation/discussion came too early in their investigation and/or they had not yet probed the value of the sources they were locating.

Once students had begun their researching, a supplemental reading, Emily Martin's "The Egg and the Sperm: How Science Has Constructed a Romance Based on Stereotypical Male-Female Roles,"[27] was introduced; students were asked to reflect on scientific writing's objective value and how authority was constructed in the assigned article and in the sources they had located thus far in their own investigations. This reading was meant to instill skepticism and help students enact the dispositions promoted in ACRL's first frame, "Authority Is Constructed and Contextual."[28] By reviewing a conflicting point of view from one they had commonly understood, and by considering their own sources, the student researchers could begin to unpack notions of authority and refine their questions of inquiry to consider relevance, divergent points of view, and information trends. Most responses to the discussion prompt acknowledged surprise at Martin's differing characterization of the scientific process. Students also seemed to begin to understand how they created an authoritative voice as researchers and professionals through their use of sources, choice of words, and communication with patients and clients.

As a whole, the discussion boards allowed students to reflect upon the information they had been presented and the information they had independently located, as well as enter conversations with each other as they examined texts. These tasks were designed to foster WPA habits of curiosity and engagement in low-stakes assignments where students could "grapple with challenging ideas [or] texts,"[29] "make connections between their own ideas and those of others,"[30] and "take risks by exploring questions, topics and ideas that are new to them."[31]

Writing for Other Professionals—Research Project

A research project was introduced, and although its effectiveness has been questioned by compositionists because it is "written to a non-specialist audience,"[32] the assignment was deemed useful since it allowed the students to investigate a topic related to their discipline and pertinent to the University's borderland region. The assignment specifically asked students to explore a topic in the El Paso region to help make the effort more relevant to students. Furthermore, since the students might not always find research regarding their selected topic that had been conducted in the El Paso area, they were expected to search strategically, an ACRL frame, for research that could be applied to the border region and to think critically about the specific elements that could be applied to the El Paso region. Thus, students were expected to identify gaps in resources and critically discern disciplinary strategies that had been practiced under different circumstances, yet could be relevant to their specific topic. To achieve this kind of exploration, students would have to understand the different scenarios and how research strategies could be adapted to a borderland setting. Furthermore, the research project established the disciplinary knowledge students would then apply in developing other assignments in different modes and for different audiences. Since the audience for this research project was established as other medical professionals, students practiced the abilities enumerated in the ACRL's "Scholarship as Conversation" frame.[33]

A recursive research-writing process was emphasized since students could modify their research topic and questions of inquiry throughout the semester as their investigation progressed. The project was presented as three separate, but related assignments: a topic proposal memo, an annotated bibliography, and the final project, an informative research paper. The three assignments were designed to scaffold students' efforts. I also intended to introduce students to different writing genres since each assignment followed different conventions: memo, bibliography, and research paper. Students were expected to consider different sources presented in different formats and how each source had relative value in the annotated bibliography and research paper. Finally, students had to practice appropriate attribution in the bibliography and research paper. To further emphasize how their research would inform subsequent assignments, students were also told their research project would serve as the foundation for two other projects: an educational brochure/instruction brochure and proposed health campaign group project.

The first research requirement was a topic proposal memo where students proposed a public health issue relevant to the El Paso, Texas borderland region that was also related to the student's major. Students chose topics such as the link between physical inactivity and chronic diseases, childhood obesity, and childhood asthma. Although these topics were initially broad, the students were allowed to narrow the topic by focusing on specific populations such as Hispanics, the largest minority population in the area. If not related to the major, the researcher had to explain why the topic interested her. As part of the proposal memo, two initial sources had to be presented in APA format;

the sources could be academic journal articles, government sources, or sources from not-for-profit organizations. This assignment was intended to foster several WPA habits of mind: student curiosity, creativity, responsibility, and flexibility. Since this assignment was due after the first information literacy/librarian-led workshop and after student-librarian consultations, students were also able to enact numerous knowledge practices in various ACRL frames. Namely, students explored notions of authority, information creation processes, information value, inquiry, and strategic exploration.

The habits of mind and frames were enacted when students began exploring topics that interested them. Rather than assigning specific topics, students were encouraged to begin their inquiries by considering current topics in the local media, developing unanswered or under-answered questions they had encountered in their disciplinary courses, and forecasting questions they might encounter once they entered the professional workplace. Since the students were responsible for their own research, they had to rediscover the curiosity and creativity that might have attracted them to their selected field of study. Because the research efforts required that students identify sources for their topic, they began exploring who was responsible for creating information within their field of study and within their topic in particular. My feedback regarding their selected sources included comments asking students to consider the timeliness and value of the information. My intent was to help students consider how the initial exploration could lead to strategic exploration that met the scope of their projects. All of these efforts are represented and grounded in the Frameworks.

Once I approved students' topics, their investigations moved to an annotated bibliography. This assignment was designed to encourage students to review, analyze, and synthesize information from multiple types of sources as presented in the library workshops. Citing sources was an important component that the instructor emphasized when discussing this task. However, the annotations were also highlighted as the most valuable element of the assignment for the students' ongoing work. The required annotations summarized the source, explained how the source fit into the student's research, identified the audience for the information and whether that audience was addressed effectively by the source, assessed the thoroughness the source provided the student, and determined whether or not the source furthered the student's inquiry process.

The annotated bibliography was the second opportunity students had to practice the ACRL frames introduced with the topic proposal memo, but in greater depth. As the students' investigations progressed, students were allowed to refine their topic or modify their research questions. Students were also reminded, while they had to produce an annotated bibliography that met the minimum source requirements, the final reference list for their research paper could include additional or different sources. A key pedagogical practice was the instructor's attempts to consistently remind students that discarding a source in favor of a more relevant or more current source is an integral part of research, discovery, and knowledge creation. Furthermore, recognizing the iterative research process allowed students to "adapt to situations, expectations, or demands."[34] Students were advised to re-examine their initial topic and refine it as they found additional information. The instructor emphasized that topic changes were appropriate and encouraged if students discovered sub-topics they found more interesting or better suited to the assignment expectation than the topic originally proposed.

As the final and major task, the informative research paper, students were to define and clarify their selected problem/condition or issue, summarize previous investigations to inform their reader of current research, identify relations, contradictions, gaps, and inconsistencies in the literature, and suggest the next step or steps in solving the problem. Thus, the research efforts were to culminate with students not merely reporting, but analyzing information and applying it to a specific location and audience. As such, students again had opportunities to enact the knowledge practices and dispositions in the ACRL and WPA Frameworks.

Writing for Patients/Clients

The bulk of the assignments through the research project had been designed with a professional audience in mind. Once the students had completed their research, the focus shifted to writing for patients/clients. Based on their investigations, students were required to develop either an educational brochure or a set of instructions. This assignment was designed to introduce students to their roles as interpreters or mediators of technical information for a lay audience: patients or clients who may or may not have the health literacy and expertise students have achieved. The assignment called for students to create succinct texts incorporating technical information and elements of visual rhetoric—layout, graphics, white space, color, spacing, balance, and contrast—for a specific target population. Through this assignment, students began constructing their own authority in a specific context and began to understand they were creating information differently than they had in the research project. They were also introduced to the value of different genres for different purposes and audiences. Since they were constrained by the brochure or instruction sheet's genre, they had to determine which information would be of most value to their intended and potentially secondary audiences.

The most effective student brochures provided information on a health issue, recommended specific steps, and guided readers to additional resources. Although the intended audiences could not always be narrowly defined, students understood their brochures had to convey information through both text and images. Three noteworthy submittals addressed varied issues such as lower back pain, suicide prevention for military personnel, and dealing with childhood asthma. In each case, the student developer provided clear and succinct definitions and descriptions of the issue to their readers as well as used images and color to illustrate concepts and accentuate the specific actions they were recommending.

Writing for the Community

The major assignment in the course was a public health campaign proposal. This assignment was a group project where one of the group member's topics would be chosen to develop a public health campaign for the borderland or UTEP community. The proposal would be drafted and presented to a government or not-for-profit organization whose values aligned with the intended benefits of the public health campaign and who would then perhaps fund the proposed health campaign. Students were to incorporate the critical analyses conducted throughout the semester to develop a workplace report for a decision-making audience. The proposal would present the public health campaign's need and purpose, target audience, potential collaborators (other organizations whose authority was recognized in the community, as the ACRL frame notes how such authority is constructed and contextual), distribution channels for the public health information (the ACRL frame of information creation and value), and specific information to be conveyed in the public health campaign. Not only was a final, written report required, but the groups presented their proposals to the class and instructor who assumed the roles of the funding organization's board of directors and executive director, respectively.

Since students completed the proposal in groups, WPA habits of mind including openness, engagement, creativity, persistence, responsibility, flexibility and metacognition were fostered through this final project. To facilitate effective group work, I provided students with potential roles group members could assume and also required that students develop a group contract which all students signed. The contract identified the topic/campaign to be developed, how the students were to meet and collaborate, how the tasks were to be divided among group members, what roles each group member was to assume, and how the group would address perceived infractions by individual group members. I emphasized differing opinions and approaches could strengthen the final proposal and reminded students that the role of devil's advocate was valuable, provided the group was respectful in listening to differing opinions and engaged with the ideas being presented. Since the topic selected was one student's area of research, by definition the remaining group members would not have the same level of expertise on the topic. However, their varied backgrounds and experiences, along with their own semester-long inquiry projects, prepared them to critically analyze how the information developed for a professional audience had to be interpreted for the community at large. Determining both campaign content and distribution channels challenged the students to think creatively and reflect on the cultural situation the students were asked to address.

The instructor presented guidelines for proposal reports and emphasized the persuasive nature of such reports—the goal was to have the proposal's audience, the class and instructor as board of directors and executive director, approve the health campaign. To achieve a persuasive proposal, students were encouraged to develop guidelines for their collaboration to enact responsible teamwork. They had to, in WPA terms, "persevere" through group member scheduling conflicts and display "flexibility" and "openness" as group members contributed divergent ideas to complete the report and presentation. While general guidelines for report and presentation were provided and discussed in class, students were given flexibility in the appearance of the final report and creativity was fostered through group/instructor interactions where the instructor asked questions regarding the purpose, intended health campaign audience, and other required elements. In many instances, the instructor reminded students to reflect on the research they had conducted regarding the health issue to inform their own presentations.

One of the strongest campaigns expanded on the research and brochure aimed at preventing military personnel suicides. "The Courage to Live" campaign sought to educate military families and soldiers about the warning signs of suicide among soldiers and ultimately to prevent suicides by providing help and removing the stigma associated with seeking help. The campaign was limited to facilities at Fort Bliss, the largest army post in the continental United States and surrounded by the El Paso, Texas community. The proposal relied heavily on the scholarly research conducted, but its strength lied in the adeptness the students demonstrated in translating that research into a proposal that effectively brought information and presented additional resources to a public affected by the health issue: military personnel, their families, and friends.

Conclusion

Assessing the impact of the Library Information Literacy Course Enhancement Grant at this point is primarily qualitative. Students' comments regarding the first workshop indicate they had not previously been exposed to explicit information literacy and were initially uncomfortable with research tasks. The second library workshop was scheduled just before students submitted the annotated bibliography. While this second workshop could not have had a significant impact on that assignment, students would have identified gaps in their research and could ask more specific and critical questions regarding information value and relevance. Unfortunately, students did not take the opportunity to do so—mostly because they had not been prepared to do so by the instructor. Greater schedule coordination along with increased coordination between the instructor and librarians could ensure that the ACRL Frameworks are more effectively integrated into the second or subsequent library workshops.

Including librarian-led workshops, however, seemed to provide students with greater confidence in the knowledge practices required to research effectively and develop alternative strategies when presented with new topics to research. One of the capstone, yet low-stakes tasks, was for students to identify a health topic introduced in the popular media within the last 12–18 months and identify a research plan identifying databases and the rationale for those sources to provide relevant and credible information. The vast majority of students demonstrated mastery of the research strategies and familiarity with appropriate databases.

Since the Frameworks' habits of mind, knowledge practices, and dispositions are so intrinsically entwined with the assignments, it is difficult to assess how well they were cultivated in the students. Final grades provide a quantitative, albeit incomplete, assessment of how proficiently students displayed knowledge practices, dispositions, and habits of mind. Twenty of the twenty-five students who completed the course during fall 2014 earned a B or better and, of these, ten (40 percent) earned an A. I taught the course during the fall 2015 semester without the enhancement grant and included only one librarian-led workshop. Although the assignments were very similar in both classes, the most recent class did not include the capstone research proposal memo. Only 22 percent, or four of eighteen students, earned an A during the fall 2015 semester, and ten of eighteen (55 percent) earned a B. My sense is the explicit inclusion of information literacy and greater involvement by librarians in the course not only augmented the Frameworks' prominence in the course, but also promoted student success. Continued collaboration and additional student reflection may provide additional qualitative data that can help librarians and writing instructors determine how students perceive courses that make the Frameworks' goals explicit and whether the students can envision how certain habits of mind or dispositions may be helpful to them both as they complete their studies and enter the workforce.

Notes

1. Krest and Carle, "Teaching Scientific Writing," 223.
2. Malcolm, "Analyzing the News," 143.
3. Ibid., 146.
4. Shih, "Content-Based Approaches to Teaching Academic Writing," 617.
5. Ibid., 621.
6. Ibid., 621.
7. WPA, Framework, 1.
8. Salome and Dulin, "The UTEP Instructor Guide to Undergraduate Rhetoric and Writing," 21–23.
9. Lindstrom and Shonrock, "Faculty-Librarian Collaboration," 19.
10. Ibid., 20.
11. Quezada, Donovan, Martin, and Agee, "Mining for Informed Technical Communication Curricula."
12. Quezada, Technical Writing Syllabus, Fall 2014 semester.
13. Ibid.
14. ACRL, Framework, 1
15. Artman, Frisicaro-Pawlowski, and Monge, "Not Just One Shot," 94.
16. Ibid., 96.
17. ACRL, Framework, 4.
18. Heifferon, Barbara A. *Writing in the Health Professions.*
19. Martin, Emily. "The Egg and the Sperm."
20. Hsieh, Dawson, Hoffmann, Titus, and Carlin, "Four Pedagogical Approaches." 236.
21. Ibid., 236.
22. ACRL, Framework, 2.
23. Artman, Frisicaro-Pawlowski, and Monge, "Not Just One Shot," 94.
24. ACRL, Framework, 9.
25. WPA, Framework, 5.
26. Ibid., 1.
27. Martin, Emily. "The Egg and the Sperm."
28. ACRL, Framework, 5.
29. WPA, Framework, 5.
30. Ibid., 4.
31. Ibid., 4.
32. Margolin and Hayden, "Reframing the Pedagogy," 603.
33. ACRL, Framework, 8.
34. WPA, Framework, 5.

Bibliography

Abraham, Charles and Marieke Kools. *Writing Health Communication: An Evidence-Based Guide.* Thousand Oaks, California: Sage, 2012.
Artman, Margaret, Erica Frisicaro-Pawlowski, and Robert Monge. "Not Just One Shot: Extending the Dialogue about Infromation Literacy in Composition Classes." *Composition Studies* 38, no. 2 (2010): 93–109.

Association of College and Research Libraries, 2016. *Framework for Information Literacy for Higher Education.* Accessed December 14, 2015. http://www.ala.org/acrl/sites/ala.org.acrl/files/content/issues/infolit/Framework_ILHE.pdf.

Council of Writing Program Administrators, National Council of Teachers of English, National Writing Project, 2011. *Framework for Success in Postsecondary Writing.* Accessed February 4, 2016. http://www.wpacouncil.org/files/framework-for-success-postsecondary-writing.pdf

Heifferon, Barbara A. *Writing in the Health Professions.* New York: Pearson Education, 2005.

Hsie, Ma Lei, Patricia H. Dawson, Melissa A. Hofmann, Megan L. Titus, and Michael T. Carlin. "Four Pedagogical Approaches in Helping Students Learn Information Literacy Skills." *The Journal of Academic Librarianship* 40 (2014): 234–246.

Krest, Margie and Daria O. Carle. "Teaching Scientific Writing: A Model for Integrating Research, Writing and Critical Thinking." *The American Biology Teacher* 61, no. 3 (1999): 223–227.

Lindstrom, Joyce and Diana D. Shonrock. "Faculty-Librarian Collaboration to Achieve Integration of Information Literacy." *Reference & User Services Quarterly* 46, no. 1 (2006): 18–23.

Malcolm, Nancy L. "Analyzing the News: Teaching Critical Thinking Skills in a Writing Intensive Social Problems Course." *Teaching Sociology* 34 (2006):143–149.

Margolin, Stephanie and Wendy Hayden. "Beyond Mechanics: Reframing the Pedagogy and Development of Information Literacy Teaching Tools." *The Journal of Academic Librarianship* 41 (2015): 602–612.

Martin, Emily. "The Egg and the Sperm: How Science Has Constructed a Romance Based on Stereotypical Male-Female Roles." *Signs* 16, no. 3 (1991): 485–501.

Quezada, Teresa. "RWS 3359-Technical Writing Fall 2014 Syllabus." 2014.

Quezada, Teresa, Theresa L. Donovan, Levi Martin, Nikki Agee. "Mining for Informed Technical Communication Curricula." *Conference of the Council for Programs in Technical and Scientific Communication (CPTSC).* Colorado Springs, 2014. N/P.

Salome, Melanie R. and Cassandra Dulin, Co-editors. The UTEP Guide to Undergraduate Rhetoric and Writing, 17th edition. University of Texas at El Paso. 2014.

Shih, May. "Content-Based Approaches to Teaching Academic Writing." *TESOL Quarterly* 20, no. 4 (1986): 617–648.

CHAPTER 11*

Dynamic Duos:

Blended Instruction and Faculty-Librarian Collaboration†

Kathleen Reed and Dawn Thompson
Vancouver Island University

Introduction

In the winter of 2014, an English Department faculty member (Dawn) and a librarian faculty member (Kathleen) at Vancouver Island University (VIU), a Canadian undergraduate university with a full-time enrollment of 6,500 students, collaborated to design and deliver a semester-long, senior-level English Research Methods course. While the course covered literary research methods and methodologies, it was underpinned by apprenticeship in scholarly communication introducing models of collaboration, production, peer-review, altmetrics, online scholarly personas, open access, and knowledge mobilization. Through instruction, course logistics, and assignments, we challenged students, and ourselves, to explore the question: what does it mean to be a scholar today? Using reflection, student feedback, and continued dialogue, this chapter reflects on our partnership as it explores how other librarians and disciplinary faculty can work together to introduce, encourage, and mentor

* This work is licensed under a Creative Commons Attribution-NonCommercial 4.0 License, CC BY-NC (https://creativecommons.org/licenses/by-nc/4.0/).

† An earlier version of this paper was published in the ACRL 2014 Conference Proceedings: http://www.ala.org/acrl/files/conferences/confsandpreconfs/2015/Reed_Thompson.pdf.

students in an increasingly complicated scholarly communication landscape. Throughout this paper, we draw on the Council of Writing Program Administrators, National Council of Teachers of English, and National Writing Project (WPA, NCTE, and NWP)'s *Framework for Success in Postsecondary Writing* (hereafter referred to as WPA Framework), where it applies to a course at the senior undergraduate level.[1] After describing our collaboration, we also consider it in light of the new Association of College and Research Librarians (ACRL) *Framework for Information Literacy for Higher Education*.[2] By examining both the WPA and ACRL Framework, we conclude that librarian-disciplinary faculty partnerships in research methods courses are an ideal setting to explore with students the complex and shifting technical and collaborative information dispositions to which the ACRL Framework refers, particularly using the vehicle of scholarly communication and how scholars share their thoughts with each other and a wider audience.

Librarians in the Classroom

As librarians seek to enhance the information literacy skills of students, embedded librarianship is increasingly discussed as a potential avenue.[3] The practice entails "[taking] a librarian out of the context of the traditional library and... [placing] him or her in an 'on-site' setting or situation that enables close coordination and collaboration with researchers or teaching faculty."[4]

While there is a significant amount of discussion on embedded librarianship, few articles focus specifically on embedding librarians in research methods classes at either the undergraduate or graduate level. Those articles that do explore this context are from a range of disciplines such as political science,[5] liberal studies,[6] and education.[7] As with much of the scholarship related to embedded librarianship, the basis of librarian participation, in all of the previously mentioned studies, is traditional information literacy instruction: developing research questions and finding, evaluating, and documenting sources. These skills are grounded in both the WPA Framework's critical thinking objectives and ACRL's *Information Literacy Competency Standards for Higher Education* (2000), the latter of which was often seen as a highly prescriptive set of standards.[8]

However, with the ACRL updating the Standards in favor of the Framework, there exists a space for librarians to consider their engagement with information literacy instruction in new ways. Of particular relevance to this chapter is an emphasis on understanding scholarly conversations taking place in all stages of research, which has not been a focus of the previous literature written by librarians embedded in research methods courses. Thus, scholarly conversations in the process of knowledge creation are part of scholarly communication, which also includes ways of sharing the research product. In this light, scholarly communication and information literacy are intimately related, and a research methods course is an ideal place for students to encounter that relationship. While librarian interest in the intersection of these two areas is growing,[9] this has not been discussed in the context of research methods courses.

Our Project

Research Methods is a senior-level undergraduate English course taught on a two-year cycle at Vancouver Island University (VIU). Despite her specialization in literary theory, Dawn had avoided teaching the Research Methods course in the past. She was hesitant for two reasons: the first was how methodologies (the connection to theory) had traditionally been approached both at VIU and similar institutions, which she felt inhibited critical thinking with regard to literary theory; the second was the fact she did not consider herself a good role model as a researcher. She comments, "I always feel as if I am playing catch-up with information technology used in research. However, a moment of inspiration on a long walk helped me to get past the first hesitation. Reading just a little about collaboration in the Digital Humanities also made me realize that I should just find an expert to help me with the latter." Having come to this realization, Dawn sought out a librarian partner.

While Dawn's initial request to the library for a librarian guest instructor did include information literacy, Kathleen was specifically recruited because of her training and experience with digital humanities, and she brought with her an interest in scholarly communication. The VIU Library does not have a significant history of partnerships between teaching and librarian faculty related to co-teaching and embedded librarianship. Librarians had been looking for opportunities to change this pattern, and Dawn's proposal was a chance to pilot a new model of working with instructional faculty. Dawn would teach the English Literature content, and Kathleen would cover information literacy, digital humanities, research technology, and scholarly communication. We worked together, though, to develop the syllabus and assignments.

Course Design & Curriculum

The course explored the multifaceted relationships between literature, literary criticism, and literary theory, as it endeavored to prepare students for the level of critical thinking required in graduate studies a concept at the core of the WPA Framework.* Together, we studied a canonical text, Mary Shelley's

---

* In this, our course further develops the WPA Framework on critical thinking (7).

Frankenstein,[10] read several critical articles on *Frankenstein* that approach the novel from different theoretical perspectives, and read some of the theoretical texts informing those critical articles. We then followed the same process with a much less known text, Canadian author Daphne Marlatt's *Ana Historic* (1988),[11] which has a strong intertextual relationship with *Frankenstein*. We discussed in detail how one literary text may be informed by another; how literature informs criticism, and vice versa; and how literary theory informs both and can be, in turn, informed by both in a literary ecosystem.

In addition to providing students with an introduction to traditional literary research methods and methodologies, we also explored how the field of digital humanities is changing how many literary scholars work. As Katherine Hales writes, "[H]umanities scholars are confronting the differences that digital media make in every aspect of humanistic inquiry, including conceptualizing projects, implementing research programs, designing curricula, and educating students."[12] We took this a step further, by also looking at the ways in which digital media is changing scholarly communication. Exploring digital humanities projects expanded ideas of what counts as scholarship, and it offered new insights into texts through the use of text mining and visualization. Students were introduced to what the WPA Framework refers to as "composing in multiple environments," viewing scholarly work packaged as a website, not the standard book or journal article with which they are used to working.[13] For example, we explored an e-book that allows readers to comment on the text and respond to each other. Instead of a solitary student or academic reading the book then publishing a reply months later, the e-book allows for public engagement with the text in real time. We discussed the implications of such projects with regard to both strengths and weaknesses. From viewing scholarly writing in website and interactive e-book form, students learned this mode of delivery offers avenues to convey meaning that standard academic papers do not.

In addition to seeing how technology is changing the study of English literature, we wanted students to experience how it is shaping the methods in which scholars collaborate and communicate. Structurally, we purposely set up the logistics of the course to emulate how scholars increasingly collaborate with each other by offering the course at a regional campus remotely via video-conferencing and requiring students to discuss scholarly material in online forums. These technologies are not novel and are, in fact, used in many courses today. However, it is not as common to metacognitively consider the impact of these technologies on our communication and our work. Moreover, our experience has shown us many teachers rarely specifically identify and stress the importance of developing related skills: being flexible with plans, ideas, and technology and approaching our work with an open, playful, resilient, and critical attitude, more ideas found in the WPA Framework. Through self-reflection, as well as communicating about and demonstrating these skills, we hoped to model a critical attitude required for twenty-first century scholarly work.

Assignments

The major assignment was designed to replicate the steps of scholarly production for an academic researcher. First, students read the texts and developed research questions. They then carried out their own research while considering the influence of different theoretical points of view on the development of their research questions. The final paper served as a vehicle to discuss several scholarly communication issues, in particular the peer-review process. In setting up the exercise, Kathleen explored the traditional peer-review system with students, considering its strengths and weakness, as well as possible alternatives. One of the alternatives introduced in this course was pre-publication peer review, in which a work is posted for peers to review before it is published in final form. We discussed this model in class, then gave the students an assignment stimulating this workflow. Once the students had written their research papers, they posted their essays online, using the course management software, where they read and critiqued each other's work. Incorporating feedback they received from their peers, students submitted the final version of their papers to the instructors one week later.

While this exercise, in itself, is not much different from an online writing workshop, by framing it in the context of the peer-review process, we hoped the students would gain a professional perspective of it. Thus, it became more than an exercise; it was also an opportunity to learn more about the peer-review process, to think critically about it, and about the new directions in which it is going.

In addition to allowing students to experience how academic work comes into being, the peer-review assignment allowed students to practice skills required to function in today's scholarly environment. Students gained experience in constructively critiquing a colleague's work in writing, as well as receiving, evaluating, and incorporating selected feedback. The feedback on the assignment we initially received from students was that they were uncomfortable with their peers seeing their work before it's done. This is unsurprising, as many English courses are not set up to allow students to see each other's work, despite the WPA Framework calling on instructors to help "develop flexible writing processes by having students [...] work with others in various stages of writing."[14] Ironically, although writing and peer-review workshops are almost always part of first-year composition courses, these soft skills are less often used and rarely explicitly taught by professors in upper-level courses, despite the fact they are vital to learning to work in a scholarly environment and other workplaces. To this end, the course tried to move students beyond the idea of a perfected, fixed piece of scholarship written in isolation, pointing out the ways in which scholars are curating scholarly thoughts that shift and change over time via collaboration, both in person and on social media.

Another exercise, related to the final paper assignment, raised the issue of knowledge mobilization—the way scholars shape and deliver research findings. After watching several short YouTube videos by scholars talking about their research, students worked with a partner to practice a one-minute speech explaining their final research paper to a lay audience. The WPA Framework refers to this as "developing rhetorical knowledge," calling on educators to give students opportunities to "write for different audiences, purposes, and contexts."[15] An opportunity to put this into practice came in the form of a serendipitously timed event: a research colloquium on how technology is changing the humanities, where several of the students volunteered to present in front of several hundred people.[16] Topics included research via the deep web, the final essay peer-review assignment, and collaboration via video conferencing. The aim of these exercises was for students to experience adapting their message and its packaging depending on audience and purpose.

Student and Faculty Feedback

Course evaluation survey data showed the students were overwhelmingly in favor of the co-teaching approach. Several students in the class recognized this collaboration made the course better than either faculty member could have produced alone, and a few urged us to go even further in integrating instruction.

Unlike our decision to collaborate, the choice to incorporate as much of the technology scholars are using as possible for the sake of introducing students to working in a technical environment was not uniformly successful. Students found video-conferencing to be difficult to deal with because people are represented as small talking heads on camera, so body language was not always clear. More problematic were one-second signal delays which caused interruptions and false starts in discussion. However, one technological element received very well by the students was an online environment to model the peer-review process. Students found it useful to both read the work of other students and receive feedback themselves. One student commented, "The process required me to take other people's feedback and apply it to my paper, resulting in a very thoughtful revision." From both our disciplinary perspectives, the assignment worked brilliantly to facilitate a discussion of the strengths and weaknesses of the peer-review process, as well as identify how it might be improved.

We received feedback from colleagues as well. At the research colloquium, even though some students were critical of some of our uses of technology, colleagues from other disciplines commented that this kind of collaboration in a research methods course should be considered by their departments. Additionally, as the English Department is nearing the end of a full curriculum review, our project has helped influence the department to revise its research methods course description to include information literacy and scholarly communication. A second result is the departmental upper-level planning committee has proposed making this course mandatory for the department's new Honor's Program. A third development is the department has proposed embedding a librarian in its new senior-level Capstone Project.

Refining the Course

We are in the midst of running the course for a second time. As we planned for this iteration, perhaps the most important aspect of the course we addressed was the level of complexity. In 2014, we leapt in with both feet and deliberately chose to incorporate a good deal of technology—some of which neither of us was familiar—all in one go. In some regards, we got carried away with the "Fascinating Technologies" (the title of the humanities colloquium at which we presented with some of our students). We recognized, in some instances, a return to the basics and away from some of the more distracting technologies would better serve our students. This time, the course was streamlined somewhat, building on the technology that worked best (e.g., the peer-editing process) and leaving out what did not work as well (e.g., video-conferencing), especially in a course with challenging theoretical content.

In addition to making technological changes, we have increased the focus given to information literacy skills. In 2014, a total of six hours of instruction time was devoted to search skills (two hours), curating a scholarly profile (two hours), and scholarly communication (two hours). In the 2016 version of the course, 7.5 hours is now used for expanded information literacy and writing instruction, including search skills, topic and question development, source evaluation, and proposal writing. A further 1.5 hours for scholarly communication and 1.5 hours for curating a scholarly profile online round out the information literacy portion of instruction.

In the current iteration of the course, assignments have also been added to enhance the information literacy skills espoused by the ACRL Framework and the writing skills discussed in the WPA Framework. Prior to discussing the steps scholars walk through when initially undertaking research, we asked the students to reflect on their own research and writing processes in the form of a short reflection paper. Students wrote about how they select a research topic and a question, their strategies for finding secondary sources, their motivations for selecting the citations they use, and their own writing process, among other questions. From this metacognitive exercise, one at the heart of both Frameworks, we noticed the class is almost perfectly divided in the approach taken to developing a research question. Half of the class formulate a question and then go to the published literature, while the other half start exploring literature and allow their question to develop from there. Out of this observation, we were able to discuss the implications of conducting research in both fashions.

In addition to adding a reflection paper, the second version of this course saw us expand upon the success of the collegial peer-review final essay process and bring this approach to paper proposals. In the first version of the course only the instructors saw final essay proposals. This time, students paired up with their classmates to discuss proposals and give each other feedback in class. This change was made to give students an additional opportunity to work collaboratively, as they will be commonly required to do in post-undergraduate employment. The exercise promotes what the WPA Framework labels as "openness" in writing, by encouraging students to "listen to and reflect on the ideas and responses of others…to their writing."[17] Additionally, it strengthened the quality of proposals, a type of writing with which most students in the class were unfamiliar. We also asked students to be "flexible" in crafting their proposals and to "reflect on the choices they [made] in light of context, purpose, and audience."[18] Dawn discussed her experience with writing proposals read by people from different disciplines or outside of academia and how this changes the content and tone of her writing. As indicated, the change to the course to allow for an additional opportunity for collaboration between students answers the WPA Framework's call for instructors to help students "develop flexible writing processes" by working with each other.[19]

As requested by students in the 2014 version of the course, we continued to work on integrating our individual subject expertise into a fluid and dynamic back-and-forth style of instruction. Exploring how researchers go about defining new research projects for themselves served as example of strong, integrated instruction. For example, in one of our class meetings on research methods, Dawn began by leading the class in brainstorming areas of research interest on *Frankenstein* and arriving at a specific research question. Kathleen then led students through search techniques that would best get students connected to the literature they required for the question selected. We both talked about evaluating sources: Kathleen from a general library perspective covering authority and the peer-review process and Dawn from a disciplinary perspective of evaluating critics' use of theoretical positions. Next, Kathleen introduced citation management software, then Dawn brought all the parts together in a discussion of how to create an effective research proposal.

Both the enhanced information literacy content and the more fluid back-and-forth approach in 2016 are bolstered by a deepened relationship between librarian and disciplinary faculty this time around. Coming from a library without previous experience working so closely with a faculty member in a classroom, Kathleen found one of the most difficult aspects of embedded librarianship is walking a delicate balance between selling the skills librarians can bring to the classroom and not overstepping boundaries, which is highly variable depending on each partner. In 2014, despite Dawn's repeated and genuine requests for input, Kathleen didn't want to make her feel like she was taking over too much of her turf or asking for too much time in the classroom. As we continued to work together and established deeper trust and respect, it became much easier for Kathleen to offer her thoughts on the design of the course and feel like a full partner in the endeavor.

The Course in the Context of ACRL Frames

At the same time the first iteration of this course was being taught, the ACRL was revising its information literacy standards following increasing calls by librarians for redefinition and reframing. As the first edition of ACRL *Information Literacy Competency Standards for Higher Education* (2000) aged, they were critiqued by many librarians for being too specific and prescriptive.[20] Scholars increasingly talked of "critical information literacy"[21] and proposed new definitions and conceptions of information literacy that went beyond traditional library and research skills.[22] Online, the #critlib Twitter community was born.[23] Recognizing the need for an update, the ACRL struck a task force in 2013 and charged it with significantly revising the Standards. Throughout 2014, the Task Force released three drafts, each a significant departure from the 2000 Standards.

The ACRL Framework emphasizes six threshold concepts, or frames, which it defined as "those critical gateway or portal concepts through which students must pass in order to develop genuine expertise within a discipline, profession, or knowledge domain."[24] The six threshold concepts are as follows:

- Authority Is Constructed and Contextual
- Information Creation as a Process
- Information Has Value
- Research as Inquiry
- Scholarship as Conversation
- Searching as Strategic Exploration[25]

The new frames permit a broader understanding of information literacy as including social and technical practices and dispositions, in line with what scholars have articulated through concepts such as "metaliteracy"[26] and information literacy as a "sociotechnical practice."[27] The frames allow teaching and librarian faculty to conceptualize information literacy as a set of skills developed over the course of a student's time at an institution.

We were midway through our 2014 version of the course when the third draft of the ACRL Framework was released by the task force. Immediately, we saw many of the ideas in this document were already in action in our course. The text provided us with a richer understanding of what information literacy is and why collaborations such as the one we are involved in are critical to the work of librarians and teachers alike. The old Standards felt restrictive and as if they were pass/fail skills. The new ACRL Framework emphasizes the development of information literacy is a process occurring over time, and it feels more flexible in terms of the pathways in which students enhance their information literacy. In shedding restrictive directives, however, the ACRL Framework has been critiqued for leaving librarians without a clear path forward for information literacy instruction. We realized we were in the process of finding just such a path.

Our partnership suggested how the new document can be deployed in an embedded librarian setting. While all of the frames are relevant to our course, two in particular are the most relevant to contextualize and ground what occurs in our course: "Information Creation as Process" and "Scholarship Is a Conversation."

Information Creation as a Process

"Information Creation as a Process," according to the ACRL Framework, "refers to the understanding that the purpose, message, and delivery of information are intentional acts of creation. Recognizing the nature of information creation, experts look to the underlying processes of creation as well as the final product to critically evaluate the usefulness of the information."[28] In our course, Dawn explored how academics create meaning and messages in the study of literature. Both Dawn and Kathleen explored the development of research questions and information literacy for research methods. Kathleen then followed up by guiding students to an understanding of how scholarship moves from the idea phase to the transmission of an intellectual product. In particular, the peer-review process exercise was helpful to explore the act of shaping scholarship.

Often in research methods classes, the focus is on the collection and analysis of research data, and how these analyses enter into scholarly and public discourse is not discussed. We really wanted the students to walk away from the course with an understanding that while the dissemination of traditional papers still has value for getting work in front of other academics, there are other models of publishing work needing to be considered apart from traditional peer-reviewed journal articles and books. In class, we explored different models for communication through a discussion of building an online scholarly profile. Key to success in developing a well-rounded profile is the ability to repackage work for different audiences. We discussed blogging, tweeting, posting videos online, composing multimedia oral presentations, and the previously mentioned digital humanities websites, and interactive e-books. Whether students go on in academia or not wasn't important; we stressed learning to present information in different ways is a critical job skill.

Scholarship Is a Conversation

The second ACRL principle, "Scholarship Is a Conversation," "refers to the idea of sustained discourse within a community of scholars, researchers, or professionals, with new insights and discoveries occurring over time as a result of competing perspectives and interpretations."[29] Dawn led the students in an exploration of how various authors, literary critics, and literary theorists engage with each other and with texts in order to develop and build scholarship. Kathleen introduced the students to non-traditional forms of conversations via digital humanities projects. Together, we built the course to reinforce the idea that scholarship is an ongoing conversation, and we tried to help students build skills in this area.

Both the content and structure of the course were designed to model current and emerging forms of scholarly communication. With regard to content, we posited those relationships between literature, criticism, and literary theory precisely as a conversation. Texts in all three categories are talking to each other. Some talk about cultural issues of concern, such as in *Frankenstein*, the ethical limits of scientific experimentation, and some talk about other texts. During research skills sessions, we explored how scholars engage each other through an exploration of tracking citations backwards via bibliographies and forwards through the use of Google Scholar's "Cited By" feature. Modeling how scholars communicate was infused into the structure of the course through assignments, such as learning collaborative skills in the peer-review essay and proposal requirements, and via the technological aspects of the course, including working collaboratively via videoconferencing and online in small groups.

Conclusion

The WPA and the ACRL Framework, taken together, offer a new avenue for understanding research-writing and new opportunities for both teachers and librarians to assist students in enhancing their information literacy skills. One highly effective way to do so is for librarians to partner with disciplinary faculty, creating dynamic instruction duos. The ACRL Framework recognizes this, highlighting the need for teaching and librarian faculty to work together to assist students in deepening their information literacy by issuing a challenge:

> Teaching faculty have a greater responsibility in designing curricula and assignments that foster enhanced engagement with the core ideas about information and scholarship within their disciplines. Librarians have a greater responsibility in identifying core ideas within their own knowledge domain that can extend learning for students, in creating a new cohesive curriculum for information literacy, and in collaborating more extensively with faculty.[30]

Collaboration at all stages of our course has opened a space for one librarian and one disciplinary faculty member to engage students more effectively than either individual could have done alone. While embedded librarianship is not a new practice, more attention should be paid to specifically embedding librarians in research methods courses. Regardless of academic discipline, this type of course is an ideal site to form librarian-faculty partnerships. Research methods curricula are a natural place to assist students in advancing their information literacy capacities and engage students in a discussion of the complex and constantly changing scholarly communication environment.

Notes

1. Council of Writing Program Administrators, National Council of Teachers of English, and National Writing Project. 2011. *Framework for Success in Postsecondary Writing*. Accessed 8 February 2016. http://www.wpacouncil.org/files/framework-for-success-postsecondary-writing.pdf.
2 Association of College and Research Libraries. 2016. *Framework for Information Literacy for Higher Education*. Accessed December 14, 2015. http://www.ala.org/acrl/sites/ala.org.acrl/files/content/issues/infolit/Framework_ILHE.pdf.
3. Barbara I. Dewey, "The Embedded Librarian," *Resource Sharing & Information Networks* 17, no. 1–2. (2004): 5–17. doi:10.1300/J121v17n01_02.
4. Jake Carlson and Ruth Kneale, "Embedded Librarianship in the Research Context: Navigating New Waters," *College & Research Libraries News* 72, no. 3 (2011): 167–170.
5. Sarah Polkinghorne and Shauna Wilton, "Research is a Verb: Exploring a New Information Literacy-Embedded Undergraduate Research Methods Course," *Canadian Journal of Information and Library Science* 34, no.10 (2010): 457–473; B. Marfleet and Brian Dille, "Information Literacy and the Undergraduate Research Methods Curriculum," *Journal of Political Science Education* 1, no. 2 (2005): 175–190.

6. Michelle Toth, "Research and Writing and Theses—Oh My! The Journey of a Collaboratively Taught Graduate Research and Writing Course," *The Reference Librarian* 89/90 (2005): 81–92.

7. Navaz P. Bhavnagri and Veronica Bielat, "Faculty-Librarian Collaboration to Teach Research Skills: Electronic Symbiosis," *The Reference Librarian* 13, no. 89/90 (2005): 121–138. doi:10.1300/J120v43n89_09.

8. Association of College and Research Libraries, 2000. *Information Literacy Competency Standards for Higher Education.* Accessed October 7, 2016. http://www.ala.org/acrl/standards/informationliteracycompetency.

9. See: Stephanie Davis-Kahl, "Engaging Undergraduates in Scholarly Communication: Outreach, Education, and Advocacy," *College & Research Libraries News* 73, no. 4 (2005): 212–222; Scott Warren and Kim Duckett, "Why Does Google Scholar Sometimes Ask for Money? Engaging Science Students in Scholarly Communication and the Economics of Information," *Journal of Library Administration* 50, no. 4 (2010): 349–372, doi:10.1080/01930821003667021; and Stephanie Davis-Kahl and Merinda Kaye Hensley, *Common Ground at the Nexus of Information Literacy and Scholarly Communication* (Chicago: Association of College and Research Libraries, 2013).

10. Mary Shelley, *Frankenstein*, ed. Johanna A. Smith (Boston: Bedford/St. Martin's, 2000).

11. Daphne Marlatt, *Anna Historic* (Toronto: House of Anansi, 1988).

12. N. Katherine Hayles. *How We Think: Digital Media and Contemporary Technogenisis* (Chicago: University of Chicago Press, 2012): 1.

13. WPA, Framework, 10.

14. Ibid., 8.

15. Ibid., 6.

16. The colloquium was recorded and is available at: http://viuspace.viu.ca/handle/10613/2485.

17. WPA, Framework, 4.

18. Ibid., 5.

19. Ibid., 8.

20. Bill Johnston and Sheila Webber, "Information Literacy in Higher Education: A Review and Case Study," *Studies in Higher Education* 28, no. 3 (2003): 335–352.

21. See James Elmborg, "Critical Information Literacy: Implications for Instructional Practice," *The Journal of Academic Librarianship* 32, no. 2 (2006): 192–199; Troy A. Swanson, "A Radical Step: Implementing a Critical Information Literacy Model," *Portal: Libraries and the Academy* 4, no. 2 (2004): 259–273.

22. Kimmo Tuominen, Reijo Savolainen, and Sanna Talja, "Information Literacy as a Sociotechnical Practice," *The Library Quarterly* 75, no. 3 (2005): 329–345; Trudi E. Jacobson and Thomas P. Mackey, "Proposing a Metaliteracy Model to Redefine Information Literacy," *Communications in Information Literacy* 7, no. 2 (2013): 84–91; Annemaree Lloyd, *Information Literacy Landscapes: Information Literacy in Education, Workplace and Everyday Contexts* (Oxford: Chandos, 2010).

23. Nicole Pagowsky, "Introducing #critlib Chats!" *Pumped Librarian.* April 3, 2014. Accessed January 28, 2015. http://pumpedlibrarian.blogspot.ca/2014/04/introducing-critlib-chats.html.

24. ACRL, Framework, 12.

25. Ibid., 2.

26. Thomas P. Mackey and Trudi E. Jacobson, "Reframing Information Literacy as a Metaliteracy," *College & Research Libraries* 76, no. 1 (2011).
27. Tuominen, Savolainen, and Talja, "Information Literacy as a Sociotechnical Practice."
28. ACRL, Framework, 5.
29. Ibid., 8.
30. Ibid., 2.

Bibliography

Association of College and Research Libraries. 2000. *Information Literacy Competency Standards for Higher Education*. Accessed December 14, 2015. http://www.ala.org/acrl/standards/informationliteracycompetency.

Association of College and Research Libraries. 2016. *Framework for Information Literacy for Higher Education*. Accessed December 14, 2015. http://www.ala.org/acrl/sites/ala.org.acrl/files/content/issues/infolit/Framework_ILHE.pdf.

Bhavnagri, Navaz P. and Veronica Bielat. "Faculty-Librarian Collaboration to Teach Research Skills: Electronic Symbiosis." *The Reference Librarian* 13, no. 89/90 (2005): 121–138. doi:10.1300/J120v43n89_09.

Carlson, Jake and Ruth Kneale. "Embedded Librarianship in the Research Context: Navigating New Waters." *College & Research Libraries News* 72, no. 3 (2011): 167–170.

Council of Writing Program Administrators, National Council of Teachers of English, and National Writing Project. 2011. *Framework for Success in Postsecondary Writing*. Accessed February 8, 2016. http://www.wpacouncil.org/files/framework-for-success-postsecondary-writing.pdf.

Davis-Kahl, Stephanie. "Engaging Undergraduates in Scholarly Communication: Outreach, Education, and Advocacy." *College & Research Libraries News* 73, no. 4 (2012): 212–222.

Davis-Kahl, Stephanie and Merinda Kaye Hensley. *Common Ground at the Nexus of Information Literacy and Scholarly Communication*. Chicago: Association of College and Research Libraries, 2013.

Dewey, Barbara I. "The Embedded Librarian." *Resource Sharing & Information Networks* 17, no. 1–2 (2004): 5–17. doi:10.1300/J121v17n01_02.

Elmborg, James. "Critical Information Literacy: Implications for Instructional Practice." *The Journal of Academic Librarianship* 32, no. 2 (2006): 192–199.

Flavell, John H. "Metacognition and Cognitive Monitoring: A New Area of Cognitive Developmental Inquiry." *American Psychologist* 34 (1979): 906–911.

Hayles, N. Katherine. *How We Think: Digital Media and Contemporary Technogenisis*. Chicago: University of Chicago Press, 2012.

Jacobson, Trudi E. and Thomas P. Mackey. "Proposing a Metaliteracy Model to Redefine Information Literacy." *Communications in Information Literacy* 7, no. 2 (2013): 84–91.

Johnston, Bill and Sheila Webber. "Information Literacy in Higher Education: A Review and Case Study." *Studies in Higher Education* 28, no. 3 (2003): 335–352.

Lloyd, Annemaree. *Information Literacy Landscapes: Information Literacy in Education, Workplace and Everyday Contexts*. Oxford: Chandos, 2010.

Mackey, Thomas P. and Trudi E. Jacobson. "Reframing Information Literacy as a Metaliteracy." *College & Research Libraries* 76, no. 1 (2011).

Marfleet, B. and Brian Dille. "Information Literacy and the Undergraduate Research Methods Curriculum." *Journal of Political Science Education* 1, no. 2 (2005): 175–190.

Pagowsky, Nicole. "Introducing #critlib Chats!" *Pumped Librarian*. 3 April 2014. Accessed January 28, 2015. http://pumpedlibrarian.blogspot.ca/2014/04/introducing-crit-lib-chats.html.

Polkinghorne, Sarah and Shauna Wilton. "Research is a Verb: Exploring a New Information Literacy-Embedded Undergraduate Research Methods Course." *Canadian Journal of Information and Library Science* 34, no.10 (2010): 457–473.

Swanson, Troy A. "A Radical Step: Implementing a Critical Information Literacy Model." *Portal: Libraries and the Academy* 4, no. 2 (2004): 259–273.

Toth, Michelle. "Research and Writing and Theses—Oh My! The Journey of a Collaboratively Taught Graduate Research and Writing Course." *The Reference Librarian* 89/90 (2005): 81–92.

Tuominen, Kimmo, Reijo Savolainen, and Sanna Talja. "Information Literacy as a Sociotechnical Practice." *The Library Quarterly* 75, no. 3 (2005): 329–345.

Warren, Scott and Kim Duckett. "Why Does Google Scholar Sometimes Ask for Money? Engaging Science Students in Scholarly Communication and the Economics of Information." *Journal of Library Administration* 50, no. 4 (2010): 349–372. doi:10.1080/01930821003667021.

SECTION 3:
Assessing Writing & Information Literacy

CHAPTER 12[*]

The Frameworks, Comparative Analyses, and Sharing Responsibility for Learning and Assessment

Teresa Grettano and Donna Witek
The University of Scranton

Introduction

With the push in U.S. higher education toward outcomes-based, rubric-driven assessment, Edward M. White's "'first law of assesso-dynamics': *Assess thyself or assessment will be done unto thee*" rings louder than ever.[1] Rubrics ushered the discipline of rhetoric and composition into assessment in the 1960s with much benefit: they legitimized the direct assessment of writing, sped up the process and made it more affordable, and provided documentation of how writing is

* This work is licensed under a Creative Commons Attribution-NonCommercial 4.0 License, CC BY-NC (https://creativecommons.org/licenses/by-nc/4.0/).

evaluated.[2] Now some fifty years later, educators are criticizing the testing-centric existence of assessment, as imposed assessments dictated by those outside of a program in order to satisfy constituencies such as accreditation groups have left many teachers feeling disconnected from actual pedagogy, seeing most assessments today as irrelevant and distracting, or in some cases punitive.[3] Rubrics seem to speak to the concerns of those who do not teach writing but instead make policy; to offer generic representations focused on formal aspects of writing rather than the complex, rhetorical writing taught in composition classes; and to falsify a messy process of meaning-making as something containable in a short skills statement.[4] At best, writing assessment founded on rubrics can seem uninspired or uninformed; at worst, unpedagogical and harmful.[5]

We present the process of our collaboration and the commonalities between our two fields of study—rhetoric and composition and information literacy (IL)—as a means by which to take more control of our pedagogical and assessment practices, to make them more intentional and meaning-driven, and to comply with outside standards while still holding true to our pedagogical beliefs. We posit that using our guiding documents—the *Framework for Success in Postsecondary Writing* (hereafter WPA Framework) and the *Framework for Information Literacy for Higher Education* (hereafter ACRL Framework), as well as the older *WPA Outcomes Statement for First-Year Composition* (hereafter WPA OS) and the *Information Literacy Competency Standards for Higher Education* (hereafter ACRL Standards)—makes visible the connections in our work, offers language with which to discuss pedagogy, and enables shared responsibility for instruction and assessment.[6]

Most writing and information literacy experts already know literacy education works best when it is integrated throughout the curriculum and responsibility for it is shared among various stakeholders on campus.[7] In fact, Barry M. Maid and Barbara J. D'Angelo call for a merging of the research and writing processes under the banner of IL in order to better serve our students. "Doing so," they claim, "allows us to more fully integrate IL into the writing process so that, from the perspective of writing, research is not simply the collection of information and, from the perspective of research, writing is not simply the presentation of information."[8] This integration better reflects what students actually do when researching and writing in the dynamic new participatory information environments in which these processes are situated.[9] Maid and D'Angelo insist our assessment practices become as dynamic as the practices we are assessing.[10]

Beyond these pedagogical benefits of integrating literacy instruction, however, a more practical catalyst for joining forces is to manage—in terms of workload and governance—the assessments of literacy we are now being pressured to produce. Instead of having assessment "done unto thee" in the form of standardized rubrics, creating collaborative initiatives grounded in the shared language and outcomes of our national documents can not only revive uninspired assessment, but also revolutionize work on our localized campuses.[11] Peggy O'Neill, Cindy Moore, and Brian Huot contend "a department-level administrator who embraces assessment—especially the kind of assessment that extends beyond the boundaries of her specific program—is in a position not only to help set the agenda for campus-wide assessment initiatives, but to affect, even 'transform,' teaching and learning across the university community."[12] This has been our experience. To be sure, such work takes time and patience, failed attempts and restarts, moments of pause and restraint, and spouts of energy and excitement. And despite the fact that this work must be contextualized always within the distinct cultures of our own campuses, we posit our collaboration as a model through which to identify shared outcomes and language in order to share responsibility for assessment across the university.

Collaboration as Conversation

Twentieth-century literary and rhetorical theorist Kenneth Burke described the act of scholarly writing in what has become known as Burke's parlor metaphor:

> Imagine that you enter a parlor. You come late. When you arrive, others have long preceded you, and they are engaged in a heated discussion, a discussion too heated for them to pause and tell you exactly what it is about. In fact, the discussion had already begun long before any of them got there, so that no one present is qualified to retrace for you all the steps that had gone before. You listen for a while, until you decide that you have caught the tenor of the argument; then you put in your oar. Someone answers; you answer him; another comes to your defense; another aligns himself against you, to either the embarrassment or gratification of your opponent, depending upon the quality of your ally's assistance. However, the discussion is interminable. The hour grows late, you must depart. And you do depart, with the discussion still vigorously in progress.[13]

Burke's parlor metaphor was the first thing Teresa thought of when she encountered the proposed "Scholarship as Conversation" frame in the ACRL Framework draft. It is through Burke's metaphor that many in rhetoric and composition teach academic writing to students. It is a way to teach students scope and move them from informative writing to persuasive writing. This metaphor speaks to many points in both Frameworks. In the ACRL Framework it speaks to the "Scholarship as Conversation" and "Research as Inquiry" frames, and in the WPA Framework it speaks to "Developing Rhetorical Knowledge" and "De-

veloping Critical Thinking Through Writing, Reading, and Research," two experiences listed under "Experiences with Writing, Reading, and Critical Analysis." It also can be used to understand the intersections for instruction in our
fields, as librarian Barbara Fister alludes to when she and her colleagues refer
to the various approaches to teaching this concept as "Burke's Parlor Tricks."[14]

The importance of this metaphor goes beyond its usefulness in communicating these concepts to students, however. Even more important is the fact
we are enacting this metaphor as we discuss the meanings of our Frameworks
in our own fields, as we collaborate between them, and as we work across our
campuses. We are in the midst of heated discussion about the purposes of
higher education, literacy instruction, meaning in our own disciplines, and
curriculum on our campuses. These discussions began long before any of us
adopted our professional identities or duties, and they are interminable. We all
simply are listening to catch up and then putting our oars in to contribute. This
chapter is an example of one such contribution.

Institutional Context

We recognize the approach we proffer has been fostered by our institutional
context. Our collaboration has been cultivated by our being employed on a
relatively small campus and at a Jesuit institution. This context has given us
leave to practice our disciplines in ways other contexts may inhibit. We acknowledge this context may not be common, yet we see value in sharing our
experience and the ways in which our disciplinary Frameworks have helped
foster the collaboration we share.

The University of Scranton is a private, Catholic, Jesuit institution located in northeastern Pennsylvania. The university matriculates about four thousand undergraduate students per year, most of whom are residential and come
from white, middle-class, suburban households. There are about three hundred
full-time faculty members protected by a faculty union, 87 percent of which
hold tenure lines. Our Catholic, Jesuit identity influences the ways in which
we approach instruction, collaboration, and assessment. We are committed to
cura personalis, or caring for the whole person, and this value manifests in a
responsibility to consider not only the intellectual, educational, or disciplinary
development of our students, but also their human formation. As Jesuit Supe-
rior General Rev. Peter-Hans Kolvenbach, S.J., declared in his 2000 address,
"The real measure of our Jesuit universities lies in who our students become."[15]
Therefore, our assessment of students' time at the institution must include outcomes that aren't necessarily measurable through the application of rubrics.

The First-Year Writing (FYW) Program at The University of Scranton is
housed in the Department of English & Theatre. The director of the program,

historically, has been a tenure-track faculty member in rhetoric and composition who is appointed by the Dean of Arts & Sciences with the support of the department. The program is responsible for teaching courses that fulfill for most first-year students the general education *Eloquentia Perfecta* FYW requirement, discussed later in this chapter. Students fulfill this requirement either by successfully completing the one-semester mainstream WRTG 107 or the two-semester developmental stretch sequence WRTG 105–106, placement decisions for which are determined by a timed writing exam administered during summer orientation. On average, the program offers close to seventy-five sections of FYW per year. Currently, the program employs two tenured faculty members in rhetoric and composition, two full-time non-tenure-track faculty specialists, and ten to fifteen part-time adjunct faculty with backgrounds mostly in creative writing and English education, with the Dean of Arts & Sciences and the Dean of the Library and Information Fluency teaching one section of FYW each year; still the program is at 70 percent adjunct dependency.

The University of Scranton Weinberg Memorial Library's Information Literacy Program (IL Program) "supports the learning needs of students as well as the teaching and research needs of faculty and staff" in the area of IL.[16] The ACRL Framework defines IL as "the set of integrated abilities encompassing the reflective discovery of information, the understanding of how information is produced and valued, and the use of information in creating new knowledge and participating ethically in communities of learning."[17] The university's IL Program supports the development of this literacy through direct instruction, research support provided by appointment or at the reference desk, and consultation and outreach to the university community including course instructors who assign work that involves IL outcomes, explicitly or implicitly. There are nine full-time, tenure-line faculty librarians, all of whom are part of the faculty union, and five of which are directly responsible for supporting the IL Program through instruction, reference, and consultation.

Collaboration through the Frameworks Serving Curriculum

In this section, we explain how we use our disciplinary documents to foster collaboration and influence curriculum development in our own programs and those across campus. We began this work before the Frameworks were available, in the fall of 2009. At that time, we worked with the WPA OS 2.0 version (updated to version 3.0 in July 2014) and the ACRL Standards. Our methodology for collaborating with and analyzing the documents has been narrated in our previous work; it involves side-by-side textual analyses of the documents in which we map like-concepts between them, coupled with in-depth conversation through which we aim to uncover the shared meaning between our fields of practice.[18] We since have applied this methodology to the Framework documents. These documents enable us to share language and outcomes and to build curricular initiatives that work toward developing literacy in our students.

FYW Program Outcomes

Teresa was appointed Director of First-Year Writing in fall 2013 and charged with developing a programmatic mission statement and learning outcomes. Her first step in doing so was to survey her current instructors using the WPA OS to gauge instructor practices, attitudes, and areas of expertise. She chose the WPA OS as the instrument through which to conduct this inquiry because it is the guiding document for FYW, as it "describes the writing knowledge, practices, and attitudes that undergraduate students develop in first-year composition, which at most schools is a required general education course or sequence of courses" and "articulates what composition teachers nationwide have learned from practice, research, and theory."[19]

Teresa invited the sixteen instructors teaching FYW courses during fall 2013, along with Charles Kratz, Dean of the Library and Information Fluency, who teaches in the FYW Program annually, to participate in the survey; fourteen of the seventeen participants invited completed the survey, for an 82 percent response rate.

Using the twenty-five total outcomes listed in the WPA OS 2.0, Teresa asked instructors to rank the importance of each outcome, the capability of the program to meet each outcome, and the ease at which each outcome is met, among other questions. Regardless of how the questions were asked, both in terms of importance of the outcome in general and in terms of reflecting on current practices, the same outcomes rose to the top of the scoring throughout the survey results, half of which related to IL instruction. Table 12.01 lists these outcomes with the abbreviations used to report the survey results.

The top-ranked outcomes FYW shares with IL instruction are (abbreviated): Writing for Inquiry, Information Literacy, Integrate, Documenting, and Digital Information Literacy. Table 12.02 maps these outcomes from the WPA OS 2.0 to the Frameworks.

In all, it was clear from the survey results current instructors in the FYW Program valued IL instruction not only as an extension of how the library could support the program, but also in what defines the program itself and the outcomes to achieve with students. What this meant to Teresa was she needed to make this sharing of curriculum and pedagogy more explicit and intentional.

Table 12.01
Top Outcomes Consistently Ranked with Survey Abbreviations

Outcome	Abbreviation
Rhetorical Knowledge	
Focus on a purpose	Focus on Purpose
Respond to the needs of different audiences	Audience
Adopt appropriate voice, tone, and level of formality	Voice
Critical Thinking, Reading, and Writing	
Use writing and reading for inquiry, learning, thinking, and communicating	Writing for Inquiry
Understand a writing assignment as a series of tasks, including finding, evaluating, analyzing, and synthesizing appropriate primary and secondary sources	Information Literacy
Integrate their own ideas with those of others	Integrate
Processes	
Be aware that it usually takes multiple drafts to create and complete a successful text	Multiple Drafts
Develop flexible strategies for generating, revising, editing, and proof-reading	Flexible Strategies
Knowledge of Conventions	
Practice appropriate means of documenting their work	Documenting
Control such surface features as syntax, grammar, punctuation, and spelling	Surface Features
Composing in Electronic Environments	
Locate, evaluate, organize, and use research material collected from electronic sources, including scholarly library databases; other official databases (e.g., federal government databases); and informal electronic networks and Internet sources	Digital Information Literacy

Table 12.02
WPA OS Survey IL-related Outcomes Mapped to Frameworks

WPA Outcome 2.0	Abbreviation for Survey	WPA Framework	ACRL Framework
Use writing and reading for inquiry, learning, thinking, and communicating	Writing for Inquiry	"generate ideas and texts using a variety of processes and situate those ideas within different academic disciplines and contexts" in the "Developing Flexible Writing Processes" experience	Research as Inquiry
Understand a writing assignment as a series of tasks, including finding, evaluating, analyzing, and synthesizing appropriate primary and secondary sources	Information Literacy	"conduct primary and secondary research using a variety of print and nonprint sources" in the "Developing Critical Thinking Through Writing, Reading, and Research" experience	Searching as Strategic Exploration Authority Is Constructed and Contextual Information Creation as a Process Scholarship as Conversation Information Has Value Research as Inquiry
Integrate their own ideas with those of others	Integrate	"craft written responses to texts that put the writer's ideas in conversation with those in a text in ways that are appropriate to the academic discipline or context" in the "Developing Critical Thinking Through Writing, Reading, and Research" experience	Scholarship as Conversation Information Has Value

Table 12.02
WPA OS Survey IL-related Outcomes Mapped to Frameworks

WPA Outcome 2.0	Abbreviation for Survey	WPA Framework	ACRL Framework
Practice appropriate means of documenting their work	Documenting	"practice various approaches to the documentation and attribution of sources" in the "Developing Knowledge of Conventions" experience	Information Has Value Information Creation as a Process Scholarship as Conversation
Locate, evaluate, organize, and use research material collected from electronic sources, including scholarly library databases; other official databases (e.g., federal government databases); and informal electronic networks and Internet sources	Digital Information Literacy	"conduct primary and secondary research using a variety of print and nonprint sources" in the "Developing Critical Thinking Through Writing, Reading, and Research" experience	Searching as Strategic Exploration Authority Is Constructed and Contextual Information Creation as a Process Scholarship as Conversation Information Has Value Research as Inquiry

Once the outcomes from the results of the WPA OS survey are mapped to the other Framework documents (see table 12.02), even more connections between the two programs on our campus and in our disciplines are evident. "Scholarship as Conversation" and "Information Has Value" are evident in all IL-related outcomes except one. Because "Writing for Inquiry" showed to be the most important outcome to our current instructors, the IL frame "Research as Inquiry" rose to top status in our programmatic collaboration. However, all frames in the ACRL Framework are represented in the WPA OS survey results because of the two major IL outcomes (abbreviated): Information Literacy and Digital Information Literacy.

FYW Committee

Using the results of the WPA OS survey as leverage, Teresa gained approval from her department to consult with Dean Kratz to invite IL librarians to join the newly-formed FYW Committee. This committee serves as an advisory board for the FYW Program and comprises multiple stakeholders: two full-time FYW faculty, two tenured faculty in the department not involved in the teaching of FYW, two part-time FYW faculty, two librarians (including Donna), and Teresa as director.

The major project for the FYW Committee for spring 2014 was to develop programmatic learning outcomes for FYW. Teresa worked from the results of the WPA OS survey and drafted a programmatic learning outcomes statement she first presented to FYW instructors. Those instructors helped revise the initial draft, then the group voted to move the document forward for review. The FYW Committee reviewed the document, further editing and revising it. The document was next presented to representatives from the national Council of Writing Program Administrators and our own institutional Office of Educational Assessment. All agreed the initial list of programmatic learning outcomes was not manageable and suggested it be reduced. The FYW Committee worked to condense the list from twenty-five outcomes to twelve (see table 12.03) that were then approved by the Department of English & Theatre.

Table 12.03
First-Year Writing Programmatic Learning Outcomes

Due to a mandate from the Middle States Commission on Higher Education, all syllabi must list student learning outcomes. Student learning outcomes identify what students should be able *to do* at the end of a course; they do not, however, describe who students *should be* at the end of a course. Your learning should be *transformative*, meaning who you are as a person and how you process the world and act in it should change through your education. Some of these changes will be "measurable" in terms of outcomes; other changes will not. Listed below are the measurable outcomes for this course, but know that through this course you will grow as a writer and as a person in other ways, as well.

By the end of first-year writing, students should demonstrate a foundational ability to perform the tasks listed in the following three categories:

Thesis Development	• Generate appropriate writing topics and research questions
	• Focus on a purpose
	• Adjust the rhetorical strategy in response to specific writing situations and audiences
	• Develop and support an appropriate thesis statement
	• Draft, revise, and edit as necessary throughout the process

Table 12.03 *First-Year Writing Programmatic Learning Outcomes*	
Using Research	• Develop effective search strategies for gathering information • Gather and evaluate information in terms of both relevance & reliability • Express their own ideas in relation to the ideas of others • Integrate the ideas of others responsibly in their own writing
Style & Mechanics	• Attribute sources of information based on disciplinary formatting and style standards • Adjust the tone, style, and level of diction in response to specific writing situations • Write in standardized written English (SWE)

The important factor in this process is librarians, who share some of the responsibility in supporting the teaching of these outcomes through the IL Program, were in the room while the programmatic learning outcomes were drafted and revised. They were present for the discussions about pedagogy, logistics, instruction, and assessment, and they were able to contribute to the development of the FYW Programmatic Learning Outcomes (table 12.03) from their expertise in teaching IL-related outcomes and to advocate for their department's role in teaching and supporting those outcomes.

Collaborative Assessment

Because the librarians participated in writing the FYW Programmatic Learning Outcomes and because these outcomes included IL-related outcomes, Teresa was able to argue successfully for the Dean of Arts & Sciences to compensate the two librarians on the FYW Committee for participating in programmatic assessment. For this assessment project, the librarians helped score the final paper in the FYW Program during the 2013–14 academic year. It was important to faculty in the library and the FYW Program that librarians be compensated for this work because it fell outside their established job duties. Librarians were given the same stipend part-time instructors in the FYW Program are given for doing the same assessment work.

Teresa chose three outcomes to assess through the reading of final papers submitted in WRTG 107 during fall 2013 by analyzing the results of the WPA OS survey and determining which outcomes could be assessed through reading final products; these outcomes were (abbreviated): Focus, Integrate, and Documenting. Final paper assignments varied across sections of WRTG 107 that semester. Eventually, there may be a requirement that all final paper assignments in WRTG 107 be designed to demonstrate the same IL-related outcomes, but for now instructors have the freedom to assign the kind of writing they want. Most assign writing necessitating IL-related skills; some assign reflections that do not. The rubric for IL-related skills (see figure 12.01) included an NA-0 scoring to reflect types of writing students submitted that could not be scored for IL-related outcomes; these scores were omitted easily from our final calculations.

Figure 12.01
Final Paper Assessment Rubric

(Documents assessed: final papers submitted to be graded in WRTG 107, Fall 2013; assessed Spring 2014)
(Rubric descriptions adapted from the University of California, Irvine 2011 Assessment of Lower-Division Writing at UCI)

Criterion 1: Focus on a Purpose
SLO: Thesis Development—Focus on a Purpose
Assessment will be conducted based on this outcome for two reasons: (1) it consistently ranked in the top 4 outcomes for most important or most met, and (2) of those top 4 it is the only outcome assessable through reading a final product.

	4. Proficient	3. Satisfactory	2. Fair	1. Insufficient
Focus	High degree of focus is evident	Generally good focus	Weak or inconsistent focus	No clear focus

Criterion 2: Integrate—Integrate their own ideas with those of others
SLO: Using Research—Integrate the ideas of others responsibly in their own writing
SLO: Style & Mechanics—Attribute sources of information based on disciplinary formatting and style standards
Assessment will be conducted based on this outcome for two reasons: (1) while instructors indicated they met this outcome about 80% of the time, only one instructor indicated it was met with ease, and (2) while this outcome is identified separately in the WPA Outcomes, it is considered part of information literacy in general, and that outcome consistently ranked high in all questions asked.

	4. Proficient	3. Satisfactory	2. Fair	1. Insufficient	0. N/A
Sources/ Evidence: Integration	Eloquently introduces and situates source material	Effectively introduces and situates source material	Sporadically introduces and/or situates source material	Fails to introduce and/ or situate source material	No sources used
Document-ation	Document-ation style is evident, appropriate, and accurate	Document-ation style is generally evident and accurate	Document-ation style is inconsistently evident, accurate, and/ or appropriate	Document-ation style is absent or inappropriate/ inaccurate	No sources used

The librarians and their FYW colleagues worked together to revise the rubric before assessment work began. Teresa provided a first draft, and all four scorers worked to clarify the language of the rubric so scoring would be consistent. The group discussed what it meant for students to focus on a purpose, what the difference was between a score of 4 and 3 for integration, among other nuances in language and meaning. All participants took ownership over the writing of the rubric and the process of assessment, creating stronger buy-in; figure 12.01 represents the final version of the rubric. Moreover, the librarians were able to view the products of their time with students, time spent both in one-shot sessions—where the librarian provides guest instruction in just one class meeting—and at the reference desk, participating in an important part of assessment to which they typically do not have access. The process led to conversations about outcomes and skills as well as language from both IL and FYW, making meaning between the programs in order to share more directly the responsibility of teaching students these skills.

General Education Revision and the Eloquentia Perfecta Program

In her capacity as Director of First-Year Writing, Teresa was able to bring this collaborative, Frameworks-based methodology and the corresponding documents to colleagues across campus who were working on curriculum development and revision. Teresa served on the faculty senate committee charged with revising what has been referred to as the skills courses in the general education (GE) curriculum. This committee developed the *Eloquentia Perfecta* (EP) component of the GE curriculum that houses literacy requirements. It comprises the oral communication, digital technology, writing, and critical thinking and reading requirements. As of this writing, the foundational level has been adopted by the senate and integrated into the curriculum, and the upper/rhetorical level has been approved for implementation in 2017.

During the committee meetings to develop the EP component, Teresa brought the ACRL and WPA documents to the attention of her colleagues, and they used the language in these documents to define and determine much of the component. Also serving on the committee were faculty in other disciplines who worked with librarians to embed IL instruction into their own courses, so they were already familiar with the documents. As a result of these collaborative relationships and the conversations that grew from them in committee meetings, IL has been infused throughout the EP component, evident in the outcomes for all of the designations.

Knowledge of each other's disciplinary documents and their use in our collaboration and curriculum development has fostered further collaboration and allowed for IL instruction to be infused throughout the curriculum. Though we admit this process has been slow and at times arduous, we are proud of the end result.

Collaboration through the Frameworks Serving Pedagogy

The purpose of this section is to illustrate targeted collaboration within the curriculum leads to more intentional pedagogy in the classroom. We will do so by sharing an example of an IL instruction lesson developed by Donna in collaboration with Teresa and another FYW instructor, Emily Denison. This lesson, titled "Research as Inquiry: Using the Search Process to Strategically Explore your Topic," was designed using both Frameworks and represents a prototype for how IL can be explicitly integrated, practiced, and assessed in a FYW context.

Instructional Design with the Frameworks

In spring 2015, Donna received IL instruction requests from both Teresa and Emily for the same day. The instruction sessions were one-shots scheduled back-to-back for seventy-five minutes each. Two sections were Emily's and one was Teresa's, which meant the assignments students would be working on differed; however, as WRTG 107 sections, they shared the same course-level student learning outcomes (see table 12.03). Those outcomes provided an anchor for Donna as she designed instruction customized to the assignments in each section, yet standardized across all three sections to deliver the instruction back-to-back. It also allowed Donna to design an easily repeatable, in-class activity that resulted in immediate formative assessment of student learning.

Donna's ability to design instruction that would meet the needs of all stakeholders—especially students—was predicated on the disciplinary connections between and curricular integration of IL and FYW described in the previous section. She began by analyzing the assignment prompts and syllabi from both writing instructors, drafting measurable student learning outcomes related to the research process facilitated through each assignment, and mapping these classroom-level outcomes to the FYW Programmatic Learning Outcomes (table 12.03), the IL Program Student Learning Outcomes (table 12.04), and the Frameworks.

Table 12.04
*IL Program Student Learning Outcomes**

SLO1	Students will investigate differing viewpoints that they encounter in their strategic exploration of topics in order to be able to develop their own informed arguments or hypotheses.
SLO2	Students will gain insight and understanding about diverse sources of information in order to evaluate and use resources appropriately for their information needs.
SLO3	Students will identify the appropriate level of scholarship among publication types (scholarly journals, trade publications, magazines, websites, etc.) in order to critically evaluate the usefulness of the information for their research need.
SLO4	Students will articulate the key elements in their research questions in order to develop and execute a search strategy.
SLO5	Students will properly distinguish between their own ideas and the intellectual property of others in order to ethically use information and demonstrate academic integrity.

*Originally endorsed by the Library faculty in June 2014, and again with minor revisions in October 2015.

The initial purpose of this mapping was to discover new meaning around Donna's classroom-level outcomes and to revise those outcomes in response to the program and disciplinary documents with which she and her writing instructor collaborators were working. The final maps of these outcomes are represented in table 12.05 and table 12.06.

Table 12.05
Program Outcomes Map for IL Lesson

FYW Programmatic Learning Outcomes	IL Lesson Student Learning Outcomes	IL Program Student Learning Outcomes
Generate appropriate writing topics and research questions	Brainstorm research questions, search terms, and information types/ formats related to their research topics	SLO4: Students will articulate the key elements in their research questions in order to develop and execute a search strategy.
Develop effective search strategies for gathering information		SLO2: Students will gain insight and understanding about diverse sources of information in order to evaluate and use resources appropriately for their information needs.

Table 12.05
Program Outcomes Map for IL Lesson

FYW Programmatic Learning Outcomes	IL Lesson Student Learning Outcomes	IL Program Student Learning Outcomes
Gather and evaluate information in terms of both relevance and reliability	Practice searching for and locating possible information sources for their research projects	SLO3: Students will identify the appropriate level of scholarship among publication types (scholarly journals, trade publications, magazines, websites, etc.) in order to critically evaluate the usefulness of the information for their research need.
		SLO5: Students will properly distinguish between their own ideas and the intellectual property of others in order to ethically use information and demonstrate academic integrity.
Generate appropriate writing topics and research questions	Use the search process as an opportunity to strategically explore their research topics and questions	SLO1: Students will investigate differing viewpoints that they encounter in their strategic exploration of topics in order to be able to develop their own informed arguments or hypotheses.
Develop effective search strategies for gathering information		SLO2: Students will gain insight and understanding about diverse sources of information in order to evaluate and use resources appropriately for their information needs.
		SLO4: Students will articulate the key elements in their research questions in order to develop and execute a search strategy.

In both table 12.05 and table 12.06, the middle column contains the classroom-level outcomes Donna currently uses for this IL lesson; these were revised in the summer of 2015 in order to simplify what students were tasked with during the seventy-five-minute instruction session. This assessment process and the resulting outcome revisions are described in the next section. The first two classroom-level outcomes, "Brainstorm research questions, search terms, and information types/formats related to their research topics" and "Practice searching for and locating possible information sources for their research projects," are measurable tasks in the behavioral/skills learning domain, while the third outcome, "Use the search process as an opportunity to strategically explore their research topics and questions," intentionally falls in the dispositional learning domain where habits, values, and attitudes are developed. Programmatically, these outcomes map in two directions: to the FYW Programmatic Learning Outcomes (table 12.05, first column) and to the IL Program Student Learning Outcomes (table 12.05, third column). On the disciplinary level, they map to the frames in the ACRL Framework (table 12.06, first column) and to the habits of mind and experiences in the WPA Framework (table 12.06, third column).

Table 12.06
Disciplinary Outcomes Map for IL Lesson

ACRL Framework (frames)	IL Lesson Student Learning Outcomes	WPA Framework (habits of mind on left; experiences on right)	
Information Creation as a Process	Brainstorm research questions, search terms, and information types/ formats related to their research topics	Flexibility, Persistence	Composing in Multiple Environments; Developing Rhetorical Knowledge; Developing Critical Thinking Through Writing, Reading, and Research
Research as Inquiry		Curiosity, Openness, Creativity, Persistence	Developing Critical Thinking Through Writing, Reading, and Research
Searching as Strategic Exploration		Persistence, Creativity, Flexibility, Metacognition	Developing Critical Thinking Through Writing, Reading, and Research; Developing Flexible Writing Processes
Searching as Strategic Exploration	Practice searching for and locating possible information sources for their research projects	Persistence, Creativity, Flexibility, Metacognition	Developing Critical Thinking Through Writing, Reading, and Research; Developing Flexible Writing Processes
Authority Is Constructed and Contextual		Openness, Responsibility	Developing Rhetorical Knowledge
Information Has Value		Responsibility, Metacognition	Developing Knowledge of Conventions

Table 12.06
Disciplinary Outcomes Map for IL Lesson

ACRL Framework (frames)	IL Lesson Student Learning Outcomes	WPA Framework (habits of mind on left; experiences on right)	
Scholarship as Conversation	Use the search process as an opportunity to strategically explore their research topics and questions	Creativity, Curiosity, Openness, Flexibility,	Developing Rhetorical Knowledge; Developing Critical Thinking Through Writing, Reading, and Research
Searching as Strategic Exploration		Persistence, Creativity, Flexibility, Metacognition	Developing Critical Thinking Through Writing, Reading, and Research; Developing Flexible Writing Processes
Research as Inquiry		Curiosity, Openness, Creativity, Persistence	Developing Critical Thinking Through Writing, Reading, and Research; Developing Flexible Writing Processes

These maps are significant for several reasons. First, they center the classroom-level outcomes Donna targets, situating the learning goals in the immediate needs of the students. This approach to instructional design—where the librarian analyzes the research assignment prompt and then puts this analysis in conversation with the course instructor's desired goals, as well as the programmatic learning outcomes for all instructors involved—situates the classroom-level outcomes within the specific research tasks students are being asked to do, tasks that will be evaluated by the course instructor for a grade. It grounds the limited time the librarian spends with the students in the very real needs of those students for that particular course, while connecting that time—and the practices and processes students have an opportunity to engage in during it—to the wider aims of programs and disciplines.[20]

Second, the maps illustrate how the conceptual and practical language used in the various outcomes statements is shaped by the Frameworks within which the instruction aims to be situated. This language, in turn, shapes how instructors think about and design their pedagogy. For example, Donna's third classroom-level outcome, as well as the title of the IL lesson, both draw directly and indirectly on the two ACRL frames "Research as Inquiry" and "Searching as Strategic Exploration," as well as the WPA Framework habits of mind "Curiosity" and "Persistence" and experience "Developing Critical Thinking Through Writing, Reading, and Research," among others (table 12.06). The FYW Programmatic Learning Outcomes and IL Program Student Learning Outcomes in table 12.05 also directly and indirectly draw from both Frameworks. These maps are intentionally cross-referential and the outcomes, as well as the pedagogy used to teach them, are continually enriched and deepened as the curricular and disciplinary language more comprehensively connects in the thoughts and experiences of the instructors doing the teaching.

Once these conceptual maps were developed, Donna used them to design pedagogy that would facilitate students practicing, demonstrating, and developing these outcomes within the scope of the seventy-five-minute IL instruction session. This second phase of the process incorporates strategies from Grant Wiggins and Jay McTighe's "backwards design" approach, as well as principles from Thomas P. Mackey and Trudi E. Jacobson's theory of metaliteracy, both which informed the development of the ACRL Framework.[21]

There are two parts to the IL lesson: a fifteen-minute presentation communicating the conceptual components of the research process students will engage in as they research and write their papers, and a fifty-minute activity during which students practice these components while the librarian provides feedback in real time. Donna composed a Prezi that she uses for the fifteen-minute presentation. For the fifty-minute activity, she adapted Shannon R. Simpson's Google spreadsheet activity, where the entire class accesses and contributes to the same collaborative, cloud-based Google spreadsheet as they accomplish the tasks and processes demonstrated by the librarian.[22]

The Google spreadsheet activity meets several needs in the context of this IL lesson. As Simpson predicts, columns within the spreadsheet correspond to learning outcomes for the lesson, making the collection of assessment data instantaneous and seamless.[23] This is also an example of designing instruction "backwards," where the learning outcome is articulated first and the activity that will provide evidence of students practicing or demonstrating the outcome is developed second.[24] During the instruction session, students carry out each research practice or process as, or immediately after, the librarian models it, populating spreadsheet cells with the evidence of this practice.

Specifically, the first four columns in Donna's Google spreadsheet activity correspond to the classroom-level outcome "Brainstorm research questions, search terms, and information types/formats related to their research topics," while six other columns correspond to the classroom-level outcome "Practice searching for and locating possible information sources for their research projects." The final two columns are students' exit ticket for the seventy-five-minute session: no matter where they are in the activity when there are five minutes remaining, students are directed to scroll to these columns and answer the questions, "What is one useful thing you learned today that you did not know before?" and "What other questions do you have about doing research on your topic/question?" Answers to these questions enable Donna to assess, indirectly, the effectiveness of her instruction, while the responses in the other columns provide data for direct assessment of student learning.

The second thing the Google spreadsheet activity accomplishes, which Simpson successfully predicts, is that students provide real-time information to the instructor about their level of understanding; this means Donna is able to adjust her instruction according to the specific needs of the students in front of her.[25] This formative assessment is useful when teaching three sections of the same course back-to-back, as it ensures the instruction is differentiated between sections yet remains standardized enough for Donna to easily repeat the lesson three times in a row. The critical thinking and research practices and processes the librarian models for students are laid out in the first row of the spreadsheet, while the second row contains a series of model submissions prepared in advance by the librarian. Students fill in subsequent rows with their own submissions. This organization helps Donna stay on task if, say, by the third back-to-back section she is experiencing cognitive fatigue.

There is at least one more significant contribution the Google spreadsheet activity makes to IL learning in the context of this lesson. The activity requires students to access the shared Google spreadsheet and toggle between the spreadsheet and the library's search tools, recording in the former their activity in the latter. Students do this activity together, where every student submits to the collaborative spreadsheet a response for their own research topic or question, prior to moving on to the next research practice or process. They are applying their learning to their own research need with the benefit of consulting the submissions of their peers in the semi-anonymous space of the shared spreadsheet. This toggling between dynamic, collaborative online spaces and search systems is a practical application of a central concept underlying both Frameworks: metaliteracy, which by definition "expands the scope of traditional information skills (determine, access, locate, understand, produce, and use information) to include the collaborative production and sharing of information in participatory digital environments (collaborate, participate, produce, and share)."[26] With this expansion in scope, the metacognitive learning domain becomes essential: awareness of one's own learning process enables the learner to learn more and better in each new context. Adaptation is essential because information systems are dynamic and ever-changing, and so must be learners' processes within and across those systems.

Metaliteracy is significant because the ACRL Framework "depends on these core ideas of metaliteracy, with special focus on metacognition, or critical self-reflection, as crucial to becoming more self-directed in that rapidly changing ecosystem."[27] Similarly, metacognition is one of the eight habits of mind in the WPA Framework, defined as "the ability to reflect on one's own thinking as well as on the individual and cultural processes and systems used to structure knowledge."[28] The Google spreadsheet activity is an example of how metaliteracy and metacognition are not always direct learning outcomes, but instead can be secondary outcomes as a result of the pedagogical design of the learning activity. During the Google spreadsheet activity, students must toggle between online, collaborative platforms and both record and reflect not only on what they find, but also on what they learn as they do so. Therefore, the direct assessment data collected through the spreadsheet provides evidence of learning in multiple domains, including behavioral, cognitive, dispositional, and metacognitive.

Assessment with the Frameworks

Our approach to outcomes-based assessment incorporates two considerations: learning domain and level. The four learning domains we consider as we develop learning outcomes in service of instructional or programmatic design are the following: behavioral, in which skills and abilities are developed and assessed; cognitive, in which knowledge and understanding are developed and assessed; dispositional, in which habits, values, and attitudes are developed and assessed; and metacognitive, in which self-reflection and awareness of thinking and learning processes are developed and assessed. The four levels in which learning outcomes can be developed and assessed include: classroom-level, course-level, program-level, and institution-level. Figure 12.02 illustrates as you traverse both lists, they become more challenging to assess.

Figure 12.02
Considerations when Developing Student Learning Outcomes

Multiple learning domains
- behavioral (skills)
- cognitive (knowledge)
- dispositional (values/attitude)
- metacognitive (reflection)

Multiple levels
- classroom-level
- course-level
- program-level
- institution-level

Outcomes are more transferable, yet harder to measure and assess, the farther you go down the list.

The scope of an outcome broadens, making it harder to measure and assess, the farther you go down the list.

In the case of learning domains, this challenge does not mean instructors and program directors should avoid developing outcomes in the dispositional and metacognitive domains. Donna's approach to classroom-level instructional design and assessment aims for a variety of learning domains, as the IL lesson in this chapter illustrates. Two of the classroom-level outcomes for this lesson fall in the behavioral domain, while one falls in the dispositional domain. Donna intentionally built this variety into these outcomes, which in turn affects her approach to their assessment.

Once the outcomes are developed, the next step for Donna is to write a rubric to assess those outcomes. Sometimes, this same rubric can inform evaluation of student performance for the purposes of a grade, though this is not required for a rubric to be effective as an assessment tool. In addition, using the rubric for grading requires collaborating with the course instructor and getting the instructor's assurance the students' IL lesson submissions will count toward their grades in some way. While Donna got this approval from both Emily and Teresa, Donna's workload as a member of the library faculty kept her from assessing student work in time to be used toward their grades.

Donna's approach to rubrics evolved during the period from spring to fall 2015 when she taught this IL lesson, in large part as a result of her experience assessing student work in spring 2015. Initially, Donna developed an analytic rubric with four classroom-level outcomes and planned to assess only the three that are easily measurable (see figure 12.03).

Figure 12.03
Spring 2015 Rubric

	Levels of Achievement			
Student Learning Outcome	Accomplished 3	Proficient 2	Developing 1	Insufficient 0
SLO1: Brainstorm research questions, search terms, and information types/formats related to their research topics [Google spreadsheet columns A, B, C, D]	Succeeded at brainstorming 3 out of 3 related to topic: • research questions • search terms • information types/ formats	Succeeded at brainstorming 2 out of 3 related to topic: • research questions • search terms • information types/ formats	Succeeded at brainstorming 1 out of 3 related to topic: • research questions • search terms • information types/ formats	Did not brainstorm any of the following: • research questions • search terms • information types/ formats

Figure 12.03
Spring 2015 Rubric

	Levels of Achievement			
Student Learning Outcome	Accomplished 3	Proficient 2	Developing 1	Insufficient 0
SLO2: Identify search tools that match their information need(s) *[Google spreadsheet column F]*	Identifies search tools that match research topic and information need	Identifies search tools in own words but not fully relevant to research topic and information need	Identifies search tools by rote from the lesson which may or may not be relevant to research topic and information need	Did not identify possible search tools
SLO3: Practice searching for and locating possible information sources for their research projects *[Google spreadsheet columns H, I, J, K, L, M]*	Succeeded at identifying 3 out of 3: • book • academic journal article • newspaper or magazine article	Succeeded at identifying 2 out of 3: • book • academic journal article • newspaper or magazine article	Succeeded at identifying 1 out of 3: • book • academic journal article • newspaper or magazine article	Did not identify any of the following: • book • academic journal article • newspaper or magazine article
SLO4: Use the search process as an opportunity to strategically explore their research topics and questions	Requires qualitative assessment which is not possible within the limitations of the one-shot information literacy instruction model.			

The assessment data resulting from applying this rubric to student work generated through the Google spreadsheet activity is laid out in table 12.07.

A brief analysis of this spring 2015 data contextualizes the changes Donna made to the lesson between spring and fall 2015. The success rate for SLO1: "Brainstorm research questions, search terms, and information types/formats related to their research topics" was consistently high across all three sections

(100 percent, 98 percent, and 96 percent), while the success rate for SLO2: "Identify search tools that match their information need(s)" was consistently low across all three sections (54 percent, 43 percent, and 48 percent). This indicates the modeling and practice of SLO1 during the IL lesson was effective and not in need of changing, while the modeling and practice of SLO2 needed to be addressed. Donna chose to address this by eliminating SLO2 from the lesson as a targeted learning outcome, as she realized during the modeling portion of the lesson that this outcome is tied to more advanced research practices and processes, whereas the students in WRTG 107 are novices. Furthermore, this outcome is less useful toward the completion of their assignments than the other outcomes in the lesson, so she justified eliminating it for fall 2015.

Table 12.07
Spring 2015 Assessment Data

IL Lesson Student Learning Outcome	WRTG 107 Grettano	WRTG 107 Denison 1	WRTG 107 Denison 2
SLO1: Brainstorm research questions, search terms, and information types/ formats related to their research topics	• 48/48 points across 16 students • 100% success across whole class	• 41/42 points across 14 students • 98% success across whole class	• 26/27 points across 9 students • 96% success across whole class
SLO2: Identify search tools that match their information need(s)	• 26/48 points across 16 students • 54% success across whole class	• 18/42 points across 14 students • 43% success across whole class	• 13/27 points across 9 students • 48% success across whole class
SLO3: Practice searching for and locating possible information sources for their research projects	• 15/48 points across 16 students • 31% success across whole class	• 36/42 points across 14 students • 86% success across whole class	• 21/27 points across 9 students • 78% success across whole class
SLO4: Use the search process as an opportunity to strategically explore their research topics and questions	Requires qualitative assessment which is not possible within the limitations of the one-shot information literacy instruction model.		

The success rate for SLO3 (shown in table 12.07): "Practice searching for and locating possible information sources for their research projects" differed significantly between Teresa's section (31 percent) and Emily's sections (86 percent and 78 percent). The reason for this difference is, for all three sections, Donna ran out of time before completing the activity, which meant the spreadsheet columns used to assess this outcome were unpopulated. Emily, however, decided on the spot that students in her sections would be required to complete the spreadsheet activity for homework and that their completion of the activity would count toward their class participation grade. As a result, the final spreadsheets for Emily's sections contained complete assessment data for all three measurable learning outcomes, while the spreadsheets for Teresa's section did not. The inability to complete the entire activity in any of the three sections told Donna there were too many learning outcomes and activity components built into this IL lesson, which gave her leverage to make changes for fall 2015.

After using the spring 2015 rubric (figure 12.03) to assess the three sections of WRTG 107, Donna decided to make two significant changes to the rubric for fall 2015. First, she chose to have fewer learning outcomes for the lesson, solving the time problem. Second, Donna wanted the criteria described for each level of achievement in the rubric to be tied to quality, not quantity; in other words, she aimed to measure how well students did, not simply that they did each research practice or process. This goal would necessarily make the assessment more qualitative than quantitative, thus potentially more time-consuming, but she predicted the rewards of moving the assessment in this direction would be worth it.

It was at this time Donna serendipitously learned about the single-point rubric, which differs from an analytic rubric in the following way: "Instead of detailing all the different ways an assignment deviates from the target, the single-point rubric simply *describes the target*, using a single column of traits.... On either side of that column, there's space for the teacher to write feedback about the specific things this student did that either fell short of the target (the left side) or surpassed it (the right)."[29] The single-point rubric is designed to be given to students in advance of an assignment or activity so students have explicit (and metacognitive) access to the learning outcomes they will be practicing and for which they are aiming, which means the audience for the rubric is not the instructor doing the assessing or evaluating, but the student doing the learning. Furthermore, the single-point rubric is designed to be returned to students with specific feedback (in the left and right columns).

Donna adapted the single-point rubric for this IL lesson, making two significant changes: she reversed the order in which the feedback is presented to students and she added a "Points Awarded" column so qualitative feedback could be quantified for the purposes of assessment reporting. Rather than the overwhelming and complex criteria lists in the spring 2015 analytic rubric (figure 12.03), the awarding of points in the adapted single-point rubric is informed by the qualitative feedback the instructor offers to each student. This change is a move away from assessing to a standard and toward assessing particular students with particular learning needs.[30] Points awarded are still based on evidence generated through direct assessment of student work and are still grounded in shared learning outcomes across the class (which in turn map to programmatic and disciplinary outcomes and goals; see table 12.05 and table 12.06). But an assessment process using a single-point rubric is better positioned than an analytic rubric to directly benefit students, one of the main factors in Donna's decision to move to a single-point rubric for this IL lesson.

The single-point rubric Donna developed for fall 2015, during which she taught this IL lesson to two new sections of Emily's WRTG 107 course, is found in figure 12.04.

Figure 12.04
Fall 2015 Rubric

"Research as Inquiry" Google Spreadsheet Activity Evaluation Rubric

The purpose of this activity is for you **to use the search process to strategically explore your research topics and questions.**

Click here to access activity.*

Advanced	Criteria	Concerns	Points Awarded
Evidence of exceeding what is expected	*Description of what is expected for you to succeed at the purpose of this assignment (see above)*	*Areas that need work*	*0 to 5*
	Brainstorm research questions, search terms, and information types/formats related to their research topics [*columns A, B, C, D*]		
	Practice searching for and locating possible information sources for their research projects [*columns E, F, G, H, I, J*]		

TOTAL out of 10: _____

Click here to learn about our Library Research Prize: 500 words could win you $500!†

---

* During class session this text is a customized link to the Google spreadsheet activity for the course section being taught.

† For all classes this text is a link to the University of Scranton Weinberg Memorial Library Research Prize web page: http://www.scranton.edu/libraryresearchprize.

There are now only two measurable classroom-level outcomes within the rubric itself, the two that fall within the behavioral domain and that correspond to specific columns in the Google spreadsheet activity. The third outcome—"Use the search process as an opportunity to strategically explore your/their research topics and questions"—has now become the overall purpose of the activity and is positioned above the rubric as a statement of purpose. The goal is for students to conceptualize the two behavioral outcomes (i.e., skills) within the rubric as components of the overarching dispositional purpose of the activity—to experience strategically exploring their topics through the search process. This revision also meant Donna could assess if students took seriously this opportunity: their completion of the activity for homework is a concrete indicator of this dispositional outcome. And so, all three classroom-level outcomes were now measurable.

The assessment data resulting from applying the revised rubric to student work is laid out in table 12.08.

Table 12.08
Fall 2015 Assessment Data

IL Lesson Student Learning Outcome	WRTG 107 Denison 1	WRTG 107 Denison 2
SLO1: Brainstorm research questions, search terms, and information types/formats related to their research topics	• 64/80 points across 16 students • 80% success across whole class	• 68/85 points across 17 students • 80% success across whole class
SLO2: Practice searching for and locating possible information sources for their research projects	• 53/80 points across 16 students • 66% success across whole class	• 74/85 points across 17 students • 87% success across whole class
SLO3/Overall Purpose of Activity: Use the search process as an opportunity to strategically explore their research topics and questions	• 8 out of 14 students completed activity • 57% success across whole class	• 14 out of 17 students completed activity • 82% success across whole class

In fall 2015, Donna taught this IL lesson to two sections of Emily's WRTG 107. The sessions were still taught back-to-back and the students were working on the same assignment for the course as in the lesson offered in spring 2015. The success rate for SLO1: "Brainstorm research questions, search terms, and information types/formats related to their research topics" was relatively high for both sections this semester (80 percent and 80 percent), indicating Donna's modeling of this outcome remained effective. However, the success rates for SLO2: "Practice searching for and locating possible information sources for their research projects" (66 percent and 87 percent) and SLO3: "Use the search process as an opportunity to strategically explore your/their research topics and questions" (57 percent and 82 percent) differed significantly between the sections. The reason for this difference is clear once the source of the data for each is considered. For SLO2, the source of the data comes from columns in the Google spreadsheet activity that were assigned as homework, and for SLO3 whether or not the entire exercise was completed for homework. Emily assigned the activity for homework to both sections and told students their decision to complete it would be incorporated into their grades as a quiz score. In Emily's first section (WRTG 107 Denison 1 in table 12.08), many students chose not to complete the activity for homework, which affected their assessment scores. Without data to assess, their scores were necessarily low. More students in Emily's second section (WRTG 107 Denison 2 in table 12.08) completed the activity for homework, and as a result their assessment scores were higher. This assessment data has been reported to the Weinberg Memorial Library's Information Literacy Coordinator for the purposes of assessment of the IL Program.[31]

As part of the reflective process of closing the assessment loop, Donna plans to make two changes to this IL lesson the next time she teaches it. First, she wants to manage her overall workload differently so her assessment of student work can be used as part of students' grades and so her feedback on the two measurable learning outcomes can be received by students during their research and writing processes. This update means turning around assessment in a week or less—a challenge during the height of the library's IL instruction season. Second, she needs to explore alternative tools to Google spreadsheets because the collaborative spreadsheet froze for some of the students, making them unable to complete the activity along with their peers. It is possible the students' frustration with the tool contributed to the low completion rate.

More important than these concrete changes, though, is the reflective process closing the assessment loop requires of the instructor. The awarding of points based on qualitative assessment of student learning—quantifying this learning for the purposes of assessment reporting—is not a positive experience for Donna as an instructor, as O'Neill, Moore, and Huot have predicted.[32] However, because it requires her to read every student submission closely, it facilitates reflection about the IL lesson and her effectiveness teaching and modeling the classroom-level outcomes she's developed. This reflection leads to specific and concrete changes she can make to her approach so students will be more likely to learn what she aims to teach through this lesson. It is this framing that gives assessment meaning and purpose for Donna, despite the ideological challenges posed by having to quantify the unquantifiable.

Conclusion

For many of us in higher education, assessment is a struggle. While we understand on a practical level that we must participate in assessment to maintain accreditation and continue to do the work we love, on theoretical and ideological levels mainstream methods of assessment counter much of what we believe to be the purpose of higher education, the important work of our disciplines, and the reasons we began to teach in the first place. As authors, we have found assessment rewarding when we have worked on it together, from engaged pedagogical and disciplinary positions. We've done so in a shared effort to better student learning, and more importantly, their literacy, so as our EP mission articulates, "they are empowered to excel as professionals and citizens to serve more fully the common good." We hope the examples of our methodology and our curricular and instructional work inspire others to engage assessment from this same perspective.

Notes

1. Edward M. White, "The Misuse of Writing Assessment for Political Purposes," *Journal of Writing Assessment* 2, no. 1 (2005): 33, emphasis in original. Bob Broad, "Organic Matters: In Praise of Locally Grown Writing Assessment," in *Organic Writing Assessment: Dynamic Criteria Mapping in Action* (Logan, UT: Utah State University Press, 2009). Peggy O'Neill, Cindy Moore, and Brian Huot, *A Guide to College Writing Assessment* (Logan, UT: Utah State University Press, 2009). Barry M. Maid and Barbara J. D'Angelo, "The WPA Outcomes, Information Literacy, and the Challenges of Outcomes-Based Curricular Design," in *Writing Assessment in the 21st Century: Essays in Honor of Edward M. White*, edited by Norbert Elliot and Les Perelman (New York: Hampton Press, Inc., 2012), 102–103.

2. Bob Broad, *What We Really Value: Beyond Rubrics in Teaching and Assessing Writing* (Logan, UT: Utah State University Press, 2003), 8.

3. O'Neill, Moore, and Huot, *A Guide to College Writing Assessment*, 3.

4. Broad, *What We Really Value*, 2–6.

5. O'Neill, Moore, and Huot, *A Guide to College Writing Assessment*, 3.

6. Council of Writing Program Administrators (WPA), National Council of Teachers of English (NCTE), and National Writing Project (NWP), 2011, *Framework for Success in Postsecondary Writing*, http://www.wpacouncil.org/files/framework-for-success-postsecondary-writing.pdf. Association of College and Research Libraries (ACRL), 2015, *Framework for Information Literacy for Higher Education*, http://www.ala.org/acrl/sites/ala.org.acrl/files/content/issues/infolit/Framework_ILHE.pdf. WPA, [2000, 2008] 2014, *WPA Outcomes Statement for First-Year Composition* (3.0), http://www.wpacouncil.org/positions/outcomes.html. ACRL, 2000, *Information Literacy Competency Standards for Higher Education*, http://www.ala.org/acrl/sites/ala.org.acrl/files/content/standards/standards.pdf.

7. Rolf Norgaard, "Writing Information Literacy in the Classroom: Pedagogical Enactments and Implications," *Reference & User Services Quarterly* 43, no. 3 (2004).

Barbara J. D'Angelo and Barry M. Maid, "Moving Beyond Definitions: Implementing Information Literacy Across the Curriculum," *Journal of Academic Librarianship* 30, no. 3 (2004). Jamie White-Farnham and Carolyn Caffrey Gardner, "Crowdsourcing the Curriculum: Information Literacy Instruction in First-Year Writing," *Reference Services Review* 42, no. 2 (2014).

8. Maid and D'Angelo, "The WPA Outcomes, Information Literacy, and the Challenges of Outcomes-Based Curricular Design," 106.

9. Ibid., 112.

10. Ibid.

11. Edward M. White, "The Misuse of Writing Assessment," 33. Bob Broad, "Organic Matters."

12. O'Neill, Moore, and Huot, *A Guide to College Writing Assessment*, 2.

13. Kenneth Burke, *The Philosophy of Literary Forms* (Berkeley: University of California Press, 1941), 110–111.

14. Barbara Fister, 2011, "Burke's Parlor Tricks: Introducing Research as Conversation," *Library Babel Fish: Inside Higher Ed*, http://www.insidehighered.com/blogs/library-babel-fish/burkes-parlor-tricks-introducing-research-conversation.

15. Peter-Hans Kolvenbach, 2000, "The Service of Faith and the Promotion of Justice in American Jesuit Higher Education" (presentation, Santa Clara University, Santa Clara, CA, October 6, 2000), http://www.sjweb.info/documents/phk/2000santa_clara_en.pdf.

16. "Information Literacy," 2016, *The University of Scranton: A Jesuit Institution*, http://www.scranton.edu/academics/wml/infolit/index.shtml.

17. ACRL, Framework, 3.

18. Donna Mazziotti and Teresa Grettano, "'Hanging Together': Collaboration Between Information Literacy and Writing Programs Based on the ACRL Standards and the WPA Outcomes," in *Declaration of Interdependence: The Proceedings of the ACRL 2011 Conference, March 30-April 2, 2011, Philadelphia, PA*, edited by Dawn M. Mueller (Chicago: Association of College and Research Libraries, 2011).

19. WPA, Outcomes.

20. Emily Drabinski, "Toward a *Kairos* of Library Instruction," *Journal of Academic Librarianship* 40, no. 2 (2014). Andrea Bear, "The Framework Is Constructed and Contextual: Context as a Starting Point for Instructional Planning," (presentation, LOEX fall Focus 2015: *ACRL Framework for Information Literacy for Higher Education*, Ypsilanti, MI, November 13–15, 2015).

21. Grant Wiggins and Jay McTighe, *Understanding by Design*, 2nd ed. (Alexandria, VA: Association for Supervision and Curriculum Development, 2005). Thomas P. Mackey and Trudi E. Jacobson, *Metaliteracy: Reinventing Information Literacy to Empower Learners* (Chicago: Neal-Schuman, 2014). ACRL, Framework, 2–3.

22. Shannon R. Simpson, "Google Spreadsheets and Real-Time Assessment: Instant Feedback for Library Instruction," *College & Research Libraries News* 73, no. 9 (2012). Donna's Prezi is accessible at http://tinyurl.com/WitekFYWPrezi, and her Google spreadsheet activity at http://tinyurl.com/WitekFYWActivity.

23. Simpson, "Google spreadsheets," 530.

24. Wiggins and McTighe, *Understanding by Design*.

25. Simpson, "Google Spreadsheets," 530.

26. Mackey and Jacobson, *Metaliteracy*, 1.

27. ACRL, Framework, 3.
28. WPA, Framework, 5.
29. Jennifer Gonzalez, 2014, "Your Rubric is a Hot Mess; Here's How to Fix It," *Brilliant or Insane: Education on the Edge,* http://www.brilliant-insane.com/2014/10/single-point-rubric.html, emphasis in original.
30. Drabinski, "Toward a *Kairos* of Library Instruction." Baer, "The Framework is Constructed and Contextual." Broad, *What We Really Value.*
31. "Information Literacy Assessment," 2016, *The University of Scranton: A Jesuit Institution,* http://www.scranton.edu/academics/wml/infolit/assessment.shtml.
32. O'Neill, Moore, and Huot, *A Guide to College Writing Assessment.*

Bibliography

Association of College and Research Libraries. 2015. *Framework for Information Literacy for Higher Education.* Accessed February 23, 2016. http://www.ala.org/acrl/sites/ala.org.acrl/files/content/issues/infolit/Framework_ILHE.pdf.

Association of College and Research Libraries. 2000. *Information Literacy Competency Standards for Higher Education.* Accessed February 23, 2016. http://www.ala.org/acrl/sites/ala.org.acrl/files/content/standards/standards.pdf.

Baer, Andrea. "The Framework Is Constructed and Contextual: Context as a Starting Point for Instructional Planning." Presentation at LOEX fall Focus 2015: *ACRL Framework for Information Literacy for Higher Education,* Ypsilanti, MI, November 13–15, 2015.

Broad, Bob. "Organic Matters: In Praise of Locally Grown Writing Assessment." In *Organic Writing Assessment: Dynamic Criteria Mapping in Action,* 1–13. Logan, UT: Utah State University Press, 2009.

———. *What We Really Value: Beyond Rubrics in Teaching and Assessing Writing.* Logan, UT: Utah State University Press, 2003.

Burke, Kenneth. *The Philosophy of Literary Forms.* Berkeley: University of California Press, 1941.

Council of Writing Program Administrators. 2000, 2008, 2014. *WPA Outcomes Statement for First-Year Composition (3.0).* Accessed February 23, 2016. http://www.wpacouncil.org/positions/outcomes.html.

Council of Writing Program Administrators, National Council of Teachers of English, and National Writing Project. 2011. *Framework for Success in Postsecondary Writing.* Accessed February 23, 2016. http://www.wpacouncil.org/files/framework-for-success-postsecondary-writing.pdf.

D'Angelo, Barbara J., and Barry M. Maid. "Moving Beyond Definitions: Implementing Information Literacy Across the Curriculum." *Journal of Academic Librarianship* 30, no. 3 (2004): 212–217.

Drabinski, Emily. "Toward a *Kairos* of Library Instruction." *Journal of Academic Librarianship* 40, no. 2 (2014): 480–485.

Fister, Barbara. 2011. "Burke's Parlor Tricks: Introducing Research as Conversation." *Library Babel Fish: Inside Higher Ed.* Accessed February 23, 2016. http://www.insidehighered.com/blogs/library-babel-fish/burkes-parlor-tricks-introducing-research-conversation.

Gonzalez, Jennifer. 2014. "Your Rubric is a Hot Mess; Here's How to Fix It." *Brilliant or Insane: Education on the Edge*. Accessed February 23, 2016. http://www.brilliant-insane.com/2014/10/single-point-rubric.html.

"Information Literacy." 2016. *The University of Scranton: A Jesuit Institution*. Accessed February 23, 2016. http://www.scranton.edu/academics/wml/infolit/index.shtml.

"Information Literacy Assessment." 2016. *The University of Scranton: A Jesuit Institution*. Accessed February 23, 2016. http://www.scranton.edu/academics/wml/infolit/assessment.shtml.

Kolvenbach, Peter-Hans. "The Service of Faith and the Promotion of Justice in American Jesuit Higher Education." Presentation at Santa Clara University, Santa Clara, CA, October 6, 2000. Accessed February 23, 2016. http://www.sjweb.info/documents/phk/2000santa_clara_en.pdf.

Mackey, Thomas P., and Trudi E. Jacobson. *Metaliteracy: Reinventing Information Literacy to Empower Learners*. Chicago: Neal-Schuman, 2014.

Maid, Barry M., and Barbara J. D'Angelo. "The WPA Outcomes, Information Literacy, and the Challenges of Outcomes-Based Curricular Design." In *Writing Assessment in the 21st Century: Essays in Honor of Edward M. White*, edited by Norbert Elliot and Les Perelman, 101–114. New York: Hampton Press, Inc., 2012.

Mazziotti, Donna, and Teresa Grettano. "'Hanging Together': Collaboration Between Information Literacy and Writing Programs Based on the ACRL Standards and the WPA Outcomes." In *Declaration of Interdependence: The Proceedings of the ACRL 2011 Conference, March 30-April 2, 2011, Philadelphia, PA*, edited by Dawn M. Mueller, 180–190. Chicago: Association of College and Research Libraries, 2011.

Norgaard, Rolf. "Writing Information Literacy in the Classroom: Pedagogical Enactments and Implications." *Reference & User Services Quarterly* 43, no. 3 (2004): 220–226.

O'Neill, Peggy, Cindy Moore, and Brian Huot. *A Guide to College Writing Assessment*. Logan, UT: Utah State University Press, 2009.

Simpson, Shannon R. "Google Spreadsheets and Real-Time Assessment: Instant Feedback for Library Instruction." *College & Research Libraries News* 73, no. 9 (2012): 528–530, 549.

White, Edward M. "The Misuse of Writing Assessment for Political Purposes." *Journal of Writing Assessment* 2, no. 1 (2005): 21–36.

White-Farnham, Jamie, and Carolyn Caffrey Gardner. "Crowdsourcing the Curriculum: Information Literacy Instruction in First-Year Writing." *Reference Services Review* 42, no. 2 (2014): 277–292.

Wiggins, Grant, and Jay McTighe. *Understanding by Design*. 2nd ed. Alexandria, VA: Association for Supervision and Curriculum Development, 2005.

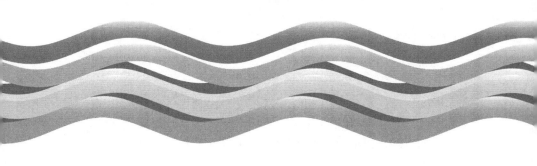

CHAPTER 13*

Leveraging New Frameworks to Teach Information Appropriation

William Duffy and Rachel E. Scott
University of Memphis

Jennifer Schnabel
The Ohio State University

Introduction

We begin with some familiar questions: What does the craft of research require? What are the skills and capacities differentiating an effective researcher from an ineffective researcher? What is information literacy, and how are definitions of this concept evolving? Can information literacy be accurately measured and assessed? There are, of course, no clear cut, universal answers to these questions, but for those of us who teach research in the contexts of library instruction and college-level writing courses, these are questions we must, nevertheless, continually ask. And for good reason. In the twenty-first century, digital technologies

* This work is licensed under a Creative Commons Attribution-NonCommercial-Share-Alike 4.0 License, CC BY-NC-SA (https://creativecommons.org/licenses/by-nc-sa/4.0/).

are not just allowing information to circulate in ways that once seemed un-imaginable, but also expanding the forms and contexts of information available to us. For example, the three of us remember sitting in composition courses as undergraduates while learning how to tell the differences between scholarly and non-scholarly sources. While we had access to electronic databases, most of the information we combed through for research projects fell into easily identifiable categories: academic journals, magazines, newspapers, and schol-arly monographs. Moreover, when it came to avoiding plagiarism, we simply had to follow the rules our instructors provided. It all seemed straightforward.

We know better now; teaching effective research practices has never been a straightforward endeavor.[1] To be sure, academic journals and scholarly press-es still publish research following processes of peer and external review that have changed very little over the years, and academic librarians still encourage students to grasp how understanding these processes will in turn help them to assess the quality and value of different types of texts. However, the questions we might ask to conduct these assessments are not as useful as they once were. Indeed, what denotes a scholarly source is hardly answered simply by asking, for example, whether or not it was peer-reviewed. Consider the following case.

In 2014, two large academic publishers, Springer and the Institute of Elec-trical and Electronic Engineers (IEEE), removed more than 120 papers from their respective databases when it was discovered these works were actually computer-generated gobbledygook papers. Writing in the journal *Nature*, Rich-ard Van Noorden explains how these papers were written using software called SCIgen that was developed in 2005 at the Massachusetts Institute of Technol-ogy. Cyril Labbé, a French computer scientist, discovered these gobbledygook papers using a technique that, as Noorden summarizes, "involves searching for characteristic vocabulary generated by SCIgen." To illustrate how easily aca-demic publics can be deceived by these gibberish papers, Labbé created a fake researcher named "Ike Antkare" in 2010 and attached the name to over 100 pa-pers generated using this software. According to Noorden, for a time "Antkare" became the twenty-first most cited scientist on Google Scholar.[2] Commenting on the significance of this deception, Konstantin Kakaes cautions while it is impressive that software sophisticated enough to produce "passable gibberish" now exists, "the wide acceptance of these papers by respected journals is symp-tomatic of a deeper dysfunction in scientific publishing, in which quantitative measures of citation have acquired an importance that is distorting the practice of science."[3] As Kakaes speculates, economic and professional pressures have left quantity not quality as the key standard in assessing academic success; and because academic publishers can charge a premium for access to their subscrip-tion services, the economics of academic authorship have assumed a new sig-nificance both in terms of how much academics are expected to publish and how much publishers can charge for access to such scholarship.

In this Springer/IEEE example, we see how the *content* of academic articles can sometimes be less important than the *citation value* of the articles. That is, the more a bogus article's citation begins to circulate across bibliographies, the harder it becomes to dispute the article's legitimacy, at least if one doesn't possess the rhetorical know-how or disciplinary knowledge to locate the article and assess its dubious status. Admittedly, most student researchers will probably not encounter texts like these gobbledygook papers. This doesn't mean, though, students won't encounter texts that blur boundaries of legitimacy and require careful, rhetorically-nuanced examination to assess their value, not to mention what counts as an appropriate use of such sources in their own writing. In fact, considering many students now turn to the open web to conduct the initial (if not all) phases of a research project, it makes sense to reconsider the skills necessary for students to assess and, in turn, appropriate the various forms of information available to them with a click of the mouse.

In this chapter, we pursue such a reconsideration while specifically focusing on how the *Framework for Information Literacy for Higher Education*[4] (hereafter ACRL Framework) and the *Framework for Success in Postsecondary Writing*[5] (hereafter WPA Framework) offer library and composition instructors a fresh perspective on the aims of information literacy and writing pedagogy.

By promoting dispositions instead of prescriptively outlining standards, these Frameworks allow stakeholders to talk about the messy, complex work of research and writing in terms underscoring the critical role habits of mind play in literacy development. To this end, we first offer a brief discussion for why questions about information appropriation should be considered alongside ones that attempt to understand the networks in and out of which information circulates, which we suggest underscore the usefulness of the ACRL Framework and the WPA Framework as pedagogical tools. Next, we turn to the Frameworks and explain how their respective emphases on the importance of dispositions can be examined alongside each other in ways promoting a robust, yet flexible, conception of information literacy appropriate for twenty-first-century students. We conclude by sharing an instructional heuristic and assignment sequence drawing explicitly on the language of the Frameworks and encouraging students to see themselves as contributors to scholarship, not just consumers of it.

Networking Information

Before discussing the significance of using a disposition-based framework to promote information literacy, we turn to the question of why it is useful to think about information literacy as something to be approached as a functional engagement with objects and practices requiring, not the acquisition of specific abilities and knowledge sets, but the cultivation of habits of mind like curiosity, flexibility, and metacognition. In his reworking of Barthes's well-known essay "The Death of the Author," John Logie argues that unlike romantic constructions of authorship, twenty-first-century composers are more networked than solitary and more responsive than originary.[6] Preferring the term composer to that of author, Logie outlines why composers should recognize how "even their most distinctive compositions have antecedents, analogs, and echoes," ones that in many cases are "accessible in the space of a few mouse clicks."[7] As networks of information becomes more profuse and accessible, it is incumbent on us to recognize how the compositions we create exist in multiple contexts that may not always be discernible at first blush. And just like these networks of information, the literacies needed to navigate such contexts are always evolving. Memorizing sets of rules about source type, for example, won't always be sufficient for effectively appropriating information from sources that evade classification.

The article from *Nature* we draw upon is a case in point. Published weekly and with a print circulation of more than fifty thousand, *Nature* is a well-known academic journal. According to the 2013 Journal Citation Reports Science Edition, in fact, "*Nature* is the world's most highly cited interdisciplinary science journal."[8] But the author of the article we cite, Richard Van Noorden, is not a scientist; he's a science journalist. And Noorden's article wasn't published in the print edition of the journal; it was published on the journal's website in the News and Comment section. The point is that Noorden's article doesn't fit into an easily definable information schema. It is not an academic article, but it is an article about academic publication that includes a reference list and is published by an academic journal. How should we assess this piece of writing as an academic text, then? More to the point, how might a librarian or composition instructor talk to students about this article as a source they might draw upon and reference in their own research? This question does not just concern the technicalities of citation; we are also asking about how instructors should encourage students to read and engage such a piece while developing a rhetorically-informed understanding of it as a networked text.

We believe part of what is required is a capacity to locate such texts in relationship to others. Rather than hold up Noorden's article as a discrete source needing to be interpreted and assessed, students might look up other articles Noorden has written; they might also backtrack to see what other types of articles have been published in the News and Comment section of *Nature*'s website. Additionally, students could follow the multiple hyperlinks included in the body of the article. These are simple exercises that can provide invaluable context. Here, we find the sociologist George Herbert Mead's notion of a "consentient set" useful, which is his term for the patterns we perceive across related events, patterns that get "grasped together or prehended [gathered together] into a unity."[9] A consentient set is thus an artificial set of perceptual relationships originating in the dynamic between an observer and a field of objects. Another way of getting at this idea is to borrow Bourdieu's concept of a field, which like a consentient set, underscores the value of relationality as the primary marker for understanding the significance of social objects in specific contexts. As Bourdieu explains, "a field may be defined as a network, or a configuration, of objective relations between positions."[10] Fields are dynamic groupings of objects and relationships necessarily influenced by the expectations and experiences of those who perceive them.

The ability to examine a piece of writing and interpret it according to various academic conventions, including systems of reference, is directly linked to the work of locating a text within the various fields that might signal which of these conventions are the most applicable. At the risk of further abstraction, Bourdieu notes how "[e]very field constitutes a potentially open space of play whose boundaries are dynamic borders which are the stake of struggles within the field itself."[11] In short, even within fields themselves, rules and conventions are dynamic. For instance, if we assigned a research paper requiring students to use a certain number of scholarly sources, and if we are not prepared to engage and affirm students who bring sources like Noorden's to the table that blur such categorization, we are ultimately doing them a disservice. Certainly, we agree with Mike Duncan who reminds us that to compose a successful researched argument "one must read a great deal, understand what one has read, reflect on the reading through analysis, and then reconsider all that has been done."[12] But this work of reading and analysis has to include careful consideration of the networks of information in which we locate texts. Shaping research instruction around standards not responsive to the dynamic nature of digital writing, for example, is not pedagogically useful to the vast multitude of students who do their research in digitally-mediated environments. Twenty-first-century composers are "almost by default" turning to networked computing to research and compose, Logie reminds us.[13] For this reason, we suggest turning to disposition-based methods of instruction more sensitive to the kinds of thinking we want students to pursue when evaluating research they locate on the web. The ACRL Framework and the WPA Framework both include related dispositions on which librarians and composition instructors can base their strategies for teaching information appropriation.

Information Appropriation in the ACRL Framework

There are substantive differences between the *Information Literacy Competency Standards for Higher Education* (hereafter ACRL Standards)[14] and the ACRL Framework: the ACRL Standards are prescriptive and the ACRL Framework encourages adaptation; the ACRL Standards are discrete and comprehensive and the ACRL Framework overlaps and makes no claim to comprehensiveness; and, most importantly, the Standards are performance-based and the ACRL Framework dispositions-based. The extensive changes should have a profound impact on what and how librarians teach. This section explores how discussions surrounding information appropriation and academic integrity have evolved from plagiarism avoidance in the ACRL Standards to informed information appropriation for knowledge production in the ACRL Framework, along with the implications of these changes for librarians and writing professionals.

The Association of College and Research Libraries approved the ACRL Standards in 2000. The document includes a definition of information literacy and a list of standards accompanied by performance indications and outcomes. The Standards are numbered one to five with the belief the student should progress through them in that order, first determining the need, then accessing, evaluating, and using the information ethically and legally. Each standard begins with the phrase "The information literate student" and concludes with competencies of which the student is to master. Although this is standard language for learning outcomes, James Elmborg notes "the student has become the 'object' of the information literacy, and by extension, the place where information literacy happens. The academic librarian…can maintain a safe objective distance from this student and assess…using the measuring stick of the Standards."[15]

The ACRL Framework, approved in 2015 by the ACRL, is a re-visioning not only of the substance, but also of the purpose of the instrument. Unlike the prescriptive ACRL Standards, which present a systematic and comprehensive measure of students' information literacy competency, the ACRL Framework recommends adapting the interconnected frames to accommodate local needs. Where the language used in the Standards suggests information literacy can be measured discretely and externally, the ACRL Framework outlines some of the knowledge practices and dispositions demonstrated by learners developing their abilities. Instead of being externally judged, the learner takes responsibility for the development of his/her information literacy. To this end, the ACRL Framework relies on metacognition to empower students to become more aware and reflective vis-a-vis information literacy.[16]

A comparison of the two documents' definitions of information literacy reveals how radically these documents diverge. The 1989 ALA Presidential Committee on Information Literacy Final Report quoted in the ACRL Standards reads: "To be information literate, a person must be able to recognize when information is needed and have the ability to locate, evaluate, and use effectively the needed information."[17] The ACRL Framework defines information literacy as "the set of integrated abilities encompassing the reflective discovery of information, the understanding of how information is produced and valued, and the use of information in creating new knowledge and participating ethically in communities of learning."[18] The shift from discrete and measurable skills to integrated dispositions is plain to see. Unlike the definition offered in the ACRL Framework, the ACRL Standards' definition does not account for the appropriation of information to create knowledge or to participate in learning; its effective use of information is not informed by an understanding of the information's production or value.

In the Standards, the fifth and final standard deals explicitly with information use: "The information literate student understands many of the ethical, legal, and social issues surrounding the use of information and accesses and uses information ethically and legally." The attendant performance indicator reads this way, "The information literate student acknowledges the use of information sources in communicating the product or performance."[19] In this document, it boils down to whether or not students cite sources, with the information literate student behaving ethically and acknowledging her use. There is no discussion of how students interact with sources, no discussion of the complexities surrounding information appropriation and the varieties of use, and no acknowledgment of the dizzying proliferation of what the ACRL labels "free" information sources in a variety of formats.[20]

Several of the ACRL Framework frames—and their related knowledge practices and dispositions—touch on aspects of information appropriation. Elements of information use are embedded in all six of the frames, but three are of particular interest: "information has value," "information creation as a process," and "scholarship as conversation." That several of the frames deal with information use is related to the ACRL Framework's expanded appreciation of students not only as consumers, but also as creators and collaborators, which is attributed to the concept of metaliteracy.[21]

"Information has value" includes the following warning: "The novice learner may struggle to understand the diverse values of information in an environment where free information and related services are plentiful and the concept of intellectual property is first encountered through rules of citation or warnings about plagiarism and copyright law."[22] By equating information use with plagiarism warnings, librarians and writing teachers lose the opportunity to discuss the deliberate and informed choices students can make when acknowledging the words and ideas of authors with whom they engage. This frame encourages librarians to go beyond teaching students to give credit to the originator of words and ideas, to challenge students to think about their role as creators of information and how they assign value to it, and to recognize that the value of information is socially-constructed and culturally-defined.

"Information creation as a process" highlights the "iterative processes of researching, creating, revising, and disseminating information"[23] that shapes the resulting product. Experts take a holistic approach to and value this process; students show reluctance to embrace the iterative nature of the process. In an article on plagiarism-detection software, Howard, for example, emphasizes the necessity of teaching an appreciation of intertextuality and process as antidotes.[24] If students can be taught to value how they engage with and question the information sources they appropriate, then they should make better use of the information in their own content.

"Scholarship as conversation" highlights the ongoing process by which academics, practitioners, and other stakeholders generate knowledge. Students often feel excluded from this conversation and, accordingly, do not fully engage with or debate the information they use. Indeed, plagiarism is blatant when students present a phrase devoid of the context of surrounding discourse. Experts are more comfortable with the complexity and dissent in scholarship, and they seek information in various participatory forums. Students may need encouragement, not only to find an appropriate venue in which to participate in this conversation, but also to recognize their responsibility when participating. Contributing to the conversation requires a developing knowledge of the discourse and a respect for others' contributions, even while critically evaluating them.

The integrative nature of these frames and the dynamic context which they seek to investigate mimic Bourdieu's fields with their "open space of play whose boundaries are dynamic borders."[25] Instead of asking students, for example, to cite only peer-reviewed sources and thus constrain their appropriation, we ask them to acknowledge and compare the networks and agents responsible for the information they are using.

Information Appropriation in the WPA Framework

Academic librarians continue to explore ways they can partner with composition and other faculty to encourage students to understand information literacy (IL) and refine their practice of source appropriation. For example, librarians at Utah State University have collaborated with writing instructors to build a series of classroom activities which employ Rolf Norgaard's theory of "writing information literacy"[26] and to conduct IL workshops for students as a way to co-develop new learning outcomes.[27] Writing instructors and librarians at Duquesne University partnered to teach information literacy and research skills in two courses within a learning community,[28] and colleagues at Chandler-Gilbert Community College in Arizona integrated two online credit-bearing courses—composition and information literacy—to increase students' exposure to IL concepts and provide immediate opportunities for application.[29]

Not all academic librarians enjoy productive partnerships with composition instructors and writing programs, however. This could be due to several factors, including time and staffing issues within the library, but some teaching faculty may not view librarians as academic peers or understand the specialized skills they can offer students.[30] Regardless, it is important for librarians and teaching faculty to acknowledge "both IL and rhetoric and composition draw from the same intellectual well, building upon more general pedagogical developments."[31] Librarians interested in partnering with faculty in writing programs should first understand how some composition instructors are using their own framework document to guide and assess their teaching practices.

Similar to the ACRL committees charged with developing learning outcomes for information literacy and then the ACRL Framework, professional organizations in the writing studies first partnered in 2000 to create learning outcomes for students in first-year writing courses, then in 2011 to produce the WPA Framework. The WPA Framework is the product of a task force created by the Council of Writing Program Administrators (WPA), National Council of Teachers of English (NCTE), and the National Writing Project (NWP). Participants included writing instructors from two- and four-year institutions as well as high school English teachers. The WPA Framework, "based on outcomes included in the WPA's *Outcomes Statement for First-Year Composition*,"[32] is intended to inform and guide members of a broader community, including policy makers and parents, who are in key positions to support students as they work toward college readiness.[33] In turn, the WPA Outcomes document, revised in 2014, includes a nod to the WPA Framework in a footnote, calling both documents aligned.[34]

The ACRL Framework requires librarians to engage conceptually with the knowledge practices and dispositions in order to generate local learning outcomes. Likewise, first-year writing instructors are encouraged to use the WPA Framework as a method for articulating outcomes by focusing on the "habits of mind and experiences with writing, reading, and critical analysis that serve as foundations for writing in college-level, credit-bearing courses."[35] These habits of mind or "ways of approaching learning that are both intellectual and practical" highlight the importance of curiosity, openness, engagement, creativity, persistence, responsibility, flexibility, and metacognition.[36] The last three habits of mind are particularly relevant to this chapter, as instructors guide students in their practice of appropriating information in their writing assignments. "Responsibility," "flexibility," and "metacognition" complement the disposition-based ACRL Framework and provide librarians with a further understanding of how the two documents can provide a solid foundation for partnerships in the classroom.

The WPA Framework defines responsibility as "the ability to take ownership of one's actions and understand the consequences of those actions for oneself and others." This habit of mind "is fostered when writers are encouraged to recognize their own role in learning" and "act on the understanding that learning is shared among the writer and others—students, instructors, and the institution, as well as those engaged in the questions and/or fields in which the writer is interested." Writers can "engage and incorporate the ideas of others, giving credit to those ideas by using appropriate attribution," and like the ACRL Framework, the WPA Framework supports the idea that scholarship is a conversation, which places the onus on the writer to view herself as a serious contributor to the scholarly discussion.[37] A student who is asked to compose a paper for a class assignment should not imagine the instructor (and the gradebook) as the only audience, but consider how the piece can impact others' understanding of a concept and contribute to the existing information landscape. Librarians, during instruction and reference consultations, can echo this message while demonstrating how to search for, evaluate, and appropriate existing scholarly and non-scholarly work on a topic, focusing not on consumerism but participation.

Flexibility, "the ability to adapt to situations, expectations, or demands," is prescribed by the WPA Framework to help students "recognize that conventions (such as formal and informal rules of content, organization, style, evidence, citation, mechanics, usage, register, and dialect) are dependent on discipline and context." This habit of mind encourages writers to respect the nature of information as context-specific and to select and cite sources appropriately.[38] Similar to the ACRL Framework, which emphasizes "information has value" and the importance of critically evaluating available sources, the WPA Framework underlines the benefit of attaining "rhetorical knowledge— the ability to analyze and act on understandings of audiences, purposes, and contexts in creating and comprehending texts."[39] As twenty-first-century students are faced with navigating a more complex information environment, writing instructors and librarians can draw on their respective frameworks and impart a common message that source selection and appropriation is specific to disciplinary discourse. Early emphasis on flexibility can prepare students to successfully translate and hone their research and writing skills in a variety of contexts.

Metacognition, "the ability to reflect on one's own thinking as well as on the individual and cultural processes and systems used to structure knowledge," encourages students to "examine processes they use to think and write in a variety of disciplines and contexts" and "reflect on the texts that they have produced in a variety of contexts." In addition, writers can "connect choices they have made in texts to audiences and purposes for which texts are intended" and "use what they learn from reflections on one writing project to improve writing on subsequent projects."[40] This habit of mind is echoed in the ACRL Framework, which empowers students to reflect on the ongoing processes entailed in research and writing; faculty who adapt this concept can "help students view themselves as information producers, individually and collaboratively."[41] Writing instructors continue to emphasize the importance of reflection and revision at all levels. Librarians can support this process by encouraging students to question the sources they've chosen and consider the possibility a source may not function in the same way in an improved, revised version of the composition. When an author has altered a purpose or identified a different audience, librarians can model how to conduct a new or revised inquiry based on initial search results.

First-year writing instructors may not be familiar with the ACRL frames, knowledge practices, and dispositions, as well as how librarians are applying them to create information literacy assignments. However, both writing instructors and librarians can identify bridges between them through the similar philosophies reflected in the Framework documents. Librarians can encourage faculty who teach composition courses to use their understanding of the habits of mind discussed in their own professional documents to relate to concepts outlined in the ACRL Framework and vice versa. These commonalities are especially useful as librarians and instructors work proactively to teach students how they can appropriate information and cite the contributions of others, encouraging them to join the scholarly conversation and avoid accidental plagiarism. To this end, the below heuristic includes strategies and examples that readers can use to engage students in the application and understanding of the relevant dispositions and habits of mind discussed earlier in in the chapter.

Information Appropriation Heuristic and Assignments

To understand the significance and meaning of a given piece of digital information, readers must be able to trace the networks in and out of which it exists. To this end, students in a semester-long research methods class taught by Rachel were asked to read James Grimmelmann's *Slate* article "Harry Potter and the Mysterious Defeat Device"[42] ("HPMDD") in preparation for a discussion of the ACRL frame "Scholarship as Conversation." On the day of the discussion, William, a composition specialist, joined the class as a guest instructor. The goal of this classroom session and the subsequent assignments was to empower students to see themselves as authors, to provide a method for interacting responsibly with texts in practice, and to encourage self-reflection of reading and citation practices.

An article about the need to revise laws that could help prevent automobile manufacturers, like Volkswagen, from building software that allow its vehicles to cheat on emissions tests, "HPMDD" is a useful example of the types of sources students increasingly come across when doing web-based research. On one hand, the article is relatively short, has a playful title, and is published in a popular online periodical. On the other hand, the author is a law professor and, perhaps more interestingly, the piece is published as a "Future Tense" feature. Co-sponsored by *Slate*, the New America Foundation, and Arizona State University, Future Tense is a *Slate* series publishing commentary that "seeks to understand the latest technological and scientific breakthroughs, and what they mean for our environment, how we relate to one another, and what it means to be human."[43] There is no list of references at the end of the piece, but hyperlinks in the article take readers to a range of sources: government documents, articles in popular magazines, and websites of various professional organizations and lobbying groups. While "HPMDD" is clearly not a peer-reviewed research article, it is also clear the article is not without scholarly value. More to the point, this article is representative of the changing information landscapes student researchers must learn to navigate, ones brought about by the confluence of new types of texts with new habits of reading through online interfaces.

Throughout the class's initial discussion of Grimmelmann's article, Rachel and William modeled question-posing strategies as a means of understanding the context in which the article was produced and might be understood. Sample questions included: What is the difference between paraphrasing and quoting and why does Grimmelmann use both methods? How does the author introduce dissent, support, context, and history? Besides avoiding plagiarism, why does Grimmelmann link to sources? What kinds of sources are they, and how can you tell? Is it possible to decipher that Grimmelmann is law professor without reading his author bio? Who can contribute to and who is excluded from this discourse and how have digital platforms changed this? To help answer these questions, students were asked to imagine the article within a citation network. By way of example, William created a Prezi illustrating one way to imagine the different networks within which Grimmelmann's article exists (see figure 13.01).

While not exhaustive, the Prezi presents Grimmelmann's network of scholarship, journalism, and op-ed content; the sponsoring bodies of Future Tense: *Slate*, Arizona State University, and New America; and color-coded nodes of cited source indicating various types of government publications such as an Environmental Protect Agency letter, articles from magazines such a *Wired*, and policy statements from groups such as the Electronic Frontier Foundation.

Figure 13.01

Prezi Illustrating How to Imagine the Different Networks in Grimmelmann's Article

As a visual representation of networked information, this presentation attempts to enact Bourdieu's field theory, namely how "one must map out the objective structure of the relations between the positions occupied by the agents" that jockey for recognition and authority.[44] Because this article, like so many digital artifacts, exists within several layers of networks that mitigate the meaning of the content itself, traditional labels of scholarly, popular, published, and edited are insufficient to critically evaluate it. Instead, students should be empowered to frame their evaluation of research in terms that help them understand the ways information is networked and the implications of these networks for their own information appropriation. While borrowing terms from Bourdieu or Mead is certainly an option, the language of the Frameworks is more accessible and suggests multiple avenues for assessing the complex work of appropriating research. Combining the ACRL frame of "scholarship as conversation" with the WPA Framework emphasis on flexibility, students researching controversies associated with the production of self-driving cars, for example, could be encouraged to read an article like Grimmelmann's as an example of research different from, but nevertheless in conversation with, questions asked about the safety of driverless cars. Tracing the networks that inform Grimmelmann's article might then reveal nodes of information more directly relevant for their own research. Or it might not. As we all want our students to understand, research is never a straightforward, one-shot endeavor always producing useable information. This was one of the points Rachel and William emphasized during the class discussion of "HPMDD," a discussion serving as the basis for two homework assignments students completed over the course of the next week.

The first assignment, offered at the conclusion of this chapter as part of Appendix 13A, required paired students to create and present a map or other visual representation of the referentiality in an assigned article.[45] Students could create a physical map or use a variety of digital platforms, such as Prezi, to realize their map. The only requirement was to create at least at one node for each source cited. Groups then presented their maps to the class and discussed patterns or relationships of particular interest. As a follow-up, the second assignment asked students to use this tracing process to reflect on their own authorship practices. Specifically, students were asked to reflect on citations and information appropriation in a previously submitted paper.[46] By asking students to reflect on their processes and answer questions about their previous appropriation of sources, we wanted to promote the value of metacognition while encouraging them to acknowledge the interactivity of information sources in their own scholarship. Our hope is by acknowledging this interactivity and recognizing their own writing in networked frames, students will be more likely to see themselves as contributors to scholarship and not just consumers of it. Indeed, this understanding and respect for the give and take of writing should help students begin to foster a respect for the words and ideas of others while promoting the responsible use of information.

Conclusion

In the end, we believe framing the research process in terms of information appropriation helps to underscore for students the idea that research is rarely an isolated activity; that every time we take up a journal article, search a database, or read an essay published in an online periodical, we are interacting with communities of readers and writers that become nodes in networks of information we have a hand in creating through our various acts of research. Of course, this level of recognition depends, in part, on the ways we both encourage and authorize students to view themselves as actual researchers, as participants in the production of knowledge. And as we all know, this is perhaps the hardest task we face as research librarians and teachers of writing: helping students recognize how research-based assignments can be meaningful in ways that go beyond the immediate parameters of course outcomes, grade expectations, and the like. Indeed, tapping into that space where research becomes consequential in unexpected ways is something that can hardly be taught in the instrumental sense. Thinking in terms of dispositions, however, pushes us beyond the realm of instrumental teaching, beyond just the identification of codified rules and conventions, and into the more fluid (and harder) work of fostering the attitudes necessary to become capable researchers who can navigate complex networks of information.

Developing the ability to successfully navigate the work of research—to understand how to assess the origins, values, and meanings of the sources we locate—does not automatically translate into the skill sets needed to responsibly appropriate sources. We obviously have to teach students strategies for using sources, in other words. And it would be irresponsible to bypass rule-oriented discussions of plagiarism, for example, but at the same time we should push against the urge to reduce the complexities of information appropriation into bifurcated models presenting research as a rule-governed process consisting of only correct and incorrect actions. When it comes to the problem of plagiarism in particular, we know the primary reasons students cheat are often time-related,[47] but providing students with a mechanism by which they can value and evaluate authors' contributions to a given discourse can empower them to appropriate information responsibly. The work of asking questions, evaluating citations, and reflecting on the purposes that motivate authors to use information in specific ways provides students with a method by which to recognize the various ways research can be valued, understood as a process, and connected to conversations beyond the immediacy of a single assignment.

None of this is easy, of course, nor should it be. But our experience with the Frameworks has been teaching us we are better equipped to work with novice researchers when we coordinate our efforts in ways that bridge the writing classroom with the library. Indeed, there is tremendous value in building collaborations between composition instructors and librarians, a point with which most of our readers are probably in agreement, but it is our hope this chapter encourages you to draw on the WPA Framework and ACRL Framework in tandem to help foster such collaboration as we all pursue the work of teaching students how to become responsive and responsible researchers.

Appendix 13A: Sample Assignments

Note: *As the ACRL Framework suggests, practitioners should customize assignments for their students and local contexts. This principle applies here as well. When it comes to the sample assignments below, professors with limited class time can choose a one-page article with which students can practice the tracing process, or they can omit the presentation component of the reference mapping assignment. In addition, online students can use the communication tools in the course management system to complete the group exercise, and they can use free online information visualization tools to co-create their reference map. As a follow-up to the in-class and homework assignments, professors may revisit the heuristic later in the semester by asking students to interview one another about the source material they appropriated in final papers that might have been assigned, therefore continuing the conversation of scholarship.*

Assignment 1: Mapping Referentiality

Working in groups of two or three, create a visual representation of the references in your assigned article. Your group may use a variety of digital or analog methods to map this information, but please do prioritize readability. Please include at least one node for each document to which the author refers. Some elements you might wish to illustrate:

- source author (government agency / corporate author / personal author (If so, is the person an academic or other "expert"?))
- source type (academic article / popular press article / social media content / digital document / statistical document)
- type of reference (quote / paraphrase / allusion)
- purpose of reference (provide evidence / introduce dissent / show conflict / stylistic gesture)
- interrelationships of sources

Sample Map: https://prezi.com/u5-pmtfhhev_/tracing-harry-potter-and-the-mysterious-defeat-device-by-j/

Assignment 2: Writing Is a Conversation

In a 500-word essay due in one week, describe your appropriation of various types of source material in a previously-submitted paper. Please submit the earlier paper along with this essay. Your essay should address the following questions:

- How do you differentiate someone else's ideas/words from your own?

- Do you only use sources to support your thesis or do you also introduce dissent or conflict?
- Who are you citing and what are their credentials?
- Do you make clear the author's relationship to the information by introducing citations with explanatory or contextualizing information?
- Does your use of published sources show engagement with and understanding of discourse? If so, how? If not, how will you more deeply engage with sources and convey your understanding of a given discourse?

Notes

1. Barbara Fister, "The Research Processes of Undergraduate Students," *Journal of Academic Librarianship* 18, no.3 (1992): 163–69; Cushla, Kapitke, "Information Literacy: A Positivist Epistemology and a Politics of Outformation," *Educational Theory* 53, no. 1 (2003): 37–53; Celia Rabinwitz, "Working in a Vacuum: A Study of the Literature of Student Research and Writing," *Research Strategies* 17, no. 4 (2000): 337–346.; and Daniel Melzer and Pavel Zemliansky, "Research Writing in First-Year Composition and Across Disciplines: Assignments, Attitudes, and Student Performance," *Kairos: A Journal of Rhetoric, Technology, and Pedagogy* 8, no. 1 (2003).
2. Richard Van Noorden, "Publishers Withdraw More Than 120 Gibberish Papers," *Nature*, February 24, 2014, http://www.nature.com/news/publishers-withdraw-more-than-120-gibberish-papers-1.14763.
3. Konstantin Kakae, "How Gobbledygook Ended Up in Respected Scientific Journals," *Slate*, February 27, 2014, http://www.slate.com/blogs/future_tense/2014/02/27/how_nonsense_papers_ended_up_in_respected_scientific_journals.html.
4. Association of College and Research Libraries, 2016, *Framework for Information Literacy for Higher Education,* accessed October 9, 2015, http://www.ala.org/acrl/standards/ilframework.
5. Council of Writing Program Administrators, National Council of Teachers of English, and National Writing Project, 2011, *Framework for Success in Postsecondary Writing,* accessed October 19, 2015, http://wpacouncil.org/files/framework-for-success-postsecondary-writing.pdf.
6. John Logie, "The (Re)birth of the Composer," *Composition and Copyright: Perspectives on Teaching Text-making and Fair Use,* ed. Steve Westbrook. (Albany: State University of New York Press, 2009), 185.
7. Ibid., 184.
8. Nature, "About Nature," accessed December 6, 2015, http://www.nature.com/nature/about/.
9. George Herbert Mead, *Selected Writings,* ed. Andrew J. Reck (Indianapolis: The Bobbs-Merrill Company, Inc., 1964).
10. Pierre Bourdieu and Loïc J. D. Wacquant, *An Invitation to Reflexive Sociology* (Chicago: University of Chicago Press, 1992).
11. Bourdieu and Wacquant, *Reflexive Sociology*, 104.

12. Mike Duncan, "The Research Paper as Stylistic Exercise," in *The Centrality of Style*, ed. Mike Duncan and Star Medzerian Vanguri, (Fort Collins, CO: WAC Clearinghouse and Parlor Press, 2013), 162.
13. Logie, "(Re)birth," 183.
14. Association of College and Research Libraries, 2000, *Information Literacy Competency Standards for Higher Education,* Accessed October 9, 2015, http://www.ala.org/acrl/standards/informationliteracycompetency.
15. James Elmborg, "Critical information literacy: Definitions and challenges," in *Transforming Information Literacy Programs: Intersecting Frontiers of Self, Library Culture, and Campus Community*, edited by Carroll Wetzel Wilkinson and Courtney Bruch, 75–95. (Chicago: Association of College and Research Libraries, 2012), 88.
16. Eveline Houtman, "Mind-Blowing," *Communications in Information Literacy* 9, no.1 (2015): 6–18.
17. ACRL, Standards, 15.
18. ACRL, Framework, 12.
19. ACRL, Standards, 14.
20. ACRL, Framework, 10.
21. Thomas P. Mackey and Trudi E. Jacobson, "Reframing Information Literacy as a Metaliteracy," *College & Research Libraries* 72, no. 1 (2011): 62–78.
22. ACRL, Framework, 6.
23. Ibid., 5.
24. Rebecca Moore Howard, "Understanding 'Internet Plagiarism,'" *COCOMP Computers and Composition* 24, no. 1 (2007): 3–15.
25. Bourdieu and Wacquant, *Reflexive Sociology*, 104.
26. Melissa Bowles-Terry, Erin Davis, and Wendy Holliday, "'Writing Information Literacy' Revisited Application of Theory to Practice in the Classroom," *Reference & User Services Quarterly* 49, no. 3 (2010): 225–230.
27. Kacy Lundstom, Britt Anna Fagerheim, and Elizabeth Benson, "Librarians and Instructors Developing Student Learning Outcomes Using Frameworks to Lead the Process," *Reference Services Review* 42, no. 3 (2014): 484–498.
28. Marcia Rapchak and Ava Cipri, "Standing Alone No More: Linking Research to a Writing Course in a Learning Community," *Portal: Libraries & the Academy* 15, no.4 (2015): 661–675.
29. Mary Beth Burgoyne and Kim Chuppa-Cornell, "Beyond Embedded: Creating an Online-Learning Community Integrating Information Literacy and Composition Courses," *Journal of Academic Librarianship* 41, no. 4 (2015): 416–421.
30. Carolyn Caffrey Gardner and Jamie White-Farnham, "'She Has a Vocabulary I Just Don't Have': Faculty Culture and Information Literacy Collaboration," *Collaborative Librarianship* 5, no. 4 (2014): 235–242.
31. Bowles-Terry, Davis, and Holliday, "'Writing Information Theory' Revisited," 225.
32. WPA, Framework, *2–3*.
33. Ibid., 2.
34. Council of Writing Program Administrators. 2014.*WPA Outcomes Statement for First-Year Composition* (3.0), accessed October 9, 2015, http://wpacouncil.org/positions/outcomes.html,1.
35. WPA, Framework *2*.
36. Ibid., 4.

37. Ibid., 5.
38. Ibid.
39. Ibid., 1.
40. Ibid., 5.
41. ACRL, Framework, 13.
42. James Grimmelmann, "Harry Potter and the Mysterious Defeat Device," *Slate,* September 22, 2015 http://www.slate.com/articles/technology/future_tense/2015/09/ volkswagen_s_cheating_emissions_software_and_the_threat_of_black_boxes.html.
43. Slate, "What is Future Tense?" *Slate,* accessed December 6, 2015, http://www.slate. com/articles/technology/future_tense/2012/03/future_tense_emerging_technolo- gies_society_and_policy_.html.
44. Bourdieu and Wacquant, *Reflexive Sociology,* 105.
45. See Appendix 13A.
46. Ibid.
47. Ruben Comas-Forgas and Jaume Sureda-Negre, "Academic Plagiarism: Explanatory Factors from Students' Perspective," *Journal of Academic Ethics* 8, no.3 (2010): 217–232.

Bibliography

Association of College and Research Libraries. 2016. *Framework for Information Literacy for Higher Education.* Accessed October 9, 2015. http://www.ala.org/acrl/standards/ ilframework.

Association of College and Research Libraries. 2000. *Information Literacy Competency Standards for Higher Education.* Accessed October 9, 2015. http://www.ala.org/acrl/ sites/ala.org.acrl/files/content/standards/standards.pdf.

Bourdieu, Pierre, and Loïc J. D. Wacquant. *An Invitation to Reflexive Sociology.* Chicago: University of Chicago Press, 1992.

Bowles-Terry, Melissa, Erin Davis, and Wendy Holliday. "'Writing Information Literacy' Revisited Application of Theory to Practice in the Classroom." *Reference & User Services Quarterly* 49, no. 3 (2010): 225–230.

Burgoyne, Mary Beth and Kim Chuppa-Cornell. "Beyond Embedded: Creating an Online-Learning Community Integrating Information Literacy and Composition Courses." *Journal of Academic Librarianship* 41, no. 4 (2015): 416–421.

Comas-Forgas, Rubén, and Jaume Sureda-Negre. "Academic Plagiarism: Explanatory Fac- tors from Students' Perspective." *Journal of Academic Ethics* 8, no.3 (2010): 217–232.

Council of Writing Program Administrators. 2014.*WPA Outcomes Statement for First-Year Composition* (3.0). Accessed October 9, 2015. http://wpacouncil.org/positions/ outcomes.html.

Council of Writing Program Administrators, National Council of Teachers of English, and National Writing Project. 2011. *Framework for Success in Postsecondary Writing.* Accessed October 19, 2015, http://wpacouncil.org/files/framework-for-suc- cess-postsecondary-writing.pdf.

Cushla, Kapitke, "Information Literacy: A Positivist Epistemology and a Politics of Out- formation," *Educational Theory* 53, no. 1 (2003): 37–53.

Duncan, Mike. "The Research Paper as Stylistic Exercise," in *The Centrality of Style*, ed. Mike Duncan and Star Medzerian Vanguri, (Fort Collins, CO: WAC Clearinghouse and Parlor Press, 2013).

Elmborg, James. "Critical information literacy: Definitions and challenges." In *Transforming Information Literacy Programs: Intersecting Frontiers of Self, Library Culture, and Campus Community*, edited by Carroll Wetzel Wilkinson and Courtney Bruch, 75–95. Chicago: Association of College and Research Libraries, 2012.

Fister, Barbara. "The Research Processes of Undergraduate Students," *Journal of Academic Librarianship* 18, no.3 (1992): 163–69.

Gardner, Carolyn Caffrey, and Jamie White-Farnham. "'She Has a Vocabulary I Just Don't Have': Faculty Culture and Information Literacy Collaboration," *Collaborative Librarianship* 5, no. 4 (2014): 235–242.

Grimmelmann, James. "Harry Potter and the Mysterious Defeat Device," *Slate*, accessed September 22, 2015, http://www.slate.com/articles/technology/future_tense/2015/09/volkswagen_s_cheating_emissions_software_and_the_threat_of_black_boxes.html.

Houtman, Eveline. "Mind-Blowing," *Communications in Information Literacy* 9, no.1 (2015): 6–18.

Howard, Rebecca Moore. "Understanding "Internet Plagiarism," *COCOMP Computers and Composition* 24, no. 1 (2007): 3–15.

Kakae, Konstantin. "How Gobbledygook Ended Up in Respected Scientific Journals," *Slate*, accessed February 27, 2014, http://www.slate.com/blogs/future_tense/2014/02/27/how_nonsense_papers_ended_up_in_respected_scientific_journals.html.

Logie, John. "The (Re)birth of the Composer." *Composition and Copyright: Perspectives on Teaching Text-making and Fair Use*, edited by Steve Westbrook, 175–190. Albany: State University of New York Press, 2009.

Lundstom, Kacy, Britt Anna Fagerheim, and Elizabeth Benson. "Librarians and Instructors Developing Student Learning Outcomes Using Frameworks to Lead the Process," *Reference Services Review* 42, no. 3 (2014): 484–498.

Mackey, Thomas P. and Trudi E. Jacobson, "Reframing Information Literacy as a Metaliteracy," *College & Research Libraries* 72, no. 1 (2011): 62–78.

Mead, George Herbert. *Selected Writings*, edited by Andrew J. Reck. Indianapolis: The Bobbs-Merrill Company, Inc., 1964.

Melzer, Daniel, and Pavel Zemliansky, "Research Writing in First-Year Composition and Across Disciplines: Assignments, Attitudes, and Student Performance," *Kairos: A Journal of Rhetoric, Technology, and Pedagogy* 8, no. 1 (2003).

Nature, "About Nature," accessed December 6, 2015, http://www.nature.com/nature/about/.

Rabinwitz, Celia. "Working in a Vacuum: A Study of the Literature of Student Research and Writing," *Research Strategies* 17, no. 4 (2000): 337–346.

Rapchak, Marcia and Ava Cipri. "Standing Alone No More: Linking Research to a Writing Course in a Learning Community," *Portal: Libraries & the Academy* 15, no.4 (2015): 661–675.

Slate, "What is Future Tense?" *Slate*, accessed December 6, 2015, http://www.slate.com/articles/technology/future_tense/2012/03/future_tense_emerging_technologies_society_and_policy_.html

Van Noorden, Richard. "Publishers Withdraw More Than 120 Gibberish Papers," *Nature*, accessed February 24, 2014, http://www.nature.com/news/publishers-withdraw-more-than-120-gibberish-papers-1.14763.

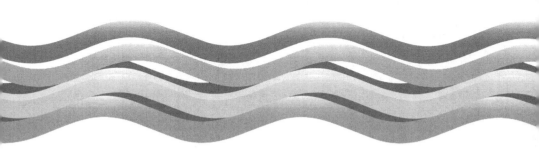

CHAPTER 14*

Can We Talk Multimodality?

Meghan Roe and Julius Fleschner
Briar Cliff University

Introduction

The landscape of libraries, writing centers, and higher education in general is shifting. Libraries have our new Information Literacy framework to interpret and implement. Writing Centers are offering a related response to the benefits and drawbacks of digital composing by focusing on multimodal composing and multiliteracy centers. Many involved in higher education as a whole seek to see their institutions' commitment to intellectual freedom survive in an era of for-profit online institutions, mass-enrolled online courses, and disposable adjunct instructors. To the future-focused individual, however, the confluence of these events presents a unique opportunity to innovate.

At Briar Cliff University, a small Franciscan private college, the retirement and decision not to replace a beloved theater professor—the only qualified person to teach the speech course required of all undergraduate students—forced our undergraduate faculty to reevaluate aspects of our general education offerings. This reduction in faculty is not uncommon. All one need do is read *The Chronicle of Higher Education* or other higher education trade magazines to see the numbers of adjuncts are increasing and tenure-track faculty members are not being replaced as they retire.[1] Being a small liberal arts insti-

* This work is licensed under a Creative Commons Attribution-NonCommercial 4.0 License, CC BY-NC (https://creativecommons.org/licenses/by-nc/4.0/).

tution located in the Midwest, Briar Cliff University is not immune from these pressures.

When it was announced the person qualified to teach our speech course was retiring and not being replaced, the undergraduate faculty was faced with several options:

1. eliminate the speech competencies
2. issue waivers for every student nearing graduation
3. create a new course incorporating speech competencies

After months of deep discussion and discernment, we decided to combine our writing and speech courses and focus the new hybrid course on twenty-first-century communication skills, with an emphasis on multimodality. The new course—CORE 131: Writing and Speaking in the Digital Age—would introduce students to the core concepts of college-level writing and speech.

As service centers, the Bishop Mueller Library and Briar Cliff University Writing Center were tasked with supporting the curriculum passed by the undergraduate faculty and assisting students with their needs. This new course presented several new challenges. Meghan, as Assistant Professor of Writing and Director of the Writing Center (located in the library), would be teaching many of the sections of the new multimodal first-year course, and she had embedded writing center peer tutors as part of the new course design. Julius, as Director of the Library and Information Services, was already teaching information literacy through one-shot workshops and presentations in classes across the university. To truly live out our particular departmental missions, we needed to reshape aspects of our offerings, create new services, and collaborate more deeply. In doing so, we found natural connections between the new ACRL Framework and the WPA Framework. The Frameworks, and in particular the threshold concepts and habits of mind that form the bedrock for both Frameworks, offer a connection to multimodal composition and to multiliteracy centers, writing centers that help students with multimodal writing projects.

One year into our new multimodal composing initiative, our experience has been positive. The library and writing center have been able to better integrate threshold concepts from library science and habits of mind from writing studies through offering support for students composing multimodal projects in the new hybrid course. The experience of creating the new course discussed in this chapter, with respect to the professional literature from library science, writing centers, and composition studies, demonstrates a new opportunity for collaboration between the library and the writing center—particularly in small schools where faculty and administrators share many responsibilities. Our collaboration has been successful so far, and it will only grow once these multimodal and information literacy initiatives are reinforced through upper-division courses in disciplines across campus.

Threshold Concepts in the ACRL and WPA Frameworks

When the *Information Literacy Competency Standards for Higher Education* was published in 2000 by the Association of College and Research Libraries (ACRL),[2] academic librarians took up the call to systematically educate our students on how to find, use, and cite information. However, over a decade and a half has since passed and the world has become a different place. College students lead even richer, more active, digital lives, and information overload has become an even greater problem. Despite the information glut, students have developed an expectation to be active participants in dialog and information creation—not just consumers of it. As the information habits of students have changed, so too has our pedagogical framework for educating them.

The groundbreaking work of Project Information Literacy (PIL) has helped librarians gain an understanding of these new information behaviors. The PIL studies have found over 80 percent of students have "overwhelming difficulties getting started on research assignments."[3] They are often lost and unable to navigate the overabundance of information. Instead of branching out and exploring, they exhibit risk-adverse strategies and only use tried and true information resources … i.e., Google searches, Wikipedia pages, course readings, etc. Rarely do they go deeper into the scholarly discourse.

To address these new behaviors and technologies, the ACRL has established the *Framework for Information Literacy for Higher Education*. By adding the Framework to the "constellation of documents used by information literacy practitioners,"[4] the association offers a new theoretical structure upon which librarians can advance the teaching of information literacy, as well as develop deeper partnerships with faculty outside the library. The ACRL Framework breathes new life into the instruction and pedagogical tools available to librarians. Built upon the pedagogical theories of "Understanding by Design" by Wiggin and McTighe, as well as Meyer and Land's "Threshold Concepts", the Framework lays out six concepts, or frames of information literacy:

- Authority Is Constructed and Contextual
- Information Creation as a Process
- Information Has Value
- Research as Inquiry
- Scholarship as Conversation
- Searching as Strategic Exploration

Threshold concepts, as we know them today, were developed by Jan Meyer and Ray Land[5] and applied to library science by Townsend, Hofer, Brunetti, and Lu.[6] Threshold concepts are analogous to a "passage, portal, or gateway to gaining a new view of a subject landscape."[7] For a topic to be considered a threshold concept, it must be transformative, integrative, irreversible, bounded, and troublesome.[8]

To identify threshold concepts in information literacy, Hofer, Townsend, and Brunetti[9] conducted a study. They sent a qualitative survey to a variety of listservs asking respondents to identify big concepts students struggle to understand. The responses were scored and concepts grouped into two meta-themes. The first involved the impact of Google. Specifically, students are failing to see information as coming from a variety of sources and that Google does not actually produce the information. The second meta-theme is described as "affect," or the students' feelings about information. As noted by the respondents, students feel strong negative emotions when unable to find useful information. The researchers went so far as to propose seven threshold concepts, which served as the basis for the six enshrined in The ACRL Framework.

By comparison, Linda Adler-Kassner and Elizabeth Wardle do not see as much correlation between threshold concepts important to writing instruction and the Council of Writing Program Administrator's (WPA's) *Framework for Success in Postsecondary Writing*. In *Naming What We Know: Threshold Concepts of Writing Studies*, Adler-Kassner and Wardle differentiate between the "concise, usable statements about best practices" in the WPA's *Framework for Success in Postsecondary Writing* and the threshold concepts of "composed knowledge," whose impact moves beyond writing studies or writing program administrators.[10] Other composition scholars have also expressed concern for the limitations of a frameworks approach. While Heidi Estrem calls the WPA Framework "productive" and "rich," she worries it can also lead students to believe they only need to follow "specific stopping points along a trajectory" in order to improve.[11] She writes, "Our field's focus on signposts (frameworks, benchmarks, outcomes) also leaves us entangled in a model that conceives of learning as a straight line (from framework at the beginning to outcome at the end)."[12]

Although she co-edited a book about threshold concepts in writing studies, Adler-Kassner was also part of the task force that wrote the WPA's Framework—the result of a partnership between the WPA, the National Council of Teachers of English (NCTE) and the National Writing Project (NWP)—that represented the expectations of K–16 writing students (though focused on postsecondary writing instruction).[13] The diversity of experience distilled in the WPA Framework increases its applicability in a range of institutional contexts, and since writing studies and library science both have threshold concepts for writing and research instruction, along with a framework for teaching these concepts, intersections between the Frameworks are natural.

At the same time, while libraries and writing programs share similar goals, their approach to instruction is different. WPAs and writing teachers value classroom instruction, while librarians are becoming increasingly suspicious of the one-off classroom presentation. Even more so, librarians argue much IL instruction happens in the library space itself, either through one-on-one interactions between students and librarians or through students' individual work. A more applicable partner for combining IL and writing instruction, and one that shares a commitment to collaborative (and often peer-to-peer) instruction may, in fact, be the writing center.

Collaboration at Briar Cliff: Multimodality and the Writing Center

Writing centers and libraries are often natural collaborators, in part due to the location of many writing centers inside libraries.[14] Recently, an increasing number of writing centers are moving into centralized learning center configurations and sharing space with other student support services. As part of this trend, the second floor of the library at Briar Cliff University became the Academic Resource Commons in 2014. It houses the offices of Academic Achievement, our Early Alert program, and the Writing Center.

The writing center and the library have obvious potential to be collaborators given our shared space and our shared vision of the twenty-first-century library. In comparison to writing programs, writing centers and libraries typically share the same perspective: both already agree most writing and research instruction happens outside the classroom, and both also share a vision of the modern library as an academic and social hub of campus activity. Purdy and Walker describe the first-year composition classroom as a "liminal space," "highlighting the nature of introductory composition classes as spaces that mark a boundary between the inside and the outside of the academy."[15] They continue: "The composition classroom, of course, is a very real and public space, but it is likewise a space where students are asked to immerse themselves in a (for most of them) new academic culture and regard as fantastical their prior (and private) experiences with research." Using this definition, the library is another important liminal space for students—public and private, social and academic. As Purdy and Walker point out, "liminality" comes from a Latin word for threshold, as in the concepts students need to understand in order to become stronger writers, researchers, and thinkers and advance in their coursework.[16] For Meghan and Julius, the Frameworks and the threshold concepts were their own opening to change writing and research instruction at their institution, and multimodal composition was the method of implementation.

As part of the team putting the original proposal for the new course together, and as one of the faculty who would be teaching the course, Meghan approached the development of the writing and speaking course through her interest in multimodal composition. The term multimodal has become the favored term in composition studies for writing that features multiple modes of communication, such as the combination of written and spoken words, images, sounds, and movements.[17] Other disciplines use multimedia or new media to describe videos, podcasts, websites, or other products that do not revolve around the written word. Students are creating these projects more and more. More importantly, these projects represent the real-world composing students will be expected to complete after college, which is one reason many composition instructors now use them in the college writing classroom.

The multimodal writing initiative at Briar Cliff University was supported first by the chair of general education, who sought the support of Julius and Meghan as directors of the library and writing center, respectively. With experience in two very different writing center environments, Meghan knew collaboration with a variety of institutional partners is a natural part of writing center work. As a whole, writing centers offer individualized writing instruction, ideally through peer-to-peer consultations, but that is often where the similarities between writing centers end. All writing centers operate in a specific institutional context and respond to the particular needs of their campuses. While some writing centers are affiliated with English departments, more and more centers operate as separate entities or within learning commons gathering various academic service departments in one location. Without a departmental home, and because writing center services are open to all students from a variety of majors, writing center administrators need to work across the university to build awareness for the center's services and improve writing instruction everywhere on campus. One important purpose of writing center theory is to respond to demographic trends or shifts in writing instruction; recently, writing centers have had to grapple with increased attention to multimodal composing in writing studies and across campus.

John Trimbur[18] first forecast the development of writing centers that could help students with multimodal compositions, and he called these centers multiliteracy centers—a reference to the New London Group's[19] call to expand education beyond word-based definitions of literacy. Literacy is not limited to the ability to read words on a page (consider computer literacy); a person can be literate in more than one method of communication. If the generally-accepted definition of a writing center is a place where students can become better writers, then a multiliteracy center is a place where students can become better writers, speakers, designers, and more. Since 2010, multiliteracy centers have become an important topic of conversation in writing center scholar-ship.[20] However, as with most writing center scholarship, it is difficult to know whether multiliteracy centers are a passing trend or cross-country reevalua-tion of the services offered by writing centers.[21]

Meghan conducted an online survey of writing center professionals, the results published elsewhere.[22] The most significant of the survey findings, especially in reference to the new multimodal initiative at Briar Cliff, imply more writing centers are encountering multimodal compositions in the center (though not at a high number compared with traditional written assignments) and that these changes are occurring even where respondents are not familiar with multiliteracy center scholarship. Indeed, one challenge of approving the new multimodal course at Briar Cliff was the undergraduate faculty's hesitance to adopt the term multimodal, or even the less discipline-specific term mul-timedia. Still, the approved proposal of the now-titled "Writing and Speak-ing in the Digital Age" describes a multimodal course, and however faculty in various departments label their pedagogy, they are already asking students to compose in multiple modes. From these examples, it appears writing centers need to build awareness for the composing currently happening on campus, and one way to accomplish this goal is through finding partners for collabora-tion, such as in libraries.

Writing and Speaking in the Digital Age

Writing in a recent collection about collaborative, technologically-enhanced "learning spaces," Kimberly M. Cuny, Sarah Littlejohn, and Kathy Crowe write:

> While it is not unusual for libraries to have digital media learning spaces, it is unusual for libraries to pair with emerg-ing multiliteracy centers in order to expand the services for media designers beyond functional support and into the crit-ical and rhetorical contexts that new media projects demand. This unique collaboration adds support beyond helping pa-trons learn how to use technology. Patrons can also become effective designers, learning how to better convey messages through shape, space, style, and form.[23]

While the authors are correct that collaborations between multiliteracy centers and libraries are rare, writing centers and libraries have a long histo-ry of collaboration. The collection edited by Elmborg and Hook[24] give many examples of successful partnerships between libraries and writing centers. As more writing centers move into centralized learning center configurations,

often sharing space with other student support services and housed in libraries, they will have even more opportunities to collaborate with their new colleagues in a shared space.

In terms of library involvement in Briar Cliff's multimodal composing
initiative, information literacy instruction has been a vehicle for additional
support of students in the writing and speaking course. So far, typical assignments for the new course have included digital narratives, online portfolios,
blogs, podcasts, and infographics. These projects have created opportunities to
teach aspects of the ACRL Framework[25] to first-year students.

While the decision to include any particular assignment is up the individual instructor, many at Briar Cliff have opted for a digital narrative. This
assignment requires students to compose a video using pictures, sound, text,
and other modes of communication to be published and shared via a video
streaming service, such as YouTube. Since it requires a composite of several
media assets, it is a perfect fit to expose students to the second frame, "Information Creation as a Process."

At Briar Cliff, we have a mixed technology environment. Students may
bring any device of their choosing to campus, as long as it is suitable for academic work. Most have chosen a laptop computer. In order to keep costs
low for students, instructors have encouraged them to compose their digital
narratives in Windows Movie Maker, iMovie, or a web-based alternative like
WeVideo. All of these programs follow a generally standard user interface.
Julius has trained Meghan's writing center consultants on the various video
editing programs, and the consultants in turn work with students during class
or in the writing center. By the end of the assignment, each student should
have a new understanding of the work required to create a video project; in
other words, they learn several knowledge practices related to "Information
Creation as a Process."

Utilizing a digital narrative has also been helpful in regard to the third
ACRL frame, "Information has Value." It would be inappropriate to have students create publicly shared videos without a basic understanding of copyright.
To facilitate this understanding, Julius has visited several classes to deliver a
one-shot copyright lecture. During the session, students watched the fourth
part of "Everything is a Remix"[26] and discussed the idea of information as property. The lecture ended with searching strategies geared towards finding creative commons and public domain material for composing digital narratives.

As libraries evolve to support the twenty-first-century needs of patrons,
creating a makerspace to support such innovative teaching may be the next
step. By harnessing the purchasing power of a library, better equipment and
software could be provided for students composing multimodal assignments.
That in turn would allow students to explore information creation more deeply and not be limited by personal financial constraints.

Threshold Concepts and the WPA Framework

The threshold concepts that underlie the WPA Framework, even if the connections are not as explicit as they are in the ACRL Frameworks, make the application of the WPA Framework easier. Unlike the ACRL Framework, we can't point to a particular bullet point or subheading we apply in our multimodal composing initiative, but we do apply the ideas of the WPA document as a whole. Indeed, an early critique of the WPA Framework was the lack of connection between the eight Habits of Mind and the five categories that make up the "Experiences in Writing, Reading, and Critical Analysis." As Summerfield and Anderson ask, "Are the habits to be taught or encouraged, while experiences are to be initiated or engaged? Do the habits precede the experiences or do the experiences engender the habits?"[27] Still, the idea that writing is a process is one of the most fundamental threshold concepts in composition studies, and the word process is repeated throughout the WPA Framework—a concept essential to the section on Habits of Mind and to the process of gaining knowledge through the act of writing. As stated in the Framework under "Developing Flexible Writing Processes," "Writing processes are not linear. Successful writers use different processes that vary over time and depend on the particular task."[28]

Writing is a process—something that both the ACRL and WPA Frameworks value—yet the thresholds holding up the Frameworks value a more recursive, messy process. As we've experienced from the digital narrative assignment, multimodal projects allow for more frustration, more nuance, and fewer discrete steps in order to end with a digital product. Threshold concepts also make more room for the process of writing instruction (rather than the destination). Estrem describes writing instruction not as a list of discrete steps but as "much more like scrambling across rocky terrain: learners make progress, slip back, try again, get a little higher, slip back again."[29] Similarly, Purdy and Walker attest, "Students need to be able to make their own investigations into these practices and to understand the complexities and contradictions in the ways that academic research practices create knowledge. We need to assist students in this learning by sharing with them examples of academic research processes as messy, tentative, and even contested."[30] They add: "Teaching research as a closed, linear, universal process prevents students from leaving the liminal space"—they can't advance as writers or researchers.[31] By comparison, the messiness of multimodality helps students understand the messy recursiveness of the research-writing process.

With the WPA Framework and the new ACRL Framework now available to us and with the current emphasis on digital research and trend toward assigning multimodal projects, it is easier than ever before for writing centers and libraries to jointly support students as they learn to research ethically and communicate effectively. With this combined effort, the library and writing center can also jointly promote information literacy and multimodal communication to other parts of campus (such as upper-division courses across majors).

Conclusion & Future Directions

Even more than their relationship with libraries, writing center scholars have long described collaboration between writing centers and writing-across-the-curriculum programs (WAC).[32,33] These collaborations often result in increased visibility for the writing center across campus, with tutors often serving as ambassadors for WAC initiatives.[34] Carrie Leverenz has also written about "supporting multimodal writing across the curriculum" by developing a grant-funded New Media Writing Studio at Texas Christian University.[35] Leverenz describes the challenges of gaining funding for the studio and losing funding at the end of the four-year grant. She writes that the Studio still operates, but "remains on the fringes, left to plan programming with 4% of our original budget."[36] One lesson Leverenz and the staff of the studio learned is to "align our interests with the interests of those in power," in other words, administrators. With the possibility of supporting a shared multimodal initiative across disciplines, the Briar Cliff writing center and library are actually in a prime position to take the lead and proactively encourage and promote writing throughout our institution, but the writing center in particular must be willing to challenge its common institutional role and demonstrate its worth to students, tutors, faculty members across the disciplines, and perhaps most especially to administrators.

Collaboration between the writing center, the library, and instructors of courses across the disciplines could be enacted successfully if all sides share a commitment to the value of multimodal composing. Collaborative efforts do not have to be revolutionary or highly disruptive to major programs of study. As part of an online survey Meghan conducted of writing center professionals, one surprising result indicated writing centers are responding to an increased number of multimodal assignments not only coming from composition courses, but also from courses in other disciplines. When asked to identify the courses assigning the multimodal projects brought to their writing centers, higher numbers of respondents said these assignments came from communication courses or non-writing intensive courses in the students' major, rather than from composition courses. From these results, it appears students understand the writing center can help them with writing in all its forms, and the writing center is not responding to a need from any one department, but has the opportunity to create the need themselves.

One respondent noted that providing a "cohesive message about the value of multimodal composition to the greater university audience (particularly administration) [could] help to further justify the existence of the center in the first place." As evidenced by this reply, one implication of the survey results is that a successful multiliteracy center could lead the institution in this area.

With the introduction of the ACRL Framework, new curriculum needs, and successes of the previous year, there are many new opportunities to grow our collaborations at Briar Cliff. After hearing about digital narratives, some members of the faculty have been asking how the library and writing center could support such an assignment in other courses. Others have asked us to present a guest lecture on finding suitable (copyright cleared) material for a digital assignment. Being a small university, we are anticipating this snowball effect to grow.

In the coming months, we will develop a technology mentor program. By hiring students who have done exceptionally well in our new multimodal course or enrolled in technology-heavy majors, training should be minimal. We are looking for those who are not just competent in the use of technology, but fluent.[37] These new mentors must be able to use a wide range of software and platforms. In other words, they must have reached a threshold understanding of key concepts in the ACRL Framework. These mentors will serve in three main capacities. They will staff part of the circulation/reference desk and provide technology assistance. We will look to Apple's Genius Bar concept for inspiration. The mentors will also go into classrooms and hold peer-led lab sessions. Additionally, they will do one-shot technology lectures at the instructor's request, which will allow the library deeper reach into the curriculum.

Although multimodal composing does not need to rely on a computer,[38] students enrolled in the digital writing and speaking course are primarily using a computer to compose their class projects. Returning to Meghan's survey, with the exception of oral presentations, the most common multimodal projects brought to the writing center are composed by combining modes on a computer: 44 percent of respondents have encountered students seeking help with website design, 40 percent with a blog, 33 percent with a video, and 31 percent with an infographic. Michael Pemberton[39] asks whether writing centers will need to hire "specialist tutors" who understand the variety of computer software necessary to compose multimodal assignments (which he calls hypertexts) or whether administrators should provide "specialized training" to teach all tutors how to operate software.[40] The former approach changes the tutor's role to something more akin to technological support, while the latter approach requires valuable time for training. David Sheridan worries "if students need to go to separate sources to get technical and rhetorical help, then many of them, for pragmatic reason, will simply skip the rhetorical support altogether."[41]

The tech mentors are a potential solution to this problem. Rhetorical and technical support would become separate, but both would still be housed in the library. Cuny, Littlejohn, and Crowe have discovered a similar solution: "It is not realistic to expect every student who is trained in the theory and practice of digital centers to also be skilled at supporting technological literacies."[42] At their joint multiliteracy center/library space at The University of North Carolina Greensboro, "the literacies are split between the units' missions, [but] the support of the literacies happens in the same physical space." Although their collaboration has had its challenges,[43] they write that students appear to be using both the multiliteracy center and the technology center (receiving both rhetorical and technical help) precisely because both are located under the same roof.

Cuny, Littlejohn, and Crowe operate at a large public university, while Briar Cliff is a small liberal arts college. These types of innovations are possible, regardless of institutional circumstances. Due to the administrative decision not to replace a faculty member, our undergraduate faculty voted to allow one course to meet both the writing and speech competencies. The Briar Cliff University Writing Center and the Bishop Mueller Library have been invaluable to supporting the new course and students' needs. Through this collaboration, we have developed stronger programs with new services that will have a long-term impact on how students approach research-writing in our increasingly digital age.

Notes

1. Scott Jaschik, "The Disappearing Tenure-Track Job," *Inside Higher Ed.*, last modified May 12, http://www.insidehighered.com/news/2009/05/12/workforce; Schmidt, Peter, "AAUP Slams Reduction of Full-Time Faculty at National Louis U," *The Chronicle of Higher Education* 59 (2013).

2. Association of College and Research Libraries, *Framework for Information Literacy for Higher Education*, last modified February 2, 2015, accessed March 12, 2016, http://www.ala.org/acrl/standards/ilframework.

3. Alison J. Head, "Project Information Literacy: What Can Be Learned about the Information-Seeking Behavior of Today's College Students?" 2013, http://papers.ssrn.com/sol3/pa-pers.cfm?abstract_id=2281511.

4. Association of College and Research Libraries, *Framework for Information Literacy for Higher Education*.

5. Jan Meyer and Ray Land, *Threshold Concepts and Troublesome Knowledge: Linkages to Ways of Thinking and Practising within the Disciplines.* (Edinburgh: School of Education, University of Edinburgh, 2003) http://www.etl.tla.ed.ac.uk/docs/ETLreport4.pdf.

6. Amy R Hofer, Korey Brunetti, and Lori Townsend, "A Thresholds Concepts Approach to the Standards Revision," *Communications in Information Literacy* 7, no. 2 (2013): 108, http://search.proquest.com/docview/1496849643.

7. Craig Gibson, "ACRL's Framework for Information Literacy for Higher Education,"

Maryland Information Literacy Exchange, http://milexmd.org/docs/GibsonMILEX-Keynote.pdf.

8. Amy R. Hofer, Lori Townsend, and Korey Brunetti, "Troublesome Concepts and Information Literacy: Investigating Threshold Concepts for IL Instruction," *portal: Libraries and the Academy* 12, no. 4 (2012): 387–405, http://muse.jhu.edu/journals/portal_libraries_and_the_academy/v012/12.4.hofer.html.

9. Ibid.

10. Linda Adler-Kassner and Elizabeth Waddle, *Naming What We Know: Threshold Concepts of Writing Studies.* (Logan: Utah State Univ., 2015): 2.

11. Heidi Estrem, "Threshold Concepts and Student Learning Outcomes," in *Naming What We Know: Threshold Concepts of Writing Studies*, eds. Linda Adler-Kassner and Elizabeth Wardle, (Logan, UT: Utah State University Press, 2015): 89–104.

12. Ibid., 92

13 Anne-Marie Hall, Linda Adler-Kassner, Cathy Fleischer, and Peggy O'Neill "Creating the Framework for Success in Postsecondary Writing," *College English* 74, no. 6 (2012): 520.

14. James Elmborg and Sheril Hook, eds., *Centers for Learning: Writing Centers and Academic Libraries in Collaboration*, (Chicago: ACRL, 2005).

15. James P. Purdy and Joyce R. Walker, "Liminal Spaces and Research Identity: The Construction of Introductory Composition Students as Researchers." *Pedagogy* 13, no. 1 (2013): 9–41, http://muse.jhu.edu/journals/pedagogy/v013/13.1.purdy.html.

16. Ibid., 11.

17. Claire Lauer, "What's in a Name? The Anatomy of Defining New/Multi/Modal/Digital/Media Texts," *Kairos* 17, no. 1 (2012).

18. John Trimbur, "Multiliteracies, Social Futures, and Writing Centers," *The Writing Center Journal* 20, no. 2 (2000): 29–32.

19. New London Group, "A Pedagogy of Multiliteracies: Designing Social Futures." *Harvard Educational Review* 66, no. 1 (1996): 60–93.

20. David Sheridan, "Writing Centers and the Multimodal Turn," in *Multiliteracy Centers: Writing Center Work, New Media and Multimodal Rhetoric*, eds. David Sheridan and James Inman, (New Jersey: Hampton Press, 2010); Jackie Grutsch McKinney, "New Media Matters: Tutoring in the Late Age of Print," *The Writing Center Journal* 29, no. 2 (2009): 28–51; Sohui Lee and Russell Carpenter, eds., *The Routledge Reader on Writing Centers & New Media*, (New York: Routledge, 2013).

21. Valerie Balester, Nancy Grimm, Jackie Grutsch McKinney, Sohui Lee, David M. Sheridan, and Naomi Silver, "The Idea of Multiliteracy Center: Six Responses." *Praxis* 9, no. 2 (2012).

22. Meghan Roe, "The Multiliteracy Center as Collaboration Tool," in *Writing Programs and Writing Center Collaborations: Transcending Boundaries*, eds. Alice J. Myatt and Lynee L. Gaillet (New York: Macmillan, forthcoming).

23. Kimberly Cuny, Sara Littlejohn, and Kathy Crowe, "The Digital Media Commons and the Digital Literacy Center Collaborate: The Growing Pains of Creating a Sustainable, Flexible Learning Space," in *Environmental Sustainability and Learning Space Design*, eds. Russell Carpenter, Richard Selfe, Shawn Apostel and Kristi Apostel, (Computers and Composition Digital Press 2015), http://ccdigitalpress.org/sustainable/s3/uncg/index.html.

24. Elmborg and Hook, *Centers for Learning*.

25. Association of College and Research Libraries, *Framework for Information Literacy for Higher Education.*

26. Kirby Ferguson. "Everything is A Remix, Part 4, (Vimeo, 2015), https://vimeo.com/36881035.

27. Judith Summerfield and Philip M. Anderson, "A Framework Adrift," *College English* 74, no. 6 (2012): 544–547, http://www.jstor.org/stable/23212915.

28. Council of Writing Program Administrators, National Council of Teachers of English, and National Writing Project, *Framework for Success in Postsecondary Writing,* (WPA, NCTE, and NWP, 2011), accessed March 15, 2016. http://www.wpacouncil.org/files/framework-for-success-postsecondary-writing.pdf.

29. Heidi Estrem, "Threshold Concepts and Student Learning Outcomes," 89–104.

30. Purdy and Walker, "Liminal Spaces and Research Identity."

31. Ibid., 10.

32. Ray Wallace, "The Writing Center's Role in the Writing Across the Curriculum Program: Theory and Practice," *The Writing Center Journal* 8, no. 2 (1988): 43–48.

33. Joan Mullin, "Writing Centers and WAC," in *WAC for the New Millennium: Strategies of/for Continuing WAC Programs,* eds. Susan McLeod, Eric Miraglia, Margot Soven and Christopher Thaiss, (Urbana IL: NCTE, 2001): 179–200.

34. Scott Johnston and Bruce W. Speck, "The Writing Center as Ambassador Pleinpotentiary in a Developing WAC Program," *in Writing Centers and Writing Across the Curriculum Programs: Building Interdisciplinary Partnerships,* eds. Robert W. Barnett and Jacob S. Blumner, (Westport, CT: Greenwood, 1999): 13–30; Carol Severino and Megan Knight, "Exporting Writing Center Pedagogy: Writing Fellows Programs as Ambassadors for the Writing Center," in *Marginal Words, Marginal Work? Tutoring the Academy in the Work of Writing Centers,* eds. William J. Macauley Jr and Nicholas Mauriello, (New York: Hampton, 2007): 19–32.

35. Carrie Leverenz, "'Growing Smarter Over Time': An Emergence Model for Administrating a New Media Writing Studio," *Computers and Composition* 29, no. 1 (2012): 61–62; Ibid., 52.

36. Ibid., 61.

37. Qian Wang, Michael Myers, and David Sundaram, "Digital Natives and Digital Immigrants: Towards a Model of Digital Fluency," *Business & Information Systems Engineering* 5, no. 6 (2013): 409–419.

38. Jody Shipka, *Toward a Composition Made Whole,* (Pittsburgh: University of Pittsburgh Press, 2011).

39. Michael Pemberton, "Planning for Hypertexts in the Writing Center … Or Not," *The Writing Center Journal* 24 (2003): 9–24.

40. Ibid., 19–20.

41. David Sheridan, "Words, Images, Sounds: Writing Centers as Multiliteracy Centers," in *The Writing Center Director's Resource Book,* eds. Christina Murphy and Byron L. Stay, (Mahway, NJ: Elbaum, 2006): 339–350.

42. Cuny, Littlejohn, and Crowe, "The Digital Media Commons and the Digital Literacy Center Collaborate."

43. Sara Littlejohn and Kimberly M. Cuny. "Creating a Digital Support Center: Foregrounding Multiliteracy," in *Cases on Higher Education Spaces: Innovation, Collaboration, and Technology,* ed. Russell G. Carpenter, (Hershey, PA: Info Sci Ref., 2012): 87–106.

Bibliography

Adler-Kassner, Linda and Elizabeth Waddle. *Naming What We Know: Threshold Concepts of Writing Studies*. Logan: Utah State Univ. Press, 2015.

Association of College and Research Libraries. *Framework for Information Literacy for Higher Education*, last modified February 2, 2015, http://www.ala.org/acrl/standards/ilframework.

Balester, Valerie, Nancy Grimm, Jackie Grutsch McKinney, Sohui Lee, David M. Sheridan, and Naomi Silver. "The Idea of Multiliteracy Center: Six Responses." *Praxis* 9, no. 2 (2012).

Council of Writing Program Administrators, National Council of Teachers of English, and National Writing Project. 2011. *Framework for Success in Postsecondary Writing*, accessed March 15, 2016. http://www.wpacouncil.org/files/framework-for-success-postsecondary-writing.pdf.

Cuny, Kimberly, Sara Littlejohn, and Kathy Crowe. "The Digital Media Commons and the Digital Literacy Center Collaborate: The Growing Pains of Creating a Sustainable, Flexible Learning Space." In *Sustainable Learning Spaces: Design, Infrastructure, and Technology*, edited by Russell Carpenter, Richard Selfe, Shawn Apostel and Kristi Apostel. Computers and Composition Digital Press, 2015.

Elmborg, James and Sheril Hook, eds. *Centers for Learning: Writing Centers and Academic Libraries in Collaboration*. Chicago: ACRL, 2005.

Estrem, Heidi. "Threshold Concepts and Student Learning Outcomes." In *Naming What We Know: Threshold Concepts of Writing Studies*, edited by Linda Adler-Kassner and Elizabeth Wardle, 89–104. Logan, UT: Utah State University Press, 2015.

Ferguson, Kirby. "Everything is A Remix, Part 4." Vimeo.2015, https://vimeo.com/36881035.

Gibson, Craig. "ACRL's Framework for Information Literacy for Higher Education." *Maryland Information Literacy Exchange*. http://milexmd.org/docs/GibsonMILEX-Keynote.pdf.

Grutsch McKinney, Jackie. "New Media Matters: Tutoring in the Late Age of Print." *The Writing Center Journal* 29, no. 2 (2009): 28–51.

Hall, Anne-Marie, Linda Adler-Kassner, Cathy Fleischer, and Peggy O'Neill. "Creating the Framework for Success in Postsecondary Writing." *College English* 74, no. 6 (2012): 520. http://gateway.proquest.com/openurl?ctx_ver=Z39.88-2003&xri:pqil:res_ver=0.2&res_id=xri:ilcs-us&rft_id=xri:ilcs:rec:abell:R04707010.

Head, Alison J. "Project Information Literacy: What Can Be Learned about the Information-Seeking Behavior of Today's College Students?" 2013, http://papers.ssrn.com/sol3/pa-pers.cfm?abstract_id=2281511.

Hofer, Amy R., Korey Brunetti, and Lori Townsend. "A Thresholds Concepts Approach to the Standards Revision." *Communications in Information Literacy* 7, no. 2 (2013): 108. http://search.proquest.com/docview/1496849643.

Hofer, Amy R., Lori Townsend, and Korey Brunetti. "Troublesome Concepts and Information Literacy: Investigating Threshold Concepts for IL Instruction." *portal: Libraries and the Academy* 12, no. 4 (2012): 387–405. http://muse.jhu.edu/journals/portal_libraries_and_the_academy/v012/12.4.hofer.html.

Jaschik, Scott. "The Disappearing Tenure-Track Job." *Inside Higher Ed.*, last modified May 12, 2009, https://www.insidehighered.com/news/2009/05/12/workforce.

Johnston, Scott and Bruce W. Speck. "The Writing Center as Ambassador Pleinpotentiary in a Developing WAC Program." In *Writing Centers and Writing Across the Curriculum Programs: Building Interdisciplinary Partnerships*, edited by Robert W. Barnett and Jacob S. Blumner, 13–30. Westport, CT: Greenwood Press, 1999.

Lauer, Claire. "What's in a Name? The Anatomy of Defining New/Multi/Modal/Digital/ Media Texts." *Kairos* 17, no. 1 (2012).

Lee, Sohui and Russell Carpenter, eds. *The Routledge Reader on Writing Centers & New Media*. New York: Routledge, 2013.

Leverenz, Carrie. "'Growing Smarter Over Time': An Emergence Model for Administrating a New Media Writing Studio." *Computers and Composition* 29, no. 1 (2012): 61–62.

Littlejohn, Sara and Kimberly M. Cuny. "Creating a Digital Support Center: Foregrounding Multiliteracy." In *Cases on Higher Education Spaces: Innovation, Collaboration, and Technology*, edited by Russell G. Carpenter, 87–106. Hershey, PA: Info Science Reference, 2012.

Meyer, Jan and Ray Land. *Threshold Concepts and Troublesome Knowledge: Linkages to Ways of Thinking and Practising within the Disciplines*. Edinburgh: School of Education, University of Edinburgh, 2003. http://www.etl.tla.ed.ac.uk/docs/ETLreport4.pdf.

Mullin, Joan. "Writing Centers and WAC." In *WAC for the New Millennium: Strategies of/ for Continuing WAC Programs*, edited by Susan McLeod, Eric Miraglia, Margot Soven and Christopher Thaiss, 179–200. Urbana IL: NCTE, 2001.

New London Group. "A Pedagogy of Multiliteracies: Designing Social Futures." *Harvard Educational Review* 66, no. 1 (1996): 60–93.

Pemberton, Michael A. "Planning for Hypertexts in the Writing Center … Or Not." *The Writing Center Journal* 24 (2003): 9–24.

Purdy, James and Joyce R. Walker. "Liminal Spaces and Research Identity: The Construction of Introductory Composition Students as Researchers." *Pedagogy* 13, no. 1 (2013): 9–41. http://muse.jhu.edu/journals/pedagogy/v013/13.1.purdy.html.

Roe, Meghan. "The Multiliteracy Center as Collaboration Tool." In *Writing Programs and Writing Center Collaborations: Transcending Boundaries*, edited by Alice J. Myatt and Lynee L. Gaillet. New York: Macmillan, forthcoming.

Schmidt, Peter. "AAUP Slams Reduction of Full-Time Faculty at National Louis U." *The Chronicle of Higher Education* 59 (2013).

Sheridan, David M. "Words, Images, Sounds: Writing Centers as Multiliteracy Centers." In *The Writing Center Director's Resource Book*, edited by Christina Murphy and Byron L. Stay, 339–350. Mahway, NJ: Elbaum, 2006.

———. "Writing Centers and the Multimodal Turn." In *Multiliteracy Centers: Writing Center Work, New Media and Multimodal Rhetoric*, edited by David Sheridan and James Inman. New Jersey: Hampton Press, 2010.

Severino, Carol and Megan Knight. "Exporting Writing Center Pedagogy: Writing Fellows Programs as Ambassadors for the Writing Center." In *Marginal Words, Marginal Work? Tutoring the Academy in the Work of Writing Centers*, edited by William J. Macauley Jr and Nicholas Mauriello, 19–32. New York: Hampton, 2007.

Shipka, Jody. *Toward a Composition Made Whole*. Pittsburgh: University of Pittsburgh Press, 2011.

Summerfield, Judith and Philip M. Anderson. "A Framework Adrift." *College English* 74, no. 6 (2012): 544–547. http://www.jstor.org/stable/23212915.

Trimbur, John. "Multiliteracies, Social Futures, and Writing Centers." *The Writing Center Journal* 20, no. 2 (2000): 29–32.

Wallace, Ray. "The Writing Center's Role in the Writing Across the Curriculum Program: Theory and Practice." *The Writing Center Journal* 8, no. 2 (1988): 43–48.

Wang, Qian, Michael D. Myers, and David Sundaram. "Digital Natives and Digital Immigrants: Towards a Model of Digital Fluency." *Business & Information Systems Engineering* 5, no. 6 (2013): 409–419. doi:10.1007/s12599-013-0296-y.

Building Meaningful, Institution-Specific Partnerships

Susan K. Miller-Cochran
University of Arizona

WHEN SHELLEY RODRIGO and I worked on the first edition of our research textbook, *The Cengage Guide to Research*, we were writing in response to some of our own frustration as writing instructors at a community college. We worked with a large number of students each semester, and we recognized that there was a palpable lack of communication between teachers of research-writing and specialists in our library who taught information literacy. While we certainly talked to and worked with each other on committees and through institutional initiatives, the work we were each doing in our respective areas didn't always inform the other in meaningful ways.

We recognized the ways in which most writing textbooks taught research lacked the nuance about evidence, research, and source use that was evident in the literature on information literacy. We were concerned that research-writing textbooks, by and large, instructed students on searching for, evaluating, and incorporating sources in a way that drew a binary between "online" and "print" sources, a distinction that our first-year college students suspected was problematic (evidenced by questions such as, "If I found this article from a journal in the library database, but it's a PDF, does it count as a print or an online source? What about if it's an article from an online journal?"). Moreover, we suspected that the discussions we have in writing studies about the rhetorical situation of writing and research might offer a bridge across the divide.

Our solution was to try to move beyond the binary and rethink how research-writing could be taught from a rhetorical perspective. Yet, even with those intentions, we didn't think to consult in meaningful ways with our colleagues next door in the library.

Colleges and universities tend to be siloed spaces where we work within our departments, programs, divisions, and units, and we don't always recognize the connections we have with the work of our colleagues down the hallway, in another building, or across a courtyard. A tremendous value of this book is the ability of its contributors to highlight the clear connections between two important disciplinary documents—the *Framework for Success in Postsecondary Writing* (WPA, NCTE, and NWP, 2011) and the *Framework for Information Literacy for Higher Education* (ACRL, 2016). In doing so, it features partnerships within a range of institutional types that have built upon the connections between these documents in ways that construct meaningful bridges for students as they develop expertise in research-writing. The chapters in Section 1 show off the ways we can learn from each other's expertise when we engage in conversation and break down the disciplinary silos that tend to separate us. The range of curricular reforms at institutions across the country showcased in Section 2 offer multiple options for how partnerships between faculty members invested in writing in the disciplines and their librarian colleagues might develop in different kinds of institutional contexts. And finally, Section 3 challenges us to think about how we assess students' research-writing development and the impact of the partnerships we develop.

As Sharon Mader mentions in the Foreword, the two Frameworks, and consequently the work of this collection, give us a shared language to determine a productive way to move forward. We can build on the partnerships that Randall McClure highlights in his Introduction to the collection to figure out what might work best for our students, on our campuses, and in our programs. To that end, I offer the following set of challenges for faculty and librarians alike:

- Establish research-writing learning circles on your campus to determine the best way to identify challenges your students face in their research-writing tasks. It is critical that you involve faculty members from across your campus, including writing faculty, along with librarians, students, and both faculty/staff development and assessment experts in these conversations.
- Have faculty and librarians on your campus read both the *Framework for Success in Postsecondary Writing* and the *Framework for Information Literacy for Higher Education* and pose this question: in what context could you introduce the tenets found in these docu-

ments to faculty members, librarians, and students along with the connections between the two documents?

- Form partnerships. Drawing on examples from this collection, determine the types of partnerships that could be built on your campus, perhaps as part of a collective response to some of the challenges students face in research-writing projects, particularly here in the digital age.
- Think ahead about assessment. While pockets of resistance to assessment remain in today's academy, it is important to consider how you will measure whether or not your responses have been effective. If we are genuinely committed to helping our students, then we need some form of measurement to gauge our practices and their learning.

On my campus, research-writing is taught in a variety of spaces, in a range of departments and colleges, and at different levels in the undergraduate experience. Conversations about the two Frameworks could provide a productive way to build needed connections between classes that will facilitate transfer of learning as students develop research-writing expertise. The scholarship published in this collection encourages me to step outside my own building and begin looking for solutions and potential partnerships on my own campus. I hope you find the same inspiration.

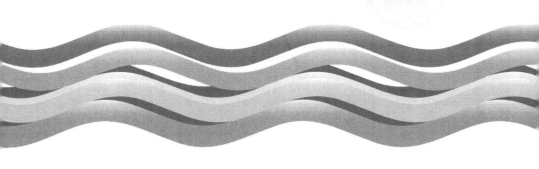

About the Contributors

Kathy Christie Anders is Assistant Professor at Texas A&M University where she serves as graduate studies librarian. Her research examines the intersections of rhetoric and information literacy as well as graduate student scholarly communications. She earned her PhD in English at the University of Nevada, Las Vegas, her MA in English from Duquesne University, and her MS in Library and Information Science from the University of Pittsburgh.

Rosalind Bucy serves as Learning & Research Services Librarian at Wheelock College in Boston. She is the liaison to the School of Arts & Sciences, with a particular focus on the first-year program. Rosalind is especially interested in empowering students to view themselves as interlocutors in scholarly conversations. She is also a past chair of the New England Chapter of ASIS&T and has presented her work with Maric Kramer at the New England Library Instruction Group.

Theresa Burress is the Humanities Librarian at Cook Library, serving the academic communities of New College of Florida (NCF) and University of South Florida Sarasota-Manatee. She is the liaison librarian to faculty in the Humanities Division of NCF, and she provides research, instruction, and digital humanities services to faculty and students. Her research interests include digital humanities, the intersecting fields of information literacy and digital pedagogy, and academic library outreach.

Kaijsa Calkins is Associate Librarian and Chair of the Research & Instruction department of the University of Wyoming Libraries and is the subject librarian for English and several interdisciplinary units, including the Honors Program. She has taught courses on library research and first-year seminars. She is a winner of the Beginning Professional Award given by the Mountain Plains

Library Association (2009) and is co-editor of *Embedded Librarians: Moving Beyond One-shot Instruction* (2011) and *The Embedded Librarian's Cookbook* (2014), both from ACRL. She is currently researching the library service needs of graduate students in the humanities.

Maribeth Clark is Associate Professor of Music at New College of Florida. As a musicologist at a small liberal arts college, she teaches classes on topics spanning Western art and music, folk music, music and the environment, and sound studies, and in doing so, she regularly integrates instruction in writing and information literacy into her pedagogical practices. She has published on music and dance in mid-nineteenth-century Paris, and her current research focuses on the history of whistling in the United States.

Donell Callender has been an academic librarian at Texas Tech University since 2002. She started out in Access Services in Interlibrary Loan. She currently serves as Associate Librarian in Research, Instruction & Outreach and is the personal librarian for the College of Education and the Department of English. In teaching Information Literacy and Freshman Seminar courses over the past 15 years, she has found a passion for information literacy and user experience.

Nancy C. DeJoy is Associate Professor in the Department of Writing, Rhetoric, and American Cultures at Michigan State University and serves as a core faculty member in the Center for Gender in Global Contexts. She publishes in the areas of first-year writing and the internationalization of higher education in the U.S.. She also writes poetry, which she uses to create art installations at galleries and other public spaces.

Gillian Devereux directs the Writing Center at Wheelock College in Boston where she also teaches creative writing and foundational writing courses for graduate students. Her research interests include multilingual writing instruction, documentation in the writing center, feminist erasure poetry, and advocacy through experimental creative writing. She is a founding editor at Coven Press, an independent publisher of experimental poetry.

William Duffy is Assistant Professor of English at the University of Memphis where he teaches undergraduate and graduate courses in rhetoric, composition, and professional writing. His most recent work has been published in *Literacy in Composition Studies, Ethos: A Digital Review of Arts, Humanities, and Public Ethics*, and *College English.*

Rick Fisher is an Associate Lecturer in the Department of English at the University of Wyoming. He teaches first-year composition, technical writing, and courses in the learning community for at-risk students, and he has won multiple awards for his teaching of first-year students. His research interests include first-year experience and students in transition, assessment of student learning, and interdisciplinary intersections of reading, writing, and research. He is a doctoral student in literacy education at the University of Wyoming.

Julius Fleschner is the Director of Library & Information Services and Assistant Professor at Briar Cliff University in Sioux City, Iowa. Prior to his promotion, he was Briar Cliff's Reference & Instruction librarian and tasked with teaching all information literacy sessions for the university. He earned his MLIS from the University of South Florida in 2010. During that time, he specialized in information literacy and intellectual property. Julius is particularly interested in furthering the mission of libraries through collaboration with institutional and regional partners. His undergraduate degree is in psychology, also from the University of South Florida.

Teresa Grettano is Assistant Professor and Director of First-Year Writing in the Department of English & Theatre at The University of Scranton. She teaches courses in writing, rhetoric, and public/political discourse. She earned her bachelor's and master's degrees in English literature from the University of South Alabama and her PhD in English studies with a concentration in rhetoric & composition from Illinois State University. Her research interests include twenty-first century literacies, critical pedagogy, interdisciplinarity, and post-9/11 discourses.

Sarah Hernandez is Associate Professor of Sociology at New College of Florida. In addition to Introduction to Sociology and Social Theory, she teaches courses on alternative work organization, social movements, development, and globalization. Her courses integrate information literacy from the basics of gathering and assessing bibliographic information to contributing knowledge through varied means. Her research explores governance processes in worker-owned and managed enterprises and transnational labor collaboration, both with a focus on Mexico.

Cassie Hemstrom is currently a lecturer in the University Writing program at the University of California, Davis. She teaches a variety of lower- and upper-division composition courses including Writing for Business and Writing in the Health Sciences. She earned her PhD in literature at the University of Nevada, Reno. She also holds an MA in literature from Boise State University and a BA in liberal arts from St. John's College, Santa Fe. Her interdisciplinary research focuses on intersections of identity theory and composition pedagogy.

Laura Heinz has been an academic librarian since 1999 and has served as Head of Research, Instruction, and Outreach for the Texas Tech University Library since 2007. Her interest focuses on academic librarian-faculty collaboration to create a meaningful and enriched academic experience for students.

Brian D. Holcomb is Assistant Professor of English at Limestone College. He earned his PhD in English from Michigan State University, with emphases in transatlantic Modernism, narrative theory, and gender studies. His literary research focuses on comic texts of the Modernist period and on twentieth-century Chinese literature, and his pedagogical research is primarily on general education assessment. He has published on the *Jeeves* stories of P.G. Wodehouse, the stage-to-screen adaptation of the Broadway musical *Sweeney Todd*, and the documentary theater of Anna Deavere Smith and the Tectonic Theatre Project.

Stacy Kastner is Assistant Professor and Associate Director of the Writing Center in the English Department at Mississippi State University. Her BA and MA degrees in English are from St. Bonaventure University, and she earned her PhD in rhetoric and writing from Bowling Green State University. At Mississippi State, she teaches courses on writing center theory, practice, and research as well as first-year composition. She's passionate about the potential of non-traditional learning environments and pedagogies, the extra- and co-curricular, to address issues of inequity within educational institutions. Her research focuses on the political, ideological, and personal dimensions of literacy acquisition with special attention to techno- and cyber-literacy, disciplinary self-identity formation, and techno-feminist community outreach activities.

Maric Kramer serves as Learning & Research Services Librarian at Wheelock College in Boston. Her favorite ACRL frame is "Authority is Constructed and Contextual." With Rosalind Bucy, she has spurred attendees at the New England Library Instruction Group to explore their own relationship to authority, while demonstrating the Question Formulation Technique to encourage students to voice authentic questions to guide research. In her own practice, she helps students make connections between their professional goals, their lived experience, and their academic work.

Amber Lancaster has taught first-year composition and other writing courses since 1998. She served as the Assistant Director of Composition for two academic years before taking on the position of Assistant Director of Online Graduate Studies, and now Dissertation Specialist and Writing Coach at a research and writing center for doctoral students. She continues to teach freshman composition as an adjunct instructor for Texas Tech University.

Sharon Mader is the ACRL Visiting Program Officer for Information Literacy, whose primary responsibility is to spearhead the launch and implementation of the *ACRL Framework for Information Literacy for Higher Education*. She earned a BA in History from Oberlin College, an MLS from Rosary College, an MS in Education from University of Memphis, and an EdD in Instructional Technology and Distance Education from Nova Southeastern University. Dr. Mader retired in early 2015 after fifteen years as Dean of Library Services at the University of New Orleans, after a rewarding career at a variety of public and private academic libraries, including University of Illinois Health Sciences, Lake Forest College, DePaul University, and University of Memphis.

Randall McClure has taught writing at several universities, including Miami University, Georgia Southern University, Cleveland State University, and Minnesota State University, Mankato. He researches in the areas of information behavior and academic writing, teaching and learning online, and academic policy. He has published articles recently in *The Writing Instructor, Inside Higher Ed, portal: Libraries and the Academy, Computers and Composition Online, Academic Exchange Quarterly, Computers and Composition, Writing Spaces, WPA: Writing Program Administration, Writing & Pedagogy*, and the *Journal of Literacy and Technology*. He is co-editor with James P. Purdy of *The New Digital Scholar: Exploring and Enriching the Research* and Writing Practices of NextGen Students and *The Next Digital Scholar: A Fresh Approach to the Common Core State Standards in Research and Writing*.

Sara D. Miller is the Librarian for Interdisciplinary Teaching and Learning Initiatives at Michigan State University (MSU), where she supports and facilitates the development of MSU teacher-librarians and pursues information literacy-related participation in campus initiatives. Sara works with first-year writing students in the information literacy classroom. She has previously served as MSU's Head of Information Literacy, co-facilitated faculty learning communities focusing on writing and inquiry within disciplines, and participated in the development of MSU's Undergraduate Learning Goals rubrics. She has published and presented internationally with librarians and disciplinary faculty on the intersections of writing, rhetoric, and information literacy. Her current research focuses on critical pedagogy and practice.

Susan K. Miller-Cochran is Professor of English and Director of the Writing Program at the University of Arizona. Her research focuses on instructional technology, L2 writing, and writing program administration. She is a co-author of *An Insider's Guide to Academic Writing* (Macmillan, 2016), *The Cengage Guide to Research* (Cengage, 2017) and *Keys for Writers* (Cengage, 2018), and she is also an editor of *Rhetorically Rethinking Usability* (Hampton Press,

2009), and *Strategies for Teaching First-Year Composition* (NCTE, 2002). She currently serves as President of the Council of Writing Program Administrators.

Nova Myhill is Associate Professor of English at New College of Florida where she teaches British literature before 1700, drama from all periods, and co-chairs the New College Conference on Medieval and Renaissance Studies. She is the co-editor, with Jennifer Low, of *Imagining the Audience in Early Modern Drama, 1558-1642* (Palgrave, 2011) and various articles on audience and reception in the drama of Shakespeare and his contemporaries.

Jim Nugent is Associate Professor and Director of the Writing and Rhetoric major at Oakland University. His research interests include neosophistic rhetorical theory, medical writing, and the teaching of technical communication. With Greg Giberson and Lori Ostergaard, he is co-editor of *Writing Majors: Eighteen Program Profiles* (2015, University Press of Colorado).

Lori Ostergaard is Associate Professor and Chair of the Department of Writing and Rhetoric at Oakland University in Rochester, Michigan. Her archival research examines the history of writing instruction at midwestern normal schools and high schools. Her collection, *Writing Stories: Composition and Rhetoric in High Schools and Normal Schools, 1839–1969*, is available from University of Pittsburgh Press. She co-edited *Writing Majors: Eighteen Program Profiles* with Greg Giberson and Jim Nugent. This collection examines writing majors at institutional sites around the country.

Jenne Powers is Assistant Professor of Humanities and Writing at Wheelock College in Boston. She teaches first-year and advanced writing courses as well as American and Russian literature. She is also the coordinator of Wheelock's First Year Seminar program. Her research interests include intersectionality and friendship in women's literature, as well as the role of writing in college students' social identity development.

Teresa (Terry) Quezada is Assistant Professor in Practice and Associate Director in the Rhetoric and Writing studies program at UTEP where she teaches first-year writing, undergraduate technical writing, and graduate professional writing courses. Her research interests include political and bureaucratic rhetoric, online writing instruction, and first-year writing instruction, and the first-year experience.

Kathleen Reed is Assessment and Data Librarian at Vancouver Island University; she's a Jill-of-all-trades working with services as varied as research help, instruction, liaison, research data management, and altmetrics.

Brenda Refaei is Associate Professor and Composition Coordinator at the University of Cincinnati Blue Ash College where she teaches basic writing, first-year composition, and intermediate composition. She earned a Doctorate of Education in Literacy from the University of Cincinnati. She has published articles in *Journal of the Scholarship of Teaching and Learning, College Teaching,* and *Writing and Pedagogy.* She is currently involved in research projects around eportfolios, information literacy, and Problem-Based Learning in composition.

Hillary Richardson is Assistant Professor and Humanities Librarian at Mississippi State University Libraries. She is the liaison to the Department of English, the African American Studies Program, and the Shackouls Honors College. Prior to earning her MLIS from the University of Southern Mississippi, she earned an MA in English from the University of Mississippi. Her research interests include information and digital literacy, pedagogy in library instruction and digital humanities, the trends and behaviors of humanities scholarship, and social justice and librarianship. She is a contributing author and project manager of "'A Shaky Truce': Starkville Civil Rights Struggles, 1960-1980," an oral and digital public history website.

Meghan Roe is Assistant Professor of Writing and Director of the Writing Center at Briar Cliff University in Sioux City, Iowa. She received her PhD in rhetoric and composition from Texas Christian University in 2014, where she worked for six years in TCU's William L. Adams Center for Writing. Meghan's primary research interest is multiliteracy centers, though she is also interested in the connections between disability studies, writing centers, and multimodal writing pedagogy. Her goal at Briar Cliff University is to implement her research through a new multimodal fist-year writing course and through increased collaboration between the long-established writing center and institutional partners both on campus and online.

Jennifer Schnabel is Assistant Professor and English librarian at The Ohio State University. She previously worked as the Assistant to the Dean for Community Engagement at the University of Memphis Libraries, where she served on the campus Writing Center Planning and Implementation Committee. She has more than ten years of college-level instruction experience, including courses in developmental reading and writing, composition, and literature.

Rachel E. Scott is Assistant Professor and Integrated Library Systems Librarian at the University of Memphis. Her research focuses on information literacy and music bibliography. In addition to teaching an introduction to research methods course, she regularly offers library instruction to students in social science and humanities courses. She has recently placed chapters in several anthologies, and articles in *Music Reference Services Quarterly, The Reference Librarian,* and *Tennessee Libraries.*

Dawn Thompson teaches in the English department at Vancouver Island University. Her areas of specialization include literary theory, North American indigenous literatures, and Canadian literatures.

Elizabeth L. Wallis is Associate Professor and Coordinator of Library Instruction in Kresge Library at Oakland University. She is co-editor (as Elizabeth W. Kraemer), with Alice S. Horning, of the book *Reconnecting Reading and Writing* (Parlor Press, 2013). Her research has appeared in *The Journal of Academic Librarianship, The Reference Librarian,* and *College & Research Libraries,* among others.

M. Lauren Wahman is Associate Senior Librarian and Instruction Program Coordinator at the University of Cincinnati Blue Ash College Library where she coordinates the library instruction program, teaches instruction classes as well as serves as the liaison to Business and Economics, English and Communication, and Foreign Language. She earned a Master's of Science in Information Studies from The University of Texas at Austin's School of Information. She is an active member in the Association of College and Research Libraries Instruction Section. Her research interests include teaching methods and professional development for teaching librarians.

Donna Witek is Associate Professor and Public Services Librarian in The University of Scranton's Weinberg Memorial Library. She provides research services and support through information literacy instruction and reference service to members of the university community. She serves as liaison to theology/religious studies, English and theatre, sociology/criminal justice, and women's studies as well as the First-Year Writing Program. She earned her master of library & information science degree from Long Island University's Palmer School of Library & Information Science, and her master of arts in theology degree from The University of Scranton. Her research interests include social media and information literacy, metaliteracy, technology and critical pedagogy, and collaboration with faculty across disciplines.